The Twentieth Century World, 1914 to the Present

The Twentieth-Century World, 1914 to the Present

State of Modernity

John C. Corbally

BLOOMSBURY ACADEMIC
LONDON • NEW YORK • OXFORD • NEW DELHI • SYDNEY

BLOOMSBURY ACADEMIC
Bloomsbury Publishing Plc
50 Bedford Square, London, WC1B 3DP, UK
1385 Broadway, New York, NY 10018, USA

BLOOMSBURY, BLOOMSBURY ACADEMIC and the Diana logo are trademarks of
Bloomsbury Publishing Plc

First published in Great Britain 2019

Cover design by Adriana Brioso
Cover image: Housing in Hong Kong, China. (© www.jethuynh.com/Getty Images)

A catalogue record for this book is available from the British Library.

A catalog record for this book is available from the Library of Congress.

ISBN: HB: 978-1-4742-9797-4
PB: 978-1-4742-9793-6
ePDF: 978-1-4742-9795-0
eBook: 978-1-4742-9794-3

Series: The Making of the Modern World

Typeset by Newgen KnowledgeWorks Pvt. Ltd., Chennai, India
Printed and bound in Great Britain

To find out more about our authors and books visit www.bloomsbury.com
and sign up for our newsletters.

To Scarlett and Sebastien, for the innumerable hours spent with my head in the history clouds.

To Tracy, for your constant support and patience.

Contents

Figures

Series Introduction

The Making of the Modern World

This world history series comprises a unique, three-volume set of books for use in the classroom or for those wishing to understand world history since 1500.

It consists of three separate volumes:

The Early Modern World, 1450–1750: Seeds of Modernity (forthcoming)
John C. Corbally, Trevor R. Getz, and Jacob Whittaker

The Long Nineteenth Century, 1750–1914: Crucible of Modernity (2018)
Trevor R. Getz

The Twentieth-Century World, 1914 to the Present: State of Modernity (2018)
John C. Corbally

The series is unconventional in its approach to understanding the world since 1500 through popular perspectives and experiences: those of common, ordinary people; of peasants, women, workers, slaves, serfs, and outsiders rather than of kings, generals, or politicians. In doing so, it aims to understand humanity's past by transcending the traditional emphasis on nations, empires, masculinity, war, or acquisition.

The authors intend for a diverse array of learners to appreciate just how connected our globalized world has been since 1500, instead of assuming separate peoples lived in separate nations with separate histories. They reveal rather than hide the complex and unappealing sides of history, outlining the history as it is understood, whether pleasing or not.

The series is purposely written in a nonacademic style, to invite students and general readers to enjoy the story while learning the broad outlines of world history. It is clearly organized, with short segments providing the opportunity for the reader to absorb one section at a time. Each chapter in each volume has a clear thesis, making a historical point supported by the sources, exploring a distinct period of the modern past through five different lenses: environmental, political, economic, intellectual, and technological history. Framed around social experience and cultural perspective, each chapter in each volume explores the development and contested construction of modernity. Together, the series forms an interpretation of the modern past that will help readers both understand and question the development of the world in which we live.

What Is This Book?

This book is a world history of the past century or so (c.1914–2017), a period of enormous transformation, tighter global connections, and new human experiences. The subtitle, *State of Modernity*, reflects the interpretation that during this century humans created a troubled modernity. The chapters of this book introduce many of the era's critical themes on a global scale. The text, like the other two in this three-part series, is built on a framework for exploring themes and events discussed in a classroom setting. Though all will not agree with this approach, it is our hope the series can be used by instructors with different outlooks in fertile conversation. Such historical debates are very good for students!

The Twentieth-Century World, 1914 to the Present is structured around five separate themes in five chapters that group historical events into categories—political, economic, intellectual/philosophical, technological, and environmental history. In our lives, these five overlapping aspects of the social environment seep into each other; combined, they shape our sense of reality, nature, and life itself. Our approach is to explore historical continuity and change through individual and collective human experiences. The aim is to say something important about how individuals and groups lived their lives, how they sought to manage and understand the changes around them—to depict history in ways we can relate to as we live today.

Not only does the past have an impact on how we live now, it is something that we all understand in our everyday lives, through nostalgia, traditions, memories, heritage projects, and popular culture. In this series, we try to emphasize these connections in the interludes between chapters, exploring ways that people in our time specifically interact with the events and experiences of the past.

Though the purpose is to relate to readers the essential stories of recent history, all societies cannot be covered equally, both for practical purposes and due to disparities in available sources. What we can do is try to examine well-known events and historical processes from the perspective of the average person rather than the politician, general, or priest. We can empathize with those who suffered rather than celebrate with the victors. We can question progress while acknowledging its virtues, and we can concede that our knowledge of the past is inherently limited.

One final note—it is often supposed that the purpose of history classes is to simplify the past and make it easier to comprehend. We feel it is important to write and teach histories that are understandable, but students must grasp how extraordinarily complex the real human past was. Often, we are left not with answers, but with more questions, questions that will hopefully stimulate an intellectual curiosity far beyond this book.

Introduction: A Wild 100 Years

In attempting to cover a century of the world's history, the reader should be warned that the author has omitted much, through necessity. The main goal has been to consider the well-known turning points (world wars, the Depression, Cold War, colonialism, capitalism, and Communism, etc.) from a new vantage point. To disregard these historical processes would be to ignore much of history. Hence, rather than reciting well-known battles or praising Western leaders or capitalism, the goal is to explore the impact of such events on the rest of the world. This is the aim of the series, to widen the lens in our scrutiny of the past.

This book is about many transformations which, placed together, might be described as *modernity*. Modernity can be defined as a set of historical experiences and perspectives, rooted in the period between 1492 and 1750 (Volume 1), debated, fought over, and contested during the period 1750–1914 (Volume 2) and thrust upon the world since 1914. Some components of modernity under study in this volume include:

- Political entities like *the nation-state, empires* and the power structures they maintain
- Technological and social transformations derived from *global connections*
- The emergence of a *capitalist* global economy and form of social organization that replaced loose knit, subsistence economies and mercantilist practices worldwide
- Global *urbanization*, population booms, the diversity of communities, and increased migration
- The development of a modern outlook that extolls *progress* as a virtue
- The triumph of modern *science*, including the earth, physical, and life sciences
- The systematized critique of *traditional values*, and emergent ideas of equality, diversity and liberty
- New *ways of acting and being* that normalized acquisition and industriousness in human life

Assumptions and key points

First, some disclaimers, so to speak. Historians are informed by theory derived from other disciplines, particularly such disciplines that relate to social and cultural history. In deciding what to emphasize, I have taken a Critical Theory approach to the past century. My aim is not to simply describe things that happened, but to ask *why* they did so, as far as we can tell. I strive to consider whose interests were sustained, who benefitted from historical processes, not to just list "what happened." This necessitates a little more editorial, or commentary, than the average history text.

Second, a central assumption that threads through the series is that we can productively compare humans and societies across time and space. Though humans differ vastly in culture and vary in biological appearance, we are genetically identical, and act in generally similar ways, most of the time. This in itself is a historical claim. Books written even as early as 1900 tacitly assumed a hierarchy of races existed, often with white Protestants supreme and the rest of the world inferior in comparison. Well into the 1970s, differences in cultural aptitude were simply assumed, supporting a view that the economic and military superiority of the Western world can explain all of history—a particularly virile, masculine version of history at that.

This brings us to a third point. The most cursory analysis of the past century reveals greater inequality, more poverty, deaths and violence. Such has been the increase in wealth and power in the developed states of the world that global inequality is greater now than it was in 1900. Though global inequity was enormous then, it has increased. A century ago, poor parts of the world were usually colonized and traditional in outlook. Today many in undeveloped nations live in similar poverty under independent, autocratic regimes. Wars of genocide occurred through the century in both industrial and traditional societies. Religious violence has increased, and material greed has become more commonplace. More environmental destruction has ensued in this century than in all of history.

Fourth and finally, this confronts us with a paradox. Even accounting for these horrors, unmistakable progress, particularly since 1945, has been central to the human condition on earth. War and civil war are now less frequent than in the past: since 1945 large-scale international warfare has been nonexistent. Global attempts to prevent genocide prevail with the spread of human rights as a philosophy. Vast improvements in living standards and public health have, if unevenly, spread worldwide. Poverty and sickness have declined, thanks to scientific research and organized aid. Many diseases are now eradicated. The last few decades have brought the normalization of democracy, albeit gradually. Even the poorest populations are more comfortable than their ancestors were a century ago. Women worldwide are far closer to a position of equality than in 1900, particularly in developed nations. The global conversation about environmental conservation, albeit with vested interests working against it, is incontrovertible. Which of the last two perspectives one takes depends on the length of one's historical outlook.

Glimmers of hope suggest that humans are cooperating more than ever. The United Nations has changed expectations from all state leaders. The World Health Organization has saved billions from early deaths. The International Court of Justice, even when snubbed by the United States or others, regularly intervenes in international disputes. Such institutions set governable rules of behavior, constraining the political or economic abuses found throughout history, and in the past century.

Five threads

The author hopes that students will have some awareness of the major stories of the twentieth century. If not, they will have five separate opportunities to scour the past from varying perspectives—first politically, then economically, philosophically, technologically and last, perhaps most significantly, environmentally. Across all five categories, the central thesis is that the many horrors of the past century offer potential for a happy ending—but Hollywood style, disconcerting twists remain unresolved. The five themes are as follows.

Political century: Autocracy and growing democracy

Politically, this was a century where strong, well-organized nation-states, captivated by ardent competition over ideas and resources, conspired to kill up to 100 million humans, wrecking countless lives in the process. Liberal democracies in the West had a head start: seventeenth-century Holland and England were more sophisticated and organized than most states worldwide now. Still today, from Africa to the Middle East and Asia, "big men," autocrats or ethnic-religious elites rule with an iron fist—notions of citizenship and human rights barely seem to cross their minds. But Western powers intervened unreservedly in the business of less powerful sovereign states through the century, and frequently supported dictatorships. Western imperialism shaped the path of many states, Communism brought little minimal political participation, while US meddling rarely brought democracy.

Yet democracy, electoral choice, and a public voice are more widespread today more than ever before. Even if, as many claim, political participation is limited by a profit-seeking, distraction-inducing media, more people now vote and speak up. And even if populations consist of mostly lethargic constituents, a century ago most humans didn't know what voting was. The question remains though, how much of a voice do everyday people really have? Chapter 1 will cover the century's political narrative to put this in context.

Economic century: Inequality and growing prosperity

Economically, as Chapter 2 establishes, this was a century in which the rich got much richer. Wealthy nations built on accumulated affluence to become even more prosperous, often at the expense of poorer states; wealthy people passed on accrued capital, both social and financial, to their offspring, keeping wealth in the family. More poor people were born into immiseration and destitution than ever before. Over a billion people live in poverty in 2018, more than were alive in 1900!

Yet, far more people were also born in this century, particularly in poorer nations. The century was also one of fantastic prosperity and mounting material possessions. Though easily romanticized, traditional life around 1900 was frequently one of poverty-stricken conventionalism, in which whole societies endured the daily threat of hunger, desperation or cold, following abstruse beliefs as a guide for life. Rural youth rarely stay in the country now as they did then: most want city life and modern playthings. Still, habits of instant gratification and consumerism as a new form of devotion may be the consequence of increased materialism. What does it mean to live a life in search of consumption-based pleasure? Does it overwhelm the human spirit? If buying "stuff" is now the true purpose of most lives, what are the costs? Chapter 2 attempts to understand these issues.

Intellectual century: Ideological certitude and growing pluralism

This brings us to Chapter 3, which explores a century replete with new worldviews, philosophies, and mentalities that intertwined with or replaced traditions, religions, and belief-systems to drive human conduct. This was a century in which religious factionalism and intellectual extremism increased. Interwoven religious and secular ideologies provided the energy to enthusiastically murder by the millions—usually to prove a national, tribal, or sacrosanct point. Fanatical Fascist and Communist rulers killed with pleasure, abandoning tradition for new state-based religions. Established Christian cultures in the West killed millions of other Christians—and millions of Jews—corralling people of various faiths into ferocious European wars. Muslim societies were humiliated by Western ideologues, while infighting among Islamic sects persisted. Hindus and Muslims fought consistently in the home of the Buddha and Mahatma Gandhi, while Buddhist and Confucian nations slaughtered from Japan to Cambodia. Muslim radicals threatened civil society globally as the century ended; Buddhist Myanmar elites slaughtered innocent Muslims.

Yet, this was also a century in which more than ever before, people became aware of the source of their beliefs. More humans learned of the assumptions within their beliefs, and, crucially, the history of their cultures. It was a century in which people increasingly encountered other cultures. By the twenty-first century, world history was taught to people on most continents, when in 1900 history was for elites. For most of the century, hyper-nationalist narratives were taught, convincing people that their country was always pure and good. A gradual respect for the diverse views of humanity emerged. The question remains, will absolutist beliefs continue to cause violence? Or can objectivity and inclusiveness become the basis of a new more relativistic worldview? Chapter 3 addresses these thorny questions.

Technological century: Well-organized violence and amazing toys

But even more than belief-systems, technology transforms the earth today. Chapter 4's subject, modern technology, now alters attitudes to politics, economics, faith, philosophy, and ideas. Everybody, it seems, loves technology. Yet, this was a century in which science and technology were employed to kill hundreds of thousands in single bombing raids, where scientific planning and organizational management helped Nazis systematically kill millions of innocent Jews for no reason. Chemical and biological warfare blinded, gassed and suffocated millions—in 1918, a young Adolf Hitler fomented his hatred of liberal democracy, while lying in hospital enduring the effects of a British gas shell. Technology always brings costs. Innovation usually stemmed from complex states, but it often translated into disruption for most worldwide.

Yet, few in the modern world doubt the value, necessity, or ubiquity of technology. Few say no to robot-made cars imbued with luxurious techno-comforts. Few refuse smartphones that offer the world's knowledge in a pocket. Who does not wish to communicate with family and friends afar? Technology has brought creature comforts, warm homes, pleasurable entertainment and longer, healthier lives to billions of people. Medical technology is the primary reason 8 billion people exist today. But is technology overtaking the human mind? Where is technology taking us? The name of one of the two dominant operating systems in phones, Android, exposes the word's established meaning—a robot with a human appearance. Apparently, nobody knows where this is going. Chapter 4 will outline how we got here.

Environmental century: Defiling nature while realizing its worth

Last, but certainly not least, Chapter 5 considers the environment's recent history— how humans have treated the source of all life on earth. None of the points mentioned will matter if we can't sustain human life in the coming century. Arguably, there is less room for optimism here: the stakes are far higher than in the four other realms. If we despoil our planet to the point of no return, we won't be taking classes in college or studying the past.

This was indisputably a century where humans extracted, employed, despoiled, and depreciated the earth's fruits more than ever before. Mountainsides were ripped open to extract ores for building materials; forests and lands were destroyed to make furniture, clothes, machines, glass, pottery, electronics, jewelry— basically, everything in the modern home. Humans obliterated flora and fauna as they fought wars, built cities, formed factories and farmed fields. Pesticides, poisonous chemicals, and pollutants poured into pristine rivers, debilitating the bodies of whole populations. The most powerful political body on earth today, the US Congress, remained packed with people—mostly men—who think scientists are wrong regarding climate change.

Yet, even in 1900, leaders knew of our disposition for abusing nature. From Republican president Teddy Roosevelt to early environmentalists like John Muir and indigenous leaders worldwide, some warned of our compulsion. Indeed, the last 50 years has seen a great awakening; environmental awareness became the watchword of culture and education in almost all nations, if in an uneven manner. It is quite apparent that humans can reflect on their place in the universe; it remains to be seen if we will be here to do so in a century. That is indeed up to the reader, and all of us! The following five chapters are intended to put this problem in historical context and hopefully provide meaning therein. I hope you enjoy it.

1

Twentieth-Century Politics: Nationalism, Imperialism, Colonization

Situating the chapter

In the last century, individual political rights expanded more than ever in history. In recent decades, democracy expanded to the point it could be anticipated or expected on all continents. More people enjoy a say in the political process than ever before. Yet, for most of the century, political elites employed new types of propaganda, controlling information and stifling dissent. Competing nation-states also utilized new forms of warfare to kill more humans—usually conscripted workers and peasants—than in any prior century.

Great powers intruded upon the sovereignty of minor states throughout the century, determining who ruled and how they ruled. Within weaker states, elites prohibited mass political participation, preferring unschooled, passive subjects. This was a century then, where power was questioned more than ever, but also where ruling classes perfected the means of preserving power.

By the end of this chapter, readers should be able to:

- Explain transformations in attitudes toward politics and policy making.
- Appraise the effects of stronger states' policies on people worldwide.
- Postulate how states impacted one another through power relations.
- Determine whether political interactions were positive or negative for humanity as a whole.
- Shape an argument regarding political rights in various regions.

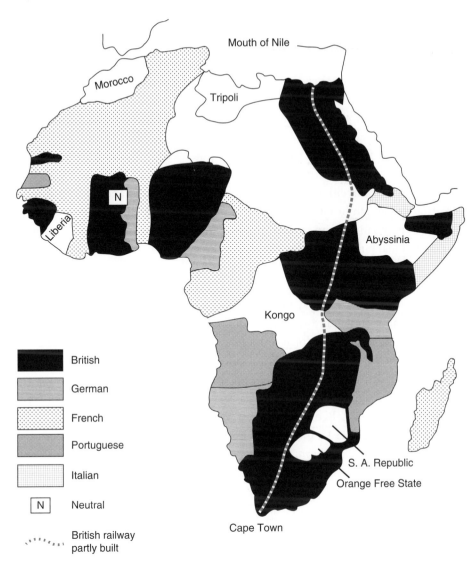

Figure 1.1 Partition of Africa after 1884.

Source: https://www.gutenberg.org/files/20531/20531-h/20531-h.htm#Page_159 (accessed June 12, 2017).

The story

A familiar twentieth-century historical narrative exists today, in which *authoritarian regimes* like Germany, Japan, or the USSR belligerently expanded, suppressing citizens' rights and threatening liberal *democracies* like Britain, France, and the United States. Though this is accurate enough, states do not function in a vacuum in world history, and there is more to the story. British and French imperial expansion, and the extension of US power throughout the century, *also* imposed itself on vast numbers of humans. Expansion from democratic states also forced people worldwide to bow to foreign influence and Western industrial capitalism. Without overlooking the horrors committed by certain regimes, it is apparent that leaders of democratic states, like authoritarian ones, considered their political causes just and honorable, regardless of the consequences.

Though the principles underlying both systems differ immensely (few would prefer dictatorship to democracy) the impact was similar enough for the vast majority of people on earth: forced participation in great power conflicts; domestic incursions and loss of autonomy; extraction of local resources; and impoverishment and political instability. In either political scenario, smaller nations and weaker societies were exploited and induced to offer cheap labor and form alliances. Aside from some indigenous populations who remain scattered around the earth, few humans escaped the gravitational pull of powerful states since 1900, regardless of whether they were democratic or authoritarian.

For those in Western democracies, the last century brought increasing political rights and representation. Yet, for the majority of humanity, it was a century of enduring domination and restricted freedom. Even in democracies, the majority of people were educated to conform to nationalist ideologies or to fight for state war machines, only slowly gaining a political voice, with limited influence.

The First World War brought the end of several ancient, autocratic empires. However new, fragmented nation-states with new types of problems emerged immediately thereafter. Between the First World War in 1914 and the end of the Second World War in 1945, the fruits of extreme *nationalism* would slaughter up to 70 million people. *Communism,* the only political ideology offering an alternative to nationalism or a voice for the working masses, was brushed aside in Western states, where capitalist political parties succeeded in keeping workers loyal to the state.

Seen from the standpoint of the Third World however, *imperialism* was the political system most apparent in everyday life. For most people were neither citizens of nation-states nor aspirants to a Communist workers' paradise; most lived under the control of foreigners, usually Westerners. Most people on earth today live in formerly colonized regions, with the effects of past power imbalances persisting. *Islamism*—the ideology of radical Muslims—is for instance a direct response to past imperialist encroachments, offering an alternative to nationalism or indeed capitalism.

1. Sovereign states and subjugated societies

In 1900, power politics mattered more than morality or justice. Such noble ideals took second place to the necessity of national interests and political aims. As the

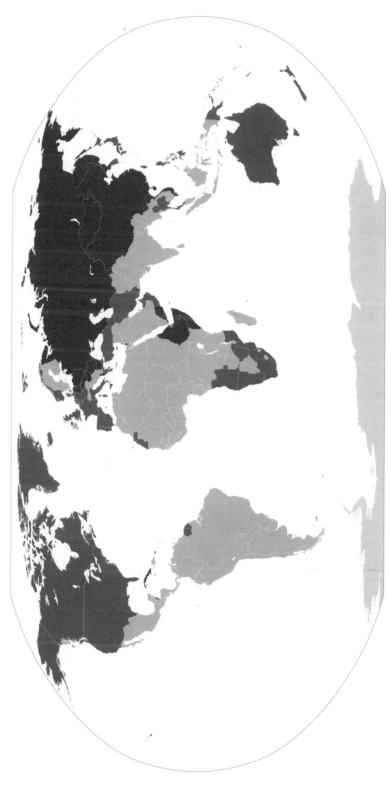

Figure 1.2 The First, Second, Third World in 1975. The "three worlds" of the Cold War era, as of the period between April 1975 and August 1975.[1]

Source: https://en.wikipedia.org/wiki/Third_World#/media/File:Cold_War_alliances_mid-1975.svg.

twentieth century began, nobody knew what was to come, but it was apparent to some that all that had been taken for granted in previous centuries seemed to be shifting seismically. "All that is solid melts into air," Marshall Berman wrote, referring to the wholesale changes in human life few could escape in the decades after 1900.[2] The world was about to change more ever before. Nobody was in control.

In Western nation-states, a new mass participation in politics emerged around 1900, perturbing traditional rulers, aristocrats, and elites. Workers in the West had mounting expectations regarding *civil rights*, wealth distribution, and class consciousness. Between 1914 and 1945, a rising mindfulness of the injustice of colonial rule captured the minds of colonized villagers, peasants, and laborers worldwide. The price of nationalism would be steep: for Westerners, it brought decades of war; for non-Westerners, poverty, humiliation, and domination.

View from the periphery: people without power

In 1900, a vast disparity in power existed between industrial states (all in Western Europe, aside from the United States and Japan) and every other society worldwide. For a century before 1914, Britain had dominated global politics. The other Western powers, America and Japan therefore purposely aspired to equal Britain's political and military prowess, employing political organization to dominate less structured societies. The ensuing worldwide expansion in pursuit of power affected all humans. By allowing greater political representation in developed states, power elites buttressed their position and maintained order, but it was contingent upon resource extraction and cheap labor from the unrepresented masses of the world.[3]

Industrial powers competed intensely, for national prestige, political leverage, and economic might. This rivalry came at the expense of the nondeveloped world, as a compulsion to govern weaker societies was normalized. This nationalistic Western power struggle set the stage for horrific world wars in the twentieth century. Though most of the dead would be commoners from developed nations, the ensuing instability would afflict the poor in less developed countries (LDC's). Few people gained much, and (notably) the only developed nation that gained economically from the world wars was the United States.

In 1900, only 30 percent of the worlds' 1.8 billion people lived in Europe or North America. A small number of Western elites directed affairs domestically and worldwide, either directly or indirectly. Most industrial citizens, like colonized subjects, were not active participants in the policy making of their homeland. Leaders of industrial states thus dominated their own populaces politically *and* the other 70 percent of the world's population. This power came from developing centralized, efficient industrial state systems that easily subjugated less organized, decentralized or traditional societies by the end of the nineteenth century.

In 1900, political life in China, the Ottoman Empire, and Latin America was dominated by elites linked to Western politicians, merchants, or financiers. Thousands of small and diverse African chiefdoms and minor states had been incorporated into European empires, and would be subsumed into forty or so fabricated nation-states after the Second World War, all the while trying to resist foreign influence. The suddenness and nature of this transition into modernity—under Western terms—guaranteed conflict in all these regions. The abrupt confrontation with Western aggression and limited means to defy the West has had enduring consequences for non-Western peoples.

Nevertheless, Communist or Third World leaders responded to foreign domination by implementing policies equally repressive or often worse than those of Western authorities. Communist leaders never offered citizens political rights, as we shall see, and after the fight for independence was won in Africa and Asia in the postwar decades, the ruling classes subjugated their own people, preferring to uphold personal ties with Western powers while guaranteeing dormant masses. Following independence, an organized, often Western-educated elite in most Third World nations lived in great comfort, while peasants and workers endured poverty. Even without European intrusions, political systems in non-Western and colonized regions never allowed for popular participation. What was left when the Europeans departed were tenuous alliances of ethnic tribes and rival political groups, with little common interest and a sure recipe for further conflict.

Eurasian people

Elites in the Middle East, Africa, or Asia prolonged the adverse effects of Western *colonization*. Middle Eastern Muslims—whether Turk, Arab, or Persian—were never organized historically in nation-states, and though nominally ruled by the Turkish Ottoman Empire, most Muslims in the region lived with limited centralized governance.

An aloof Ottoman ruling class had seen their influence on Muslim populations diminish in the nineteenth century. Rejecting large-scale military or political modernization, the ruling class invited dissent among modernizers who proposed reforms. Conservative sultans tenuously ruling the various provinces and smaller tribes of the empire would prove easy prey for expansionist Western states in the early twentieth century.

The Young Turk revolution of 1908 brought some hope for constitutional government and democracy, but the sultan and his supporters restored sharia law a year later. Sultan Mehmed V opted to collaborate with Kaiser Wilhelm of Germany, allying with the defeated side in the First World War. The region was thus open to British and French influence thereafter. For Middle Easterners, the twentieth century brought not only the onslaught of Western power, but also the implementation of European political concepts such as the national state.

Western interest in the strategic value of the Middle East was amplified by a thirst for newly discovered oil after 1908. Rival powers like Russia, France, Britain, and the United States formed alliances to extract oil. The shared goal of manipulating loosely organized Muslim states brought consequences through the century. Most Muslims carried on lives of tribal piety, nomadic wandering, or everyday village existence, often heedless of Western notions such as nationalism or capitalism, unaware of the influence that foreign powers possessed upon their rulers.

In the north and east of Africa, populations had long been dominated by Arab powers, and most regions were ruled by Muslims by 1900. All these societies had to confront Western encroachment, particularly when European nations came to control most of Africa after 1884. The Berlin Conference that year sliced the vast continent into colonies controlled by Western states. This meant that few African societies avoided the influence of European powers. The majority of African people continued to live far from capitals and official legislation, and many subsisted on lands as they had for centuries, but their rulers would bend to the economic will and political dictates of foreign politicians.

Centuries of isolation from the wider world ended in Sub-Saharan Africa by 1900, and the ensuing century would be a tortured one for much of the continent. The only option most people had was to keep farming, hunting and gathering, or fishing. Many joined armies to fight for or against Europeans. Those closer to cities worked in large enterprises like factories and mines that exported ores to the developed world. Only in the 1950s would a younger generation of leaders oust European colonial powers.

In India, British rule had increased between 1857 and 1939. A few hundred thousand British bureaucrats, supported by a mostly Indian army, coerced hundreds of millions to labor at the whim of a foreign power. When the First World War came, many Indians were loyal to Britain. Such loyalty would lead many to expect independence from Britain by the 1940s.

European domination in Southeast Asia also increased after 1900, as French and Dutch powers joined the British as colonial overlords in that region. Traders and elites from all three nations restricted political rights for the majority of people. French colonists exploited Indochina mercilessly, using the land as an economic fiefdom. Though rebellions were persistent, power resided firmly in the hands of the French and local collaborators. The French exploited concession areas in Laos and in Chinese ports such as Shanghai well into the postwar era. Dutch power increased in Indonesia between 1900 and 1945, with similar violence and exploitation. During the Second World War, Japanese imperialists ousted the Dutch. However, the new colonizers treated Indonesians even more brutally than the Europeans had. Postwar independence would bring either Communist or authoritarian governance.

People in the region, as in Africa, India, and the Middle East, were considered by Westerners unfit to rule themselves. In any case, most people had little sense of statehood—a European notion—and demonstrated minimal loyalty to the monarchs or princes who ruled them, whether Arab, Indian, Asian, or European. Political representation is still not common in parts of the world that were colonized by Europeans, though nor was it prior to their arrival.

After the Second World War, European colonists struggled to hold on to power as local groups sought autonomy. Britain enlisted up to half a million colonial soldiers in the war, treating them like subordinates, showing little gratitude to Asians, Africans, West Indians, or Indians for their services. The French treated African and Asian conscripts similarly. Unsurprisingly, after the war, millions of people fought ferociously for colonial independence.

The peoples of Central Asia were accustomed to living far from centralized state power. Most had long persisted as nomads and peasants in a subsistence lifestyle. When the First World War broke out, many were forced to fight in Ottoman or Russian armies. They were swept up in great power diplomacy, with little local context for national identity and no choice but to fight in foreign wars. A life of basic existence was transformed into one of brutal conflict in the name of distant rulers. Mongolian and other smaller tribal groups tried to resist Russian or Chinese influence, but as the First World War approached, Chinese and Russian settlers took over a quarter of the lands of Kazakhstan and Turkestan, expanding to compete with Europeans.

The Soviet military put rebellions down ruthlessly—political revolts were frequent, massacres common. In the 1920s, the USSR forcibly absorbed over 10 million Central Asians into its new Communist empire. Ethnic minorities like Mongols or Muslims were now considered Communists, whether they liked it or not. Millions of tribespeople died or were sent to labor camps for resisting. Just as in North America, indigenous leaders were callously killed to thwart rebellion.

East Asian people

In 1900, like most people on earth, Chinese peasants lived in villages or rural areas, barely concerned with national politics or great power rivalries. Unless called up to fight in wars or forced to revolt in uprisings, peasant life continued as before. Even after Chairman Mao's Communist victory in 1949, a small cadre of party elites drove policy, just as the imperial elite had for centuries before 1900.

China's century began badly with the Boxer Rebellion of 1900. Chinese rebels, weary of European, Japanese, and US interference, fought to expel foreigners and gain administrative control over their country. Naively thinking that martial arts would protect them against the industrial artillery of an eight-nation alliance, the rebels failed to wrest their country back. The ensuing struggle led to the collapse of the 300-year old Qing Empire in 1911, bringing decades of fragmented "warring states" and constant, violent Japanese incursions.

Humiliated by Western condescension at the *Treaty of Versailles* in 1919, Chinese leaders such as Mao Tse-Tung pursued an independent path. Whether China would take republican or communist road was not clear. Sun Yat-Sen's Nationalist Party, the Kuomintang, wanted land reform to benefit the masses, working within the established international system. After 1926, a new leader Chiang Kai-Shek gained in influence but failed to win broad support from the population. Thereafter, over a decade of civil war erupted between Chinese nationalists and the Communist Party led by Mao. War with Japan brought even more turmoil through 1945. By 1949, the Communists forced the Nationalists into modern day Taiwan, turning China into an authoritarian Communist society.

The 1911 revolution inspired by Sun Yat-Sen offered some hope for democracy, but a generation of internal warfare and Japanese interference precluded it. This was thus one of many nationalist uprisings that repelled foreign tyranny in the century, only to bring more oppression after independence. In China, tens of millions would die from incompetent Communist rule in the 1950s and 1960s, as Mao aimed to institutionalize a futile peasant form of Marxism. Life for Chinese citizens arguably worsened through the century. Japanese aggression destroyed domestic security from the 1890s until 1945. Centralized authority fragmented, descending into a chaotic world of anarchy, warlord rule and resistance to Japanese imperialism. Millions would be forced to fight for a living in squalor due to conflict arising from Japanese cruelty and inept Chinese governance.

Indeed, into the 1980s most Asian people beyond China had endured decades of political domination by small cadres of legislators: from the Far Right in Japan, the Far Left in China, or in the case of Cambodia or Vietnam, between military control or conflict. Japanese conservatives annexed Korea in 1910, and until 1945, submission and humiliation shaped daily life for Koreans. The nation was in turn divided in 1954 by vying Cold War superpowers in the Korean War. North Korea became the most repressive, desperately poor state on earth, run by family despots. The people of South Korea endured authoritarian governance until the 1990s, albeit with incremental improvements in participation and rule of law. Tibet was taken over by China in 1950 and since the 1959 rebellion, Tibet has existed as an exiled state protesting Chinese control.

Until defeat in 1945, Japan's militarized state demanded complete fealty to the state and those with higher standing. The result was compulsory national pride founded on racist dictums—the Japanese imagined themselves destined to conquer other "inferior" Asian populations. Such sentiments were bolstered by Japanese victory over a "European" army in the 1905 war with Russia, leading Japan down a path to authoritarian military control, Second World War atrocities and ultimate loss. US intervention in the 1950s purposely shaped a democratic and capitalist allied state.

American people

If most of the world's Asian population enjoyed few rights and lacked political options through the century, Latin American people endured similar political fortunes. In 1900, from Chile to Guatemala, everyday people lived disconnected from the state apparatus, though over time they were brought under the shadow of the state. Farmers and peasants produced food to survive but could expect no aid from officialdom in distant state capitals. Though nominally citizens of Latin American nations, they were peripheral to party politics for the most part, besides paying the required taxes. The lives of South and Central Americans were greatly impacted by distant powers. Though elites in Latin American capitals were often pressured or coerced by foreign nations, those in power also benefitted from the connection. The most common reflex when economies slowed for instance was to pass on harsher taxes to the majority.

After gaining independence from European rule in the early nineteenth century, states in Latin American slowly fell under American influence. The Roosevelt Corollary of 1904 proclaimed the United States could and would intervene whenever its interests were threatened anywhere in the Americas. Washington interfered freely in the region until the 1930s, continuing to pursue indirect influence afterwards. Leaders across the Americas always had to consider US opinions. American *Dollar Diplomacy* provided a rationale to intervene at will to support US interests, often proclaiming the intention to assist poorer states. In the 1930s, a more benevolent Good Neighbor policy persisted, lasting until 1945, again with limited benefits for the majority populations.

In the 1920s, people in Latin America were increasingly incorporated into centralized states. Dictatorship and autocracy became the norm, however. Parties representing the masses formed as peasants became more aware of their rights and joined populist groups. Though some political liberties were generally permitted, inequality kept a tiny cadre in high standards of living while most remained mired in poverty, frustrated by political impotency.

In Latin America, impoverished peasants possessed only a limited sense of political rights. In Argentina, Brazil, and Mexico, wealthy landowning elites controlled national politics with little concern for the masses, let alone for indigenous populations. Inequality was (and remains) vast. The maltreatment of indigenous people across the Americas also persisted through the twentieth century. Brazilian and Argentine authorities used intimidating methods to coerce natives into European cultural norms. Brazil's ruling class banned slavery only in 1888, and attempted to exterminate Canudo Indians well into the 1900s.

Massive inequality derived from the Spanish colonial past was further prolonged by elite venality. The Mexican dictator, Porfirio Diaz (r.1876–1911), brought stability but no democracy. By 1910 German interests in Mexico prompted conflict with the United States, with foreign interference stimulating the Mexican

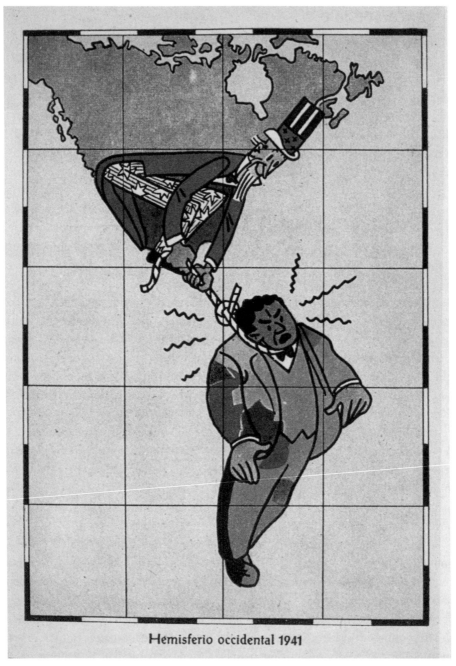

Hemisferio occidental 1941

Figure 1.3 The Monroe Doctrine in action. Card from 1941 showing Uncle Sam strangling the neck of South America, according to the terms of the Monroe Doctrine. (Michael Nicholson/Corbis via Getty Images.)

Revolution that year. Violence was endemic, as a staggering 2 million people died in Mexico in the first decade of the century, with recurring assassinations through the 1920s and 1930s. Power remained in the hands of the conservative PRI (Partido Revolucionario Institucional) party, who won support by promising land to farmers in 1929, and remained in power until 2000. Separatist uprisings by the indigenous Zapatistas in 1994 demonstrate ongoing discontent. The very poorest in Mexico continue to be excluded from political participation. Indigenous groups like the Maya still remain marginal to Mexico's political process.

Latin American ruling classes fervently resisted popular participation in the twentieth century. Prodigious US power projected into the lives of common people throughout Central and South America, often exacerbating domestic inequalities. Only since the 1990s has some semblance of democracy transpired in the region. The United States itself was comparably far more representative, but white Anglo-Saxon elites perpetuated a political system to benefit people of European origin. Native Americans were mistreated or ignored politically. People of color in general—black, native, Asian, or Hispanic—were excluded from political participation and growing prosperity through the 1960s, possessing neither political rights nor opportunity until recent decades.

Resistance was futile

Narrow political participation paled in comparison to outright massacre however, which was the affliction of many colonized people. In 1898, when a Prussian politician witnessed British guns slaughtering close to 10,000 Muslim soldiers in the Sudan, he deduced that Germany must urgently develop similar military prowess. While Western masses would be plagued by war through the first half of the century, colonial resistance against western elites would necessitate violence for the colonized.

In the first decade of the century, European powers were consumed with the urge for imperial and economic competition. This rivalry prompted unpardonable German abuses toward Africans, frequent Dutch and French violence in Southeast Asia, and British violence in India and Ireland. Until the 1940s, the notion of extending rights to colonial subjects remained absurd to the elites of Western states. Local populations were deemed unfit to govern their own societies. Force was thus perceived to be essential to maintain order.

Colonial nationalist movements developed in the first decades of the century, with aims of overthrowing foreign rule. The First World War provided an opening for Indian and Irish campaigners to remonstrate against British rule, while Mahatma Gandhi inspired millions of Indians to oust the British presence in South Asia. In 1919 British soldiers responded to a peaceful protest in Amritsar by massacring hundreds of people, only provoking greater Indian thirst for voting rights and the end of British rule. The Indian National Congress fought to gain local authority during the war, winning greater political rights from a grudging British power elite between 1917 and 1935. Followers of Gandhi mixed Western ideals of individual rights with Indian notions such as Satyagraha (truth force), working toward the ultimate goal of independence without violence.

Though people of color suffered immensely at the hands of Western powers, so too did the Irish. Southern Catholic rebels, long weary of British rule, took the opportunity to fight for independence during the war. Partial victory was achieved in 1921, with Catholic southern Ireland receiving dominion status, while majority Protestant Northern Ireland remained part of Britain. The IRA (Irish Republican Army), representing Irish Catholics, contest the division of Ireland throughout the twentieth century both peaceably and through terrorism, with solutions only emerging in the 1990s.

To counter growing violence, British officials devised home rule, in which Irish people would coordinate local politics under the umbrella of British authority. For Indians and Africans, Frederick Lugard devised a similar system after 1922, *Indirect Rule*. This paternalistic concept proposed allowing local customs and practices, while bidding elites to carry out British demands in the political sphere.

Local populations everywhere offered armed resistance, typically with limited success due to superior European firearms and military organization. Resistance

GROUP OF OFFICERS AT HEAD QUARTERS ON THE EVE OF DEPARTURE OF MR. E. FRASER, OFFG. AGENT, DEC. 1930.

Figure 1.4 Railway officers, Bombay, India, December 1930. (SSPL/Getty Images.)

was met with dreadful brutality. The Dutch and French slaughtered rebels whenever necessary. Belgian colonizers massacred Congolese natives before and after 1900, putting even other Western abuses to shame in comparison. Germany's military-aristocratic ruling class instigated the first genocide of the century in 1907, killing up to 100,000 Herero in Southwest Africa. British soldiers violently rounded up Boer rebels in South Africa into concentration camps by 1900.

Violence toward the Herero or Congolese was premised upon a firm belief in the inhumanity of inferior races. British rulers considered Irish and Indian people as politically backward and genetically inferior. Aborigines in Australia, where white settlers gained independence from Britain in 1901, were treated with similar savagery, lacking political rights up to the present. Everywhere, badly equipped or unarmed tribal warriors were wiped out mercilessly. Civilians were slaughtered while fighting to keep ancestral lands, which often contained diamonds, minerals, or gold required to sustain industrial economies.

Western rivalry also impinged upon the Muslim world, particularly after oil was discovered in Persia in 1908. Mostly decentralized, weakly organized tribal and regional polities provided easy targets for organized Western power. The slow collapse of the 700-year-old Turkic Ottoman Empire invited geopolitical interference in Arab, Turk, and Persian affairs from French, British, German, or American interests, all of whom aimed to challenge Russian influence in the region. Western interests negotiated concessions from local rulers to export oil to industrial economies. Those Arab tribes that collaborated became rich from the proceeds and usually ended up as ruling dynasties, while profits or political rights were kept from wider populations. Arab tribal populations had already suffered centuries of Ottoman rule, and though some elites gained autonomy after the First World War, the whole region would be swept up in Western power ploys. Most Arab people lived traditional lives, eking a living without political participation in the empire. Peasants who worked the land offered allegiance to local tribal and religious elites rather than to nation-states.

This was the case when the adventurer T. E. Lawrence advised British politicians to offer independence to certain Arab tribes during the war. This seemingly enlightened idea though conflicted with promises English politicians like Arthur Balfour made to the Jewish diaspora. British support for a Jewish homeland in the region would clash with contradictory promises to Arab tribes. Conflict was already prevalent by the 1920s, with abuses on both sides. Jews had suffered for decades from horrific pogroms in Russia, forcing families to flee to survive, and inspiring the Zionist movement in search of a Jewish homeland. Arab populations would soon be displaced by incoming Jewish families.

Other populations suffered as they strove for autonomy. In southeastern Europe, Balkan Muslims and Christians had lived, mostly peacefully, under Ottoman or Habsburg rule for centuries. Victory in the Balkan Wars of 1912 and 1914 brought liberation from the Ottomans and bolstered ethnic confidence for Serbia, Greece,

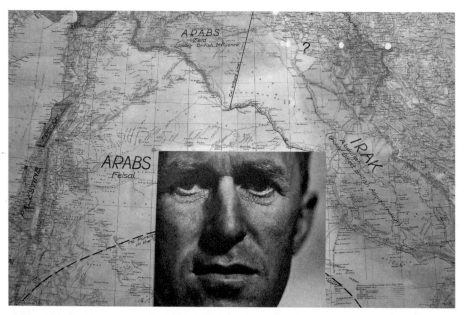

Figure 1.5 The map shows Lawrence's proposals for the reconstruction of the Middle East at the end of the First World War. (Photo illustration by Peter Macdiarmid/Getty Images.)

Montenegro, and Bulgaria. The Austrian Habsburg Empire however annexed Bosnia in 1908, prompting rising frustration in the region, particularly among Bosnian Serbs. Croatia would win independence from Austria in 1918 only after the empire finally fell.

In all these locales, the actual amount of imperial power varied. Often Westerners or Ottomans offered persuasive guidance rather than direct force. But local elites were compelled to act in accordance with the wishes of colonial officers, sultans or foreign officials, with the obvious threat of superior gun power in the background. Many local elites served as active middlemen, working to achieve gains for their own benefit; the collaboration of local elites suited Western and non-Western rulers.

The vast majority of people in Africa, the Middle East, Asia and Latin America enjoyed no basic political or indeed human rights in the first half of the century. Nationalism in Europe had motivated imperialism and colonial rule. This in turn aroused a separatist, pro-independence response from resentful, subjugated people, with limited results.

The power of national identity: the price of nationalism

In the first half of the twentieth century then, most humans lived under the influence of local elites, who were in turn dominated by foreign powers in differing degrees.

Once the First World War began, whatever stability global populations enjoyed in this system was shattered, as the world became ever more entangled politically, and far more violent.

Just as Western power widened the gap between industrial societies and the rest, European states turned the guns on one other. Nationalist rivalries were expressed through new violent industrial technologies in the First World War. The Maxim Gun provided power far beyond anything previously seen, and those few powers who possessed it—Britain and Germany, initially—dominated non-Western forces at will. Tanks and planes would complement such guns. While military technologies provided new ways of killing, new ideologies provided justification for forcing ideas upon others. Powerful nations thrust capitalism or Socialism upon less developed societies, while incorporating workers, artisans, or peasants into new forms of loyalty to the state.

Nationalism was an ideological force for expressing state power that evolved in a primitive form in medieval Britain and France. By the twentieth century, it generated an intoxicating shared identity, explaining the world to mostly illiterate people in the form of an imagined, imitation religion. Pride in self and nation was strengthened through education, symbolized daily in ubiquitous flags, monuments, and other symbolic representations of national authority. Nationalist elites recognized the benefits of providing state welfare, security, education and something all humans require, belonging.

Most people in 1900 were illiterate and uneducated, searching for a sense of dignity. Nation-states, whether autocratic or liberal, offered jobs and housing. For those in growing cities, hunger was staved for the first time in history thanks to directed national economies. In the decades before 1945, authoritarian states required only compliance and submission, while parliamentary and constitutional democracies expected and shaped conformity through education and mass media.

National identity presented a convenient outlet for hatred and prejudice, providing the means to exclude those who were different. Foreigners were derided based on difference or unsubstantiated myths. It was easy to loathe people of a different skin color; but white Germans could also hate white Frenchmen. Those of different religions could scorn each other even more: Jews, as they long had been, were despised simply for not being Christian or Muslim. Indeed, this explains the first calls for a Jewish state, as the Zionist movement sought Jewish autonomy that would culminate in the state of Israel in 1948. Jews, the most persecuted religious minority in Europe, thereafter developed a staunch nationalist ideology, to become the most powerful and militarized state in the Middle East.

Extraordinarily high casualties would come from fervent nationalist identity, as millions died for their nation, out of a sense of loyalty and a hatred of others. If any one idea can be held most responsible for the madness that lead to some 38 million deaths or casualties between 1914 and 1918, it is the manner in which power elites harnessed mass nationalist loyalty to the nation-state, a relatively new type of political ideology in history. In an era when most lacked the basic needs to survive, it made perfect sense to fight for a national homeland that provided material sustenance and a sense of identity. After 1914, millions would die for it.

The interventionist warfare state

National governments often intervened positively in the lives of citizens, but they also prepared citizens for warfare. States evolved into abstract entities of citizens partaking in a perceived political role, acting with imagined autonomy, sensing empowerment from that role. Politicians in capitals provided state benefits and services neither the free market nor village life had provided. The rising impact of government in citizens' life brought housing, hospital care, and fresh water in cities. Rulers could offer a good career to men who enlisted; the only qualification being average height and weight, and a willingness to fight other peoples. Implementing vast state-run war machines *Interventionist states* also induced citizens to join armies and navies.

Nationalism was especially attractive in totalitarian, antidemocratic countries, though it shaped industrial liberal states too. Democracies like the United States, France, and Britain purposely inculcated a sense of nationalist pride also, but they had developed with diverse power centers: the state shared power with society, through voluntary groups, churches, towns, private organizations, and competing political alliances. This diversity was crucially lacking in authoritarian states.

But even in democracies, politicians typically made pronouncements behind a veil of secrecy. Rulers in Europe found that they could get the citizenry to do almost anything if they let them have some voice. Partial democracy thus offered a win-win situation—the elite class conceded to electoral participation, while the masses felt involved. Outside the West, power elites enjoyed considerably more control; sultans, emperors, or dictators, whether in South America, the Muslim world, Asia, or Africa more easily prevented popular participation. A few men with no need for broad consultation usually made decisions for all.

After the First World War, previously loose social groups were more sharply demarcated into unified nations. Obligation to the state was cemented through new symbolic means via passports, identity cards, jobs, and even stamps. National bureaucrats busily marked out state boundaries, delineating who was who, and highlighting who and what was not acceptable.

Though national police and legal systems provided safety for families and career opportunities for loyal men, the state increasingly enjoyed the legitimacy to pursue violence in the name of security. State systems of governance controlled actions and thoughts, often claiming to be democratic or benevolent. All states, democratic or otherwise, suppressed free speech, civil liberties, and dissent. Free and compulsory schools, an enlightened notion if ever there was one, mainly educated the young to be loyal to the state, not to think critically. One of the key outcomes of this complex process was far greater loyalty to nation and far more violence.

German aggression

While liberal democracies afforded only narrow political participation, authoritarian states hoodwinked whole populations into extreme nationalist violence. This would bring the world ghastly conflict after the 1930s. Democratic states colonized and killed but should not be considered equivalent to authoritarian states. The best, or rather worst, example of this proclivity for nationalist extremism is a nation that straddled democracy and autocracy through the century, Germany.

It is hard to dispute the fact that German aggression prompted both world wars. Nonetheless, German aims to create a global empire, though no more morally acceptable than any other acts of imperialism, merely imitated other nation's practices, particularly France, Britain, and the United States. Kaiser Wilhelm in fact met with the American imperialist admiral Alfred Mahan to discuss the means of attaining sea power worldwide. By 1900, German elites harnessed national pride in their populations, incorporated citizens to pursue the military aims of the state, and propagandized worldviews through education. Military-industrial expansion was a political practice purposely pursued by all the great powers, though it was exemplified best by German conservative elites hell-bent on possessing global power through naval expansion.

Perceiving that they had missed out on nineteenth-century colonial gains, German elites militarized at breakneck speed following national unification in 1871. By 1914, an army with over 120 divisions of soldiers forced other states to pay attention. Though Britain possessed a larger navy, it could muster only ten divisions. This prompted frantic British alliances with nations such as Japan and France to counter growing German power.

Though US leaders were less involved outside the Americas, they pursued openly xenophobic expansion in Central and South American economies to add to obey the doctrine of "Manifest Destiny," which justified American influence across the Americas. After conquering the American West in North America, the United States government took the Philippines from Spain in 1898, then annexed Hawaii, Cuba, Guam, and Puerto Rico before 1914. By 1899, China was forced open, to free American businessmen to reap profits along with Europeans and Japanese in the imperial open-door policy.

Japan was the sole non-Western power playing this game of aggression. Having recently militarized and modernized, Japan defeated Russia in 1905, pushing that weak imperial state toward Communist revolution in 1917. This victory earned Japan international prestige, inspiring its military elite to expand across Asia, as a supposed "superior race." Conservative Japanese leaders purposely emulated Germany, even adopting its constitution in 1889. Japanese militarists annexed Taiwan and Korea in the 1890s and pursued a brutal expansion until eventual defeat and humiliation in 1945.

Political alliances were cemented among European nations after 1900. By 1914, France, Russia, and Britain formed the entente cordiale, while Germany, Austria, and the Turkish Ottoman Empire allied into the Central Powers. Alliances were supposed to deter other groups from aggression but served instead to put all states on knife-edge. Nationalist extremism and national alliances prompted an absurd series of events and miscommunications in July and August 1914 that led to the catastrophe of the First World War.

2. A thirty-years' war? 1914–1947

The First World War did not occur solely due to nationalist ideology, however. Imperialism, an associated dogma, enriched Western states and drove them toward conflict. As ancient as imperial expansion was historically, a new more virulent type of foreign control known as *New Imperialism* emerged after 1880 to exacerbate rivalries. Industrial and military competition required resource extraction from weaker regions, while a self-perpetuating military arms race created "better" guns, tanks, and machines using those materials. By the summer of 1914, a conflict between nationalist Balkan rebels and imperial Habsburg traditionalists set humanity on a tragic and unnecessary course, with worldwide consequences.

The First World War

The usual period cited for the war are the years 1914 to 1918. But if we include the imperial ambitions that drove states to conflict, the war arguably began with the Berlin Conference in 1884, which sliced the continent of Africa into European properties. Asian conflict increased after 1894, when Japan encroached upon the sovereignty of China and Korea, bringing 51 years of combat. For those in the Islamic or Indian world, the war was merely a continuation of past oppression, since they were caught up in the fighting whether they liked it or not.

Long-suffering non-Westerners endured war in the Middle East and Africa also, as hundreds of thousands died for foreign causes. Up to 4 million colonized African, Asian, and Indian soldiers fought in Europe's war. After the crumbling Ottoman Empire allied with Germany to maintain domination of the Arab world, it provided justification for the victors Britain and France to shape the Middle East. Bad as this was, Germany had intended to colonize the region after victory, so it could have been worse for the Arab world. Ottoman Turkey had already lost most of its Balkan territories by 1913, and internal dissent grew after the Young Turk movement of 1908 aspired toward constitutional democracy. After losing the war, Turkey would follow the political model of Western states.

The position of most states prior to war can be defended on certain levels: German leaders wished to counter Britain's empire; French rulers resisted German strength to regain earlier dominance; Britons defended their colossal empire; Russians defended Slavic pride and aspired to equal power status; Austrian elites wished to keep an ancient dynastic empire in place, and could not conceive of independent nations in their midst; and Serbs understandably desired autonomy to end historical domination and foreign rule. At the same time, no power was prepared for war, let alone a modern war unlike any prior.

The immediate, direct cause of the war is usually blamed on a radical Serb who assassinated the Habsburg, Archduke Franz Ferdinand. This act, labeled terrorist by the great powers, was however the culmination of decades of Bosnian and Serbian frustration toward aloof Austrians. Russia encouraged Serb nationalism in hopes

Figure 1.6 The First World War memorial in the forest near Victoria Falls commemorating Northern Rhodesia's sacrifice. (Jason Edwards/Getty Images.)

of countering German and British power and increasing Slavic pride in the region. Diplomatic efforts —even among royal European families connected by bloodlines— ultimately broke down, as a spiral of nationalist overconfidence prevented peaceful resolution.

The war had deep roots in the chest-thumping nationalist ideologies of preceding decades. And for all the nationalist propaganda marketed by elites, those who suffered most were the crippled and mangled masses that did most of the fighting. Though many in power also lost sons and fathers, they did so from a social position of considerably greater comfort. Millions of women lost husbands, countless children lost fathers, and a whole generation of people, in Europe and outside, endured senseless pains to add to a life already fraught with scarcity.

As noted before, Germany was the chief aggressor. Armed with imperialist and nationalist beliefs, German conservative aggression kick-started armed combat in August 1914. By invading Belgium, German bellicosity provoked national commitments to treaty alliances. The invasion violated Britain's 1830 treaty with Belgium, so British rulers declared war on Germany. France, eager to fight Germany anyway, was bound to support Russia. Britain, in turn, was bound to defend France. Austrian Habsburg obstinacy had prompted the assassination in the first place, and imperial Austrian collapse after war facilitated German domination in Central Europe—leading to the Second World War.

As the famous 1929 novel *All Quiet on the Western Front* expressed so well, the first year of war mixed tedious periods of quiet with intermittent slaughter. Well into 1915, military commanders strategized across Western Europe, with barely any forward moves. Defense was far simpler than attack. Stalemate and trench life persisted, soldiers lived in misery for no apparent reason, minor naval battles took place, and politicians made threats in newspapers. In the Crimea though, 80,000 Turkish troops froze to death while fighting Russian advances in the winter of 1914. The slaughter had begun.

The war went worldwide in 1915. Mesopotamia (Iraq) became a theater of conflict between Ottoman and Allied troops. At Gallipoli, though Turkey and Britain lost the most soldiers, large numbers of Irish, Indians, Australians, and New Zealanders died too, slaughtered by Turks while fighting for indifferent British commanders. Balkans troops were embroiled in the conflict, losing around 150,000 men at Gallipoli. In 1915, Armenians were decimated by Turkish troops in what has been labeled a genocide. British imperial forces also took Baghdad in 1915, a major blow to the Ottomans and Arab world. The British also occupied numerous Polynesian islands for naval bases, while conflict increased in North Africa between British and German troops. In 1915, Germany resorted to chemical warfare, firing canisters of gas at French and Belgian soldiers.

In 1916, all-out war developed in Europe, and deaths increased accordingly. Lacking proper military organization, men died relentlessly in appalling conditions.

Elite incompetence and low food supplies brought disease, while horrifying battles in France slaughtered hundreds of thousands of men for no strategic gain. Over 300,000 died at Verdun, while close to a million died or were wounded in the Battle of the Somme. The naval battle at Jutland in May was a similarly meaningless ocean stalemate. In 1916, the Russians lost vast numbers of men to German assaults, as both nations vied for Romanian oil fields. Russian soldiers were already stretched thin fighting Turkey in Central Asia, enduring merciless heat and bleak cold there.

> One French soldier, later killed in the war, perhaps represented the view of many soldiers, writing in 1916:
>
> *Humanity is mad. It must be mad to do what it is doing. What a massacre! What scenes of horror and carnage! I cannot find words to translate my impressions. Hell cannot be so terrible. Men are mad.[4]*

Russian deaths numbered well over 2 million by the end of the war—it is little surprise that Communism appeared a good alternative to imperialist capitalism. By 1917, Russian peasants were starving, and soldiers lost morale while fighting for Tsar Nicholas and his imperial cronies. Imperial government capitulated to popular revolt that year. The chaos of war thus thrust new leaders in the rising Communist Party such as Trotsky and Lenin into position. The Communists won support among the people by leaving the conflict in 1917, and swiftly murdered the imperial family. Well-intentioned but timid Liberals in the temporary government were pushed aside and by late 1917, Moscow came under Communist rule. Timid Russian liberals prevaricated in taking power in Russia. They also lost support among the people through their desire to continue fighting a futile war. Three attempts at democratic coalitions brought a civil war lasting through 1921 between moderate Mensheviks and Communist Bolsheviks. When Communist victory came, as many as 10 million Russians were dead.

1917 also introduced new ways of killing at sea through submarine warfare, as underwater stealth attacks from all sides sunk enemy ships. Naval warfare had brought American interest in the war when Germany sank the *Lusitania* in 1915, a ship carrying American citizens. Most Americans remained isolationist and reelected Woodrow Wilson because of his promise of neutrality. But by 1917, German threats of sinking any and all enemy ships infuriated Americans. The eventual entry of US soldiers to the war in spring 1918 supported the Allied effort crucially, tipping the balance. US participation (as an "associated power" rather than an ally) certainly helped the Western democracies win the war. It also prompted an already growing American economy to soar from massive munitions sales and increased employment. This would ironically be the foundation of America's new status as a global force.

Hostilities continued through spring 1918, when a final German offensive took place amid domestic unrest and antiwar marches at home. The German people had had enough. Through the summer, Allied soldiers defeated a crumbling German army, and a cease-fire came in November. Four years of defensive warfare had passed without any clear victories, many murderous battles of attrition and unimaginable slaughter. Years of stalemate, monotony, and frigidity dogged soldiers in trenches, along with vermin and lice. National economies were ruined, millions died, countless people were traumatized. By 1918 all sides were drained, with the exception of the geographically isolated United States. America soon gained in stature and prosperity, while Britain and France extended earlier imperial influence in Africa and the Middle East.

Country	Population in millions	Total deaths	Deaths as % of population
Serbia	4.5	Up to 1,250,000	16.67% to 27.78
Ottoman	21.3	Up to 3,271,844	13.26% to 15.36
German Empire	64.9	Up to 2,800,720	3.39 to 4.32
Russian Empire	175.1	Up to 2,254,369	1.64 to 1.94

Source: https://en.wikipedia.org/wiki/World_War_I_casualties. France lost around 5 percent to deaths.

But no nation "won," and the consequences of war lasted well past the Second World War, in effect an extension of the first conflict. The Turks lost large territories in the Middle East, leaving Britain and France to partition the Muslim world. Aside from Serbia, the Ottoman Empire lost the highest proportion of men. As different tribal Muslim kingdoms had sided with the Allies or the Turks, the Middle East became a prime source of oil and site of strategic jostling thereafter. Austria lost Serbia and became a weak, conservative appendage of Germany. Italy, having joined the Allies in 1915, at the end of the war hoped that Britain would share Middle Eastern and African colonial possessions. It ended up frustrated, weak and divided, leaving a vacuum for Mussolini and Fascist extremists to exploit in the 1920s. Japan joined Britain's side in 1914 in order to dominate China, and soon careened toward a Fascist military dictatorship.

Germany was ruined. Conservative leaders in the military and aristocracy who had started the war were now terrified of neighboring Communist states, and by association, all progressive, leftist political parties. Germany lost its navy and lands to the west of the Rhine River. After two revolutions, both of which failed, civil violence between left and right-wing extremists increased, and would help produce the Nazi Party in 1923. Divisions among progressives and Socialists facilitated Fascist coalescence on the right. The Kapp Putsch in 1920 showed that the nation leaned toward right-wing extremism well before Hitler came to power. Right-wing extremists conveniently blamed leftists and Jews for Germany's loss rather than the conservative generals who caused it, and who maintained power after the war.

Though the First World War was a war of patriotism, not all men rushed to war, and many doubted, even in the midst of battle, the logic of dying for the nation. Wilfred Owen's famous poem from 1917 argued that to die for one's country was a "lie":

Dulce et Decorum est

Bent double, like old beggars under sacks,
Knock-kneed, coughing like hags, we cursed through sludge,
Till on the haunting flares, we turned our backs
And towards our distant rest began to trudge.
Men marched asleep. Many had lost their boots
But limped on, blood-shod. All went lame; all blind;
Drunk with fatigue; deaf even to the hoots
Of tired, outstripped Five-Nines that dropped behind.
Gas! Gas! Quick, boys!—An ecstasy of fumbling,
Fitting the clumsy helmets just in time . . .

. . . Come gargling from the froth-corrupted lungs,
Obscene as cancer, bitter as the cud
Of vile, incurable sores on innocent tongues,
My friend, you would not tell with such high zest
To children ardent for some desperate glory,
The old Lie; *Dulce et Decorum est*
Pro patria mori.[5]

The 1920s: A scarred settlement

After previously unimaginable depths of carnage, a question became apparent to leaders in industrial societies: What was to replace this flawed system of international relations, where stronger nations colonized weaker societies, and economic profit motivated political decisions? Some thought that humanity could do better. Woodrow Wilson earnestly offered a new order, aiming to maintain peace through his forward-looking Fourteen Points.[6] The principled US president offered sensible suggestions to prevent future conflict, outlining the first widespread attempt to protect the independent sovereignty of smaller nations.

Elites from the major Western democracies met in 1919 to determine the new order. Outwardly high-minded ideals would inadvertently bring decades of worse conflict, however. Though Woodrow Wilson, France's Georges Clemenceau, Britain's Lloyd George and Vittorio Orlando of Italy—the "Big Four"—aspired to find peace, their nineteenth-century mind-sets could not permit dissent from supposedly inferior peoples in colonized, non-Western societies, and the conference restricted representation from the wider world. National self-interest remained foremost for the great powers.

The Paris Peace Conference concluded with the Treaty of Versailles in June 1919. Wilson's enthusiastic desire for the self-determination of all peoples would not materialize. The democratic principles he espoused inspired millions in non-Western nations but left them increasingly disappointed after Versailles. The *League of Nations* did form however, with the noble intent of removing warfare from international relations and providing a global forum for diplomacy. Nonetheless, much of the ensuing conflict stemmed from the consequences, often unintended, of this conference.

Outside Europe

The exclusion of non-Western representatives prompted decades of animosity and disappointment for the vast majority of people outside the West. Asian, African, and Arab representatives received the brunt of Western racism—African and Arab officials were not consulted. Japanese calls for a Racial Equality clause in the League of Nations covenant were brushed aside, inspiring zealous Japanese militarism. China's future overlord Mao Tse-tung felt betrayed when Western powers gave Germany's portion of China to the Japanese. Chinese rebels pursued a path to Communism motivated by irritation at Western duplicity. Ho Chi Minh, who would fight US military intervention in the Vietnam War, was similarly condescended to when he attempted to represent the Vietnamese people.

African people were simply not represented, their territories further shared among Europeans. No Arab leaders were present to see France and Britain carve new territories in the Middle East. Jewish leaders did attend to raise the issue of European anti-Semitism, prompting further indignation among the shunned Arabs. Indians and Muslims were not consulted, considered merely junior members of the British Empire. Hindu and Muslim leaders spent the next three decades working to oust British rule, led by Mahatma Gandhi.

Political decisions had enormous consequences. A month prior to the war, Winston Churchill ensured that Britain controlled Middle Eastern oil via a 51 percent stake in the Anglo-Persian Oil Company (today's British Petroleum). Britain's plan to convert its navy from coal to oil meant Middle East resources would shape decisions made in London or Paris. Bent on gaining influence in the Middle East and Africa, Britain and France created *mandates* to protect newly created states such as Jordan, Iraq, Syria, and Lebanon. Though the proposition was to gradually prepare independent Arab states, access to oil was central to national strategies. European leaders thus shaped new nations in the Middle East, mixing together rival ethnic groups with little in common.

Western decisions thus shaped the Middle East's entry into modernity. The Sykes–Picot Agreement, made between Britain and France in 1916, divided Middle Eastern territories. Since Britain possessed the only large military force in the region, it could act at will against small Arab tribes or kingdoms with limited capability. Control of the Suez Canal was necessary for British access to India, giving Britain nominal control of Egypt. In 1917, Arthur Balfour and other Anglo-American elites pronounced support for a Zionist state, supporting the Jewish desire for a national homeland in Palestine, after over thousand years of diaspora. In 1948, Israel became a modern state, amid Palestinian Arabs who had lived in the region for millennia who lacked a modern state apparatus.

The Sykes–Picot Agreement: 1916

It is accordingly understood between the French and British governments:

> That France and Great Britain are prepared to recognize and protect independent Arab states or a confederation of Arab states (a) and (b) marked on the annexed map, under the suzerainty of an Arab chief. That in area (a) France, and in area (b) Great Britain, shall have priority of right of enterprise and local loans. That in area (a) France, and in area (b) Great Britain, shall alone supply advisers or foreign functionaries at the request of the Arab state or confederation of Arab states.
>
> That in the blue area France, and in the red area Great Britain, shall be allowed to establish such direct or indirect administration or control as they desire and as they may think fit to arrange with the Arab state or confederation of Arab states.
>
> That in the brown area there shall be established an international administration, the form of which is to be decided upon after consultation with Russia, and subsequently in consultation with the other allies, and the representatives of the Shereef of Mecca.[7]

Arabs had been dominated by the Ottoman Turks for centuries, and a modern Turkish nation-state formed after the war through the exclusion of non-Turkic Muslims. As noted earlier, in 1915, the Ottoman military had slaughtered minority Armenians—in sufficient numbers that many now consider a genocide. Turkish generals had suspected alliance between Armenian Christians and Russian Orthodox Christians, and in the fury of war, acted as they found necessary. Within Turkey, protests from the Khilafat movement—a group that wished to maintain Muslim traditions—were brushed aside by secular reformers. The emergence of a Western-style republican government after 1923 led by Kemal Ataturk displeased many. However, a moderate democracy of a sort was bestowed upon the Turkish people, and Turkey emerged as the most modern, developed Muslim nation in the region.

In Egypt, British influence persisted as it had since 1882, supported by a collaborative Egyptian monarchy. The Muslim Brotherhood formed in 1928 to protest

Figure 1.7 circa 1916: Mustafa Kemal Ataturk. Turkish general, nationalist leader and president. (Keystone/Getty Images.)

this partnership with foreigners, becoming one of the earliest regional organizations intent on ousting foreign influence through violence. Iran was run by the corrupt Pahlavi dynasty, whose willingness to sell oil to the West kept the family in power until 1979, and most Persians impoverished. This followed a century of inept rule by the Qajar dynasty which left the Shia state poor and undeveloped.

Indian agitators had long protested British power and the end of war brought a steep rise in political consciousness. Moderate political participation was achieved following the limited Government of India Act of 1919, though it both dismayed British conservatives and frustrated Indian nationalists. By 1935, only one-sixth of Indian adults could vote in their own nation, further stoking the anger of nationalist advocates who would win independence in 1947

Within Europe

The war's consequences played out over decades worldwide, but in the short term the impact was felt most within Europe. New European nations were hammered together, and few were satisfied. Millions of men who had been mobilized to fight now looked to leaders to configure new nations aligning with ethnic identities. Newly independent nations like Czechoslovakia and Yugoslavia expected minorities to assimilate to a wider national identity. Poland gained earlier lost lands from Germany and Russia, enraging extremists in both nations. Italy's desire for colonial lands in Africa was rejected, offending Italian patriots. Austria lost territory and was forbidden from merging with Germany, turning that nation further to the Right. Bulgaria and Hungary also lost land for siding with the Entente Cordiale. Everywhere some faction was dissatisfied. Aside from Czechoslovakia, all Eastern European states turned toward conservative authoritarianism by 1930. Thus, a volatile set of relations was left in place that would embroil the region once again in war.

Those in democracies felt assured of German blame for the war, but Germans did not. Germans considered Liberalism as the root cause of the conflict: Communists considered capitalism as the problem. Though British politicians insisted on the *War Guilt Clause*, payment of reparations and German disarmament, they were less bent on punishment than the French. France bordered Germany directly (and suffered over 4 million lost or wounded) so the desire for retribution was understandable. Both Britain and France needed German reparations to recover the cost of war, and both had to remunerate colonial supporters. France soon took the key economic region of Alsace-Lorraine back from Germany. German irritation at the treaty terms should not be given too much credit though: Germany had punished Russia mercilessly at Brest-Litovsk in 1918, taking huge swathes of land when the Communists quit the war.

Germany though soon reeled from instability. Insolvent after the war, with rampant poverty, a detached elite and violence in the streets, there was little room left for political ideals such as women's or worker's rights. The Left-wing Spartacist Uprising of 1919 scared conservatives and moderates, who saw radical Communists loyal to Moscow. Right-wing militarists, responsible for the war in the first place, preposterously blamed progressives for losing the war. By 1920, repetition of such propaganda empowered the conservative Freikorps, who began threatening or murdering leftists. A new conservative myth, that Germany was "stabbed in the back" by the Left (and Jews) would inspire Hitler and the Nazis.

Decisions made in Washington also impacted Europe. US economic elites refused to cancel Allied war debts to US lenders, so Britain and France had no choice but to penalize Germany. Consequently, Germany bore the cost of the war alone, reluctantly submitting to demilitarization, harsh repayments and lost territories. Since essential coalmines in the Saar region went to France, Hitler had plenty of ammunition with which to incite humiliated Germans in the 1920s. US Congressional elections in late 1918 had given conservative Republicans the power to force an agenda of isolationism. Though Wilson craved independent nations and the rule of law, he could not enforce his ideals in a Republican Congress that favored harsh chastisement of Germany. Most Americans preferred disengaging anyway, and Republicans exploited this to dominate the 1920s. The Versailles Treaty would be ratified by all the powers except the United States.

A lack of American participation and weakened French and British democracies proved incapable of stemming the approaching totalitarian tide. In the 1920s centrist compromise seemed possible in the semi-democratic Weimar Republic led by the moderate German chancellor Gustav Stresemann. The Republic lasted until 1933, when Hitler was appointed chancellor. The center-left that aspired to counter aristocratic, Prussian militarism could not compete in a Germany further impoverished by the Great Depression after 1930. This gave Right-wing extremists the opportunity to capitalize on national humiliation, and drive humanity to another world war.

End of empire, or new empires?

Imperial prejudices carried over from the nineteenth century prompted Western leaders to make narrow-minded decisions after the First World War, with grave consequences. Many hoped the days of empire were numbered, and indeed the First World War ended oppressive dynastic empires in Russia, Austria, and Germany. After the Romanov, Habsburg, and Hohenzollern dynasties crumbled, ending centuries of purportedly sacred rule, all three states however adopted intensely nationalist ideologies. The vast majority of people would find themselves no better off. China's imperial Qing Dynasty, already fragmented and massively indebted to Westerners, saw its last emperor worshipped in 1917, bringing only decades of anarchy. Chinese people enjoyed no central authority until 1949.

Rising powers: United States and USSR

After the war, the most ancient form of rule, imperial authority, declined. But British, Dutch, and French imperialism would persist into the 1950s. Outwardly, the United States and the USSR, both opposed imperialism, but in the interwar period, they became new types of empires. They touted two opposing visions for humanity. While Woodrow Wilson spoke of democracy and liberty, the United States forced markets open worldwide. While Vladimir Lenin spoke of the workers' paradise and equality, the USSR subjugated people at home and outside Russia.

1917 was the year these two distant nations started down separate political paths that would intertwine them permanently. The United States joined the war reticently in 1917, only after American civilian deaths at sea caused outrage. Thereafter, it would use its power to promote unchecked capitalism and the development of overseas economic interests. Communist elites in the USSR began to implement a workers' revolution in 1917, proposing a supposed workers' paradise, while in the process subjugating millions of people and exporting revolution.

Wilson and other Western leaders zealously abhorred the notion of Communism. And, in the 1920s, an obsessive fear of left-wing internationalism began to cloud national decision making in Europe and the United States. Following Russia's 1917 Communist Revolution, a *Red Scare* shaped policies laid out at Versailles, convincing establishment elites to fight leftist governance wherever it emerged. Eastern Europe's newly independent nations were partly intended to fend off leftist revolutions and provide a buffer between the West and Russia. A forceful commitment to Western, industrial capitalism fervently countered the apparition of Communism for the next six decades.

In the 1920s, Western elites talked benevolently of a League of Nations, universal human rights, and the independence of nations. Meanwhile Russian elites aspired to engineer a social experiment and achieve true equality. Neither would ensue: Soviet leaders claimed to eradicate the profit motive in a new utopia, but poverty ensued and human rights found no fertile ground in Communist societies; while Westerners criticized political dominion, they increased global economic exploitation.

Capitalizing on war

American leaders loudly criticized Anglo-French imperialism, but Americans nonetheless profited from war. The United States certainly supported the Allies, offering manpower, a basic army and capital in the form of purchases and loans. But Conservative principles prevailed in the 1920s to focus on profit rather than peace. French and British conservatives refused to give up on empire, and US Conservatives did not wish to assist in European, or world, affairs other than through loans and trade. American bankers refused to write-off loans to struggling European states, calling in debts from British or French borrowers regardless of the political situation. These in turn refused to write-off German debts, ultimately leading to economic collapse, and German extremism.

American capitalism enriched domestic life and brought stability at home. Piecemeal though it was, political representation brought gains to middle-class and wealthy white people. Those of color, including descendants of slaves, immigrants from Asia, Hispanics, and indigenous people endured poverty and racism through the Second World War, not partaking in the nation's newfound affluence or political democracy.

Communist control

If political impotency was the lot of most in the United States, for those in the USSR it was worse. Like the poor masses in the United States, workers and peasants in the USSR had access to only restricted political participation. The anticipation of a workers' paradise with a political stake instead became one of the most oppressive societies in modern history. Famines killed 6 million people in 1921 and even more in the Ukraine in 1933.

Figure 1.8 Striking workers on the first day of the February Revolution, St. Petersburg, Russia, 1917. (Fine Art Images/Heritage Images/Getty Images.)

The Bolshevik Revolution in 1917 was supposed to make an impoverished, mostly agricultural nation a major power, and it did by the 1950s. The USSR though was vast in size and diversity, composed of many ethnic peoples. Long-suffering Russian and minority peasants had endured autocratic emperors and violent nobles, ruling blindly in their own interests. By the end of the 1920s, a controlling Communist elite from Moscow simply replaced imperial authority.

No tradition of political representation existed in Russia. Its imperial military had been humiliated in 1905, losing a war to the supposedly inferior Japanese. Ensuing protests forced the tsar to make concessions, setting up the first elected parliament in 1906. But wealthy landowners connected to the imperial family ran the state for personal gain. In February 1917, urban rebels and Communists overthrew the Tsar to install a provisional government. Marching mothers gathered in St. Petersburg to protest hunger and start the uprising. This forced the failing state to recognize widespread frustrations, and further emboldened revolutionaries. After the provisional government voted to stay in the war, a second revolution in October toppled it, leaving power in the hands of a tiny vanguard of Bolshevik Communists.

During the ensuing civil war, the more conservative Mensheviks proposed broad participation for the masses, finding support from Allied powers who intervened on their behalf. Vladimir Lenin and the Bolsheviks preferred an industrial proletariat led by a small leadership of revolutionaries. When Leon Trotsky coordinated a vast, efficient Red Army of 3 million men, a small stratum of better-organized Bolsheviks defeated the Mensheviks and their foreign suitors to secure a new Communist state, doubly wary of foreign capitalist nations.

Though many urban Russians became politically active after 1917, only a small group held power by 1921. Theoretically bringing social and political equality to human society for the first time ever, the Communist experiment was immediately hijacked by a small number of cadres whose zeal was a continuation of near-religious obedience to the imperial family. Though Communist elites purported to implement universal theories of Leninist–Marxism, they were never carried out, replaced by 1928 with Josef Stalin's megalomaniac personal rule.

Such theories were in any case dubious when applied to human experience. Marxist ideology predicted that workers would take over the state, and then it would disappear. The opposite happened in fact; an all-pervasive state emerged. Lenin had no faith in the conservative and compliant Russian peasantry, and few showed interest in the dogma of Marxism. Faced with reality, an elite group, or vanguard, took over the state to control all aspects of life for the inferior masses. The elect few such as Lenin and Stalin manipulated the population to further the interests of the party, not the people. People in the USSR merely went from imperial dynasty to Communist oligarchy.

Lenin's claim that capitalism led inevitably to imperialism was a plausible historical argument. But after he died in 1923, Stalin conspired to take control, forcing the Russian people down a path of inequity, oppression, and national paranoia known since as Stalinism. His more conservative, nationalist form of Communism vied with Trotsky's revolutionary version in the 1920s. By 1928, Stalin though had ousted Trotsky, facing no political opposition until his death in 1953.

Though victorious in resisting the Nazi threat in the Second World War, Stalin left a legacy of KGB torture, hunger, poverty, and violence toward trade unions! His political purges perpetuated a culture of insecurity even for party loyalists. From 1934 to 1938 domestic terror was relentless. Intellectuals who dissented were slaughtered and over 2 million Russians and minorities were imprisoned. Millions more were forced to labor in lives of torment. In 1940, Stalin's agents killed his sole living adversary Trotsky, for endeavoring to expose Stalinism from Mexico.

Theoretically, Communism would spread globally to the "workers of the world." The USSR was in fact immediately isolated, and pursued a one-nation form of Communism. Stalin immediately contradicted Marxist theory with his program of "Socialism in one country"—a more practical, self-serving ideal rather than the more ambitious world revolution. However, the mere fact that the Soviet Comintern espoused international revolution spooked Western elites. Throughout the Western world, well into the 1980s, the mere mention of the menace of Communism served to shepherd citizens toward state loyalty.

Democracy in the 1920s: Manufacturing consent?

While workers in the Soviet Union suffered, western Europeans hardly fared better prior to the Second World War. In Western Europe, it was mostly the common people who died during war. They faced hunger and violence in the 1920s. But more than anywhere else, Western workers were emboldened to fight for political rights as payback for wartime sacrifices. People worldwide had to survive a massive flu pandemic first in 1919, which took up to 100 million lives worldwide, far more than the war itself!

The war's origin stemmed from political dissent in the Balkans. In the decade before 1914, mass politics had become an infectious new form of thought in Europe, threatening the comforts of pampered nobles and aristocratic dynasties. Though the war's origins were attributed to terrorism, frustrated Balkans activists ultimately aimed for a broad national Slavic sovereignty and political respect.

Following wartime sacrifices, workers in Europe understandably expected participation and representation. The first workers' party, the Labour Party, had formed in Britain in 1906 to purposely advocate for the workforce. British Liberals had usually emphasized gains for the middle classes and consequently lost votes after the war. In places under British colonial influence such as Australia, Canada, New Zealand, or the United States, comparable populist parties formed to fight for (white) workers' rights, ignoring people of color or women. Though limited in scope, Western democracy began to develop in the 1920s.

Those in power knew that the simplest way to prevent revolution in democracies was to enable, but shape the votes and minds of the uneducated masses. Populations received limited schooling and had little understanding of the political process, so authorities could promote conformity and unquestioning obedience. Still, nations with more literate workers experienced greater political upheaval after the war, since workers had both the freedom to protest and the intellectual means to do so. In Western Europe voter participation gradually improved, while in southern and Eastern Europe, as elsewhere, it remained impracticable. Around the world otherwise, a mixture of colonial condescension and elite disdain for educating the masses meant voting rights were inconceivable.

In some ways, war interrupted the struggle for equality in the West, as millions of men, (some dubious about the virtue of the conflict, most oblivious of its origins) went off to die for causes leaders proclaimed were national problems. Women's rights were stifled during the war due to pressing military issues, though increased voting rights emerged for Western women afterwards. In the 1920s, suffragettes provoked male politicians physically and intellectually to eventually win the vote. Though representation was still impossible for women around the world, in the West, in Western-derived Latin America, Japan, and some Communist states, it became a partial reality in the 1920s. Limited, popular voting rights emerged in the 1920s, offering the seeds of popular participation in industrial nations.

In line with Wilson's ideals, the mid-1920s offered hope for democracy. At the Washington Conference of 1921–1922 the United States proposed limitations on navy sizes, striving to decrease warfare and shipbuilding among naval nations such as Britain, France, Japan, and the United States. This succeeded until 1936, when Japan rejected the agreements to reconstruct its navy for authoritarian imperial power. The US-led Dawes Plan of 1924 also defused tensions by lowering German repayments and pressuring the French to allow German access to the Ruhr region.

The League of Nations also contributed to peace in the 1920s, establishing assemblies and councils to avert war. After the Locarno Conference in 1925, there was optimism in Europe. Though arbitration between Germany and France was tense, disputes over European borders were resolved without great conflict. The Kellogg-Briand Pact of 1928, signed by sixty-five states, even proclaimed that war must no more be a national instrument of policy. Indeed, between 1924 and 1929, Germany appeared to be on the path of moderation. Its most notable statesman Gustav Stresemann worked to ease crippling war loans, encouraged international engagement and liberalized its political culture, even proposing a *European Union* in 1929.

Stresemann's untimely death that year seems a tragedy in retrospect, as he might have been able to counter German extremism. In any case, in 1929 worldwide economic depression spread from US markets to punish Germans and others again. Western capital markets once again seemed to offer only conflict and insecurity. Anybody who could end the hunger, humiliation, and instability would find power. Nazis and other Fascist parties would soon provide much needed bread and pride in the 1930s.

Popular authoritarianism

Popular political participation brought more than the vote and state loyalty; in authoritarian states it linked the masses to belligerent extremists, who easily manipulated populations. One obvious example, among many, was Germany, where an Austrian-raised Catholic named Adolf Hitler spent the 1920s working to discredit traditional sources of power—aristocrats who lost Germany to war, intellectuals who questioned patriotism, and liberals committed to international diplomacy. When his 1923 insurrection failed, Hitler was imprisoned, but he worked thereafter to build a new Far-Right party with private militias. The Nazis took advantage of a weak state, and by 1933 were producing a new Germany that normalized political violence.

To understand German extremism, it helps to understand the economic circumstances. After Versailles, massive reparations (132 billion gold marks) were forced upon the beaten nation. Though the rich or powerful did not suffer from this, the masses did. By 1923, Belgian and French soldiers occupied the Ruhr, further humiliating German pride. A culture of victimhood soon emerged in response to a war that German elites had started, as Far-Right agitators won over workers by blaming democratic nations or Jews.

German xenophobia toward foreigners and Jews was not unique however. English writers such as Karl Pearson had decades earlier legitimatized racist beliefs regarding supposedly superior and inferior races. American racism was extensive and encouraged German nationalists, whose bigotry was respected by US politicians. Elite and popular culture in America, as in Europe, was openly hostile toward Jews and people of color. Indeed, 1920s America saw the highpoint of the anti-Semitic and racist KKK (Ku Klux Klan), with over 4 million active members. The first blockbuster movie in America, *Birth of a Nation*, celebrated white supremacy: Woodrow Wilson played it in the White House. Mostly black people, but also Mexicans and Asians, were strung up on trees in American towns during and after the 1920s. Racism in all Western nations was normal in the 1920s and 1930s, not exceptional. Though none could predict the murder of millions of Jews, intolerance was the norm.

A desperate decade: 1930s

The 1929 Wall Street Crash provided powerful fuel for extremists. By the time the depression ended in 1933, Hitler was chancellor of Germany, Mussolini ruled Italy and Fascist militants had destroyed burgeoning democracy in Japan. Trade worldwide dropped by almost three-quarters between 1929 and 1932. The prosperous lost large sums of wealth, but the poor became ever poorer, providing fertile ground for racist ideology.

Though hopes for peace and prosperity persisted through the 1920s, the 1930s were wretched. A World Disarmament Conference in Switzerland in 1932 offered hope for peace, but Germany ominously withdrew. By 1932, reparations ended and German confidence rose. Hitler was appointed chancellor a year later via a predominantly democratic process, and Germany immediately quit the League of Nations, rejecting demilitarization.

Increasingly in the 1930s, German authorities blamed Jews and leftists for fictitious crimes. A militant police force was created in 1933 to counter political opposition. The Gestapo began purging Jews, communists, progressives, gypsies, and gays, taking the jobs, homes, and lives of innocent people. A fabricated account blaming a Dutch Communist for a fire in government offices in 1933 created a culture of fear, in which all progressives were considered Communists, terminating any hope of even moderate opposition. Few dared speak out thereafter, though some such as the singer Marlene Dietrich made the point of leaving Germany in disgust.

By 1935, modernizing the military became the political goal for German conservatives, who ignored the disarmament clauses of Versailles. A year later, German generals remilitarized the Rhineland, and the Luftwaffe air force developed revolutionary technologies for airborne bombing, practicing cutting-edge maneuvers such as flying over enemy territory to bomb civilians directly. British and French governments could neither afford nor approve rearmament, partly as a result of the democratic process, which tied decisions to debate and delayed conclusive agreement.

The 1930s was a decade of broad *autarky*, where domestic economies separated from others, ending 70 years of open trade among nations. Political diplomacy plummeted also, as separatist parties took extreme positions and offered uber-nationalist aims, preferring not to solicit ideas from other nations' representatives. Self-sufficient countries decreased trade and diplomatic relations with other countries, slowly sliding down a path to conflict. Nationalism became the central explanatory idea for both personal and collective identity.

Indeed, dictatorship emerged in over fifteen European states by the mid-1930s, as leaders of fledgling nations manipulated extremist ideologies. Catholic states in particular succumbed to authoritarian rule, with little opposition from the church hierarchy. By 1935, Mussolini had the support of the influential Roman Catholic hierarchy in Rome. Brazenly expanding into Africa, he soon proclaimed Italian expansionist aims. In the Abyssinian Crisis of 1935, Mussolini invaded Ethiopia, gassing opposition soldiers, and exposed the Allies' unwillingness to intervene. In 1936, he partnered with Hitler in the Rome–Berlin Axis. The two Fascists states were now allied.

Spain's monarchy lost standing in 1921 when Moroccan Muslims massacred its army. A moderate dictatorship governed through the 1920s, then extremism increased in the 1930s. Leftist Republicans, supported nominally by Russia and tainted by the association, tried to counter violent right-wing nationalists. The immensely influential Catholic Church, bitterly opposed to left-wing parties, supported conservatives and gave them the support of devout Spaniards. In the ensuing Civil War (1936–1939) Republican rebels in the Catalonia and Basque regions fought for independence from the Fascist state, but conservatives led by General Franco won through a church, army, and royal alliance. Franco ruled until 1975; Spain enjoyed no free elections until 1977, and military rule thwarted wide Spanish political participation for decades after the war. In neighboring Portugal, the dictator António de Oliveira Salazar ruled in similar vein from 1932 until 1968. Both countries were undemocratic and poor into the 1970s.

The vicious civil war afforded right-wing Fascists the opportunity to exploit and to expand intolerant views. It was also a perfect practice ground for experimentation in using murderous new weapons such as warplanes and tanks to slaughter civilian populations. Since neither Britain, France, nor America were prepared for war, militarists freely pushed their agendas in the 1930s, providing political participation not so much through votes, but through membership in aggressive nationalist organizations and the army.

By 1938, Fascist parties were on the ascent throughout Europe. In the March *Anschluss* Germany occupied Austria without resistance, professing to unite German-speaking peoples. In September, Britain's Prime Minister Neville Chamberlain met Hitler at the Munich Conference. He left convinced Hitler was reasonable, that there would be "peace in our time." Hitler duped him to buy time for coming expansion. Chamberlain has been ridiculed ever since for his *appeasement* of a tyrant and provided justification for hawkish foreign interventions.

In October 1938, Germany invaded the industrial Sudetenland of Czechoslovakia, a supposedly sovereign, democratic nation. This prompted the British and French to promise to protect Greece, Romania, and Poland, while the United States remained strictly isolated. Hitler had long been looking east to expand into Slavic lands, with no apparent intent of invading Britain or France. While his desire for *lebensraum*, or elbowroom, was not aimed at Western nations, Russians, and Stalin in particular, had great cause for concern.

Hitler's Nazi accomplice, Herman Goering, is purported to have emphasized the ease with which leaders could prime people for war in the 1930s:

Naturally the common people don't want war: Neither in Russia, nor in England, nor for that matter in Germany. That is understood. But, after all, it is the leaders of the country who determine the policy and it is always a simple matter to drag the people along, whether it is a democracy, or a fascist dictatorship, or a parliament, or a communist dictatorship. Voice or no voice, the people can always be brought to the bidding of the leaders. That is easy. All you have to do is tell them they are being attacked, and denounce the peacemakers for lack of patriotism and exposing the country to danger. It works the same in any country.[8]

Joining the party

Fascism was a ghastly political ideology that disavowed ideas of freedom or democratic representation. For the intolerant millions of opportunists who joined right-wing parties, it was a chance to thrive in life. Fascist nations were one-party states that provided jobs, stability, and benefits to the masses in a time of hunger and conflict. When channeled through extreme nationalist propaganda the party provided confidence and pride. Mass media such as newspapers and radio promoted party ideals, and a common identity was forged through songs, clothing. A generalized reassuring uniformity offering reverent worship to the leader, the party, and the state. Those who joined found themselves enjoying great sudden power over others, even those with more means: young people could order elders around, as the Hitler Youth monitored and purged people of all ages in search of ideological purity.

Traditional conservatives and nationalists (who were not always Nazis) had initially intended to harness Hitler's power to promote business and social policies in their interests. Hitler's foreign policy gains in the 1930s impressed many Germans of note though, and those opposed had little opportunity to voice dissent anyway after 1933. Established institutions of power such as church, courts, police, and big business worked openly with the Nazis as they did with Fascists in Italy. All knew of Nazi aims by 1938, but were unable to transcend national vanities or institutional gains.

Fascism affirmed both antidemocratic and anticommunist principles, producing a new type of faith. The cult of the *führer*, or autocratic leader, expected and received obedience throughout society. Germany had a new religion by 1938, with Hitler as God. Fascism was extremely contradictory: Fascists offered loyal women opportunities to work in the system, though it was officially antifeminist. Though antigay, many Nazis enjoyed partners of the same sex. Though Fascists were anti-individualistic, personal gains flowed from devotion to the party. As impressive as Nazi power appeared, the regime essentially made a virtue of winging it, as Hitler and his henchmen spewed out maniacal commands on a whim. This unpredictability would ultimately be its downfall in the war.

Italian Fascism was as deceitful as the German form, though less totalitarian. Italy suffered from a feeble military, a weak government, and regional disunity in the 1930s. After 1929, Wall Street's financial meltdown enabled Mussolini to offer alternatives to a liberal capitalism that already disillusioned most Italians. Tired of hunger and conflict, millions willingly followed Mussolini, as he trumpeted pride in the ancient glories of Rome. Mussolini was a Socialist before he was a Fascist, and like most tyrants, desired power however he could get it. He made ample use of extreme violence and secret police to silence critics. His final overthrow came in 1943, when he was hanged with his girlfriend in public, at which point Italian moderates joined the Allies to fight Germany.

Mussolini gained the support of power elites in Italy because—as in Germany, Britain, France, and the United States—Communism was a far greater threat to those in authority than right-wing Fascism. Though the king and pope remained sources of influence, Mussolini ruled Italy by 1930. Through the decade, wealthy people paid off the party to maintain personal liberties. The papacy was also willing to work with the anticommunist Mussolini. The Lateran Treaty of 1929 paid the pope in Rome a large sum of money; through alliance with the Fascists, Catholicism would remain the state religion, in a suitably arranged church-state concord.

Democratic failure

Elite institutions and traditional power centers failed in Fascist Europe in the 1930s. But in liberal democracies too monarchy, parliament, and church focused on countering Communism more than on spreading democracy to the people. In the 1930s, establishment elites in the United States, Britain, and France did not heroically dispute the depravities of Fascism as some later contended. High placed conservatives in England listened to Hitler through the 1930s. Many with power and affluence found Fascism a preferable alternative to Communism. British and French conservatives mostly wished to maintain global superpower status through imperial influence. Communists had after all openly disparaged imperialism: they were the enemy, not Hitler. This explains why after 1938 Western elites ignored Stalin's warnings that Hitler was planning widespread war and domination.

In the 1930s, even well-intentioned Western elites, long habituated to acting through racist or imperialist lines of thought, ignored the strains of virulent hatred coursing in Europe. Elite disdain for leftist politics, particularly Communism, empowered the growth of authoritarian states and a nightmarish recurrence of war. The democratic forces of the United States, Britain, and France were in any case racked by the Depression after 1930, unable to consider military action when capitalism had failed. Unwittingly, they left totalitarian states a free hand to dominate Europe until it was too late.

Japan: Imperial Fascism

By 1930, Japanese people too lived in a militarized, Fascist state, even though the 1920s seemed to offer hopes for democracy and civil rights. A culture of violence was worsened by the Depression, as impoverished men joined the army for food and shelter. People were easily convinced of the virtues of militarism in Japan. As in Germany, military build-up created jobs and political identity. And as in Eastern Europe, literacy was low. In East Asia it hovered around 33 percent, so the majority willingly accepted the schemes of those in power, with dreadful consequences for most of Asia.

Constrained by its island location and limited resources Japanese state policy since the late nineteenth century had been imperialist, and rulers could expand and colonize without the hindrance of political opponents. Like Germany, Japan had no tradition of parliamentary debate, and its constitution emulated Prussia's. Corrupt military leaders hijacked democratic reforms in the 1920s, making male suffrage contingent upon military service. Hence, a radical right-wing military state emerged, in which the establishment made it punishable by prison or death to even contradict the imperial state and emperor.

As Japanese ultra-nationalists intimidated democratic opponents in the 1930s, violence became endemic toward Koreans and Chinese. The Japanese empire annexed Korea by force in 1905. Koreans resisted, assassinating Japan's prime minister in 1909 and attempting to take the emperor's life in 1932. Tensions with China grew through the 1920s, culminating in the Mukden Incident in 1931, where Japan officially occupied Manchuria in China after inciting violence, using secret police thereafter to root out Chinese Communists. Chinese appeals to the international community proved futile, so Japanese leaders demonstrated disdain for international diplomacy, leaving the League of Nations in 1933. In 1937 the Japanese invaded China, killing 300,000 Chinese, assaulting countless women and innocent people in the Rape of Nanking. The Japanese assault on China persisted from the 1890s through to 1945, in the eyes of Chinese patriots.

Latin American Fascism

Autocratic rule spread in 1930s Latin America too. Leaders in key nations such as Brazil and Argentina adopted right-wing Fascism to counter Western economic influence, maintaining dictatorial rule with military support. Nations across Latin America used secret police to oppress leftist opponents through the 1980s. Mass support increased for autocratic rulers in the region, since dictators often provided workers' rights and land reforms for the poor. Military rulers, or caudillos, supported by the Catholic Church, kept the illiterate masses in poverty to ensure political conformity and loyalty.

This did not bring political stability or representation, however. Revolutions, assassinations, and revolutionary coups became a staple diet of Latin American politics for much of the twentieth century. US influence further intensified instability, since Latin American dictators typically had to bend to Washington's demands. Whenever a left-wing government in the Americas threatened United States military or business interests, elites would increase pressure to counter progressive parties or democratic populism.

The "American century" began with US intrusions into the politics of Cuba, Haiti, and the Dominican Republic prior to 1914, typically to maintain US economic interests. In Mexico, US interests complicated matters when the pro-democracy Francisco Madero overthrew Porfirio Diaz, a corrupt ruler who relied on US connections to maintain dictatorship for 40 years. Madero was ousted with US help. US interests also intervened when the rebel Pancho Villa stirred revolution in 1910. Indeed, Mexican desires for Wilsonian independence were prevented by US interference. In Nicaragua, the pro-US Somoza family controlled the state until 1979, until Sandinista rebels, intent on helping the poor, ousted the murderous regime. Nicaragua was the poorest country in the Americas, and US foreign policy worsened the situation by helping the Contras, right-wing rebels who fought the Sandinistas, through the 1980s. Conservative interests in Latin America aligned with conservative interests in the United States well into the 1980s. The Organization of American States formed in 1948 among Latin American nations to counter US power, although with minimal impact. Into the 1980s, while Washington pushed an anti-leftist or anticommunist regional agenda, and dictators preserved a corrupt political status quo, often supported by the Catholic Church and the military.

Figure 1.9 A meeting of the Chilean Nazi party, circa 1940. (FPG/Hulton Archive/ Getty Images.)

In the United States in the 1930s, Fascism did not emerge. But the American people were slowly inculcated into the belief that their country was the preeminent source of freedom worldwide, a blessed nation, with the most open political system and a mission to spread peace. Official government views were diffused through an efficient, nationalist media trained to propagate loyalty to the state, along with a school system that taught enthusiastic pride in the nation.

The 1940s: Second World War

By the early 1940s however, American help was needed desperately to support democracy, as the Second World War (1939–1945) threatened to destroy Europe. This war is easily viewed as a simple battle between dark and light forces, and the darkness of totalitarianism is of course undeniable. Yet, from the perspective of most people worldwide, this was another Western confrontation between authoritarian tyrants on one side and democratic overlords on the other. Again after the war, as in 1918, both authoritarian and democratic leaders remained incapable of conceiving that non-Western people merited political autonomy.

Democratic leaders like Britain's Prime Minister Winston Churchill and US President Franklin D. Roosevelt unquestionably fought a just war to end totalitarianism, but the prevailing political attitudes from the elite class they belonged to had, for a century, immiserated millions in colonies or dependent states.

When Japanese, Chinese, or Arab leaders endeavored for impartial treatment after Versailles, Western leaders dismissed them out of hand. After 1945, intervention in the Middle East, Africa, and Asia would persist, as democratic leaders searched for markets, oil or rooted out governments they considered Communist.

That said, the stimulus for a second horrifying war came, not from flawed democratic ideals but from Japanese elites, Mussolini, Hitler, and the many right-wing extremists who valued their cruel worldviews. By May 1939 Hitler and Mussolini signed the Pact of Steel to cement their expansionist alliance. Hitler then duped Stalin into signing a nonaggression pact in August. A week later the Germany army invaded Poland, secure now in the belief Stalin would not protest. Germany was invading Europe.

If the First World War had been mostly stagnant battles of soldiers holding positions in trenches, the second was offensive and dynamic, with planes, soldiers, tanks, and ships travelling afar to slaughter civilians in their homes. In fall 1939, German and Russian armies easily overran smaller nations like Poland and Lithuania. Then, as in 1914, a period of quiet occurred once war was declared, in this case through to spring 1940. By April that year, German armies dominated Scandinavia and could move freely around northern Europe. In May, they easily occupied Belgium, Holland, and France. Nothing could resist the new blitzkrieg methods of sudden, mechanized attack, supported by planes and tanks. In May 1940, the entire British and French armies miraculously escaped from the beaches of Dunkirk, to later regroup and return to battle.

In June 1940, Italy entered the war at the precise point when German power seemed irresistible. By September, the Italians, Germans, and Japanese were assertively allied in a Tripartite Pact, and appeared destined to conquer vast areas. Britain stubbornly refused to make peace with Hitler. A massive German air invasion in late 1940 left Britain alone among European powers, facing the enormous air power of the Luftwaffe as it bombed the ancient buildings of London without respite through the winter. The British endured the attacks and using radar, hit back by striking German cities.

There was an enormous escalation in violence in 1941. In June, Hitler turned on Russia and attacked his former ally with a huge force. Stalin was astonished, apparently bedridden for weeks in dismay. The German ambassador Joachim von Ribbentrop then pressured Japan, confiding that Germany would declare war on the United States if Japan agreed to attack. The Japanese did so in December 1941, bombing Pearl Harbor and killing over 2,000 personal, bringing the sizable US military into war. The United States and Japan had been skirting each other with animosity for decades with aims to dominate the Pacific, so this was simply the culmination of existing tensions. Japan resented American domination of the Philippines, and the United States had war plans in place since 1911 to counter Japanese expansion in the Pacific.

Demonstrating the megalomania of Hitler and Mussolini, both leaders declared war on the United States the day after with ridiculous short-sightedness. The 1941 Atlantic Charter agreement between the United States and Britain specified that an Anglo-American alliance would counter Fascism at all costs, which it did in due course. After Pearl Harbor, US help would be decisive in helping Britain and France destroy Fascism.

But in July 1941, the situation was dark. Japan occupied southern Indochina, taking ports from the Dutch and British. Through 1942, Japan's military conquered most of East and Southeast Asia, conceitedly claiming to be the protectors of Asians worldwide. The Japanese would enforce brutal rule, ignore international law, and treat Western and Asian prisoners of war savagely. People in Southeast Asia found colonial rule replaced by Japanese brutality. Japanese political militarism would bring immense abuses. Prior to the end of war in 1945, Japan let famine kill hundreds of thousands of Vietnamese, while soldiers forced up to 100,000 Korean "comfort women" to provide sexual services. Japanese abuse of Allied soldiers was rampant, as its military paid no attention to war conventions for the treatment of prisoners.

In Europe in 1942, Germany also appeared supreme. The chances for democracy surviving anywhere on earth outside of the United States seemed slim in 1942 and 1943. Only later would it become apparent that the 1942 battles of Stalingrad in Europe and Midway in Asia were turning points toward ultimate victory for the Allies.

Churchill, though unmindful of British abuses toward others, famously proclaimed the resilience of the British in their stand against Nazi tyranny. His rhetoric is justly famous. Speaking in 1940, he said:

Even though large tracts of Europe and many old and famous States have fallen or may fall into the grip of the Gestapo and all the odious apparatus of Nazi rule, we shall not flag or fail. We shall go on to the end, we shall fight in France, we shall fight on the seas and oceans, we shall fight with growing confidence and growing strength in the air, we shall defend our Island, whatever the cost may be, we shall fight on the beaches, we shall fight on the landing grounds, we shall fight in the fields and in the streets, we shall fight in the hills; we shall never surrender, and even if, which I do not for a moment believe, this Island or a large part of it were subjugated and starving, then our Empire beyond the seas, armed and guarded by the British Fleet, would carry on the struggle, until, in God's good time, the New World, with all its power and might, steps forth to the rescue and the liberation of the old.[9]

Allied leaders spent most of 1943 and 1944 secretly preparing for an invasion of Europe to defeat Germany. On June 6, 1944 (D-Day), a huge planned assault landed in France, and after a year of further conflict, this turned the tide for the remainder of the war. By May 1945, defeat of the Axis Powers was imminent. Hitler shot himself as the Allies approached Berlin.

Though war in Europe ended in May, it continued in Asia through August, when US President Harry S. Truman made the decision to drop nuclear bombs for the first time in history. Hundreds of thousands of Japanese civilians in Nagasaki and Hiroshima were killed, countless more lived with the effects of radiation for decades. Perhaps justifiably unwilling to commit more soldiers to fight in Japan, the United States thus inaugurated a new era of nuclear warfare in human history, citing the bombing as a means to finally end the conflict. The United States thereafter became a unique nation, both in its capacity to wage war and its power to shape a new world order. It would reshape Japan in its own image after 1945.

However, it immediately became apparent in 1945 that this was a different type of war: as victorious Russian, British, American, and French soldiers converged on Germany and Berlin to determine the fate of postwar Europe, they found concentration camps littered with millions of murdered Jews in German held lands, in the most unimaginable atrocity in human history. Gas chambers, ovens and other gruesome apparatus of organized murder exposed the depths of depravity that authoritarian politics had reached in Nazi Germany. German guilt was not up for debate after this war. Germans had started it, and Germans had committed acts of horror against a minority people, unrivaled in barbarity even in a century of horrors.

> Concentration camp survivor Viktor Frankl concluded his account of a hellish existence in a Nazi concentration camp with these words:
>
> *So let us be alert . . . Since Auschwitz we know what man is capable of. Since Hiroshima we know what is at stake."*[10]

United Nations—civilized internationalism

Well over 60 million people died in the war. Millions of non-Westerners suffered and died from the conflict. In Europe, everybody's life was torn apart by death or destruction. Reflecting on such inhumane behavior, those in power were now forced to ask what could change politically. Western wars had once again been fought on Arab, African, and Asian lands, once again contributing to death and dislocation outside of Europe. Much of Asia had been ravaged by Japanese despotism. Surviving Jews not only had to live with the horror of attempted annihilation, but had to find somewhere for safe haven. (Still, none of the Western nations welcomed Jewish refugees—the US Congress voted to deny Jews entry.) Notably, the USSR endured disproportionally huge losses. The war is remembered in Russia as the Great Patriotic War and considered a war mostly won by Russian sacrifice, not Anglo-American heroism.

DEATHS PER NATION

Russia lost 26 million people (as many as all other nations combined.)
Poland lost the most by percentage, around 17 % of its population.
China lost 15–20 million in the war period.
Around 2–3 million people in Dutch Indonesia died.[11]

Considering the sacrifices made by so many in wartime, elites in Western nations had to justify their position more explicitly after this war. Political leaders in the West stayed in office by offering policies to diminish inequality. Heavy state intervention in Europe would finance public programs to educate, provide health, immunization to counter disease, and the construction and financing of hospitals and housing. Mass participation in the nation finally came after the worst war in history.

Outside of Europe, aspirations for political representation and fairer world governance also increased, through the formation of the *United Nations* in 1945. The horrors of war necessitated an international political means to prevent war, since nationalist ideologies supported by militarism had caused the conflict. With millions of deaths from nationalist extremism, those at the center of global power aimed to shape a system to prevent a recurrence of global war, with some success since. Directly after the war the UN relief agency provided a billion dollars' worth of aid, including food, blankets, clothing, and medicine to prevent famine and disease.

Formed by a US-European alliance and seated in New York, the United Nations offered smaller nations the opportunity to remonstrate with great powers through diplomatic means. It was however centered on a Security Council of Britain, China, France, Soviet Union, and United States, so it seemed that the great powers were unwilling to offer "lesser peoples" full representation. Although intentions were positive, from the perspective of most of the world, these five powers now policed the planet. Third World dissatisfaction with the United Nations would be persistent and loud.

Following the war, people in the Middle East, Africa, and Southeast Asia were still colonized by European powers and were hence "represented" by Westerners. This would change with growing independence movements in the coming decades. Colonized societies would gradually win political autonomy, only to find they had to contend with the geopolitical interests of Washington or Moscow. Even amid talk of new orders, two opposing blocs appeared by the late 1940s that would shape the postwar world.

3. 1947–1991: Cold War and replacement empires?

In early 1949, Western nations formed NATO to counter potential threats to democracy, now primarily Communist states. In 1954, after West Germany joined, Communist states united in the Warsaw Pact, setting up two major alliances headed by Moscow and Washington.

Three key changers occurred in the postwar political world: the Cold War, decolonization, and the formation of the European Community, bringing in turn, conflict, independence, and unity. The Cold War is often imagined as a battle between a well-meaning capitalist West and closed-off, corrupt Communist regimes, and there is certainly some truth to this interpretation. But for most people on earth, the 40-year conflict was merely a continuation of mastery by other means. For the Third World, a century of Western global influence was replaced by two hostile superpowers. Though both declared anti-imperialist policies, both extended their power worldwide. For the weaker nations on earth, the new superpower structure was no less disruptive than the old, colonial one.

In fact, the reach of the new powers would be greater due to the vast, modern state apparatus that developed. As Europe's century of domination ended, the United States and the USSR worked to weaken European power and expand their own influence: the United States to support political elites that embraced capitalism, the USSR to spread Communism. This global battle between two opposing ideologies shaped the lives of people from Manila to the Congo. Throughout the Third World, most nations, even once independence came, remained politically impotent, as local elites served the superpowers, enriching themselves to maintain local power.

American empire?

There were frequent criticisms of excessive US influence in postwar Europe, but Western Europeans certainly needed to receive US aid in the 1940s. Russians felt manipulated by "Saxon" nations, and though Stalin was a maniac he was justifiably dismayed with Anglo-American leaders. Soviets considered Allied assistance to Mensheviks in 1917 as treachery, and were convinced the Allies had delayed the invasion of Germany until 1944, to purposely wear down the Communists along with the Nazis.

A major postwar question for the victors was what to do with Germany and Japan? Neither nation's military elite had respected wartime conventions of human rights. Both treated Allied prisoners despicably, leaving surviving representatives of both nations no moral position from which to expect sympathy. But mindful of the cost of punishing Germany in 1918 however, the Allies chose to forgive as many German elites as possible. The US military remained in Japan until 1952, specifically rebuilding society in a democratic capitalist guise without punishing surviving Japanese.

US power was unrivalled by the 1950s, stretching across Europe and Asia. It could now extend its commercial interests and political influence. The United States offered aid to Europe while developing markets for US businesses. Germany, France, Britain and other western states received over 13 billion dollars in loans and gifts from the United States in 1948's Marshall Plan, which funded broad European recovery. Welcomed in the West, Russians considered it as ideological expansionism, just another threat to Russian sovereignty from an Anglo-Saxon empire.

There were strings attached for the Allies; the British pound had to convert to the dollar, creating British political dependency that forced postwar prime ministers to heed Washington's advice (and repeated currency crises). French leaders such as Charles De Gaulle stubbornly resisted American influence but were constrained by economic reality. The Germans, like the Japanese, had no choice. European nations were wrecked by war and threatened by hunger through the late 1940s, however, so they gained from United States aid. Bolstered by loans and soon developing booming economies, the ensuing decades saw increasing political freedoms in Western Europe, and a widespread centrist political approach from both Conservative and Liberal parties to avoid a return to extremes.

Concomitant with economic aid, US foreign policy after 1947 assumed the right of intervention anywhere on earth where the threat of Communism was perceived, let alone overt. Far beyond Europe, any regime that resisted US power or even tended to the left was broad-brushed as Communist. The Truman Doctrine of 1947 hardened attitudes between the two titans. The famous telegram in 1946 from George Kennan, the US ambassador to Moscow, was interpreted loosely to assume that Russians fully intended to spread Communism globally, in retrospect this was an overstatement of Russian goals. Churchill, in a famous speech at a US university in 1946, declared an emerging partition in Europe that fulfilled its own prophecy, creatively depicting an "Iron Curtain" that closed off half of Europe to freedom.

In fact, Stalin's moves were mostly defensive, aiming to protect Russia with Eastern European buffer states. From a Russian view, Anglo-American disloyalty had caused millions of needless Russians deaths by invading Europe in 1944 rather than 1943. Churchillian speeches and intemperate US hawks now made concord impossible. Stalin's suspicion toward the West was hence further inflamed by Western words.

Though the conventional image of 1950s America is one of apple pie and happy homes, US politics were undemocratic too—if in a consumerist-conformist mode rather than an authoritarian one. McCarthyism, an ardent anti-leftist scare in 1950s America, fostered a fearful, intolerant culture focused on irrational hatred toward Communists anywhere or progressives at home. Films shown in schools and the home warned of "Reds under the bed." While espousing political openness in rhetoric, a wild paranoia in fact swept the United States in the postwar era. Presidents enjoyed wide-ranging powers to counter a permanent national security threat from Communists worldwide.

When Korean Communists moved south to take the Korean peninsula in 1950, US troops intervened to stop the spread of Communism in China's backyard. Politicians warned of a far-fetched "domino effect" in which any Communist state might infect the next nation, all the way to American shores. When Kim Il-sung invaded the south using Soviet equipment, the United States responded with force. China then responded to defend North Korea's Communists. Over 50,000 Americans, and a million Chinese and Koreans, died in the conflict. Korea remains split in two. With China and Russia supporting North Korea and the United States supporting the south, suspicion now increased greatly among the great powers. Both the USSR and China considered this a distant US adventure, labelling it the "War to Resist U.S. Aggression and Aid Korea."

US global influence became Washington's central focus in the 1950s. Through the CIA, the United States would attempt to topple sovereign leaders in China, Central America, Southeast Asia, and the Middle East through the decade, which did not go unnoticed by those who feared the spread of US power. In 1952, the United States unveiled the NSA, a new intelligence arm of the military, to fight Communism through global and if necessary domestic information gathering. James Bond-style spy games became everyday politics in the 1950s.

With new technologies developing, Washington had reason for concern of course. By 1957 Russian thermonuclear testing created considerable panic in the West. The United States developed intercontinental missiles that year, inaugurating a frantic rush to build deadly arsenals capable of explosion around the globe. The arms race cost billions, while also creating millions of jobs. A policy labeled MAD (mutually assured destruction), ironically forced caution upon both superpowers in the coming decades.

After Stalin died in 1953, a suspicious coexistence ensued under the milder Nikita Khrushchev, who ruled until 1964. In that decade, nonproliferation treaties between the United States and the USSR slowed down the production of missiles. This was only after the Cuban Missile Crisis of 1962 put the world on a knife-edge, when US President John F. Kennedy threatened to release nuclear missiles over the Soviet presence in Cuba. Thankfully Khrushchev backed down in 1962: he was soon pushed out thereafter. An era of Détente (declining tensions) followed during Leonid Brezhnev's time in power (1964–1982).

Soviet empire?

Still, no matter how much US foreign policy deliberately intervened in other nations politics, nothing compared to the iniquities of Stalinism and the political suppression of Soviet Communism. Labor camps and purges were more common than political debate in Soviet life. Moscow forced compliance on ethnic minorities in the USSR in the thirteen republics, as well as on the satellite states in Eastern Europe. This was in indefensible regime.

If the superpowers practices of foreign interference were perhaps two sides of the same coin, life within the two spheres of influence was not. The best evidence of this, aside from the fact that protest was banned in the USSR until the 1980s, was the constant desire of Eastern Europeans to escape Moscow's sphere. Through the 1950s East Germans, Poles, and Hungarians tried to flee to the West in the thousands. In 1961, Moscow built the Berlin Wall to confine those on the eastern side of Germany, signifying the political failure of Communist rule.

All the Soviet satellites pushed back on Moscow. Yugoslavia's Marshall Josip Broz Tito fended off Moscow, personally governing the Balkans after 1949. In 1953 Poland revolted, only to see Moscow crush opposition. In 1956 those in the West who still romanticized Communism saw a democratic Hungarian uprising crushed with Russian tanks. When Imre Nagy attempted to leave the Warsaw Pact he paid the price for questioning Moscow with execution.

Also in 1956, Khrushchev turned on Stalin, conceding to a stunned Communist world that Stalinism had been tyrannical. When Khrushchev expressed interest in peace with the West, Communist elites turned on him however, putting Brezhnev in power for two decades. Only in 1985 did Mikhail Gorbachev have to accept that Communism had failed and the disastrous economy could no longer be sustained. But since no tradition of democracy existed in Russia, even after Communism fell in 1991, autocratic rule returned, from Boris Yeltsin to Vladimir Putin in the present. The transition from Communism to a free economy in the 1990s brought greater political participation, but Russia is still not free politically.

Chinese Communism

China, though weak and impoverished, influenced both powers policies. US anticommunism was intensified by the triumph of the Chinese Communist Party in 1949. US Conservatives blamed the Democrats for having "lost China" and exploited this easy narrative to win elections through the 1950s. Fear of global Communism increased, even though Russia and China rarely agreed. Where Westerners saw one global monolithic Communist threat, little unity existed in the Communist world. As early as 1956, relations between the two major Communist states were strained. China emulated Russia, employing a system of state propaganda, government control, with a tiny party elite making decisions for hundreds of millions. After Stalin died, Chairman Mao accused the Soviets of being "capitalist roaders" due to industrialization and modernization programs. China was isolated and impoverished into the 1980s.

However, Chinese efforts against the Japanese had aided Western Allies during wartime, so a powerful seat at the United Nations indicated China was finally a recognized power. But Chinese Communism terrified Western elites. As in the USSR, a besieged mentality persecuted China's rulers, particularly with the United States reconstructing nearby Japan. As in the USSR, the long-suffering Chinese people endured a continuation of elite rule, corruption, and disenfranchisement.

Fragmented and war-torn since the nineteenth century, China remained politically repressed through the postwar decades. Impassioned party comrades pillaged peasants in villages across China. Tyranny was the norm. Chinese elites were even more isolated and anti-Western than the Soviets, criticizing Khrushchev when he amicably met with US President Dwight Eisenhower in 1959. US and Western Allies had also supported Chinese Nationalists' attempt to defeat Communism, so fear of American influence was obsessive. When the Communists won in 1949, the Nationalists retreated to the island of Taiwan, maintaining close ties with the United States thereafter and bringing political tensions with Beijing.

Chinese Communists strove to create a uniquely Chinese peasant form of Marxism named Maoism, where worship for a supreme leader and the political glorification of the semiliterate peasantry would somehow modernize the country. For all the propaganda in favor of "the people," few enjoyed a voice, particularly minorities. The Manchus, one of the largest minorities, found their language forbidden and were forced to assimilate to the dominant Han culture. Chinese Communists, comprised almost solely of the dominant ethnic Han, dominated fifty-five diverse ethnic groups.

By 1957, the party mandated a message of total loyalty in villages throughout China, collectivizing the national economy. Decision making was undertaken in a vacuum by ill-informed party ideologues. Bereft of wide counsel or debate, projects rarely proved fruitful. In 1958, Mao ignored Russian advice, lurching China into an absurd experiment called the *Great Leap Forward*, aiming to build a new nation with glib sloganeering, village communes instead of modern cities, and mass agriculture instead of mechanization. While the West industrialized and prospered, up to 30 million people died in China through widespread disease and famine. In 1959, China invaded Tibet, killing Buddhist priests and over 100,000 people to assert its power in the region. Tibet's Dalai Lama remains in exile.

The 1960s were no better. Mao inaugurated the *Cultural Revolution* in 1966, focusing popular energies on persecuting intellectuals, to somehow inculcate a purer version of Marxist doctrine, killing another 500,000 humans. Red Guards, led by youthful fanatics, purged anybody insufficiently committed to party slogans, prompting banishment and humiliation for skilled individuals, intellectuals, and elders. At least 3 million people were sent to labor camps for "wrong thinking" during the 10-year revolution of fear and loathing.

Mao died in 1976, having shaped a new and proud independent China. He also left a legacy of hardships, failures, and authoritarian rule. Close to 60 million people died under his rule after 1949—far more than even in the horrors of war and colonization. Only after 1976 did the new premier, Deng Xiaoping, open up markets and limit overt oppression, focusing instead on modernization and trade with the West. Many still regard Mao as a national hero in China, akin to Stalin in Russia.

In the late 1970s, looking to democratic Japan as an example, young Chinese began to question Communist rule. A Democracy Wall, hesitatingly permitted by the party, was put up in Beijing in 1978 to allow political voice. Criticism of Mao however worried the rulers and it was quickly demolished. Students grew in confidence and awareness of the wider world in the 1980s, and as in the USSR, aspired to political liberties. By 1989, as it became clear that the Soviet experiment had failed, student's revolted in Tiananmen Square in Beijing. The Peoples' Army killed between 2,000–3,000 people in response. Today corruption persists and political criticism is still frowned upon, with the prospect of imprisonment for "political or economic crimes" still pervasive.

Cold War battlegrounds—limited choices

By the 1950s, the world was split into three camps: democratic nations with increasing political representation; Communist societies with barely any participation; and colonized regions with only elite participation. Democratic states offered rewards to loyal citizens even while they subjugated people overseas through war or colonization. The Second World War had broken Western powers to the point where they could not hold on to their colonies—a weakened France, Britain, and Holland finally departed colonial lands between the late 1940s and early 1960s.

Once independence came, leaders in Africa, Asia, and India had no choice but to adopt a Western nation-state political model to participate in global institutions. Long-standing ethnic religious rivalries that simmered under colonial rule were now unleashed, however, once the common colonial enemy departed, surfacing immediately to incite internal conflict in postcolonial nations. Ethnic rivalries continue to scar societies across Africa, the Middle East, and Asia. Independence arrived in the context of the Cold War, necessitating alliance with the United States or the USSR. The vast majority of Russians and Chinese (and minorities in both states) suffered political oppression in the postwar era. The Cold War brought conflict even for people far from the superpowers.

Second World War devastated Russia, China, Europe and Japan. It destabilized other regions. Though many Americans sacrificed their lives, war ultimately helped the United States politically. Its military could now act freely around the globe to secure its own interests. Between 1947 and 1991, the CIA or Pentagon intervened in regional conflicts in Burma, Guatemala, Nicaragua, Iran, Cuba, and Chile and up to thirty other places. In all cases, local populations suffered from US interference, while the goal of eradicating Communism or leftist governments rarely succeeded. Moscow also spread its influence whenever possible, bolstering leftist governments from Cuba to Angola. As the two superpowers spread their tentacles, newly independent states with little political infrastructure were forced to take sides.

Korea represents the complexities of the Cold War context well. Violent Japanese rule in Korea ended in 1945 when US forces defeated Japan. The USSR sent forces to support Communist Korea, and by 1948 two separate governments existed—the north supported by China and the USSR, and the south occupied and supported by the United States. The Korean War, fought between 1950 and 1953, artificially split the nation into two countries, with dire consequences for the isolated and impoverished Communist North. A family dynasty paying lip service to Communist ideology has ruled since. Kim Il-sung and his successors formed a family state for their own purposes, and today threaten the United States with nuclear arms, keeping millions close to starvation - repression is the rule. South Koreans too endured autocratic rule through the postwar decades but opened up in the 1980s. People in the south now enjoy political participation and a prosperous society.

Decolonization—self-serving cliques and neo-imperialism

Within the overarching Cold War struggle, over forty new nations formed between 1945 and 1975, enveloping around a billion people. Postcolonial independence brought forth an unparalleled scale of change in the political status of humans worldwide. Violence escalated in the late 1940s and 50s as rebels from Algeria to India resisted ongoing interference from France and Britain. Across Africa, leaders rose to oust the British and French. Across Asia, Western imperialism was challenged too. Asian nations were generally independent by the 1950s, while African nations won independence through the 1960s.

The Less-Developed Countries (LDCs) of the world began to ally together in the 1950s through the Non-Aligned Movement, targeting self-government and the end of foreign intrusion. The 1955 Bandung Conference, hosted by Indonesia, was attended by leaders representing a quarter of the world's people. To resist influence from the West and the USSR, leaders of ex-colonized populations formed UNCTAD[12] in 1964 to advocate for poorer nations through the United Nations. In the 1960s the Non-Aligned Movement openly declared its intentions to counter past injustices. After 1964 the G77 worked to unite developing nations and improve trade terms with wealthy nations. However, once the zeal of independence declined, so too did Third World unity. The movement faded in the 1970s after decades of political factionalism and ruptures among LDC states.

Asian independence?

After 1945, Asian independence movements ousted British, French, and Dutch colonial authorities. Japanese political domination brought vicious exploitation of much of Asia, and young leaders were exposed to Western ideas of nationalist independence and self-determination. Everywhere in Asia, Western powers were overthrown in the 1940s and 1950s, to be replaced with Cold War coercion and token independence. Locally entrenched autocrats enjoying the support of military elites countered those who desired an open society, with limited political freedoms in Asia. Cold War coercion, like colonialism, brought relocation and political oppression for Southeast Asian populations, with little power or prosperity. Only Thailand was stable in the postwar era, though Thais still endure military and royal autocracy.

Like Koreans, the people of Southeast Asia and India were pawns in the Cold War as they sought national liberation. French control of Indochina, Vietnam, Laos, and Cambodia weakened due to rebel resistance in the 1950s, many of whom saw Communism as a reasonable alternative to capitalist colonialism. Ho Chi Minh wished to emulate the US Constitution to build a new Vietnam, even writing to Truman in 1945 to partner with the United States. Influenced by anti-leftist crusaders, the president ignored the letter, insulting Ho and his followers. The United States and Vietnam would intertwine further in the 1960s with grave consequences.

Having fought off Japanese imperialism in 1945, followers of Ho Chi Minh were now pitted against reactionary French imperialists. Violent uprisings persisted until 1954, when the French finally left to focus on Algerian resistance closer to home in North Africa. Vietnamese rebels still had to fight the pro-French, anti-Buddhist Catholic Ngo Dinh Diem regime through the 1950s, ardently supported by Conservative American officials who advised Eisenhower to counter Communism worldwide.

By 1963 the United States was transferring money, equipment and soldiers to support Diem's right-wing Southern Vietnamese, Christian regime. US troops arrived in 1965 and would stay until they were expelled in 1973. From 1961 through 1975, North and South Vietnamese people fought, leaving a ruined environment, a desperate population and another million dead in Vietnam and nearby Laos. Communist rule after 1975 plodded along without much growth, until the 1980s when Vietnam began to copy China, allowing moderate political expression. China continues to pose a political threat to Vietnam as it has for centuries: Vietnam fervently guards its hard-won independence.

While Vietnamese in the North and South died, peasant populations in neighboring Cambodia faced similar horrors, exacerbated by the war, US and Soviet interference, and despotic local warlords. Cambodia had been a French protectorate through the Second World War, with local princes willingly doing the bidding of French colonists for personal gain. The United States and its Vietnamese allies mercilessly bombed the nation in the early 1970s, entrapping it in a war of strategy, leaving a murderer in power.

Cambodia's impoverished people fell under the rule of the cruel dictator Pol Pot. He took control to counter foreign interference, adopting yet another personal brand of Communism. Pot proceeded to murder adversaries with his appalling Khmer Rouge regime. Peasant soldiers using Chinese arms slaughtered anybody opposed to Pot. The awful "killing fields" of Cambodia left close to 2 million dead; millions more disappeared, usually those educated or Westernized. Cambodians have suffered from a violent culture of tribal infighting since.

> The Vietnamese military overthrew Pot in 1979, remaining in Cambodia to maintain order until 1989, when amnesty was arranged for him and his warlords. He nonetheless claimed, as most tyrants do:
>
> *"I want you to know that everything I did, I did for my country."*[13]

Indonesia, a sprawling Muslim nation in Asia, also ousted Japanese oppression following Dutch rule, and focused on resisting Cold War influence in the postwar period. The dictator Sukarno won independence in 1950 with the support of Communists who helped him maintain personal rule. Sukarno led with an iron fist from 1945 to 1967, proclaiming democracy and republican ideals while ruling autocratically with a strong military. H. Muhammad Suharto, a military general who ruled until 1998, succeeded him and maintained political rule. Indonesia has been authoritarian for most of the period since.

As in Indonesia and Vietnam, aspirations for political independence and the expulsion of colonial oppression inspired rebels in Burma. Burmese leaders desired rule based on Buddhist values, not foreign influence. Though Burma gained independence from the British in 1948, it fell to military rule by 1962, which persisted for decades. Only in the last few years has a lone voice espoused free speech and political openness. The military imprisoned the democracy activist Aung San Suu Kyi for over a decade. Her release offered hope for democracy in a nation newly renamed Myanmar, but now she is accused of allowing the slaughter of Muslim minorities.

> Though we habitually label nations Communist or capitalist, the reality is much more complex. Elites usually rule in their own interests, as indicated in Korea and in Indonesia, whose dictator Sukarno tellingly wrote in 1941:
>
> *What is Sukarno? A nationalist? An Islamist? A Marxist? . . . Sukarno is a mixture of all these isms . . . I have made myself a meeting place of all trends and ideologies. I have blended them . . . until finally the become the present Sukarno.*[14]

The Philippines gained independence from the United States in 1946 after 50 years of US control, though it remained heavily reliant militarily and economically on American support. Decades of corrupt governance and military dictatorship, in particular the murderous Marcos regime from 1972 to 1986, left a nation impoverished with limited political participation. As few as a hundred families well connected to US power have shaped the nation, where oppression toward Muslim minorities and autocratic rule persists.

India gained independence in 1947 after 90 years of direct British rule, concluding decades of resistance. Hindu leaders such as Jawaharlal Nehru were wary of Cold War powers, so aspired to neutrality. When the British departed, political and religious violence immediately erupted between Hindus and Muslims who wished to form a new Muslim state, Pakistan. Key figures like Gandhi and Jawaharlal Nehru desired a vast multicultural Indian state, based upon the British parliamentary model. However, Muhammad Ali Jinnah and his Muslim League wanted a specifically Islamic state, fearing oppression of minority Muslims in a mostly Hindu nation. Partition of the continent persists, as do tensions between two rival nuclear powers. India has become a democracy with a parliament, albeit with a largely disenfranchised population. Conflict persists in Pakistan, which was sliced in two in 1971 after Muslim Bengalis fought off Pakistani military abuses. Pakistan has mostly been run by military elites since and has limited political freedom.

Figure 1.10 Libya's Colonel Gaddafi, celebrating 37 years of rule. (Credit: Danita Delimont.)

Middle Eastern independence?

Middle Eastern politics was also dominated by Cold War policies. Most nations had been created by Western colonial powers during the First World War. Among Middle Eastern societies, only Turkey and Israel has enjoyed political stability or democracy in the postwar era. Dictatorial, absolute or at best constitutional monarchs supported by military regimes have run most Arab states, with national political participation uncommon. Iran has also been autonomous but lacks wide participation. Politics remain authoritarian with limited mass influence in a *theocracy*, where religious elites hold political power.

From 1945 on, autocratic states in the region allied with one or other of the superpowers. Weak, inefficient local rule dependent upon profits from oil exports to Western economies dominated governance. Family-based or tribal Muslim regimes prospered in the Gulf region by providing oil to the world, with incredible inequality and political oppression the norm in the Middle East.

By the 1960s, younger Muslim activists began to foment change. Local regime change or political reform became a focal point for progressives, while energy was focused on ejecting Western influence. Iraq, Syria, and Egypt experimented with Pan Arab Nationalism in the 1960s, using Socialist principles to fend off foreign powers. Disunity and disagreement brought abject failure however. Divisions between diverse ethnic groups and Muslim sectarian animosities, which long preceded that Western intrusion, prevented harmony. Gradually, fundamentalist Islamism rose as a means to provide political unity in the Muslim world. By the 1970s, a broad desire rose to refute the Western nation-state, secular model. Instead a global Muslim community premised on religious authority would replace political statehood in the minds of radical Muslims.

Though Muslim states were no longer protectorates after 1945, Western influence persisted due to the huge power disparities between industrial states and the Islamic world. British financial interests supported a monarchy disinterested in democracy in Egypt until 1952. Colonel Gamal Abdel Nasser freed Egypt from British influence in 1956, but immediately instigated military rule. In the 1950s and 1960s he tried to unite the Arab world. Like most Egyptian dictators since, he denounced Muslim Brotherhood to counter fundamentalist Islam. Under Nasser's guidance, Egypt positioned itself as a nonaligned nation, with political participation nonexistent. Nasser's interest in Socialism and acceptance of Russian aid spooked American and Israeli Conservatives in the 1960s, inviting strategic intervention.

The state of Israel had been created in 1948 with the support of the United Nations and Western leaders. In the decades prior to 1948, Britain had helped Jews fight Arabs who resented Jewish immigration from Europe, although the British also fought Jewish extremists. After the war, Jewish people fleeing Western prejudice and Hitler's genocide created a homeland in Palestine among existing Arab populations, adding to the population of Zionists who had moved to the region for 70 years earlier. The enduring Arab-Israeli conflict still prevents political stability.

Immediately in 1948, Arab states allied to attempt to destroy the young state. Mutual loathing exploded in 1967, when Israel defeated Egypt convincingly in the Arab-Israeli War. A new power arose in the Middle East, a Jewish nation sat amid Arab Muslims, with far more military clout. In 1973, Egypt attacked Israel but lost again as Israel, supported by the United States, proved to be far more powerful than its surrounding neighbors. Egypt was humiliated by the defeat, as were many in the wider Arab world.

Positive efforts in the 1970s from US President Jimmy Carter brought the Egypt-Israeli Peace Accords in 1979, which seemed designated to end the conflict. However, the Egyptian leader who signed the accords, Anwar Sadat, was assassinated in 1981 by a jihadi Egyptian officer. Arab troops from Syria and Palestine fought with Israel in Lebanon in 1982, when Palestinian and Israeli counterattacks exploded into conflict. The result was 657 dead Israelis, 15,000 Arab deaths and the decimation of Lebanon.

In the 1960s the conflict brought the rise of the Palestinian Liberation Organization (PLO), with the aim of ousting Israel from the region. The PLO was founded in 1964 to aim for independent Palestinian statehood. Ignored by the international community, helpless against the Israeli military, impoverished Palestinians rose up in 1987 in the *intifada*. Decades of unrest followed as Palestinian Arabs pursued independence against Israeli domination, often willing to die as suicide bombers. Anti-Israeli groups such as Hamas in the Gaza Strip and Hezbollah in Lebanon remain committed to ousting Israel. This invites retaliation from Conservative Israelis, peppered by periodic, unproductive peace talks. Hardcore Conservative opinion in Israel refuses to accede to the concerns of Palestinians who desire separate statehood. No peace is in sight.

Israel endures persistent pressure from Iran, a Muslim nation with a strong military that reshaped itself in the 1979 Islamic Revolution. Also opposed to Sunni Saudi Arabia, Shia Iran, like most societies in the Middle East, lacked autonomy after the First World War. Oil discoveries by Western companies in 1908 meant that resources were extracted to the benefit of foreign states and dynastic elites with no stomach for democracy such as the Qajar dynasty.

Between 1925 and 1979, Iran was run by the despotic Pahlavi monarchy, with Western oil experts providing advice to the dynasty and their cronies. Cold War Soviet influence disrupted the Qajar dynasty's oppressive hold on power, as young people were lured to Communism. By the 1950s, Conservative Iranians pushed back, craving independence both from Western capitalism and Soviet Communism, preferring to return to Shia Islamic principles.

The CIA interfered in Iran to counter a leftist government, helping overthrow the democratically elected Muhammad Mossadegh in 1953, in order to keep in power the pro-American Shah's brutal regime. Through the 1970s, US economic interests helped preserve the Shah's power. In 1979, Islamic fundamentalists rebelled in the Iranian Revolution. Hardline clerics outmaneuvered secular democratic reformers and the leftist youth movement that initiated the rebellion. Islamists overthrew the Shah's pro-Western regime, putting in place a theocracy that resents foreign interference or internal dissent to this day and threatens Israel frequently.

> The American journalist and critic of empire, John Flynn, wrote disparagingly of earlier American overseas interventions in 1944:
>
> *The enemy aggressor is always pursuing a course of larceny, murder, rapine and barbarism. We are always moving forward with high mission, a destiny imposed by the Deity to regenerate our victims, while incidentally capturing their markets; to civilise savage and senile and paranoid peoples, while blundering accidentally into their oil wells.*[15]

In 1980 Iran was invaded by Saddam Hussein's neighboring Sunni Iraq state. Hussein claimed that Shia minorities in Iraq were agitating against his authoritarian realm. Eight years of slaughter and close to a million deaths proved pointless. However, US support for Iraq later in the war, to counter Soviet aid to Iran, embittered Iranians immensely and brought the United States deeper into the regions conflicts.

In 1991, with Soviet power gone, US forces went to war with Iraq when Saddam Hussein invaded Kuwait over oil disputes. The Kuwaiti ruling family enjoyed the support of the West, having long provided oil. US intervention quickly toppled Iraqi forces, though Hussein was left in power with his powerful personal army. US military leaders advised President George H. W. Bush that the United States should not further embroil themselves in the region's conflicts once oil was flowing again.

The 1991 Gulf War, as it became known, embroiled the United States deeper in the Middle East. It also enflamed radical Muslims such as Osama Bin Laden, who saw more Western interference and occupation of Muslim holy lands. This culminated in the terrible attacks of September 2001 in New York, to which President George Bush responded by invading Afghanistan to demolish Al Qaeda. This impoverished nation had just begun recovering from a Soviet Communist invasion between 1979 and 1989, with up to a million deaths. The United States had supported the anti-Marxist Afghani *mujahedeen* in that war, an Islamist group that later morphed into the Taliban—the group the United States now fights in the region. US troops remain there today, with the repressive Taliban regime that took control in the 1990s stronger than ever.

The US invasion of Afghanistan was understandable in the circumstances: Al Qaeda, the radical Islamic group based in Afghanistan had carried out the 9/11 attacks, and Islamists from US allies such as Pakistan, Saudi Arabia and Egypt flew planes into US buildings. But in 2003, the Bush administration invaded Iraq again. Conservative US military leaders convinced Bush to invade, citing false information that Iraq had nuclear warheads and blaming Saddam Hussein for 9/11 without evidence. Though the tyrant Hussein was killed, Iraq soon collapsed as a state. Its neighbor Syria has since collapsed, and today ISIS (Islamic State) controls much of the region.

The region remains politically volatile, with ISIS carrying out terrorist attacks worldwide and an increase in Islamism in Europe. The conflict in Syria and Iraq now sees the United States and Russia arguing vociferously about the region in a renewed Cold War standoff scenario. Since the 1970s, anti-Western sentiment has increased, while repressive Arab rulers have nowhere embraced democracy or allowed distribution of power to the people along Western lines.

Postcolonial Africa

As in the Muslim world, African societies were plagued by a blend of local despotism and foreign intervention. After 1900, the continent had been sliced into puppet states that exported raw materials and soldiers to the West. Few African people had lived in centralized states prior to nineteenth-century European colonization. Very low literacy prevented any culture of mass politics through the century. Since African states only gained independence in the 1960s, the effects of colonization persist into the present. In the postwar era, the diverse inhabitants of Africa went from being impoverished colonial subjects to disenfranchised citizens of corrupt states. Colonial rule was thus replaced by ethnic conflict and corrupt dictatorship. Indeed, the relative stability of foreign rule collapsed soon after independence.

Between 1945 and 1975, over forty new countries were created in Africa. Often Western-educated African elites repackaged colonial political ideas, using African nationalism to achieve independence from white rule. They rarely offered political participation however, and conflict was endemic. British military abuses in Kenya in the 1950s saw hundreds of thousands of rebel Mau Mau fighters slaughtered for craving autonomy. The French killed similar numbers of Algerians before departing in 1962. European Colonialism finally ended in 1975, when Angolan Marxists expelled Portugal.

Centuries-old tribal and ethnic identities were quickly crammed into newly constructed modern political entities along the lines of Western models. Ethnic divisions in almost every country prevented unity after European domination. Western-educated elites held the reins of power over populations, corruption became the norm, and democracy failed in favor of nepotism and sinecures. The departure of colonial powers was usually replaced by military coups that prohibited political participation. From the 1950s until the 1980s almost all of north and central Africa was governed by military or tribal rule. Separatist movements and internal civil wars also emerged after independence, as insurgencies, Marxist governments and civil strife prevented any rule of order.

The humiliation of colonization was thus replaced by ethnic rivalry and clique control in much of Africa, as dictatorial rule and strongmen regimes became the norm. The regional cult of personalities put "big men" in power, with the proclivity to pillage state coffers for personal gain. Even African heroes—such as Kwame Nkrumah who won Ghanaian independence from Britain in 1957—ran one-party, military states. Thus, the euphoria of independence in the 1960s succumbed to local political factionalism. This deterred global investment once the colonial powers departed, and left a dearth of functioning political institutions.

Kwame Nkrumah of Ghana worked to expand exports and increase prosperity. Offering the view of most African elites, he pointed to the ongoing influence of Western powers in 1965:

> In place of colonialism as the main instrument of imperialism we have today neo-colonialism. The essence of neo-colonialism is that the state to which it is subject to is in theory independent and has all the outward trappings of international sovereignty. In reality its economy system and its political policy is directed from outside.[16]

None of the new nations transitioned from political independence into effective and organized powers. All remained economically dependent upon foreign trade or loans, and few made use of use massive native resources. Profits from extracted resources went to political elites with foreign connections, while the majority of people remained poor.

As elsewhere, the Cold War motivated Conservatives to look to Washington for support while leftists looked to Moscow. Frequent proxy wars (between pro-Western or pro-Soviet groups) brought civil unrest, as popular rebellions and guerilla movements vied for power and Soviet or US aid. By the 1980s, half of Africa was pro-West and half pro-Soviet, premised upon the need of loans or military resources. In the ex-Portuguese colony of Angola Communist and tribal parties fought each other for decades, with elites and soldiers abusing local populations depending on left- or right-wing tendencies.

The end of the Cold War brought new dilemmas, as Moscow abandoned its African allies. Dictators lost support from the Soviets then proceeded to plunder resources and increase political violence. African elites reliant on superpowers lost authority, and ethnic, clan, and warlord rivalries flourished. The Horn of Africa suffered ethnic rivalry through the 1990s, with Eritrea and Somalia persistently at war. Somalia fell into famine and political disarray once Soviet monies dried up. It has persisted in stateless violence and remains a pirate base and no-go zone. Ethiopia, together with Eritrea and Somaliland, had fallen under Italian rule in the 1930s. It became independent under the firm rule of Haile Selassie, who remained emperor until the 1970s. Factions there vied for support from the superpowers too, and after the 1990s increasingly repressed rival tribes in semi-anarchic rule. The Sudan split into religious rivalries: Christians and Muslims remain at war.

In Central Africa, civil war also persists in the Congo. Over 5 million died between 1994 and 2003 alone, with reports of tribal massacres and even cannibalism. The Congo split into rival factions immediately after independence from Belgium in 1960. The tyrant Joseph Mobutu assassinated his rival Patrice Lumumba, probably with US help, since Lumumba was left-wing and fit into the anticommunist model of US foreign policy. With around 150 different tribes in this region alone, collaboration proved impossible, and the Congo has become the symbol of corruption, billionaire rulers and impoverished masses.

Nearby Rwanda had been dominated by French and Belgian rule until the 1960s, and the most horrific slaughter in recent decades occurred there after tribal rivalries exploded following economic collapse in 1994. Colonial rule left two major tribes in opposition, and past ethnic differences turned into political competition. When global coffee prices dropped precipitously in 1994, the country succumbed to genocide. Up to 800,000 Tutsis were killed by rival Hutus in indescribably violent circumstances, including machete attacks, mass rapes and murders in churches. Many of those involved still hold political position.

Attempts at supranational political organization in Africa, as in the Arab world, failed because of local rivalries. The Organization for African Unity formed in 1963. Though it brought political unity, it could not prevent conflict. As Cold War rivalries impeded stability, rulers in Africa enriched themselves, holding power close. The United Nations has been heavily involved in Africa since the 1970s, working to bring stability, and empower African states to impact global politics. A quarter of the nations today in the United Nations are African, albeit with limited political power.

In the 1990s, stability and prosperity did emerge in some parts of Africa. In perhaps the most overt case of political inequality derived from the colonial past, the South African nightmare saw a white-ruled nation offer black people no representation until 1994. Almost three-quarters of the country were Bantu, living in dreadful squalor with no political voice. The 1960 Sharpeville Massacre of black protestors by white police, and ongoing atrocities through the 1970s, led to the rise of resistance inspired by Nelson Mandela and others.

1994 brought the end of *apartheid* in South Africa. The white minority that held complete power finally succumbed to international political pressure, working with the all-black ANC whose imprisoned leader Nelson Mandela was released after 27 years in prison. Mandela formed a new party to govern the nation in 1994, when

Figure 1.11 Sign in District Six Museum, Cape Town, Western Cape Province, South Africa. (Denny Allen/Gallo Images.)

a tolerant minority of white rulers like President F. W. de Klerk acquiesced. Though poverty and political impotence persists, the nation is now democratic. Elsewhere there were hints of democratization in Africa in the 2000s. Nations with democratic elites like Botswana, and more recently Tanzania, have prospered thanks to open institutions.

Other nations like Zimbabwe however sustained a private fiefdom under the violent dictator Robert Mugabe, who lived in splendor off the nation's labors for decades. Nigeria, the wealthiest, most militarized African nation, is the clearest example of enduring tribal rivalry, persistent poverty and corruption. Nigeria is a major player in Africa, and other West African states look to it as an example. It has switched back and forth between civilian and military rule, and made little or no use of its vast income from oil reserves. Only in 2015 was an incumbent president first freely voted out of power.

African leaders possessed very narrow choices after independence, forced to borrow from Western nations or to export commodity crops at low cost. The first challenge for African rulers was the preexisting condition of colonial rule. Before European dominance, African states were divided along ethnic identity lines; in 1900 up to 10,000 tiny political units existed. By 1960, they were crammed into fifty new countries, with mixed populations, divergent interests, and no proclivity to work with enemy communities. Nonetheless, those who came to power elected not to spread political participation. Democracy was never the goal, since African politicians had no experience with its institutions in the first place. As in the Middle East, ethnic divisions resurfaced after independence to prevent unity or democracy.

The Americas

Latin American societies had gained independence from Spanish and Portuguese colonists in the early nineteenth century, long before African or Middle Eastern states. However, political power across the region remained in the autocratic rule of caudillos, authoritarian strongmen who often demanded reverence from the masses. Latin American dictatorships ruled with populist support, promising to thwart foreign power but usually friendly to foreign investment. Typically, a powerful man propped up by the military and the Catholic Church persuaded people that elite rule was for their benefit. Personal trust remains a key component of Latin American politics, with charm and presence standing in for legal contracts or political transparency. Since the Second World War Conservative and Liberal elites contrived to maintain privileges. Only since the 1990s has a mass electorate emerged, as education and literacy levels slowly rise. While Latin American elite's repressed popular participation, national sovereignty was constrained by Cold War pressures. Guatemala represents well how superpower ideology destroyed stability in small nations. In 1954, the CIA helped overthrew Guatemala's democratically elected president, to prevent an overtly leftist government in the region. This inspired Marxist rebels like Che Guevara to fight to counter US policies thereafter. The ensuing civil war of two decades left well over 100,000 mostly indigenous people dead at the hands of Conservative militias. Such US-supported actions were presented in American media as heroic counter-rebellions in the name of anticommunism and US national security. Revolutionaries such as Guevara inspired others to adopt radical politics as the only way to mobilize the masses and overthrow Washington-friendly elites.

US policy shifted over time, but was always intrusive. Nineteenth-century gunboat diplomacy persisted through Theodore Roosevelt's "Big Stick" policy, intended to induce fear into smaller states via the threat of military power. In 1904 his *Roosevelt Corollary* proclaimed Washington's right to intervene at will in the Americas. Until the 1930s US pressure came through Dollar Diplomacy, where subtle financial influence replaced direct physical aggression. After 1933, the United States introduced the Good Neighbor Policy, avowing to recognize the independence of Latin American states while keeping a close eye on parties or groups that threatened US interests. US actions in Latin America shifted from economic aid and trade liberalization on the one hand, to harsh containment of Communism and repression of leftist governments in the 1970s and 1980s. US interventions in Guatemala in 1954, Cuba in 1961, Brazil in 1964, the Dominican Republic in 1965, Nicaragua in 1979, and Panama in 1989 brought instability, violence, and political disenfranchisement, enthroning dictators more often than removing them.

Soviet influence in the region also persisted into the 1980s. Fidel Castro is a representative example. Castro took over Cuba in 1959, after the Cuban Revolution ousted corrupt US cronies and Conservative elites who lived in comfort among an impoverished Cuban population. Though nominally Communist, Castro's aims were simply Cuban independence and better conditions for the masses. Like Ho Chi Minh in Vietnam, he was simplistically labeled as a Communist enemy by US hawks.

The US could not stomach the idea a Communist state in its own hemisphere. A US economic boycott left Cuba desperately poor and dependent upon Soviet aid. The 1961 Cuban Missile Crisis almost brought nuclear war, when the United States discovered Soviet missiles located just south of Florida in Cuba. The Soviets backed down at the last minute, and the United States agreed to remove its missiles from Turkey (in Moscow's sphere of influence). Castro remained in power until his brother Raul took over in 2006, in a poor, isolated nation lacking wide franchise.

From 1968 Operation Condor, with US support, enabled brutal regimes to counter left-wing rebel groups all across South America. The region was incorporated into a Washington-led system of anticommunist, political repression. Populist elites were typically neither capitalist nor Communist, preferring to maintain a status quo that suited their situation, ordinarily through right-wing authoritarian rule.

Irrespective of US or Soviet meddling, democracy was unknown in Latin America anyway. Conservative elites welcomed US power, while leftists welcomed help from Moscow: most people gained from neither. Even nations less influenced by outside power, such as Argentina, were dominated by small cliques. The authoritarian Juan Peron built up a military regime after 1943, allowing no voice for opposition. Military rule was the norm into the recent era. Argentine military régimes killed tens of thousands of leftists from 1976 to 1983.

From the 1960s to the 1980s, civil war and unrest plagued Latin America, as leftist rebels working for the masses were attacked or assassinated by state military units. The CIA helped overthrow the democratically elected Chilean leader Salvador Allende in 1973. Allende was ousted since he threatened US business interests and veered to leftist politics. This was again too close to Communism for Washington, and since Allende also traded with Cuba he had to go. Claude Pinochet, the brutal military dictator left in place by the United States, would kill tens of thousands of left-wing dissenters, remaining in power until 1998.

Chilean poet Pablo Neruda's poem "The United Fruit Co." speaks to US influence in Latin American life:

When the trumpet sounded, it was
All prepared on earth,
And Jehovah parceled out the earth
To Coca Cola Inc., Anaconda
Ford Motors, and other entities:

The Fruit Company, Inc
Reserved for itself the most succulent,
The central coast of my land,
The delicate waist of America. . .

Meanwhile Indians are falling
Into the sugared chasms
Of the harbors, wrapped
For burial in the mist of the dawn:
A body rolls, a thing
That has no name, a fallen cipher,
A cluster of dead fruit
Thrown down on the dump.[17]

Central America and the Caribbean also remained in poverty through the century. Haiti endured brutal dictatorship through the postwar decades, with poverty, dictatorship and famine. Caribbean nations broke away from British rule in the 1960s but faced political corruption and relied on tourism for survival. Civil War in Nicaragua and El Salvador through the 1980s finally ended corrupt military rule. But when Nicaraguan rebels aimed to oust a brutal family dynasty the United States countered their efforts, again from fear of left-wing governance. Mexico, with one-party rule for most of the century, rarely represented the masses. The poor from Central America continue to move desperately across the US border for work, to flee political instability.

Increased political representation has come in recent decades across the continent however, and democracy increases in the region. The 1990s saw the end of the Washington Consensus, considered by most Latin Americans as a convenient system of economic policies that benefitted the United States more than the people of the Americas. Decades of conflict nonetheless lessened after the mid-1990s and a moderate democratic process emerged in most nations.

Since then, most countries have elected democratic governments, often opposed to the United States. Venezuela returned to left-wing rule under Hugo Chavez, who regained control of his nation's oil but then bankrupt the nation. Since his recent death, the nation has collapsed. Brazil and Argentina have pursed separate democratic paths since the 1990s. Argentina was impoverished by US-led IMF policies and political corruption persists. Brazil's aimed for a third way, mixing state intervention with free markets, but Brazil remains poor and he is accused of corruption at present. Colombia has long had a weak state, with a secondary system of governance in which drug lords support large portions of the population through private income from the international sales of drugs. In Peru, the democratically elected President Fujimori took power in 1992 but was found guilty of corruption and jailed. The trend in the region is slowly becoming more democratic, though with persistent patterns of corruption and limited democracy.

As in most of Africa, Asia, and the Middle East, Latin American people have enjoyed minimal political participation, even after the shackles of colonial rule and foreign intervention were broken. The legacy of Western colonialism was replaced by Cold War Soviet and US influence, followed by an aversion to democracy from established elites.

Western nations

Western Europe generally prospered after war, with centrist political parties committed to peace and political participation. Since 1945 the political process has been open in the West, from Europe to Canada and Australia. Following the economic boost from the US Marshall Plan, the European Union formed in the 1950s to bring economic growth and political stability, from the 1960s to the present. For those in Eastern Europe in contrast, Communist rule excluded most from political life until 1991, though participation has increased since.

1956 was an important year for Europe. When Egypt's Nasser took over of the Suez Canal, it marked the end of Anglo-French domination of the Arab and African world. US refusal to support Britain, France, and Israel's invasion of Egypt humiliated both imperial nations. Clearly, they were no longer great powers. Both focused thereafter on providing for their own people, with generally positive results. Also, in 1956 Communists in the West were forced to concede that Soviet politics were brutal and authoritarian, when invading Russian tanks crushed Hungarian and Polish attempts at autonomy and burgeoning democracy. They would do the same in Czechoslovakia in 1968. The *Berlin Wall,* built in 1961 to prevent widespread defection, symbolized clearly much people wished to depart from Communist societies to reach Western freedoms: many were willing to die in the effort.

By the 1960s, Westerners became more habituated to political protest. As in the United States, massive protests against the war in Vietnam broadened political dialogue beyond stifling 1950s conservatism. Though the civil rights movement in the US 1960s stemmed from widespread racism there, it merged with European movements to highlight prejudice, sexism and inequality at home. In 1968, Europeans frustrated at the political status quo exploded in student-led revolutions. Protests in Europe and America introduced a new era of political dissent that spread as far as Mexico. Cynicism toward politicians and openly defiant criticism of those in power became normalized. Western protests inspired the 1968 Prague Spring, where Czech rebels failed in an attempt to oust Communist rule.

These movements did not bring revolution or power to the people—Mexican protestors were met with massacres for instance. But the movements inaugurated a culture of political protest that has remained the norm in the West. In the 1970s radical dissent came from rebel groups willing to resort to violence. Baader Meinhof and other anti-capitalist groups propagated violence against elites in Germany and

Italy, often without popular support. The IRA practiced guerrilla violence against the British army in Northern Ireland, although without the support of most in Britain or Ireland. Broadly, the push for political change and reform became normalized in the West, even amid relative prosperity and stability.

The 1970s saw enormous political dissent, partly due to economic problems stemming from Organization of Petroleum Exporting Countries (OPEC) oil cuts. European states, Canada and Australia, remained stable overall however, and a political reaction set in against progressive and leftist ideals in that decade. Countering left-wing critics of excessive capitalism, the late 1970s Thatcher–Reagan revolution brought an era of political conservatism and the diffusion of free-market capitalism after 1980. The clear failure of Communism in the 1980s left the world's ruling elite to pursue politically Conservative policies for the rest of the century, though left and center parties participated and fought for wider participation in *Social Democracies*.

By the 1980s, Westerners generally enjoyed stable politics, with minimal historical memory of past encroachments worldwide. Willy Brandt's *North-South Report* of 1980 aspired to aid previously colonized states, to inculcate a culture of wealth sharing among Western states. Though this met with some success, the West was focused more on internal domestic growth and stability, with only limited interest in human rights issues abroad. As the new century began, Europeans considered themselves mostly united in the European Union (EU), with separate states whose interest was their own well-being. This situation is now in flux, with right-wing nationalists in some states, including Britain, wishing to break away from the EU to return to 1930s style nationalism.

4. From communism to terrorism: Since 1991

In 1908 workers in a Polish shipyard unknowingly began the process of dismantling the vast Communist apparatus. In that year, strikes in Poland, a nation persistently invaded by German and Russian neighbors, inspired the mass social movement, *Solidarity*. The movement combined Catholic anticommunism with trade union membership, aiming to counter military elites and Communist rule and to legalize political opposition. This was the first blow in a steady deterioration of the Communist experiment and by 1991, the end of the USSR. Though pushback came from Moscow through the 1980s, by the end of that decade, most of Eastern Europe had followed the Polish example of ousting Communist parties.

Few expected this in 1980. Though Communism differed significantly in specific regions, almost a third of the world lived under some form of Communist rule in the 1970s. From the Western, particularly American, perspective, one uniform ideology polluted Cuba, East Africa, Vietnam, Cambodia, Laos, and Korea. In reality, these nations had little in common with each other (or indeed with Marx's theoretical notion of an industrial proletariat). Typically, a tiny elite promoted pithy slogans to maintain personal, political domination in Communist states. This was what the Poles, and then other Communist satellites, overthrew to attain democracy.

Soviet Communism collapses

Increasing communist-capitalist compromises in the 1970s suggested that Communist leaders recognized the flaws in their political system. After 1970, China and the United States enjoyed better relations (*rapprochement*) and growing trade following President Richard Nixon's visit to China. The Helsinki Accords of 1975 further improved relations between West and East, signifying that neither side desired nuclear Armageddon. Between 1975 and 1986, a vast industrial nuclear arms race continued, with persistent saber rattling between the superpowers, but little threat of outright war.

Political resistance in Soviet satellites, propelled by economic decline, ultimately ended Communism. By the 1980s, Communist Europe floundered in poverty, prompting dissent among younger, worldlier people who saw Europeans enjoying political liberty and consumer comforts. Communist regimes lost grip on power and any legitimacy they had held. The 1986, Chernobyl nuclear disaster ultimately exposed the corruption and incompetence of the Soviet state. The Western press made this readily apparent to the world, and a new generation of leaders such as Soviet President Mikhail Gorbachev came to recognize there were better political options. Gorbachev's reforms between 1986 and 1991 brought the hope of uniting Europe from east to west.

Glasnost represented a new Soviet willingness to open up politically, while perestroika conceded the need for reforms. Gorbachev ended the futile and draining Afghan War in 1989, working toward amity with China and the West.

Gorbachev's admission of the Soviet state's ineffectiveness opened the floodgates across Eastern Europe. Hungarian Communists were forced to accept political opposition by 1989, Czechs had fought for it for decades, and all the Soviet satellite states moved in the direction of independence in the coming year or two. When Hungary opened its border with Austria in summer 1989, those trapped in Communist Hungary fled west: they immediately did so by the thousands. In November, the Berlin Wall was knocked down without response from Moscow. These were heady times for peace.

Thereafter, most Eastern European states moved peacefully toward democracy. The only major confrontation came from Romania's ruling despots, the Ceausescu's. Reformist Romanian soldiers shot the cruel president and his wife on Christmas Day 1989, with mass approval. Communists in East Germany resisted change, but by November 1989 people were moving to the West to unite with family. German reunification worried some in Europe, but compromise created a workable German state with considerable efforts to absorb East Germany's less literate and poorer population into a greater Germany. Independence for the Baltic States was restored and Soviet rule ended by 1991. Following 40 years of Communist rule, after the Berlin Wall was smashed, the vast apparatus of Soviet power simply evaporated in a somewhat farcical conclusion.

The internal disintegration of the Soviet Union in 1991 also left Eastern European nations free to pursue their own paths. In 1989, Gorbachev remained committed to a more democratic Communist Party. He was ousted by Boris Yeltsin, who became president in 1991 and pushed for further free-market capitalist reforms. The 1990s did not bring stability, however, in Russia. Instead, a new vanguard of well-connected super-capitalist elites took over in Moscow, enriching themselves and dominating politics. When Vladimir Putin replaced Boris Yeltsin in 2000, autocratic rule returned, backed by a billionaire oligarchy providing for very limited political freedom. A tougher attitude to regional territorial disputes returned, with a Russian state bent on resisting neighboring states that wished to Westernize or Americanize.

New traumas

The consequences of the Communist catastrophe endure. Just as African and Asian societies met new problems following postcolonial independence, the end of Communism presented ongoing dilemmas. A Russian Federation was proposed in 1992, but diverse peoples wanted independence. The independence of ex-Soviet republics was only partial, as they were kept within Russia's sphere of influence. People across Central Asia, from Mongols to Ukrainians, were still threatened by Moscow's edicts, and secession usually required violent resistance. The Caucasus region had long been a point of tense interaction between Christian and Muslim cultures and it returned to this state after Communist rule withered. Bitter minorities formed rebel movements to protest Russian domination, particularly in Muslim societies that fought for autonomy such as Chechnya. Russian soldiers invaded Chechnya in 1994, leading to horrific abuses on both sides.

As usual oil was a source of conflict, with crucial reserves in Chechnya and Kazakhstan triggering a struggle to control the region. In Kazakhstan, Tajikistan, Turkmenistan, and Kyrgyzstan huge mixed ethnic populations faced issues similar to African postcolonial regimes. Weakened nations like Mongolia remain pastoral and face great uncertainty in the modern world after losing autonomy for a century. What remained in the Soviet republics after 1991 was poverty, political autocracy and ethnic tensions exacerbated by decades of Soviet control and as always, corrupt indigenous political elites. Other efforts to break from Russian influence met varied success. Ukraine's Orange Revolution of 2004 followed the Georgian Revolution of 2003, demonstrating dogged disapproval of Russian authority.

Post-Communist independence brought new nightmares, however. A discouraging and unexpected consequence of the end of Communism was vicious war in the Balkans. After Nazi Germany occupied Yugoslavia in 1941, the Communist dictator, General Tito, brazenly resisted Stalin and brought unity to diverse Balkan populations. Jews had been eradicated from the region during the Nazi period, but the area was still a bewildering mixture of faiths: Catholic and Orthodox Christians mingled with various Muslim groups who had lived together for centuries under Muslim Ottoman and Catholic Habsburg rule.

Hammered together without Balkan peoples' consultation at the Treaty of Versailles, Yugoslavia functioned well enough as a fragmented composite of ethnicities during Tito's relatively benign authoritarian rule. When he died in 1980, bitter hatreds slowly resurfaced. After Communism fell in 1991, a Serb minority led by ruthless nationalist leaders took up arms in the name of Slavic pride, aiming to dominate the newly independent pro-Western states of Slovenia, Macedonia, and Croatia. When the people of Bosnia-Herzegovina declared independence in 1992, they found their home a battlefield between political factions. Over 100,000 deaths occurred, and half of the population of 4 million became refugees. Between 1991 and 2001 all sides in the conflict ignored Geneva conventions and abused enemies. Serbian right-wing nationalists committed genocide against Muslims in Srebrenica, and horrific conflict ensued through the decade between Muslim minorities and Croatian and Serbian nationalists.

International intervention came from the United Nations, with US and NATO forces helping to end the slaughter. The US-led Dayton Agreement of 1995 brought some harmony to the region. Slobodan Milosevic, the Serbian radical who prompted much of the slaughter, was placed on trial in the International War Crimes Tribunal, dying while under investigation in 2006. The separate Balkan nations remain poor and politically fragmented, but have since joined the EU, slowly adopting Western parliamentary systems.

Soviet control ironically provided overarching unity within a system of Communist domination, similar to European imperial rule in previously colonized regions. Both post-imperialist and post-Communist societies have seen little political stability. From Africa to the Middle East, the Balkans to Central Asia, political fragmentation has plagued small states with limited power and resources, bringing interminable political conflict. The region just south of the USSR is a cause celebre of political volatility, where Central Asia becomes the Middle East in Afghanistan.

The Middle East

The Middle East was not always volatile. Afghanistan for instance, was run by a pro-Western Islamic monarchy for most of the century and was generally stable. Political autonomy ended when Soviet Communists invaded in 1979, to support a dissident Marxist faction. The KGB thereafter endeavored to marginalize noncommunist ethnic factions in the region. The Soviet invasion ended in Russian humiliation in 1989—a Soviet version of America's Vietnam nightmare. But perhaps more importantly for the present, the United States allied with the Muslim fundamentalist mujahedeen who later became the Taliban.

From an Afghani perspective, Cold War rivalries created chaos, hardening men in an already impoverished, factious tribal region. In the 1990s Afghanistan became the breeding ground for Islamist radicals itching to join Al Qaeda, particularly after a UN coalition led by the United States invaded Iraq in 1991. Soviet and US operations toward the end of the Cold War thus inflamed countless young Muslim fighters who committed their lives to Al Qaeda, and later ISIS, to terrorize the Western world.

Options for Muslim states were meager in the postwar world. By the 1980s Muslim radicals were embittered toward the West. Instead of liberal democratic modernity, they saw a world of Western violence and political reach, most clearly represented by the United States. The West, in their view, had for centuries oppressed Muslims and Africans. France, Britain, and the United States had killed millions, from Algeria to Kenya to Vietnam, in the name of capitalist expansion, under the guise of liberal democracy. For many Muslims, Western political systems offered hypocrisy, corruption, nepotism and ongoing intervention in their homeland. Though an extreme viewpoint that underlay a horrific terrorist worldview, this was not wholly ahistorical.

> Mikhail Gorbachev, in the 1990s, also noted the violence in Western history:
>
> *Let us not forget, however, that the metastases of colonial slavery spread around the world from Europe. It was here that fascism came into being. It was here that the most destructive wars started. At the same time Europe, which can take a legitimate pride in its accomplishments, is far from having settled its debts to mankind. It is something that still has to be done.*[18]

Gorbachev of course failed to note rampant political violence in Communism in this statement. Western democracy was far superior to the Communist alternative, which promised so much but delivered so little. And certainly, the aim of Islamists, a worldwide Muslim Caliphate community, or *umma*, is not only impossible; it ignores inter-Muslim violence within the region disconnected from Western influence that reaches back centuries.

After a century of Western political dominance, a new millennia loomed in the first year of the twenty-first century. Hope proliferated that the truly positive components of Western politics—democracy and representation—might spread worldwide. Yet, the other side of Western ideology—imperialism and intervention—prompted a brand-new form of political violence, manifest most horribly in New York on September 11, 2001. That day, a non-state, non-nationalist, non-imperial group founded on religious and ideological radicalism, Al Qaeda, mercilessly killed 3,000 people, baffling the world's political elite and shocking the world.

Here, the authoritarian tendencies of Islamic political regimes utilized the humiliation of US, Russian and European interference in the Middle East since oil was discovered in 1906. Millions of Muslims with no stake in the continuity of the existing political system now provide the chief threat to political stability worldwide. Iraq and Syria have collapsed. Israel and Palestine are no closer to concord. Billions around the world lack the means for political engagement. So much had changed since 1900. Yet, perhaps nothing had changed.

Key terms

Authoritarian [3]
Democracies [3]
Nationalism [4]
Communism [4]
Dollar Diplomacy [11]
New Imperialism [20]
League of Nations [26]
Treaty of Versailles [10]
Mandates [26]
Indirect Rule [14]
War Guilt Clause [29]
Red Scare [31]
Interventionist State [18]
Autarky [37]
United Nations [46]
Great Leap Forward [51]
Cultural Revolution [51]
Colonization [7]
Theocracy [57]
Intifada [58]
Apartheid [62]
European Union [35]
Civil Rights [6]
North-South Report [68]
Solidarity [68]
Mujahedeen [59]

Social Democracies [68]
Islamism [4]

Further reading

Keylor, William R., *A World of Nations: The International Order Since 1945*. 2nd ed. New York: Oxford University Press, 2009. Clear exposition of the issues facing international organizations, and nations, since the Second World War. Emphasizes power relations and the necessity of strategic interests in driving national decisions.

Robbins, Keith. *The World Since 1945: A Concise History*. Oxford, England: Oxford University Press, 1998. Short, readable, and succinct account of the major events in world history since 1945.

Keylor, William R., *The Twentieth Century World and Beyond: An International History Since 1900*. 5th ed. New York: Oxford University Press, 2006. Comprehensive coverage of the century, focusing on links between nations rather than the great powers.

Interlude 1: Propaganda

After 9/11

Political propaganda

In 1900, a small number of industrial nation-states dominated most societies on earth through the process of imperial power. Between the First and Second World Wars, traditional empires crumbled. By the 1960s the, British and French empires disappeared, replaced by the global superpowers the USSR and United States. One continuity across these diverse political forms was the perpetual justification of political interference in the name of national security-and the habitual exploitation of domestic fears to justify overseas actions.

By the 1970s, scores of new nations emerged worldwide, with either democratic or authoritarian systems of governance. A contradiction existed in both political systems, an understandable desire for national autonomy and self-preservation required the darker consequences of nationalism: xenophobia, exclusion, conflict, and environmental ruination. By the end of the twentieth century, the sovereign state was an assumed entity, bringing security and stability for citizens: the only seemed to be anarchy or chaos.

Political leaders in dictatorships, theocracies, and traditional societies certainly controlled information flow to the governed masses. But, as the philosopher Michel Foucault noted, democracies did so too. The possession of power meant control, persuasions and coercion even in the most open democracy, and while the United States and Britain were indubitably the most open societies, elites in these countries shaped ideas and opinions, both at home and abroad. After the 1930s television and radio provided a means for leaders in all societies to influence the opinions of populations. Particularly in wartime, leaders demanded that the country needed men and women to make sacrifices, suggesting it was in their own interest to do so. Everywhere, typically unschooled people, believed whatever was broadcast. From the First World War to the twenty-first century, the interests of those in power are still defended by everyday soldiers.

In the United States and the West, advertising from the 1920s on shaped the image of a new consumer-citizen, specifically to counter Socialist ideas. Influential,

Figure 1.12 Digitally restored war propaganda poster. This vintage First World War poster features Lady Liberty waving the American flag. Behind her, American troops are rushing into battle. (John Parrot/Stocktrek Images.)

well-connected men such as Sigmund Freud's nephew, Edward Bernays, supported fastidiously by business and political leaders, assertively molded the views of Americans, compelling them through psychologically focused advertising to consume—in the name of patriotism and for social control.

Autocratic societies were, and remain, even more manipulative. Middle Eastern leaders routinely inundate people with images of religious or political cult idols to incite violence, as do Asian and African sovereigns. South and Southeast Asian populations have only recently been able to question autocratic rule, and Latin

American political and religious elites have long inundated citizens with images of supposedly friendly dictators, to be trusted on word.

The omnipresent political act of shaping minds helps explain how such different worldviews could collide on that terrible day of September 11, 2001, when American national security was so shockingly breached by a gang of terrorists attached to no one state. The US Congress and the hawkish President Bush could only contemplate one response—to bomb Afghanistan and then Iraq, two Muslim nations from whence none of the terrorists originated! Americans rightly saw an attack on a political system that had been an ideal of democratic governance worldwide. They did not see what much of the world did however, that American capitalism had long been a force for overseas coercion. As the most powerful power on earth, like Britain in 1900, the United States naturally invited resentment. Like Britain in the nineteenth century, US operations and political reach had made many enemies over the decades.

After the attacks of 9/11, a short-lived national unity in the United States soon fractured into a divided polity. Conservatives hell-bent on reasserting American power demanded revenge in the Middle East and even greater overseas interventionism. Some clamored for outright US imperialism. Most historians and thinkers however cited imperial history, noting the longstanding duplicity of Western political ideologies. They cautioned against risky overseas adventures, suggesting a globalist rather than a nationalist approach. Conservative hawks in the Bush administration, supported by centrist Democrats, nonetheless led the US military into Afghanistan in 2001.

Invading Afghanistan was understandable as noted above. But the ill-informed invasion of Iraq in 2003 was a disaster, creating global violence, more failed states, the deaths of many soldiers, the rise of ISIS and the collapse of both Iraq and Syria. No connection was ever shown between Iraq's horrendous ruler Saddam Hussein and the possession of Weapons of Mass Destruction. No apparent ties existed between his crony state and Al Qaeda (other than both being Muslim). False claims and outright lies from US politicians engineered a second war in the region that brought the death of up to half a million Muslims and thousands of US soldiers, More than a decade of invasion and combat in the heart of the Muslim world then inspired the more brutal radical group ISIS to threaten civil society worldwide. Though difficult for Westerners to grasp, the horrific acts of Muslim radicals were justified historically in the minds of those who committed them, and their supporters worldwide.

The message the US population received was one of America spreading democracy and free trade in the Middle East, of nation building. Little mention was made in the US media or political circles of decades of official or covert CIA interventions in the Middle East, or a century of strategic power plays for cheap oil extraction. Western European nations, ironically the source of so much twentieth-century conflict, today criticize both US aggression and increasing Russian expansion in the Middle East.

A proxy Cold War continues in the region, with Islamic terrorism as its object rather than capitalist-communist competition.

> The terrorist Osama Bin Laden wrote a letter to the US government in 2002, which contained some historical logic even if some facts were embellished:
>
> (d) You steal our wealth and oil at paltry prices because of your international influence and military threats. This theft is indeed the biggest theft ever witnessed by mankind in the history of the world.
> (e) Your forces occupy our countries; you spread your military bases throughout them; you corrupt our lands, and you besiege our sanctities, to protect the security of the Jews and to ensure the continuity of your pillage of our treasures.
> (f) You have starved the Muslims of Iraq, where children die every day. It is a wonder that more than 1.5 million Iraqi children have died as a result of your sanctions, and you did not show concern. Yet when 3000 of your people died, the entire world rises and has not yet sat down.[19]

For many worldwide, including Russia, the response to 9/11 from the sole remaining superpower and its ex-imperial allies replicated old patterns of Western arrogance—intervention, slaughter, and senseless entanglement in barely understood societies. History helps explain why people fight against seemingly impossible odds, as Al Qaeda and ISIS do. The vicious terrorist group ISIS may be the most notorious example of outright violence, but in their minds, they have historical reasons for their fury. History cannot tell us who was or is right or wrong, but it can show us many complex perspectives and provide better understanding. Indeed perhaps the key question from a world historical, as opposed to a nationalist stance, is 'Why do people dedicate themselves to such political violence?"

Political violence

The 1900s began with discontented rebels in the Third World raising consciousness to oust colonial European powers. In Europe, disgruntled workers aimed to end imperial government, to earn rights for the working masses or excluded minorities. This sense of political grievance has equivalents today, as rebels around the world work to undermine established states by expressing anger with violence.

Political rebellion today has similarities to many through the century. Those who ruled Ireland from London dealth with Irish rebellions for most of the century. The IRA killed thousands over decades, to protest British troops in Ireland into the 1990s. Spanish rulers still deal with protest from those seeking autonomy in the Catalan and Basque regions, as the French do in Corsica. Rebels in Latin America protest oppression

Figure 1.13 French Tradition. Demonstration and protest of French workers and students against French first minister Dominique de Villepin. (Credit: Julien Brachhammer.)

from autocratic states. Colombia is finally negotiating with FARC (Revolutionary Armed Forces of Colombia in English) rebels, after decades of massacres between rebels and the state. Russian leaders struggle to prevent breakaway states in the Chechnyan region, Crimea, and Ukraine. China rules Hong Kong, Taiwan, and Tibet against their wishes. Political conflict is endemic in recently formed African states and the Middle East lacks strong state rulers with authentic legitimacy.

Today up to fifty "nations" pursue political autonomy worldwide, though the international community does not recognize them. Countless people are outcast in the nation they live in, as migrants, refugees or excluded groups. Every recognized nation possesses minorities within who are either repressed or ignored. Perhaps little has changed since 1900. Conflict exists worldwide, as it did then. Political inclusion is an ongoing and intractable historical process. The most stable states remain in Western Europe, Canada, Australia, Japan and the United States, where more than elsewhere representation and participation is offered to historically excluded groups.

On the other hand, the century as a whole offers many positive changes in the political realm. Political power includes working-class people today, and far more women. Angela Merkel in Germany, Margaret Thatcher in England, Indira Gandhi in India, Ellen Sirleaf in Liberia and others suggest that women might win power in coming years. Most states worldwide provide suffrage or concede to growing aspiration for political representation. Almost half of the world's 184 nations enjoy the rule of law, civil society, and human rights - as recent as the 1970s only about thirty nations enjoyed such elementary workings of democracy. By the standards of twenty-first-century ideals, there is perhaps little to cheer regarding the ongoing litany of political slaughter and oppression worldwide, but by the standards of 1900, much has changed for the good. Indeed, a primary source of political conflict is economic circumstances, and to this we turn now in Chapter 2.

2

Twentieth-Century Economics: Natural Inequality

Situating the chapter

In 1900, Western capitalism appeared an unstoppable force, *the* universal mode of economic organization. Along with political domination, Western states enjoyed global economic command at this time. Britain, France, and Germany, and those who emulated their industrial model such as the United States and Japan, freely intimidated poorer states, gaining easy access to essential raw materials, cheap imports and inexpensive or free labor.

After the First World War, Communist states proposed an alternative, fairer distribution of national and international wealth, via Socialism. By the 1950s, indigenous or traditional economies would be governed or compelled by either

Figure 2.1 US President Ronald Reagan with British Prime Minister Margaret Thatcher, 1984. (Photo by Rogers/Express/Getty Images.)

capitalist or Socialist powers. Communism failed, and at the end of a century of unparalleled violence, free-market capitalism had won, spreading to the most remote areas of the planet and into all aspects of life. Whether this was positive or not for humanity is an important question for students of history.

Progressive political parties formed specifically to increase workers' wages around 1900 and won many gains. A century later they had generally acceded to Conservative economic programs and the influence of big business. Symbolically, the first "party of the people," Britain's Labour Party, accepted Conservative economics in the 1990s, bowing to Margaret Thatcher's and Ronald Reagan's ideology that the poor must help themselves, unions abolished, and government programs be cut back. Left-wing parties in Europe and Democrats in the United States, emulated Conservative policies after the 1990s - free-market capitalism now reached worldwide. Levels of inequality were even greater than in 1900, as the rich became richer and the poor looked on. While in 1900, the wealthiest nations were typically three or four times richer than the poorest ones, by 2000 they were hundreds of times wealthier. Nevertheless, even as the wealth gap increased, the fact remains that more wealth was created in the twentieth century than in all of history.

By the end of this chapter, readers should be able to:

- Explain twentieth-century economic inequality within and among nations.
- Illustrate the outcomes of global economic competition.
- Analyze diverse attitudes to wealth accumulation around the world.

- Shape an argument regarding variations in capitalism and Socialism since 1900.
- Formulate a position on overall economic change since 1900.

The story

Imperial economics—wide-open markets, worldwide competition

Domination by 1900 gave Western societies first-mover advantage. Industrial states could assertively enforce an ideology of free markets and global trade upon weaker societies, the consequences of which persist. Military supremacy enabled industrial states to enforce trading privileges, while protecting their domestic industries. After 1900, Western nations set up terms of trade for their gain, a pattern that persists today. Economic profits acquired in the past century still divide the world between the rich and poor, with vast disparities in standards of living worldwide.

A billion previously colonized people achieved independence between 1945 and 1975, in nations forced to utilize banking and finance institutions controlled by colonial powers. Few societies were acculturated to a culture of capitalism; most were comprised of diverse groupings of ethnic populations with contradictory interests. Unsurprisingly, most colonized states have since endured endemic poverty. In almost all postcolonial nations, *Extractive economies*—where goods are made for elites or overseas export rather than for local use—have transferred resources from poorer to wealthy nations, creating ongoing disparities.

Social Darwinism

Economic competition is of course as old as states, but economic rivalry between 1900 until 1945 was more than simply exploitative, it was premised upon racist contempt for nonindustrial peoples often considered as inferior species. European, American, and Japanese traders and officials extracted essential resources from Africa, the Americas, the Middle East, and Asia. A world of linked markets developed in the decades before 1914, premised upon rapacious national competition to control key sources of power such as timber, coal and oil. The outbreak of the First World War demonstrated the human costs of industrial competition. After the war, economic activity declined markedly, and already poor nations and people suffered more than wealthier ones. Oil soon became vital to developing economies and a source of persistent conflict.

Between 1917 and 1989 capitalist and Socialist economies pursued separate paths, competing worldwide. Third World economies were jostled between the two systems until Communism's collapse in 1989. Since then weaker economies have been swept up into one large globalized open market, primarily driven by capitalist financiers in rich, Western nations.

Inequality persists, but over the past century previously unimaginable levels of wealth were created for billions of people. In material terms, this was the most luxurious century in human history. Citizens in rich nations progressed from basic sustenance to expectation of indulgences which monarchs would have coveted a century ago. However, many in the poorest nations gained relatively too, enjoying basic goods and steady food supplies unimaginable in 1900.

Such gains were diluted over the century by large population growth, particularly in poor societies. Previously colonized regions remained impoverished, and most wealth went to small cliques of oligarchs in much of Africa, Asia, the Middle East, and South America. Thus, not only did elite greed and the long-term consequences of colonization hinder poorer societies, but after the Second World War, improved technologies enriched industrial nations even further, creating an ever-widening gap.

1. Western economics: not for everyone

In 1900, a few modern states organized the global economy without obstruction. By industrializing first, they possessed a competitive advantage over traditional societies, from China to Chile. German and US industrial growth surged between the 1870s and 1914, as those nations caught up and surpassed Britain. The First World War boosted the US economy immensely, helping make it the world's richest society. By the 1930s, the USSR and Japan industrialized, albeit in authoritarian style, with great worker repression. Modernizing after 1868, Japan immediately expanded into Asia, extracting resources violently from China, Korea, and Taiwan. Japan, like the United States, profited from the war, exporting vast amounts of textiles, military supplies, and arms to combatants. These profits helped both nations prosper in the 1920s and 1930s as they placed crosshairs on one another.

The gap between Western economies and the rest of the world was colossal in 1900. The United States, Germany, and Britain produced almost all the world's industrial goods, while the rest of the planet mined or shipped raw materials to Western factories. Indeed, a second form of industrial capitalism formed in Germany, developing sophisticated modern chemical and electrical technologies. Businesses like Siemens, Krupp, Mercedes, and Daimler made more goods than most nations on earth combined could in 1900, while American industrial production and administrative productivity soared to lay the ground for later affluence.

Since Britain had dominated nineteenth-century trade, in 1914 British businessmen governed a global economy, playing by the rules that Adam Smith had devised in the eighteenth century, based on free-market ideals. The nineteenth century was one of integrating markets connected by British (and European) capital, companies, and commercial adventurism. This continued into the Second World War, after which the United States became the dominant player in global trade. Britain dictated the course of world trade between 1840 and 1880 more than any nation ever had, exporting industrial goods, machinery and expertise, saturating markets all over the world with capital from London.

No country had ever possessed so much wealth derived from other societies. In 1900, almost half of the planet's economic assets were connected to British investors, who managed prices on all continents. British workers wore clothes made with cotton from Egypt or Uganda. British bankers and businessmen got rich on trade with countries worldwide—their counterparts in Germany and the United States wanted in on the game. Britain's ruling elite therefore played a particularly decisive role in the creation of the twentieth-century global economy. They controlled the market for gold, the standard currency after 1880, by tying it to the British pound.[1]

Nonindustrialized countries

Discoveries of gold in white settler nations like California, Australia, and South Africa in the late nineteenth century further spread Western domination. But extraction of gold for use as legal tender worsened the exploitation of indigenous and peasant labor, prompting the near enslavement of non-European workers worldwide (decades after slavery had been abolished). Though Western laborers toiled in terrible conditions, they were usually better paid, with more protections, than workers of color in mines, plantations, and factories worldwide. Since nonindustrialized societies could not compete economically, most of the 1.6 billion people on earth—including all of Latin America, the Middle East, Africa, and most of Asia—produced or exported to developed nations.

Colonized nations could not industrialize even if elites wished to, as they were not politically united or independent. Nineteenth-century African states, for instance, were small, poor or isolated. Many inland societies subsisted without European, Arab, or other foreign interference. Large African states had in fact traded on equal terms for centuries, but by the 1890s, aside from Liberia and Abyssinia, all of Africa was controlled by Europeans. The Middle East was similarly fragmented and impoverished, with a failing and corrupt Ottoman Empire disdainful of industrialization. China also remained rural and imploded in 1911 due to an internal revolution, Western interference and Japanese incursions, thriving economically only since the 1980s. Most of Latin America was economically dependent on Europe and the United States in 1914, with massive landownership supporting a tiny Latin elite. India's economy modernized only since independence in 1947, and poverty persists for most people.

Everywhere, local ruling elites worsened the impact of Western interference. Rarely inclined to share economic wealth, cliques in colonized regions benefitted from Western connections, and many were transformed into royal or privileged families in the past century. Hence, an upper class of collaborators in colonized regions thrived from links to Western investors and markets. Foreign influence was often welcomed, as elite colonial subjects in Africa and the Middle East gained from access to Western funds. Egypt's local rulers lived playboy lives on loans from London; princes and rajas in India were happy to comply with British rule; Ottoman elites welcomed German investment, even siding with the Germans in the war; French money built the Trans-Saharan Railway across the Arabian Desert, opening up Saudi Arabia. And though railways often interrupted tribal trade, some in Africa such as the Malinke encouraged French investment.

For most people though, integration into Western capitalist economies meant stricter work discipline and enduring poverty. Asians, Africans, Arabs and Latin Americans were ultimately subject to economic rules set in London, New York, or Paris. In Africa and the Middle East, agriculturalists, pastoralists, fishermen, or hunters and gatherers found that they were suddenly part of new European-contrived nations. Only Japan outside of the West industrialized, and though Japanese people reaped benefits, they were thrust into a militarized economy in the 1930s.

Exploiting labor

While Western nations subjugated colonized people worldwide, they also exploited workers at home. In the decades after 1900, Western capitalists made increasingly productive use of human labor, natural resources, and liquid assets to generate wealth. Western workers were probably better off than colonized subjects, but they faced a new work regime that chased quick profits without contemplating the human costs. Western factory workers endured incredibly wretched conditions, forced to work faster to meet productivity goals set by management, whose sole purpose was to satisfy business owners or shareholders. Colonized peasants too no longer worked in ways that they were acclimatized to, toiling faster for foreign companies, spending longer hours and harder days producing for distant markets. Thus, families worldwide long habituated to slower lifestyles found their customs and habits disrupted in the twentieth century. Working for companies or factories tuned solely to the demands of faraway markets and abstract spreadsheets, people on earth everywhere worked harder to subsist or survive.

In industrial nations, the drastic pace of change in the first decade of the century required intense work habits. Assembly workers in Ford's auto production line needed 151 hours to make a car in 1906; by the early 1920s they could make a car in 37 hours. Such automation made cars cheaper for all, but it required frenetic labor practices that were later normalized across the United States and worldwide.

After the First World War though, Western workers protested vigorously for reform legislation to improve working conditions and pay rates. The growth of trade unions, combined with increasingly literate members, brought campaigns for social insurance and other assistance. Growing defiance from the industrial poor, usually due to Socialist-inspired ideas and raised consciousness, pressured wealthy capitalists to accept the need for more humane working conditions in the first decades of the century. Lacking comparable education or literacy, workers in colonized countries had little hope of gaining from organizing, and could not expect to share in the wealth of their societies. Consciousness of inequity raised by Socialist thinkers and growing literacy were rare outside the West.

In Europe, but particularly so in the United States, employers united to counter workers' movements, enjoying support from government elites, to essentially form "anti-union unions." US government and business elites committed deep resources to advertising and marketing, convincing workers that a life of consumption was preferable to revolution, protest, or indeed Socialism. Continuous worker strife and violence proliferated in the United States prior to the 1920s, but rising consumerism served to counter Socialist ideas and state militias physically assaulted those with leftist ideals. The diverse, ethnic nature of the vast, fragmented population made it easier for American elites to stall workers' resistance and unity, so business and political rulers successfully thwarted class consciousness at home. Fearful of Socialism, they persecuted activist labor leaders through the 1920s, killing some. Reasonable workers' rights claims were broadly painted as Marxist revolution, quieting dissent in favor of pro-business attitudes.

Britain was the origin of the ideology of free trade in the nineteenth century. It was also the site of the first workers political party. The following is an excerpt from the Labour Party manifesto of 1906, which placed the burden of providing necessities such as water, sanitation and heating on the state and the wealthy. Much of this was accepted thereafter in reformist Western Europe, serving to counter workers' revolution:

1906 Labour Party General Election Manifesto

This election is to decide whether or not Labour is to be fairly represented in Parliament.

The House of Commons is supposed to be the people's House, and yet the people are not there.

Landlords, employers, lawyers, brewers, and financiers are there in force. Why not Labour?

The Trade Unions ask the same liberty as capital enjoys. They are refused.

The aged poor are neglected. The slums remain; overcrowding continues, whilst the land goes to waste. Shopkeepers and traders are overburdened with rates and taxation, whilst the increasing land values, which should relieve the ratepayers, go to people who have not earned them.

Wars are fought to make the rich richer, and underfed schoolchildren are still neglected.[2]

For better or worse, Western capitalism encircled the colonized world by 1914, infiltrating the lives of indigenous people, peasant farmers, and urban paupers.

Industrial capitalism uprooted people from their homelands, forcing tens of millions of people, both white and nonwhite, to move to find work in hostile wealthy nations. It mostly benefitted those with existing wealth who were well connected to international markets. It also provided work for many, particularly the Western industrial masses, although work was inconsistent and brutal.

Explaining inequality

Economic theory

In the early twentieth century, few but Socialists thought to even question or explain inequality. Those in power considered it perfectly natural; most workers doubted that it could ever change. The gospel of nineteenth-century classical liberalism preached belief in unfettered markets and unregulated working conditions—profits were the moral goal. This remained the economic creed in 1900, with no verses on the injustice of inequality.

Karl Marx was unquestionably radical, but he demonstrated first that the rules of capitalism favored those with existing wealth. Richer nations and richer people had the upper hand, and used it to accumulate greater wealth and power over time. Other more reformist thinkers built on his critique, preferring to work outside of his revolutionary framework. Motivated by restless workers, some Western intellectuals began to question the creation of wealth and its unequal distribution. In 1899, Thorsten Veblen published his *Theory of the Leisure Class*, in which he depicted the richest as barbaric, stealing from the lower classes via Darwinian exploitation. This idea resounded with many around the world, offering an argument to contest the assumption that rich people were superior and deserved or earned their fortunes. Some criticized liberal capitalism as inherently imperialist, noting the exploitation of peripheral regions *and* European workers. Both the Englishman J. A. Hobson and the Communist Vladimir Lenin argued that capitalism was unstable, discriminating, and premised upon the manipulation of markets to favor wealthy people and nations.

Karl Marx's ideas about economic disruption had enormous influence. He wrote in 1848:

The need of a constantly expanding market for its products chases the bourgeoisie over the entire surface of the globe. It must nestle everywhere, settle everywhere, establish connexions everywhere . . . All old-established national industries have been destroyed or are daily being destroyed. They are dislodged by new industries, whose introduction becomes a life and death question for all civilised nations, by industries that no longer work up indigenous raw material, but raw material drawn from the remotest zones; industries whose products are consumed, not only at home, but in every

> quarter of the globe. In place of the old wants, satisfied by the production of the country, we find new wants, requiring for their satisfaction the products of distant lands and climes.[3]

The major challenge to nineteenth-century liberal capitalism came in the 1920s from Communist state-run, planned economies, and we will see how these economies flourished but later faltered. After the First World War exposed the hazards of industrial capitalist competition, a third way was offered between state Socialism and free-market capitalism. John Maynard Keynes posited a theory later known as *Keynesianism*, arguing that government intervention to create work and social programs would boost lagging economies and get people back to work. This would in turn stoke consumption, increase sales and demand, and help economies grow in downturns. Keynes's middle-ground approach has proven more applicable than Socialism or runaway unlegislated capitalism. All these thinkers addressed fundamental questions about the division of labor and the distribution of profits (although none considered the social, psychological, or environmental effects of economic life, which would have to wait until the end of the century).

Western critics of capitalism struggled to gain influence however since the intellectual advocates of capitalism ruled Western states. Wealthy political and economic families in Britain, Germany, or the United States, and their companions in academia, finance or banking, controlled the international economic system. Some, like the Rothschilds and J. P. Morgan, built economic empires, possessing more wealth than most nations. Some millionaires became philanthropists to aid the poor, and President Theodore Roosevelt was an outspoken critic of corporate greed. As the century proceeded, Conservative economists often derided both the Keynesian and Socialist critique of capitalism, preaching instead a new faith where profit chasing and soaring consumption were considered virtuous.

Wealthy families then, as they do now, heavily influenced leaders in powerful nations, advising monarchs and presidents on economic matters. Some amassed sufficient power to make or break political parties. J. P. Morgan in the United States was so wealthy that he single-handedly saved the US economy after a banking panic in 1907. Though he acted for the public good, this scare followed decades of economic fluctuations which nobody could explain. The panic inspired the creation of the Federal Reserve System in 1913, a national central bank that stabilized the economy and works to steady the global economy today.

Wealthy capitalists could literally move the earth. US businessmen like R. G. Letourneau developed huge earth-moving machinery, stimulating the development of global oil and mining industries. Though such entrepreneurism created vast wealth, and later brought consumer comforts such as plastics and nylons, vast areas were mined and ruined, and people worldwide were forced to toil to supply Western markets.

JACK AND THE WALL STREET GIANTS.

Figure 2.2 Theodore Roosevelt holding a sword that says, "public service" as he faces the great robber barons, 1904. (Fotosearch/Getty Images.)

Capitalism impoverished traditional societies both large and small, and inspired many to turn toward Socialism. But it was vastly more productive than traditional or Socialist systems. By the 1940s, Western political and social institutions promoted economic growth worldwide under the guise of capitalist norms. Millions of jobs were created by utilizing surplus private capital and government investment. Capital financing, particularly after 1945, meant that wealth could be generated from existing profits or even debt; new earnings paid off earlier debts and then provided more capital for reinvestment. After the Second World War, government, organized labor, and private enterprise worked in a triad of uneasy but functioning relations in most Western democracies.

But since capitalist economies depended on materials and labor from the whole world, the global impact was enormous. Those nations that advocated capitalism provoked as much conflict as Socialist states through the century, as the wild effects of boom-and-bust swings crushed non-Western markets. The world's poorest people became increasingly dependent on imbalanced trade with the core industrial nations and, once traditional lifestyles were eliminated, the only option was to produce for the global economy. Unfair and brutal though it was, by the end of the twentieth century, most accepted the approach that economic competition and resource exploitation were normal, even though this economic system contributed to what was at the time the greatest military catastrophe in history, the Great War. Socialism was in fact a response to capitalist abuses in the first place.

2. 1914–1945: war and scarcity, for all

The most dreadful, if inadvertent, consequence of capitalist rivalry was the First World War. Between 1914 and 1918, industrial competition among nations sent a generation of workers to their deaths, as over 10 million men died for causes that few comprehended. Strategic struggles for economic assets were usually situated in the non-Western world. The mutual antagonism of a small number of industrial states created a general ethos of economic envy.

1910s—Communist collectivism or democratic capitalism?

A crucial economic outcome of the war was the Communist Revolution of 1917, which thrust a utopian experiment theorized for industrial economies on archaic Eastern European subsistence economies. Persistent industrial discord since the turn of the century failed to improve workers conditions in Russia, as Conservative nobles and the emperor stubbornly resisted land reforms or workers' rights. Bitter misery paved the road to Socialism, leaving no option but violent revolution. When the Bolsheviks won the civil war in 1921, European states refused to trade with them, partly from fear of Socialism spreading, but also because Communists wrote off huge debts to France and other capitalist states, a mortal sin in the eyes of Western bankers and financiers.

Communist coercion

From the outset, Communist leaders failed to create affluence and stability, offering only confused policies. Wartime Communism implemented during the civil war provided only for a strong army until 1921. To build infrastructure, Lenin's NEP (New Economic Policy) instituted a mixed economy through the 1920s, chasing foreign capital (ironically) similar to Western economic policies. After Lenin died in 1923, Stalin created "Socialism in one Country"—hardly the intended global Marxist

Figure 2.3 Russian Government Troops Firing on Demonstrators, July 4, 1917. (Fine Art Images/Heritage Images/Getty Images.)

world revolution. Conceding that the world's workers had not risen up to overthrow capitalists, he instead focused on national economic planning similar to that in the West. His 5-year plans, implemented from 1928 until after the Second World War, brought rapid industrial growth, mainly through military expansion and steel production however, not through widening consumption.

Until 1928, the Soviets combined state control of the economy with modest entrepreneurialism. Stalin's power grab slowly moved the USSR toward his dictatorial ideology though. Private agriculture and enterprise were outlawed, and Stalin's system of state-run *collectivized agriculture* would punish workers for decades. As would be the case for most of the Soviet era, peasants and factory workers had little incentive to produce willingly. Innovators had no incentive to create new products or technologies and were discouraged from doing so. Low productivity and low-quality work became the trademark of Communist economies, as fabrication of production and output figures substituted for fabrication of actual products.

Communist states lacked foreign capital, which of course resided in the banks of capitalists! Lacking investment from abroad, only Soviet labor and wealth was available, requiring a disciplinary work environment. Mechanization produced more food, but results were even more unpredictable than in capitalist economies. Famine and poverty killed millions of laborers, and Stalin moved millions more into gulags to work as slaves, rotting away in a life of forced labor. The Communist Party forcibly shifted different ethnicities around the vast Soviet region to diffuse dissent, with consequences still felt today in post-Soviet satellite states. This forced production gradually turned the USSR into an industrial power, but Stalin's mandatory program of collectivization worked peasants to despair.

The USSR in the 1920s and 1930s, like China in the 1960s, produced large amounts of low-quality steel and coal. But heating and food shortages were constant torments for cold, hungry people. Famine was endemic in both Communist states. Soviet dissidents were exiled into Siberian wastelands for criticizing the party, their lands seized. Into the 1930s, wealthy farmers with more means (kulaks) were wiped out, labeled "class enemies" of the Soviets. The victimization of party adversaries meant that those who made money, fairly or dishonestly, were jailed, beaten, or imprisoned. The general population in Communist states spent as much time accusing, or avoiding persecution, as they did working or producing.

Nonetheless, before after the Second World War, the Soviet economy grew, particularly in the 1940s and 1950s when industrial production outpaced all but Germany and the United States. Though defense spending spurred the economy, limited investment in the domestic economy and isolation from global capital markets brought stagnation. By the 1980s, the disparity between stagnant Socialist economies and the consumerist capitalist West was indisputable.

Capitalism and conflict

Fortunately, the victors in the First World War were democratic. They were also capitalist, committed to spreading an economic system suited to their needs. The US economy grew substantially from the First World War. Big businesses, shareholders, and the well-connected made vast profits, as enterprises and government agencies supplied arms and materiel to combatants, prompting a huge increase in the size of the US economy. Though the United States lacked aristocrats or royal families to speak of, the wealthiest businessmen enjoyed tight connections to Congress. Though lacking titles, they were in effect economic royalty, influencing government at every turn. After the war, New York took London's role as world banker, and the United States became the center of the global economy.

The other victors, Britain and France, suffered immense economic loss. During the war, both nations deployed wartime economies to maintain munitions production, compelling men and women to work for the war effort rather than for enterprises and profits. When war ended, output declined, economies shrunk and workers were unemployed. Since much of France and nearby regions like Flanders were besieged by combatant soldiers, food production was reduced. British workers suffered from economic stagnation, hunger, and poverty well into the 1930s. Britain and France were established imperial powers though, who reached markets around the world. They persisted with economic expansion, making use of Middle Eastern, African, or Indian markets to sustain their economies, exploiting resources such as oil, cocoa, or cotton into the 1940s.

During the war, farmers and peasants in Africa and the Arab world watched bewildered as divisions of soldiers marauded over their homelands armed with industrial weapons. Hundreds of thousands of African and Indian men died fighting for European allies. Arabs were conscripted to fight for Britain, France, or Germany, bringing social disruption to villages left behind. When trade with Western nations declined after the war, greater poverty followed conflict, as wars end further disadvantaged non-Western economies. Terrible effects of trade declines in colonized societies included famine, poverty, and wide social dislocation.

Everywhere, the end of the war brought inflation, unemployment and rising national debts. By the 1920s, Latin American nations could no longer afford to buy European goods, as US businessmen, increasingly convinced of the virtues of capitalism, dominated markets. Everyday people suffered from inflation, with rising prices for basic items increasing poverty everywhere. Thus, business interests gained from the war, while poorer states and individuals were indebted or forced to endure inflation.

1920s—Boom time and economic insecurity

Once peace came, wages generally rose through the 1920s in developed nations, though a great many workers did not share in the affluence. In the United States, the 1920s saw the *roaring twenties*, an economic boom premised upon a new phenomenon of mass markets, consumer-focused advertising and government-funded infrastructure. The United States became a country with a high standard of living, even though most people remained excluded, particularly those of color. This was a period of reckless, unregulated capitalism, where businessmen acted almost free of legal or government constraint. Great riches were accrued by well-connected families, while most lived in poverty on farms or in slums, enduring squalor similar to others worldwide.

Though those of color—ex-slaves, natives, or immigrants—did not partake of economic prosperity in America equally, African-American, Asian and Latino immigrants generally found work. Happy to live in a new country, they seldom risked protesting against employers at the ready to fire them. Strikes were met with brutal police responses; thousands were injured when strikes were called. Those with the fortitude to rebel were attacked verbally, typically accused of Communist sympathy or anti-American treason. This was not an open society by modern standards.

The economy in the 1920s suffered from the Christian evangelical-inspired prohibition of alcohol sales, which created a huge, untaxed black market. Illegal liquor sales generated a huge mafia underworld, dishing out violence and murder, ending only when alcohol was legalized in 1933. Even accounting for endemic corruption and brutal tactics from business leaders, workers saw upward mobility in the United States.

Europe in the 1920s was less prosperous. Besides the very rich, most Europeans lived in terrible hardship. Britain's economy suffered from declining imperial trade, meaning workers suffered great privations even as those in colonies remained poor. French and British wealth accrued through past industrial expansion and imperialist exploitation slowly evaporated, while economic clout passed to the United States. France lost vast wealth in the war, and a ruined economy stimulated French fury toward Germany, with vociferous demands for compensation. When Germany fell behind on payments, France extended no sympathy, punishing German people for the actions of its military and ruling class. France occupied the Ruhr Valley in 1923, so Germany's central source of energy and raw materials was lost, worsening conditions.

Thus, after 1921, when hyperinflation arrived in Germany, a bankrupt, humiliated nation collapsed economically. 20 German marks bought 1 English pound in 1918: by 1923 it took 21 billion marks to earn a pound! Germans burned worthless money to stay warm or bake bread. Though the working class suffered most, the middle class lost life savings. Both classes gradually fell prey to extremist political groups committed to fixing the economy through militarism, promising to avenge the capitalist powers that castigated Germany.

German vitriol was not wholly fictional. US bankers collected loans from its Allies with no concern for economic conditions in Europe or the impact on Germany. A cycle of debt flowed from the United States, through the Allies, on to Germany. America's closest ally Britain spent half its national budget to repay US war debts in the 1920s. Both French and American banks hoarded gold, making shrill demands for debt repayment from Germany, punishing the aggressor nation, unwittingly generating conditions for zealotry. Reparations meant that millions went hungry, so Fascist right-wing ideologues like Hitler could promise economic expansion, enticing Germans with exhilarating plans to grab Slavic lands to the east.

US loans and policies helped and hindered at different times. Sporadic efforts to aid Germany such as The Dawes Plan in 1924 eased German privation, stabilizing the economy and lowering some payments. And the Young Plan in 1929 further reduced reparations. The damage had been done by then though; Germany was already veering to the Far Right. By the late 1920s, when depression came, economic troubles highlighted not only the disparity of wealth between capitalist nations and the rest, but also the instability of free-market capitalism Western states so proudly propagated. Communists suitably highlighted the aggression and exploitation of Western capitalists; Fascists offered common people economic hope and pointed to the iniquities of liberal capitalism.

In the booming 1920s, American financiers treated European nations as items on a worksheet. The firm belief that "business was business, debts were debts," punished Europe, left poor states poorer, and inspired resentment and instability everywhere. Bankers and politicians believed in the competitive spirit, not conversation, collaboration, or contemplation. From the vantage point of Western financiers, all was fair in love and business, and contracts had to be enforced. From the standpoint

Figure 2.4 Berlin: Riots and looting caused by 1923 inflation. (Gircke/ullstein bild via Getty Images.)

of German workers or colonized people, such deals were inked in harsh economic contracts. The price for humanity would be heavy, bringing German belligerence in the Second World War, then the Cold War and postcolonial poverty.

Less developed countries

Eastern Europe was highly undeveloped, with rural peasant fiefdoms still prevalent and agricultural life being the norm. After the war, these already small economies imposed high tariffs, bringing a period of economic nationalism and increasing autocracy. European economies suffered more than America's, and the smaller economies of the world suffered more in turn due to imbalanced industrial and colonial commercial connections. Western powers ceased purchasing raw materials and commodities from colonial regions worldwide. By calling in debts, they forced hardship on poorer nations with corrupt elites. The volume of items exported from LDCs, such as tea, cotton, beef, oil and more, fell precipitously. Diminished food production hurt the poorest as always.

Though US loans had in part promoted 1920s prosperity, the Wall Street Crash of October 1929 ended all hope of peace. From 1929 to 1933, the global capitalist economy completely collapsed due to the barely understood consequences of overproduction. The growing US economy of the 1920s, with its well-run businesses working at full speed, simply produced too many goods. Demand could not match supply because poorly paid or poor people possessed insufficient income to purchase the goods. This simple imbalance, rooted in inequality, slowed US economic growth, and then spread to shatter the world economy.

When the US stock market collapsed, the fall of the sole healthy industrial economy sent a tidal wave of instability first through European markets, and then the world. The Crash dried up bank lending and stalled investment, which hit Germany particularly hard, leaving a population ripe for radicalization. Credit earlier extended to too many people was now called in. Global trade declined by up to 35 percent, and its effects brought authoritarian governance in Europe and worldwide. Japan suffered greatly due to US tariffs; its rice-based agricultural sector collapsed and wages sunk. Japanese men could only find work in the military now.

Genuine economic investment and job production was replaced by greed and short-term financial gain in the late 1920s. A key cause of the Depression was the search for quick profits and wild speculation from financiers and industrialists, less interested in production than personal profits. The Depression invited blunt questions regarding the virtues of capitalism, which Communists and Fascists exploited this well.

1930s—Alternatives to free-market, liberal capitalism

When the economy contracted so quickly after 1929, the immediate response of those in power was classical nineteenth-century liberalism. Employers lowered workers wages (deflation) to cut costs and stay in business. When those masses out of work ceased purchasing, the economy contracted further! For four years, international trade declined and poverty increased globally. The 1930s would bring the terrible fruits of this economic failure.

Western economics: Keynesianism

Between the extremes of unregulated capitalism and the forced labor of authoritarianism, there had to be another economic system. The English economist John Maynard Keynes exposed the downside of competitive capitalism, noting the persistent inequality and instability of free trade. Keynes compelled government officials to purposely intercede, providing housing, job training, and education for those suffering, intentionally boosting infrastructure spending - priming the economy to jump-start it, or as the term went, pump-prime it. Since both the war and the Depression already brought a larger role for government in regulating economic life, Keynes ideas were timely.

Significantly, US President Franklin Roosevelt applied his ideas to stabilize the 1930s US economy. The New Deal set of programs were Keynesian, using national funds for public spending programs, lubricating the economy with a mixture of private and public investment, maximizing the relationship between the state and the private sector for the good of all. For the first time in history, extensive social security, state welfare, and minimum wages were provided for American workers. Agencies were set up by Washington to regenerate labor markets. Work groups built bridges, freeways, and cleared national parks. Though this alone did not prompt the postwar US boom, it kept the largest economy plugging along through the 1930s. The New Deal demonstrated that the government could employ and inspire millions of ordinary people, while providing basic protections against the wild swings of unfettered capitalism. Roosevelt fought successfully through the 1930s to control Conservative business elites who wished to profit without state directives. In fact, during this decade, Conservative and business elites in Europe were happy to trade with whomever they could, including Mussolini and Hitler.

The upper-class philosopher Bertrand Russell, one of many Western critics of capitalism, in 1928 pointed out the practical consequences of the capitalist system:

Advocates of capitalism are very apt to appeal to the sacred principles of liberty, which are embodied in one maxim: The fortunate must not be restrained in the exercise of tyranny over the unfortunate.[4]

Authoritarian autarky

If unfettered markets were unpredictable, the approach of both democratic and authoritarian states in the 1930s was worse. Autarky—economic separation from other trading nations and a domestic focus—was the typical response in this decade, stifling commerce. The United States focused on repairing its terrible economic downturn; Germany turned toward home production of armaments; Italy industrialized and militarized; Japanese and Russian workers labored long and hard for authoritarian military states. International trade further declined along with diplomacy.

Disdainful of the virtues of capitalist markets, authoritarian states in Europe, Asia, and Latin America turned inward toward autarky. Many adopted *corporatism*, developing industries aided by government in service of the state. In Fascist states, private property was permitted, but the economy was built around one-party control. Opposition was forbidden, which streamlined decisions and facilitated planning. This brought efficiency to the economy, providing work and income for the masses more readily than capitalist economies. Indeed, the wealthy in corporatist states, as in capitalist ones, had the same overarching fear in the 1930s, Communism—the one ideology that aggressively espoused equality and workers' rights, not to mention the redressing of past inequalities.

Fascist states created full employment in the 1930s, something unheard of in capitalist economies. They prompted pride in work and membership in a flourishing one-party system that tied worker's goals to state goals. Instead of business elites gaming the economy under the supposed "invisible hand" of a free market, single-minded decisions came from Fascist leaders. In Germany after 1933, Hitler's charisma even inspired those struggling financially to accept hardship in the name of the party, a feature lacking in capitalist states, where envy was directed at those in power. By adhering to Nazi Party demands, farmers were remunerated well, and those in business well connected to the party won privileges and influence.

Unionization or worker protest was implausible in authoritarian states. Trade unions, which grew in Western democracies in the 1930s, were purged in Germany. Workers could not risk protest, even though Fascist ideology pretended that all workers were members of one state family. Private militarized armies enforced the law, containing crime and keeping people hard at work. Barely educated factions of young men joined Fascist paramilitary groups like the SA (Brownshirts) and, after 1934, the murderous SS to persecute opponents at will, sanctioned by those in power.

As in Germany, Italian workers had no voice; those who dissented were brutally beaten by state thugs. By the early 1930s, Italy had dismembered its parliamentary system, allowing Mussolini to make economic decisions alone. Mussolini cunningly allied with the Catholic Church and the standing monarch, King Emmanuel III to maintain wide support. As in Spain, both church and royalty favored Fascism, since it revered tradition and challenged nonreligious Communism. Italian industry grew through the 1930s, with a stable currency and vast public works delivered jobs to a mostly gratified people. Italians responded by bearing more children, enjoying a culture where all aspects of life, including leisure and health care, were provided by the state. As in Germany, nationalist pride returned to the Italian masses. Mussolini provided jobs and food for Italians, and state-run industry delivered an economic boom that fed masses more concerned with bread than complex ideologies.

Though locked in mutual hostility, authoritarian Communist and Fascist states were similar economically, forcing top-down decisions upon an intimidated mass. Horrific famine in the Ukraine in 1932 exposed the gruesome toll on those excluded from party preference; imprisonment and murder were common in Germany or Italy. Communist states, like Fascist ones, were run by fundamentalist elites who controlled the economy and society. Communist leaders echoed Marxist ideology, while benefitting economically as much as Tsars or Western capitalists. The global impact of the Great Depression cannot be underestimated. It is feasible that Fascism and Communism may have remained localized, disagreeable systems of political and economic ideology, were it not for the fact that global depression hit the world so hard in the 1930s. While millions lost work or went hungry in Western nations, authoritarian economies appeared to succeed in the 1930s. The two totalitarian systems—Fascism and Communism—hence found adherents in the wider world, apparently offering an alternative to capitalism, free of the rule of law or respect for individual rights. Indeed, all of Eastern Europe and most of Latin America succumbed to dictator-led poverty in this decade, as autarky and dictatorship went hand in hand.

LDCs and the colonized world: limited options

While workers endured desperation in democracies and toiled for the state in authoritarian nations, those in the poorer parts of the world endured the spiraling effects of the Depression. LDCs remained dependent upon industrialized nations for trade, so when demand dropped precipitously or prices plummeted, they were at the mercy of market forces centered in Western capitals. Long-standing colonial connections between Western Europe, the United States and the world meant that economies worldwide foundered in the 1930s. Suppliers of coffee, copper, rubber, and agricultural exports all lost markets when Western economies contracted. Poorer nations found already imbalanced commercial relations worsened. In regions like India, Africa, the Middle East, and Latin America, economic disorder brought more poverty and greater subjugation from traditional elites disinterested in modernizing.

Exporting produce

Latin America is representative of conditions worldwide. Since Latin American markets depended primarily on exports to Western nations, the collapse of advanced economies hurt the Americas. Tin or copper prices fell in global markets and purchase orders were cancelled. When wealthy landowners lost capital on international deals or trades, they cut back on wages or provisions for the poor workers, so people lost work in regions with very limited state support. Already harsh terms of trade hardened as Western powers called in debts to nonindustrialized nations. Wealthy investors chasing quick profits then withdrew currency from poor countries, chasing higher returns in other markets.

   Foreign intrusion was one thing, but the chief reason that developing nations in the Americas failed to industrialize in the first place was because entrenched landowners preferred an agricultural economy to maintain a status quo they preferred. The poor suffered most from this reluctance to modernize. The majority of people still farmed in Latin America, with many peasants in effect living as serfs on massive *latifundia,* landed estates owned by elites. Along with ruling-class intransigence, US power limited progress in the region. American troops occupied Haiti, the Dominican Republic, and Nicaragua in the 1910s and 1920s to secure important commercial resources. In 1917, Puerto Rico was annexed to the United States. Mexico had to go through a revolution to seize its oil industry away from Anglo-American financiers. Only after 1933 did Roosevelt's Good Neighbor policy ease up on oppressive colonial interference, but influence persisted.

The combination of Western exploitation and elite obstinacy meant that Latin America, like much of Asia and Africa, remained underdeveloped. The region lacked capital and large-scale industry and suffered from a dearth of technical knowledge. Those states that eventually created more complex economies, such as Brazil and Mexico, industrialized only after the Second World War, remaining limited in scale compared to Asian and European nations. For much of the world as in Latin America, to trade meant to trade with the United States or Europe, since no relationships existed with other regions. Latin American dependency on the US economy benefitted ruling classes, but no economic growth from within transpired, and nor was there entrepreneurial spirit. The only positive for most Latin Americans was that they escaped the horrors of the Second World War.

Peasants and workers in the Middle East, Africa, and India were less fortunate, enduring colonial exploitation *and* entanglement in global conflict. Through the 1930s, permanent resistance against European imperial rule hampered economic activity. Conflict in British India, many African states, and the Middle East through the decade prevented the stability required for economic growth. Intransigent imperial elites paid no heed to such concerns until after the war and the rise of independence movements.

The consequences of the Great Depression were thus felt globally. Instability enabled authoritarian states to control and centralize economic activity in Latin America, Europe, and elsewhere. Over time, the aggressive militarization of authoritarian societies would prove a short-term gambit, doing little to inspire genuine innovation or fresh economic ideas, something that democratic states would excel at after the Second World War. By then most economists argued that connected economies were superior to isolated ones, which brought decades of modern globalization. Most recognized too that paying workers better wages would prime the economy for growth. First though, the world returned to the horrors of global conflict, between 1939 and 1945, as authoritarian aggression, in particular Fascism, brought catastrophe to the world again.

1940s—Wartime economies

Economic circumstances clearly led the world to war in 1939. Lost savings and job insecurity inspired Germans to accept Hitler's extremism. France and Britain were too insolvent to resist militarily, and the United States remained insulated for economic protection. Authoritarianism assured people food and work, but it created the worst imaginable abuses of human rights, even within the sphere of economics.

Figure 2.5 Soldier with Nazi treasures taken from Jews. (National Archives.)

Slave labor oiled Russian and Japanese economies, while conquered people were forced to work for totalitarian states around the world. This was democracy's darkest hour.

Most horrendous of all, Nazi Germany profited from actual human bodies, using gold in teeth, stolen jewelry, and in the most depraved cases, the skins of Jewish people murdered in the Holocaust. Countless people died from forced labor as well as in gas chambers. The infamous Buchenwald Report of 1945 exposed the extent of Nazi depravity. Jewish people, homosexuals, Communists, and gypsies were worked to death for companies such as IG Farben, producing rubber and petroleum products for the war. Jews and others became line items in Nazi finances, as the Holocaust—the systematic murder and of up to 7 million humans—was carried out in the manner of an efficient, orderly German business enterprise.

Inconceivable loss and destruction

As this suggests, the economic cost of the war was incalculably high, from lost productivity and broken economies to property damage and lost lives. Between 1939 and 1945, war totally destroyed already weak economies. Worldwide, industrial and agricultural output fell by half compared to 1939, leaving hungry people worldwide. Combat ended in 1945, but its destructive effects did not fade for a decade even in wealthier nations, where rationing continued into the 1950s. The physiological and mental costs of the war never left most survivors.

And war was not limited to Europe, of course. Colonial powers drew heavily on resources from colonial regions, where subjects found themselves again exploited or sent to fight. Italy invaded Ethiopia in 1937 to access resources, and other Western powers fought across North Africa and the Middle East through to 1945, showing no concern for local populations and despoiling lands. Wartime desperation pushed Britain and France into even greater exploitation of minerals and resources in India and Southeast Asia. The French exploited labor and materials across North Africa, irritating many Muslims. Though the United States provided large quantities of oil to combatants, oil from Iran and Iraq, as well as southeastern Europe, kept war machines churning. India provided coal and metal ores for Britain's war effort, while other parts of the British Empire supplied crucial materiel. Japan also dominated and impoverished vast regions of Asia, taking oil from ex-Dutch and British colonies in Southeast Asia with brutal efficiency.

While Europeans fought a second war, colonized people were forced to labor to support one side or the other. Once war ended, the colonized of the world would push aggressively for autonomy. In Western states, the ever-increasing role of the state in daily life during wartime would paradoxically turn out to be an economic blessing. After the slaughter of the 1940s, wartime powers provided politicians with the technology and means to forge fairer and better economic solutions for Westerners. Official planning and state investment to support the private sector and technological advancements would create a global surge in trade, and better working conditions in the developed world. In the colonized world though, political independence would not bring economic prosperity.

3. 1945–1973: Economic miracle, for some

US Aid

War wrecked economies worldwide, leaving the United States as the sole source of capital. As in 1918, America was physically untouched by war (aside from Pearl Harbor in Hawaii). Consequently, American leaders could shape the postwar economy, instituting the US-dominated Bretton Woods System in 1944. This provided for the International Monetary Fund (IMF) to stabilize global trade, promote investment and encourage the integration of economies and currencies. The system also forced open markets upon Third World economies. Criticism of the IMF persists from poorer nations and from the newly industrialized BRIC (Brazil, Russia, India, and

China) nations, who criticize US domination. World Bank programs have also been censured for implementing "shock therapy" since the 1980s, in which LDC nations are forced to cut spending on social programs for the poor, to hopefully encourage foreign investment.

After 1946 however, the World Bank loaned monies to weaker economies, providing capital to fund large infrastructure projects in regions lacking investment. Though usually on terms that suited American or foreign investors, this provided desperately needed income to poorer nations. General Agreement on Tariffs and Trade (GATT) was signed in 1947 to regulate international commerce while opening trade barriers and lowering tariffs.[5] The World Trade Organization (WTO) replaced GATT in 1995. Both programs brought capital to the undeveloped world, though their impact on ex-colonized regions remains in dispute.

Either way, US assistance was crucial after 1945, and the Marshall Plan in 1948 saved Europeans from hunger. Europe's farmlands were ruined and livestock had been slaughtered in war. Surviving workers were often disabled or psychologically traumatized. The United States provided $13.5 billion in loans and gifts to Europe, in a complex mixture of self-interest and aid: aid required Allied commitment to anticommunism and also ensured customers for American businesses. Purposely preventing Europe from "going Red," the plan created new markets for US exporters. Europeans were thus compelled to buy US food, goods, machinery, and clothes. Moscow rejected Marshall Plan monies as the US–Soviet relationship soured. Though Roosevelt expressed disdain for European imperialism and for Communism, by 1947, Truman was simply anticommunist. Most outside the United States considered the plan an extension of the anticommunist Truman Doctrine and the United States soon found itself embroiled in overseas exploits.

Outside of Europe, the United States also shaped Asia economically, maintaining personnel in Japan until 1952 to forge democracy and rebuild the economy. Investment and land reform were forced upon disgraced military leaders, along with democratic ideals and US-friendly capitalist institutions. Japanese industry boomed in ensuing decades, with stable governance and steady growth. Japan had the largest economy on earth by the 1980s, even lending to the United States and Europe, prior to an economic collapse in the 1990s.

Following the economic stagnation and material devastation of war, massive rebuilding was Western Europe's general response. Since the war had eradicated any sense of normalcy, radical new economic ideas were bandied around and modern factories could be built anew. Investment and entrepreneurship pleased Conservatives, while social programs to protect all members of society pleased progressives. The postwar boom in Europe would protect the poorest through welfare programs as Europe prospered. Western Europeans reindustrialized quickly after 1945, avoiding extremism and generating enormous progress into the 1970s, enjoying a high standard of living akin to that in the United States.

Industrial growth

Transnational economic institutions were thus stacked to support US or Western capitalist aims, but they were nevertheless clearly preferable to authoritarian alternatives, autarky, or rural economies. After the 1950s, financial and physical impediments to global trade were gradually removed. Organized container shipping moved huge volumes of easily tracked goods to fill homes and businesses; lower tariffs moved goods fluidly around the planet, as the science of logistics rationalized commerce efficiently. The total volume of trade increased five times over after 1950 and continues to increase.

Nations such as Japan and South Korea who emulated industrial capitalism developed into commercial giants, raising income levels and standards of living. The spread of global capitalism brought states into closer diplomatic relations. Important entertainment events such as the Olympic Games and soccer's World Cup resumed in 1949, driven by capital profits, but also knitting diverse cultures together.

Western riches were also used for the common good. A century ago, oligarchs like the Rockefellers and Carnegies spread humanitarian relief to the desperate in society, and after 1945, the Rockefeller and Ford Foundations worked with the United Nations to fund research and improve crop yields. The United Nations sent medical and food provisions to poorer nations, facilitated the birth and survival of billions of people, and at least partially offset the abuses of local autocrats.

Developing nations nonetheless struggled to disentangle themselves from subservient relations with Western states, and nations that did not modernize struggled to feed themselves. Though independence came politically, economic self-sufficiency was more challenging. A combination of overseas pressure and domestic corruption kept the Third World in penury as compared to developed nations. Tiny groups of elites often stole national wealth in LDCs. Those in power maintained crony networks to levels considered unimaginable in the West. In the postwar decades, authoritarian rulers in states from the Middle East to Asia and Africa enjoyed palatial grandeur while the masses lived in poverty, as economies were either mismanaged or openly exploited for personal gain. Emerging markets thus suffered from bad leadership and a scarcity of capital. As such, they had to turn to Western powers, borrow more, creating further debt in a vicious circle that persists today.

From the 1930s until the 1980s, Latin American nations attempted to break this pattern of dependence through Import Substitution Industrialization, aiming to produce supplies at home rather than import from the West. Countries purposely limited imports from industrial nations to cut reliance on foreign goods. This however produced further debt and inequality, since it proved difficult to compete with more established, larger economies that made better quality goods at a lower cost. The shadow of the past loomed large into the postwar era.

1950s—Capitalism vs Communism: a false dichotomy

Social Democracy

Though there were differences among capitalist states in the West, first world economies generally boomed in the postwar decades. European social democracy differed markedly from American free-market economics, moderating and softening inequalities. In both regions, the sacred tenets of capitalism - private property and profit motive - could not be questioned. Social programs were slim in America, leaving minorities poor and excluded from opportunity. The beneficiaries of economic growth in the United States were typically investors and shareholders, not workers in the wider society, and the middle class that developed in the postwar era was almost exclusively white. Workers of all colors, however, gained from strong membership in trade unions through the 1960s, until unions were attacked in the 1980s.

In Europe, government provision of public services offered a safety net to broad populations in *social market economies*. Strong trade unions fostered a culture where business leaders were held responsible to the wider community. The European approach, a social democratic system that encouraged business innovation but provided cradle-to-grave benefits for all citizens, thus reestablished a wealthy society by forming institutions that bolstered growth and stability.

Learning from the disorderly 1930s, the European Coal and Steel Community (the ECSC) was organized in 1952 to encourage amicable trade relations among Western European states. This developed into a common market, which after 1957 helped Western Europe develop robust open markets and high standards of living without exploiting workers or colonies. From 1959 the European Free Trade Association widened participation further to promote trade worldwide. A clear pattern emerged in democracies: a strong middle class, with trade unions providing better lives for workers, something expressly lacking in one-party, Third World, or Communist states.

Collective scarcity

Stalinism

Following the failure of right-wing despotism in Germany and Italy, the only postwar alternative to capitalism seemed to be left-wing Socialism. Like capitalist societies, Socialist states varied greatly from region to region. Nonetheless, Western economists grouped Socialist states together as *Second World* nations. Due to Anglo-American wartime cooperation, a generalized paranoia emanated from the USSR regarding the

West's wealth in the 1950s. Soviet economic production, driven by fear, stimulated high levels of spending on nuclear arms, heavy industry, and defense. Related job security provided stability through the 1950s and 1960s, though homebuilding and consumer comforts were notably lacking. Soviet economic growth by the 1960s suggested that planned Socialism could be an alternative to American free-market fundamentalism.

Though dogmatically anti-imperialist in theory, Stalin's Russia also gained from economic expansionism. Eastern European satellite states were forced to accept Communist economic dictums from 1949. Though policies imposed from Moscow were a superior alternative to Nazism, they seldom provided material comforts for populations beyond Communist Party members. Resistance in Poland through the 1950s and the collapse of Hungary's economy by 1955 foreshadowed the omens of Communist failure. These protests were crushed.

Stalin and his successors also harshly exploited Central Asian states. All remained impoverished, with economies based on subsistence agriculture serving elites and Moscow. Central Asia was in essence one large cotton plantation for Soviet exports. This had long been the case; while Americans were annihilating native populations from the Midwest to California in the nineteenth century, Russians were subjugating Kazakh or Mongolian khans, making similar claims to "civilize" natives and integrating them into Russia's sphere of influence. Millions died in Central Asia in the first half of the twentieth century from poor health, harsh living conditions, and oppression from Soviet incursions. The area remains poor.

Maoism

Though Socialism brought some growth in the USSR, the fiasco of Maoist Communism in China was already apparent by the 1960s. Since the Chinese Communist Party opposed external relations, it ploughed forth alone to feed and clothe a huge population. Mao's model of a peasant-run utopia paled miserably in comparison to the industrial Soviet economy.

In 1949, Chinese Communism was a reasonable response to the encroachments of industrial capitalism and imperialist competition. A century of Western and Japanese intrusions on Chinese sovereignty in search of raw materials left China in chaos in 1900. Following four decades of violence and disorder, Chinese people now endured Communist self-destruction, as Mao's failed experiments in collective farming and village economies brought more poverty. Those who made money, like landlords and entrepreneurs, were killed, their land redistributed to peasants. Though intended to force equality on society, up to 2 million people were executed for greed, owning land, or just for saying the wrong thing. Between 1958 and 1962, while Westerners thrived materially, millions of Chinese starved.

Chinese leaders claimed to find a practical middle way between Western capitalism and Soviet Communism, irrespective of declarations of Marxist ideology. The following excerpt is from 1953:

The present-day capitalist economy in China is a capitalist economy which for the most part is under the control of the People's Government and which is linked with the state-owned socialist economy in various forms and supervised by the workers. It is not an ordinary but a particular kind of capitalist economy, namely, a state-capitalist economy of a new type. It exists not chiefly to make profits for the capitalists but to meet the needs of the people and the state . . . The People's democratic dictatorship needs the leadership of the working class. For it is only the working class that is most far-sighted, most selfless and most thoroughly revolutionary.[6]

Reality never met such theories however. The idea of sharing tools, food, and machinery perhaps made sense, but when Maoists tried to manage a massive regional economy from the center, inefficiency and corruption followed. Since all decisions were made from the capital in Beijing, an over-centralized set of commands with no connection to economic reality victimized millions. China is only recovering now.

During the inaptly named "Great Leap Forward" from 1958–1961, Chinese peasants were compelled to live in communes akin to military barracks. Mao believed that small-scale backyard production of steel and other commodities could modernize the economy. So unproductive was this system that around 20 million people died from famine. Most of the steel produced was unusable, though few dared to point it out. In place of productivity, party cadres scoured the nation purging people for verbal slipups, offering ideological incompetence as the rule of law. In spite of rather than because of this, industrial production grew over the decades and gradually, China's economy grew since the 1980s, although inequality persists.

While inadequate administration assailed Chinese people, Socialist economies in Southeast Asia, Latin America, and parts of Africa also achieved little in terms of material wealth. Inefficient economic practices, self-serving ruling classes, or both, were usually the culprit. Constant disruption from capitalist powers, either overtly or through covert action, also obstructed progress.

Winston Churchill, no friend of the left or the colonized, offered the following typically pithy summation of Communist life:

The inherent vice of capitalism is the unequal sharing of blessings; the inherent vice of socialism is the equal sharing of miseries.[7]

Cuba's Fidel Castro paid a high price for criticizing Western capitalism. After Castro ousted a brazenly pro-American dictator in 1959, Cuba had little chance of economic development, suffering revenge from irritated anticommunist US hawks. When Castro nationalized Cuba's foreign controlled assets, implementing a popular revolution to repel American business influence, the United States placed sanctions on the economy, impoverishing the mass of Cubans for decades. Castro inevitably turned to the Soviet loans for food, arms, and support. While he kept Cuba independent, the people remained poor, excluded from global trade and with limited national assets. Cuba's economy nonetheless provided health care and education to far more of its people than the United States did. Women's work opportunities were comparable to men's in Cuba, China, and the USSR. In the West, women were often restricted to home life, persuaded to consume appliances while minding children.

Though Castro called himself a Communist, most Latin American leftist parties were less ideological than China. Most remained in favor of property rights and entrepreneurialism and supported contract law. As a result of US and Soviet interference, economic stability could not develop, however. US interventions in Guatemala, Costa Rica, and Ecuador cost hundreds of thousands of lives, and left vast estates in the hands of right-wing elites, who employed peasants as modern-day serfs.

Global inequality

For previously colonized peoples, political independence only helped few materially. Colonized countries, almost without exception, remained poor and industrially undeveloped. While European states prospered minus the imperial connection, global capitalism continued to encroach upon the economic life of distant societies. Elites in LDCs negotiated with representatives of Western nations, taking on loans, failing to build adequate infrastructure, and using profits for personal use.

LDCs persisted with unequal gender relations and undeveloped markets, failing to utilize female labor or intellects. One of the hallmarks of Western democracies was a declining agricultural sector, which indicated a modernizing, better-off society (though most wealth still went to men). In most of the undeveloped world, agriculture remained the bulk of economic life. Women toiled in fields and tended to children, with minimal participation in factory, office, or public life. Typically, small groups of male elites and their families were enriched, while the majority remained impoverished, particularly women.

Decolonization and economic dependence

Postcolonial institutions in LDC's tended to lag behind because elites resisted practices from other cultures, preferring indigenous traditions. The interests of entrenched elites were easier to satisfy by staying in power than by moving toward new practices of capitalist states. Since cultures change slowly, the suddenness of independence thrust young countries into modernity, and brought decades of instability. In addition, access to simple economic information was lacking, possessed only by rich nations with long-standing connections. Capital supplies were low, requiring loans and debt accrual. So as African nations proceeded to decolonize for instance, they had no option but to take strict loans from Western-dominated institutions or banks. Lacking access to the technologies or resources of Western corporations, they could not compete on international markets.

To break Western colonial control, powerful leaders and their followers fought for liberation through the 1950s and 1960s. Between 1945 and 1975 more than fifty new African nations emerged.[8] By 1975, political freedom had come to most in the colonized world, but economic growth was slow. This perhaps is not surprising. As recent as 1941, only Liberia was independent among African states, and as elsewhere, a single foreign company, the rubber manufacturer Firestone in Liberia, could dominate the economy.

Forced to join the extant economic system at a disadvantage, new nations in Africa and Asia struggled to develop markets. Western financial institutions influenced the economies of developing countries. Foreign banks imposed terms upon weak nations, and foreign investors cared only for returns on their money, not the development of poor societies that most considered primitive. Persistent racist condescension toward colonial peoples prompted leading intellectuals such as Franz Fanon to claim that even after independence, *neo-imperialism*, was as pernicious as direct colonization. Before 1945, Western officials living in colonies had to explain their actions, usually justifying them in paternalistic terms. Postwar economic policies sent via the push of a button from financiers in New York or London or from the diktats of Moscow impoverished previously colonized peoples.

Failed leadership

Imperialism left a legacy of humiliation and anger for the colonized. Postindependence African leaders such as Ghana's Kwame Nkrumah took control of state economies, agreeing with Lenin that governments must dictate all economic practice. Repelling British and US interests in 1957, Nkrumah provided inspiration for others, as independent Ghana took control of cocoa plantations, its main export. However, like others, Ghana had to borrow to build dams and other projects. He promoted Pan-Africanism, though tribal conflict between ethnic groups proved impossible to transcend. Kenya's Jomo Kenyatta was more open to capitalist influence, but he too struggled to counter nepotism or tribalism. After winning independence in 1963, Kenyan tribal conflict and diverse regional identities hampered stability there.

Figure 2.6 Mahogany Logging, 1956: Large tree trunks are cut down in a Nigerian forest. (Dorothy Hope-Smith/BIPs/Getty Images.)

Generally, control over natural resources after independence bestowed great affluence upon well-connected cronies instead of wider populations in Africa. A deficiency of institutions to provide transparency or develop markets prevented stability, which suited dictators bent on maintaining personal fiefdoms. After Nigerian leaders ousted British colonists in 1961, its oil wealth was soon squandered, serving as a prime example of a nation with immense resources that remained poor and conflict-ridden after independence. African nations blessed with resources such as oil or minerals typically succumbed to the "resource curse," in which a tiny stratum of male elites creamed off wealth for families and friends instead of investing and supporting their own specific tribe rather than a national economy. From Zambia to Congo to the Sudan, kleptocracy's dominated the economy in most states—theft replaced economic endeavor.

Internal miscalculations from African elites stifled economic growth. Independence movements succeeded in countering foreign influence, but they trained the population for dissent rather than education or economic growth. After the colonial adversary departed, ethnic tribal divisions thwarted healthy economies. Reliance on commodity exports brought terrible repercussions from fluctuations in the prices of goods when global markets shifted. Poverty and inequality persisted across North Africa and sub-Saharan states, as raw materials were exported to the world and little internal infrastructure was developed. Colonization was thus replaced by a system where the legal or illegal extraction of resources kept Africans impoverished.

Middle Eastern economic growth suffered similarly, exacerbated by Cold War rivalries and elite venality. While the Marshall Plan helped Europe rebuild, it also facilitated acquisition of cheap oil from the Middle East. Aside from ensuring European markets for US products, the plan required US and European mastery over Arab oil production, with ongoing consequences. When the democratically elected Iranian leader Mohammad Mossadeq tried to oust American influence in 1953, he was overthrown by CIA agents, who left in place a US-backed and pro-Western shah. His family dynasty traded oil with the West, slaying tens of thousands of opponents through the 1970s, ultimately provoking the fundamentalist Islamic revolution of 1979 in Iran.

Some postcolonial states succeeded in wresting back economic control through the nonaligned movement. In Egypt, Nasser took the crucial Suez Canal back from Britain and France in 1956, nationalizing assets such as the oil industry. In India, Mahatma Gandhi had protested British economic exploitation since the 1930s, inspiring millions to resist in a Salt March to protest taxation policies. Indian leaders like Nehru implemented 5-year plans to feed the population in a mixed Socialist-capitalist economy, bringing some prosperity. President Sukarno in Indonesia was strident about not relying on Cold War powers for national fortunes.

Foreign Direct Investment

Capitalist institutions constrained developing nations, but they also provided financial assistance, with strings attached. In the 1960s, developed nations responded to Third World dissent, sending vast amounts of *Foreign Direct Investment* (FDI) to boost weaker economies, conveniently chasing easier profits than in developed markets. Nations like South Africa and India benefited significantly, industrializing and creating prosperity in emerging economies (although for Indian elites or South African whites only). Access to overseas investment helped South Africa develop its gold and mining industries, though as the economy integrated into global markets, Western elites were reluctant to question its divided, openly racist apartheid society. In the 1970s, Western nations did however begin to boycott South Africa, as resistance from people of color merged with growing contempt abroad. Activists worldwide called for the regime to address the repression and poverty endured by the majority black population. India also slowly democratized, and millions entered the middle classes, though its poor remain as poor as ever.

> India, influenced by Gandhi's wisdom, also tried to steer a middle course between capitalism and Socialism. Gandhi argued: "Capital as such is not evil; it is its wrong use that is evil. Capital in some form or other will always be needed."[9]

In Latin America, the US-led Alliance for Progress provided capital after 1961, though it was harshly criticized. Promoting investment and growth under the auspices of American capitalism, it did not require land reforms or social assistance of well-placed elites. Though up to 20 billion dollars was sent, the program helped extend US influence as much as lessen poverty. It also deeply entangled the US military in the region, supporting dictators who were favorable to US policies. Indeed, over ten nations retreated from democracy to military dictatorships in the 1960s.

With or without US dollars, Latin American economies remained small and corrupt, failing to cooperate regionally. Most nations remained agrarian well into the 1980s, functioning as single-crop exporters, lacking a diversity of manufactured product. As in colonized areas worldwide, entire economies depended upon one product. When overseas markets signaled a decline in that product's price, elites lost profits and economies crashed, causing further poverty. Even though the ruling classes publicly criticized foreign domination, they offered little help to the poor. Huge land tracts called *latifundia* were passed down from Spanish colonial times to families who remained influential. Inequality persists in the region; more Latin Americans are in poverty today than were 25 years ago.

LDCs in the Americas, Middle East, or Africa had no option but to connect to Western economies on terms they could not dictate. Hence, even when local rule aspired to growth, weak new states had to compete in global capital markets. But rulers in poor countries generally exacerbated inequalities, with either too little state intervention in the economy or too much autocratic control. Most failed to invest in education or enterprises, providing few services or economic opportunities for their populations.

Third World debt

In the 1960s, the noted Chilean economist Raul Prebisch underscored how ongoing economic dependency from the past extraction of wealth was perpetuated as capital

Figure 2.7 Idi Amin being carried by British after independence, 1975. (Bettmann/ Contributor.)

markets moved wealth perversely from poorer LDC's to wealthy nations. The Third World's economic woes thus persisted even when industrial nations sent aid. Billions of dollars were sent to indebted nations in the postwar decades through what most Westerners regard as altruism. From the perspective of poor countries, the terms of loans or aid were a means of pursuing sustained foreign influence. Western banks often lent money to corrupt states, to be squandered. Massive debts thus increased in the 1970s. By the end of the century, the apparent failure to improve material life for ex-colonized or undeveloped countries exasperated donor wealthy nations.

In LDC's, chauvinist personal fiefdoms disregarded the potential resource of at least half of the population: women rarely enjoyed the opportunity for education, let alone to occupy positions of influence. In most LDCs, birth rates remained so high that women normally raised families with limited or no opportunity to contribute directly to economic growth. High population growth undermined economic growth in LDC's. Low literacy persists to this day, hampering development.

There were success stories. African states such as Tanzania and Botswana joined South Africa to create prosperity by the 1990s. In some Middle Eastern states like Syria, Iran, and minor oil states, Western-educated elites developed education systems and literate societies to boost economic growth, although inequality and female marginalization remain the norm. In Latin America and India, economic growth was slow but gradually improved over the postwar decades, though massive inequality persisted. Brazil's economy grew tremendously in the 1960s, and East Asian states used foreign investment to develop through mostly stable—if authoritarian—governance. High literacy rates and more female participation in Asian economies brought higher standards of living than elsewhere.

Inequality in the First World

Inequality persisted in the developed world too. The United States, fixated on competing with Communism, developed a robust economy premised on mass consumption. Productive investments in the population, such as the GI Bill, rewarded veterans, providing free college education, work training and a return to noncombatant civilian life. A postwar population boom gained from government-supported innovative research and development, which helped companies like IBM kick-start the computer revolution. Investment in infrastructure such as freeways, hospitals, schools, and suburban neighborhoods prompted an incredible level of spending. Consumption thrived, as a well-trained workforce committed to materialism attained high standards of living across the Western world.

All was not rosy in the United States, however. The white population prospered the most in an openly racist society, and advancement to the middle class was almost impossible for nonwhites. Though some people of color and many in the white working class eventually shared in economic growth, it was limited. Business elites successfully designed policies to help people with money keep it by lowering taxes. In a purportedly transparent system of fair economic practice, American businesses actively shaped tax laws to remove tax burdens from corporations, which in turn kept white, middle- and upper-class people affluent. Americans staunchly resisted the redistribution of wealth that became standard in Europe. "What was good for business was good for America" became a US mantra, though it business was clearly not good for immigrants, people of color, most women, or workers overseas who supplied cheap goods for US homes.

1960s—Western abundance, Communist misfortune

Intriguingly, amid rising prosperity, dissent exploded in Western societies in the 1960s, where family ties, inherited wealth, and class privilege persisted. Economic protest transpired in the democratic West far more than in poor states, where autocrats simply shot demonstrators. In the 1960s, activists aimed high, pursuing greater social equality premised upon a new ideology of universal human rights. Motivated by Martin Luther King's inspirational civil rights movement and Gandhi's criticism of materialist greed, progressives fought for fairer wealth distribution.

The women's rights movement thrived in this environment, exposing the enduring inequality between the sexes. There were gains. In Europe, Conservatives and Liberals increased government policies to end scarcity, implementing programs to aid the poorest and women. In the United States, Lyndon Johnson's Great Society programs reduced poverty in the 1960s, bringing modern comforts to the masses and a basic standard of living for those previously left behind.

> Though many feminists consider capitalism as inherently exploitative of women by objectifying them, the prominent feminist Camille Paglia argued otherwise:
>
> *It is capitalist America that produced the modern independent woman. Never in history have women had more freedom of choice in regard to dress, behavior, career, and sexual orientation.* [10]

Inadvertently, the total warfare states established during war spurred vast economic growth. Thwarting repeat of the contraction, autarky, and isolation of the 1930s became a driving motivation for Western leaders. While the Communist and Third World suffered scarcity, surplus wealth created in the West empowered a generation to aspire to even higher living standards. Everyday people moved from basic sustenance to expect new levels of mental and spiritual perfection. This ironically lead many to question materialism, capitalism and consumerism! Optimism increased, with high hopes of eradicating poverty for the first time in human history.

By the late 1960s, material abundance suffused Western life in previously unthinkable ways. It became ordinary to expect good food and nice clothes. Abundant food was available in well-packed stores: Westerners soon had to fight weight gain instead of hunger, in what became known as the *age of affluence*. Disposable income increased across all classes: millions could now own a car, the ultimate symbol of materialist success and personal autonomy.

As Westerners produced and purchased consumer goods, Communist elites subjected their people to squalor or at best basic sustenance, prohibiting creative thought or freedom of innovation. Even amid industrial growth, consumer goods were scarce for those outside party elites across Eastern Europe. Most people lived bland lives in concrete cities or on impoverished farms. Communist economies such as those in the Balkans and East Germany grew impressively in the 1960s, but they were small in scale to western ones, and black markets prevented tax collection or investment. By the 1980s, Eastern European economies were empty shells close to collapse.

Chinese life was worse. The Cultural Revolution squandered natural and intellectual resources. Between 1966 and 1976 the most productive people were persecuted or banished from society. Instead of debating Liberal or Conservative principles as in the West, economic planners obeyed simplistic slogans pronounced by Chairman Mao. After 1964 over 700 million printings of his *Little Red Book* were handed out, read and memorized by Chinese people, while Westerners read anything they pleased. Coincidentally, Chinese emigrants thrived in the economies of Southeast Asian nations or in the West. Freed of Maoist constraints, ethnic Chinese served as middlemen between different groups, facilitating trade and prospering, in sharp contrast to Chinese at home.

1970s—Economic slump

By 1970, incredible wealth had been produced in capitalist societies. Elites with connections to the business world and finance lived in great luxury, while a growing middle class owned homes and enjoyed material comfort. Westerners could consider hunger and cold ancient curses, enjoying basic but warm homes, assisted by the government when necessary. States such as Japan, India, or South Africa that linked with Western markets gained similarly high living standards.

But the recurrent volatility of capitalist economic cycles intervened to impede progress in the 1970s. This was coincidentally the decade when more societies on earth than ever were ostensibly Communist. By 1973, around one-third of humans on earth lived under Communist economic systems. It was still unclear which system would dominate, and the slump in the West suggested that capitalism was failing again.

Something was clearly awry in capitalist states. 1973 was a landmark year. Industrial growth ceased and *stagflation*—unemployment *and* inflation—confounded economists. Usually, economic downturns brought lower prices, but higher prices persisted, and the cost of basic goods hit now unemployed families hard. The Bretton Woods System created by US economists ended in 1973 - US gold reserves no longer matched the actual strength of the dollar. Constant devaluations had made key currencies worthless, so the major trading regions of Europe, Japan, and the United States moved to a floating exchange-rate system, abandoning the security of a fixed-rate system, and signaling the end of the postwar boom. Communism in the 1970s, as in the 1920s, seemed a plausible alternative to Western, particularly American, capitalism.

Human costs never form part of the equation in capitalist economies. CEO's are inherently disinterested in foreign affairs or military interventions, so long as tax breaks and cheap supplies pleased shareholders. Fidel Castro once said with regard to this:

They (westerners) talk about the failure of socialism, but where is the success of capitalism in Africa, Asia and Latin America?[11]

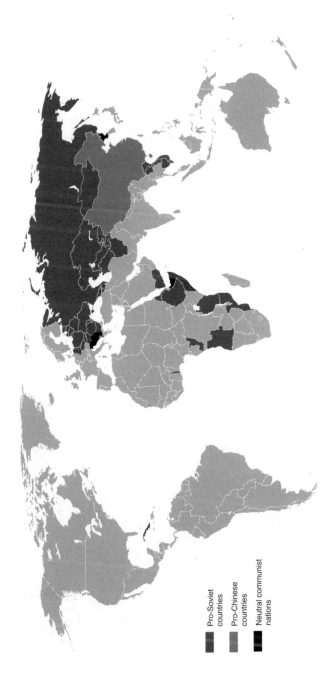

Figure 2.8 Communism at its 1970s highpoint.

Source: https://en.wikipedia.org/wiki/Sino-Soviet_split#/media/File:Sino-Soviet_split_(1980).png

OPEC[12]

With markets already contracting in 1973, a further hammer blow came from the Middle East in the OPEC crisis. Major Arab oil exporters cut off essential supplies to the West due to irritation over ongoing support for Israel. Though few consumers knew it, oil had been a central component of all developed economies for decades. Practices such as the Golden Gimmick, where Arab elites and US corporations connived to avoid taxes, pumped oil into prosperous Western economies at low cost and made those well-connected Arabs the richest people on earth.

Western powers had dominated oil rich areas of the Middle East since the First World War, ousting those in power who threatened to cut off supplies and rewarding collaborating groups. By the 1970s, oil entered the public consciousness in both oil producing and oil consuming nations. Mostly Arab OPEC nations organized, determined to gain from local control of vital resources. Rising energy prices caused economies to slump disastrously across the West. The OPEC crisis saw a colonized region of the world fighting back, using oil as an economic weapon.

The United States, like Britain after the First World War, would run trade deficits hereafter. Symbolizing this change in status, Americans lined up for hours for gasoline, while many in Britain went for days without electricity or heat, due to cutbacks or the need to conserve energy. Some might have thought Communism might be in the ascendancy in 1973, but they would have been very mistaken.

Figure 2.9 Britain's Queen Elizabeth and Prince Philip Host a dinner for Saudi king, 1979. (Tim Graham/Getty Images.)

4. Since the 1970's: Information technology and debt, for most

But by the end of the 1970s, Western economies would adapt, develop and find new sources of oil, and grow anew, creating innovative industries based upon technology and information. OPEC members soon divided among themselves, and the OPEC crisis did little to help people in those countries anyway. The crisis had a detrimental effect in regions like Latin America, where millions suffered from huge increases in basic energy costs. The majority of Arabs certainly saw no gains from the standoff. The poorest suffered more as always. In one extreme example, El Salvador subsided into a vicious civil war due to the oil crisis, when leftist forces were slaughtered by US supported military and Conservative elites. Tens of thousands died, and half a million were forced to flee as migrants.

> The Venezuelan politician who helped form OPEC, Juan Pablo Pérez Alfonzo, cautioned those states that lived off revenues from one resource such as oil, warning in 1976:
>
> *Ten years from now, twenty years from now, you will see, oil will bring us ruin . . . It is the devil's excrement.*[13]

A new type of economy

After 1973, global wealth creation once again flourished, driven by markets centered in Western and later East Asian economies. Tightly integrated markets expanded through the 1980s and 1990s, reaching most of the world by 2000. In the 2000's, a new world-historical economic system emerged, based on information and technology as much as consumer products.

Made in China

Also, however, Communist China's entry into global markets would transform the structure of capitalist economies worldwide. Amid Western economic doldrums and oil crises, economically isolated China began to open its doors to global markets. In 1976, after Mao died, younger leaders introduced four special economic zones, specifically for exporting products to the West. These ports became the factories of the world in ensuing decades, as Chinese laborers provided vast quantities of cheap labor and raw materials to the world market, eradicating higher-wage Western manufacturing jobs in the process. As jobs were lost in the West, demand for cheap

Figure 2.10 Child labor in Mexico, 1970.

imported goods continued apace. The insatiable desire of Westerners and people worldwide to fill homes with low-cost Chinese goods facilitated rapid Chinese industrialization. By the late 1970s, China integrated fully into global markets, progressing from a weak position of importing foreign goods to exporting produce in astonishing volumes, filling millions of containers each year with products for the world, moving tens of millions into the middle class.

In line with China's policies, Western leaders turned increasingly toward open markets, free trade, and deregulation of economies in the late 1970s. New neoliberal policies endorsed a globe of connected nations in one single market, intended to promote business and prevent the stagflation of the 1970s. Institutions dominated by the United States stimulated greater integration. The G7, a group of the wealthiest seven nations, met for first time in 1978 to accelerate worldwide commerce between the richest nations. Working closely with the IMF, the organization however excluded emerging economies and generated dissent from BRIC nations (Brazil, Russia, India and China).

In 1979, European nations expanded this system, setting up the European Monetary System to link European currencies and world markets. In 1980, the United Nations agency UNCTAD (The United Nations Conference on Trade and Development) adopted international economic growth initiatives, with the aim of spreading wealth to developing economies. The process of tightly integrating capitalist markets continued, reaching almost all parts in the 1990s, particularly after the fall of the Soviet Empire.

Newly industrializing countries

China's impact was enormous, and other Asian nations such as Japan and South Korea also changed strategy in the 1970s, moving toward free markets. A preferred policy was EOI (Export Oriented Industrialization), which was emulated in Latin America once it became apparent that ISI (Import Substitution Industrialization) had failed. In the 1970s, Asian export markets soared, adopting Western capitalism within closely managed state economies. Asian nations produced goods feverishly and exported incredible quantities of goods, particularly electronics but also clothing. NICs (Newly Industrializing Countries) such as Hong Kong, Taiwan, Singapore, and South Korea copied Japan's model and pursued export-oriented growth, catapulting ahead of other Third World countries, evanden developing stronger economies than Western states.

Southeast Asian economies grew in volume too. Vietnam opened its economy in the 1980s, mixing capitalist-fueled growth with authoritarian governance. After 1980, the regional economic organization ASEAN leveraged market power to boost Southeast Asian economies.[14] None were democratic, and harsh working conditions prevailed, with limited individual rights in the workplace. States like Singapore and Brunei developed a class of educated middle-class elites, who gained from autocracy so long as the economy boomed. Many prospered in the region, but the great majority did not. Cheap sweatshop work and child labor was pervasive all over the globe, particularly in Asia - and remains so.

1980s—Neoliberalism supreme

In democratic, partly autocratic, or authoritarian economies, capitalism was in the ascent by the 1980s. Over 40 years of Keynesian economics since 1945 was replaced by an influential new school of ideological theory—*neoliberalism.* Austrian and Anglo-American Conservative economists won the economic war with a message of limited government, unfunded social programs, and open, deregulated markets after 1980. Communism's collapse and its loose association with leftist economics, contributed to this victory. By the1980s, even the slightest association with Socialist economies tainted progressive economic proposals. Progressive parties had to turn to the right to win votes in the West.

Nineteenth-century liberalism called for the promotion of free trade, open markets and if individual rights. Keynesianism had been a twentieth-century reaction to this, offering social mobility and opportunity to millions of families in democratic states. After the 1950s neoliberalism emerged as a new form of libertarian economic theory espoused by Conservatives: those with money should keep it, not pay taxes to the state for redistribution; those without means should work harder; and most importantly, the government must not interfere in economic life or business practices; unions were slowly bust in the 1970s as "business values" replaced human values. Somewhat confusingly, the counterpoint to this new ideology came from Western liberals or progressives who argued that moderate state intervention should soften the excesses of capitalism, and high taxes on the rich should be redistributed across society to fund infrastructure, education, and health.

The two most powerful devotees of neoliberal ideology were Britain's Prime Minister Margaret Thatcher and US President Ronald Reagan, who ruled through the 1980s and whose fellow Conservatives shaped the global economy. Self-regulating open markets would provide growth and security for all it was argued, repeating with zeal the flawed ideas of nineteenth-century classical liberalism. Conservatives propagated a dogma that only self-reliance should promote personal success, without state assistance. Faith in market forces encouraged harsh moral criticism of those in poverty. Social relief for the less fortunate should come from charity, not the taxpayer. Those born in harsh historical circumstances must "pull themselves up the bootstraps" instead of asking for "handouts."

Friedrich Hayek, the noted Conservative economist, doubted that either common people or those in power could be trusted to understand economics, concluding that nobody should therefore plan economic growth:

The curious task of economics is to demonstrate to men how little they really know about what they imagine they can design . . . probably it is true enough that the great majority are rarely capable of thinking independently, that on most questions they accept views which they find ready-made, and that they will be equally content if born or coaxed into one set of beliefs or another. In any society freedom of thought will probably be of direct significance only for a small minority. But this does not mean that anyone is competent, or ought to have power, to select those to whom this freedom is to be reserved. It certainly does not justify the presumption of any group of people to claim the right to determine what people ought to think or believe.[15]

After 1979 neoliberal, laissez-faire policies replaced government planning across the Western world, slashing food and work programs that had attended to all sectors of society, benefitting the poor, the aged or those with mental health issues. Inherited historical circumstances related to poverty, racism, or colonialism were of no concern in this system. As long as the rich and well-connected benefitted from free-market fundamentalism, history was irrelevant. Conservative policies such as monetarism kept interest rates high to ensure financial lenders were flush and could then lubricate finance and trade. Businesses enjoyed sky-high profits, while cities fell derelict from lack of investment. Shareholders enjoyed the gains of this new world of finance, not everyday workers. In Britain and the Midwest of the United States, whole sections of populations lost their livelihoods in the coal or shipping industries through the 1980s.

Of course, many also did well in the 1980s. If one overlooks the social or environmental costs of neoliberal monetarism and focuses only on aggregate numbers, it was a success. Through the decade, rising wealth spread globally, seemingly supporting the new financial gospel based upon the scriptures of Conservative economists. Growing markets were indeed lubricated by great flows of investment capital. Economies from Asia to the West were more integrated, spurred. From 1970 to 2000, world trade grew at an average of 5.7 percent annually, an impossible notion in earlier history.

Japan's economy particularly boomed, with massive productivity per person creating profits and products. Japan's prosperity invited complaints that Japanese exports flooded foreign markets—an ironic claim coming from nations, particularly Britain and the United States, who had long done this worldwide. Japanese workers did not benefit as much as managers of corporations, enduring a culture of austere efficiency, making goods for export without enjoying increased levels of consumption domestically. Workers could expect secure lifetime employment far more than in the West, but they received low wages and inadequate means to address workplace grievances. When Japan's economy stagnated and receded in the 1980s after four decades of high growth, what was left behind was an aging population, ongoing cycles of economic depression and a culture of high stress workaholism. Suicide remains rife due to East Asian business culture.

In Japan as in the West, the rush to produce propelled national economies, while negligible attention was paid to environmental costs or the effects on the bodies or minds of workers. Those concerned with the ecological effects of worldwide production and shipping, or critics who expressed workplace grievances and unequal access to opportunity, were hushed in a culture of satisfied materialism. Those who protested inequity or those who critiqued materialism were swatted away with the wide-ranging accusation of being "socialist" or "communist." In the 1980s greed was good, very good.

Communist fiasco

This was an easy accusation to make, given the state of Communist economies in the 1980s. If the high-octane capitalism of the 1980s failed to share the spoils of wealth, little good could be said for socialism. While workers in Europe or Asia wearily protested the indifference of business elites, those in Eastern Europe simply ran out of patience. In 1980 *Solidarnosc*, a small Polish trade union movement, began to fight for workers' rights, protesting poverty, corruption and inequity, daring to criticize Communist leaders' ties to Moscow. Within a decade, this small movement stirred the collapse of Communism across Europe. In 1986 the house of cards of Communist economies crumpled. Soviet Premier Mikhail Gorbachev gave up the ghost: he announced new economic policies of perestroika in 1987, conceding the need to restructure the economy and allow open debate.

Oil embargoes had tripped up Western economies in the 1970s; oil was a core part of the problem in the Communist bloc. By the late 1970s, Soviet oil was intolerably expensive, forcing Eastern European nations to look elsewhere for supplies, where they became accustomed to trading outside the Communist system. By the end of the 1980s, a gradual recognition of the virtue of open markets would inflame independence movements in many Soviet satellite states. The desire for Western consumerism was impossible to ignore.

In the 1980s, China's Communist Party continued to proclaim the merits of Maoism even as they joined the capitalist materialist bandwagon. Premier Deng Xiaoping famously proclaimed in 1986 that it was okay for Chinese people—meaning members of the party—to get rich through open markets. Chinese capitalism since then has remained driven by state-owned industries, though some smaller businesses thrive through entrepreneurship. Hundreds of millions of Chinese have gained from entering world markets. Worker abuse was and still is accepted a part of making money and entrepreneurship, with massive inequality and poverty going unchallenged. Workers' rights remain a Western concept, of little interest to Chinese Communist-capitalists.

North and South

While Communist economies floundered, the West deregulated markets through the 1980s: workers unions were attacked by government officials and business leaders. Along with great wealth came greater inequality, leaving millions dissatisfied even in rich nations. Comparably, circumstances were far worse in the Third World, where economic elites focused on accruing personal wealth. But few Western leaders cared to address the social, personal, or environmental effects of economic life. Nor was there much will to address the growing inequality between the northern and southern nations of the planet.

Figure 2.11 Members of Solidarnosc, the Polish trade union, gather to welcome British Prime Minister Margaret Thatcher, 1988. (Derek Hudson/Getty Images.)

The celebrated Brandt Report in 1980 aimed to expose global inequality, proclaiming there were now only two worlds, not three—a rich north and a poor south. It found that 70 percent of the poorest people on earth consumed only 30 percent of its food, while rich nations such as the United States, with roughly 5 percent of the global population, enjoyed 30 percent of the world's food! In the non-unionized Third World—Africa, most of Asia, the Middle East, and South Asia—exports to wealthier nations had brought income for elites but no progress for those who produced.

In the 1980s, research revealed that aid and loans sent to poorer nations from World Bank loans was squandered by corrupt, connected local cliques. Intended to help developing countries build infrastructure, it was poorly diverted toward foolhardy schemes that benefitted those in power, as influential people in the Third World distributed investment funds and profits to those they knew. Corrupt "big men" who ran African, Asian, or Latin American countries were enriched by foreign aid and investment schemes. Oil billionaires in the Middle East lived in luxury, while most were excluded and taught to blame the West. Though the World Bank's intentions were positive, one report in the late 1980s argued it was run like a Soviet factory, doing far more harm than good through its persistent inefficiency. Human rights abuses actually increased as groups scrambled to access foreign loans.

1990s—Prosperity and inequality

In the 1990s, capitalism became the new norm. Russian leaders, like China's, abandoned Communist economics, if not autocratic rule. Russia embraced a free enterprise economy more abruptly than China had, with instability and disruption for workers throughout ex-communist societies. Minorities in ex-Soviet regions suffered most when Russia's currency devalued to the point that it was worthless. Only huge oil and gas reserves sustained Russia's economy, as the old Communist elite quickly transformed from party cadres into a group of billionaire oligarchs with easy access to international capital markets.

> Russian premier and authoritarian leader, Vladimir Putin, expressed his views on wealth in 2013, proclaiming, "I am the wealthiest man not just in Europe but in the whole world. I collect emotions, I am wealthy in that the people of Russia have twice entrusted me with the leadership of a great nation such as Russia—I believe that is my greatest wealth."[16]
>
> Coming from a man worth tens of billions of dollars who still evokes nostalgia for Communism, this suggests that little has changed in ex-Communist nations.

In ex-Soviet states, as in Russia, economic life worsened after 1991. As it had been for colonized societies, the transition to open markets was predictably rough. In 1992, the new Russian president, Boris Yeltsin, opened up the economy, letting product prices meet global market demands, even if it meant massive inflation or shortage of basic goods. Ex-Soviet citizens were now thrust into the wild vulnerabilities of capitalist market forces. Eastern Europeans saw vastly higher prices, as shady private enterprises began extracting wealth from black-market economies. Though politically repressive, Socialist state economies had at least offered steady work and security for most. Conditions for the majority were no better in this new free market Wild West of crony capitalism.

The growing middle class in Russia was mostly comprised of loyal people closely connected to the state through employment in the Communist era. Likewise, China's commitment to Western-style materialism put well-placed individuals in positions of newfound wealth. Tens of millions of Chinese people left lives of poverty to enjoy a modern standard of living, though minorities and the poor did not partake in this. As in the West, those who inherited wealth and position made the most of newfound opportunities for affluence as Communism petered out.

In the 1990s, East and Southeast Asian states prospered too, urbanizing and modernizing, if failing to address massive inequality. India and Brazil, like China, developed enough to become donor nations to the IMF by 2000, indicating great

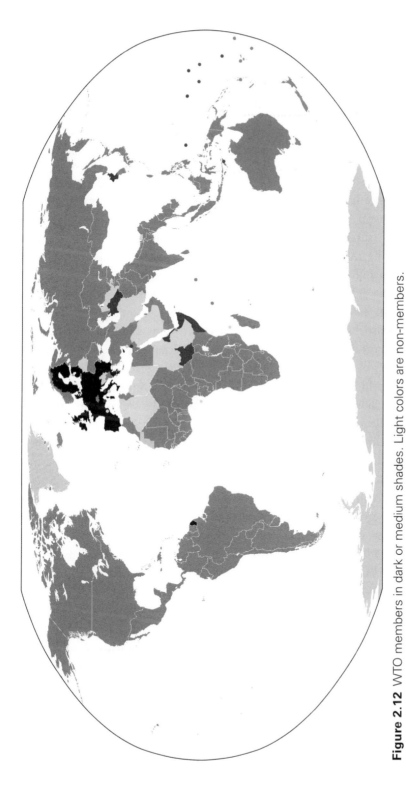

Figure 2.12 WTO members in dark or medium shades. Light colors are non-members.

Source: https://upload.wikimedia.org/wikipedia/commons/thumb/9/9a/WTO_members_and_observers.svg/2000px-WTO_members_and_observers.svg.png

progress. Symbolizing the primacy of global capitalism, the World Trade Organization formed in 1995, to promote open markets across the whole world.

Cost-benefit Analysis? Insecurity and disparity

Given the erratic nature of capitalism, the 1990s brought greater global economic uncertainty with growing wealth. The IMF's aim of promoting security generally served the interests and priorities of wealthier nations. Its coercive "advice" forced austerity upon poorer states and the poorest people therein. States such as Argentina and Malaysia in fact flourished by rebuffing IMF advice and restrictions. Epitomizing the vagaries of late twentieth-century capitalism, Japan's economy imploded after the 1980s surge. An economic bubble imploded, as wealthy investors chasing short-term profits exposed a culture of voracious moneymaking. Other East Asian nations, known as the "Asian tigers," thrived until 1997, when a huge regional collapse occurred, again from reckless investment and corruption.

IMF loans did also prop up badly run states though; through the 1990s Russia borrowed to solve economic insolvency and control inflation. Southeast Asian economies also flourished in the 1990s, particularly those that embraced transparency like Malaysia and Singapore. The Communist alternative had clearly failed anyhow. And the last remaining Communist state faired far worse than even the poorest in the Third world. In North Korea's family-run fiefdom, economic life was horrendous. Almost 3 million died due to famine in the 1990s, enduring economic stagnation, as cronies connected to the dictator's family lived in Western-style luxury.

Recognizing the limitations of command, or planned, economies, the major Latin American governments (Chile, Argentina, Brazil, Mexico, and Peru) joined the capitalist bandwagon and sold off state enterprises to the wealthy in the 1990s, liberalizing economies in a decade of turmoil and economic stagnation. What became known as the Washington Consensus, in that it was presented and supported by the United States, once again punished poorer people in the hemisphere. Some South American leaders tried to develop their economies through a regional banking system, separate from the mechanisms enforced by the IMF and Washington. Uruguay, Chile, Venezuela, and others traded with China as an alternative to challenge the United States and the IMF, a growing pattern in the twenty-first century.

Even with substantial upsurges in trade and wealth, half of the population in most Latin American nations remains mired in poverty. Inequality is probably higher today in Latin America than it was a century ago in Europe or the United States. Mexico's economy continues to flounder, as drugs sold to Western and Asian markets weaken central state authority and splinter the official economy. Mexican cartels support or undermine leading politicians, who are often connected to drug lords. Colombia's economy has been largely supported by cocaine sales to the United States for decades. Private security guards protect malls in Latin America, so those with access can shop in safety. Unions are subject to political party elites' whims where they exist.

> Brazil practiced a balanced mixture of capitalism and socialism in recent decades to build economic growth. Eduardo Paes, a prominent politician, expressed optimism in 2016, via a new democratic form of technological driven economics:
>
> > What we are witnessing is the birth of something I call Polisdigitocracy. This is a form of government that counts participation and transparency as its cornerstones and uses technology as its guide. The digital revolution is allowing democracy to recall its foundations and evolution is modernizing and reinforcing our fundamental values. And we are only at the beginning of that journey.[17]

While Asian nations prospered, and many in Latin America saw a rise in standards of living, much of Africa remains impoverished. The legacy of imperialism constrained African economic development. Colonial tensions remained in segregated South Africa, with a huge, impoverished black majority persisting. Embittered peasants in Zimbabwe seized white lands in 1990s as payback to white landowners. Economic stagnation endured with uninterrupted conflict in numerous places. Famine arrived in the 1980s and 1990s in Ethiopia, exacerbated by incompetent governance and environmental change, killing millions. Genocide between rival tribes in Rwanda slaughtered close to a million in 1994, prompted partly by falling coffee prices on international markets. African states with abundant resources often fell victim to the "resource curse," where elites sold oil or other commodities to foreign markets for personal profit. China is now investing immensely in Africa in what is considered by some a new Chinese imperialism.

> African leaders now increasingly accept that entrepreneurship and investment—the key components of capitalism—can alter that continent's dependency on aid and limit corruption. One CEO, Julian Roberts, claimed at a conference in 2015:
>
> > We wouldn't be investing as much in the rest of Africa if we didn't believe. Africa will be the success story in the next decades . . . Africa is on the move and it is moving forward.[18]

The transition from imperial domination to independence proved particularly painful in the Middle East. The 1980s and 1990s saw bitter fighting between Israel and Lebanon, and Iraq and Iran. In a desperately violent climate, hope for economic growth was impossible. Everywhere but in Israel, dictatorship and elite venality pervaded economic life. Israel is exceptional economically, both for its industrial growth and its tight connections to Western economies. Some Arab states such as Saudi Arabia, Qatar, or the Emirates enjoyed astonishing wealth from oil sales, though elite families exploit immigrant and slave labor to sustain a tiny elite; poverty is pervasive. Regional giants Iran and Iraq were both autocratic, with weak, small economies, and vast military establishments into the 1990s. After a decade of war with in the 1980s and a million deaths, both were focused more on bitterness toward each other and the United States rather than on internal growth.

Even in wealthy America, job losses and insecurity increased after the 1990s. Most Americans lived in a state of economic anxiety even while US wealth increased. Manufacturing jobs were shipped to nations offering lower labor costs in Asia or Mexico, providing profits for shareholders but job losses for everyday Americans. North America became one unified market in 1994 following NAFTA (North American Free Trade Agreement),[19] which aimed to integrate Mexico, the United States, and Canada economically similar to the European Union. This was achieved for the most part, and goods flowed cheaply. But lower worker protections and lost union jobs punished America's working class, embittering millions who had possessed well-paid jobs prior to the 1990s. Though Mexico's national economy had been growing for decades, most Mexicans remained poor, forced to emigrate without documentation to work in the toughest jobs in the United States. The white working class in America blames Mexicans immigrants for taking their jobs at lower wage rates.

Unquestionably, with regard to efficient business organization and manufacturing and commercial capacity, the United States proved exceptional in the postwar era. Over half of the world's production came from America in the 1950s; by 2000, it was 20 percent, though that decline was relative. Even with less global influence the US economy was and is still enormous compared to all others. US businesses controlled global communications through ownership of most satellites in the sky; its national budget was larger than the next eight nations combined in 2000; its multinational corporations governed economic activity worldwide, often more than other national governments. California alone is today the world's sixth largest economy.

By 2000, the United States, European Union, and China managed over half of all global trade. US-style capitalism conquered the world, premised upon secure and private property rights, commercial consumerism, global investment and contract security. Entrepreneurism stimulated the use of venture capital to start companies and produce new goods and services. Even with great corruption in finance, contractual agreements in the West were usually enforced and adhered to, a stark comparison to circumstances almost everywhere else.

Debt and credit

The United Nations today categorizes nations into three levels: rich, middling, and poor. Today's rich countries were either wealthy in 1900 or have since industrialized. The middling nations industrialized recently. The poor were colonized or remain agricultural. By the twenty-first century, there were 196 countries on earth, divided into nation-states, theoretically enjoying sovereignty over their own economic destiny, but in truth, the majority were impeded by past imperial influences or mismanaged by homegrown tyrants. Few could counter the power of multinational corporations based in the richest nations.

Once the exuberance of political independence dwindled into postcolonial economic dependency, many in the developing world perceived inequality as a form of neocolonialism. By the 1980s, Third World debts were enormous, and IMF loans, of which the United States was the largest shareholder, only increased national debts and interest payments. In the past few decades, a revolving system has developed where wealthy nations have sent large sums to corrupt Third World elites, who halfheartedly built infrastructure, creamed most of the wealth, leaving nations more indebted than when they were colonized.

Neoliberal economics drained Latin American nations for decades. A continent-wide Latin American debt crisis in the 1980s was the result of massive borrowing from foreign financiers interested only in returns. Both Brazil and Argentina experienced major debt crises, creating hardship for the majority, huge losses and political instability. Because of connections to world markets, Mexico's currency collapsed in 1982, forcing devaluation and further poverty. When oil prices collapsed in 1986, Mexico's economy fell apart, with the only option more IMF loans to escape bankruptcy. African debts spiraled out of control, to the point that postcolonial nations were often worse off than when they were colonized, and with far more people and higher expectations.

After 2000, emerging economic powers like Brazil and Argentina rejected uncompromising US- and IMF-driven structural adjustment programs on weaker economies. Such programs brought high unemployment, exacerbated an unstable labor force and forced millions to emigrate to make a living. In Venezuela, where oil wealth had seeped to a tiny group of elites serving overseas corporations, Hugo Chavez ousted American and other foreign interests. Nonetheless, the economy collapsed, indicating that local cronyism was as much a problem as foreign investors.

The capitalist world

By the twenty-first century, debt was a problem not only for poor nations, but for Western citizens too. Wealthy Western nations like the US owed China and diverse international lenders vast amounts, running higher national deficits than ever

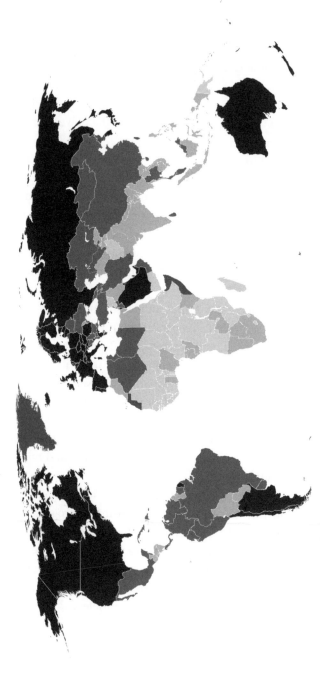

Figure 2.13 Human Development Index by region. Dark means wealthy nations, lighter is poorer. Western states are high income, ex-Communist middling, colonized regions mostly low income.

Source: https://en.wikipedia.org/wiki/List_of_countries_by_Human_Development_Index

before. Personal consumer debt surged along with sovereign debt. Though market deregulation brought those in finance and banking incredible windfalls, debt built up for working people in developed nations in the past three decades.

While most workers possessed more material goods after 1990, they lost earlier job benefits, protections and holidays, working longer days with less security. US manufacturing declined, moved overseas for cheaper labor costs so jobs were lost. Creative financial innovations made vast fortunes for some, often through backdoor deals and connections, and insider trading replaced real industrial growth. Debt levels by 2018 were sky high for the majority—the rich were richer than ever.

Opposition to free-market economics from Communist or postcolonial nations failed. But many in the West dreaded the instability of free-market capitalism too. Scandinavia, France, Britain, and postwar Germany maintained a commitment to the welfare of wider populations, while pursuing capitalist economics, even if it slowed economic growth. These countries provided for a wide array of services not normally associated with economic growth, such as libraries, mental health services, cultural appreciation, and greater literacy. These were mixed economies in practice.

Across developed nations, organized unions crumbled in the 1990s, succumbing to a global system dominated by Conservative economic elites. The largest worker's union, the International Labour Organization, had formed in 1919 with the express goal of fighting inequality and corruption to sustain workers worldwide. Most of the poorer countries on earth had joined it by the 1970s after it became a UN agency. After 1980 however, blue-collar jobs were lost and union-busting continued, increasing wealth for those in finance, law, government, or banking. The business world won the century, shaping a Conservative anti-legislation, anti-union agenda in developed and undeveloped nations.

While 35 years of neoliberal economics built up great wealth for many, nations and individuals were saddled with massive debt in the 2000s. Wealthy countries were reluctant to forgive debts to poorer nations. Banks actually gained from increasing debt levels, and the fundamental premise of capitalism remained to reward shareholders, not workers. Inequality in 2017 in the United States was at its highest since 1900. The English historian E. P. Thompson's decades-old call for a *moral economy*—where markets would be subordinated to human needs—seemed quaint and improbable in the new century, particularly once Donald Trump was elected and Conservative parties swept elections throughout the West.

2008

This is all the more remarkable given that in 2008, following three decades of neoliberal deregulation, open markets and increasing inequality, financial markets once again spiraled out of control. The US economy nearly collapsed, as the policies of President George Bush brought turmoil in the biggest economic downturn since the 1930s.

The US government used taxpayers money to bail out wealthy investment banks and their shareholders in 2008. Financiers and bankers who had brought the economy to its knees met with no punishment, while those who stole small items from stores saw jail time. Popular protests were all but ignored, as working families went into bankruptcy, and a decline in manufacturing caused the economy to contract. Most European economies faltered in turn as in 1929; some, such as Greece, Ireland, or Spain nearly collapsed. The poor, minorities and the underemployed suffered most in all cases.

The United States still shaped the global economy more than any nation after 2000. The most important decision-maker in Western economic life, Alan Greenspan of the US Federal Reserve, argued for decades—following the ideas of Milton Friedman and Friedrich Hayek—that banks must be unregulated to chase profits, repeating the mantra that government must not police business or industry. After corruption, insatiable greed and predatory lending exposed the dark side of such neoliberal policies, Greenspan admitted that he was mistaken in 2008, when the US housing market collapsed. Bad mortgages premised upon predatory lending to poorer people (and those of color) exposed Greenspan's monetarist miscalculation and left millions in great debt. This had already happened before, when 1987's Black Monday global market collapse eradicated vast sums of wealth. In both cases, billions were lost in savings, hundreds of thousands of people lost their jobs, and households were further in debt. Greenspan apologized for his miscalculation, but it was soon forgotten.

Part of the explanation for the 2008 crisis was that great wealth was accrued upon mountains of debt, in the United States and among consumers worldwide. Credit cards had emerged in the United States in the 1950s, and the consequences of easy spending were hard to predict. The Bank of America and American Express offered plastic cards by 1959 to enable freer spending, with options for repayment usually in monthly installments. This helped create a huge boom in consumption, as millions purchased on credit, purchasing home products, luxury items, or foodstuffs.

The 2008 meltdown stemmed from debt accrual and an associated ideological neoliberal belief in unfettered free markets, as the Keynesian notion of government intermediation to protect workers, producers, or pensions was abandoned in the 1980s. Economic elites' obsession for tax breaks for the wealthy, combined with low public spending and investment, brought the economy dangerously close to collapse. US workers paid the price after 2008, with over 20 trillion dollars of personal debt added to the economy. Decades of determined lobbying by the American business community shaped legislation in Congress that favored profits for the few over the wider population. The election of the businessman Donald Trump in 2016 with vast evangelical support suggested that Prosperity Theology—the notion that rewards in heaven would follow for those who enjoyed material success on earth—had become the American way.

Technology and capital

While economic shenanigans proliferated, technology proved to be the fundamental transformative factor in global markets. After the 1990s, technology transformed economies more than either Liberal or Conservative economic theories ever had. US postwar economic growth derived significantly from technologically driven production and consumption. It came too from decades of vast government investment in military technology, necessitated by Cold War competition. US wealth and military adventurism thus mirrored each other. President Eisenhower's fears of a Military Industrial Complex from the 1950s proved apt, but military driven trade provided a Keynesian pump-prime effect, with vast industries arming the nation, employing millions and paying well.

Technologies for producing electricity and oil had emerged in industrial Britain, America, and Germany over a century ago. By 2018, industrialized, mostly Western nations possessed as much technological and industrial advantage as they had in 1900 because, after the 1960s, new computer technologies emerged in those same nations. Data processing machines brought huge increases in efficiency, massive transmission of information, ideas, goods, and services, providing even greater comparative wealth to advanced economies. Particularly in the West (but also in East Asia) new types of companies based on computer technology emerged in the 1980s. Computers initially provided organization and management of profits for businesses, but by the 1990s, they became essential to personal life as well as professional.

The term Information Economy emerged in the 1960s. Financial transactions flowed worldwide in seconds rather than in days, or for much of modern history, months. By 1975, a small company named Microsoft began to sell software programs for basic office tasks. Costs kept coming down for processing power: a computer that cost $20,000 in the 1970s sold for $300 by 2000. When CompuServe began connecting users and businesses in 1980 in an online environment, exponential connectivity suddenly became available to users at home and for businesses. In 1984, the Apple Macintosh invited everyday users to manage their economic lives at home: by 2018 the company dominated almost every aspect of personal computing. By the mid-1980s, mobile phones enabled faster deal making worldwide, replacing slow faxes or long trips to visit clients.

The Internet economy that emerged in the 1990s transformed the global economy as electricity and oil had before, but on a far greater scale. As with electricity and oil, most people can't live without the Internet now. Businesses and governments can't function without it. Today's juggernaut of computer technology demolished previous lifestyles that had lasted centuries, or millennia. Time is money more today than ever before.

If time seems scarce for twenty-first-century workers, in the new century nonetheless anything seemed possible. Companies shipped goods worldwide at low cost; products were cheaper than ever before; almost anything could be purchased online, and enterprises or individuals made millions overnight by going public or writing code for an app. The information economy seemed like a win-win world compared to the poverty of the past.

> Evo Morales, the notable president in Bolivia, presented a critical view of capitalism in 2010:
>
> *We cannot have equilibrium in this world with the current inequality and destruction of Mother Earth. Capitalism is what is causing this problem and it needs to end.*[20]

After 2000, perhaps the greatest modification to economic attitudes was the gradual recognition that economics is a subset of the environment, that all wealth production was premised upon resource extraction and an interrelated problem, population growth. The wealthiest areas of the world were shown to be essentially extracting products from the earth, then discarding them into landfills as waste. The exciting technological computer revolution symbolized this quandary well: even as it created unprecedented levels of wealth, computer technology utilized gadgets made from rare earth materials dug up in poorer countries, whose workers were forced to export natural resources and cheap labor. By extracting resources from poor societies, capitalist manufacturers produced smart phones or tablets to delight citizens in rich nations. So much had changed economically since 1900, but perhaps some things hadn't changed at all.

Key terms

Extractive economies [84]
Keynesianism [90]
Collectivized agriculture [93]
Roaring Twenties [95]
Corporatism [99]
Second World 107
Neo-imperialism [111]
Foreign Direct Investment [113]
Age of Affluence [117]
Stagflation [118]
Newly Industrialized Countries [123]
Neoliberalism [123]
Moral economy [135]

Further readings

Phillips-Fein, Kim, and Julian E Zelizer. *What's Good for Business: Business and American Politics Since World War II*. Oxford: Oxford University Press, 2012. Edited set of essays showing the tight combination of interests between those in power politically in the United States and the people who drive the economy through entrepreneurship and innovation.

Screpanti, Ernesto, and Stefano Zamagni. *An Outline of the History of Economic Thought*. Oxford: Clarendon Press, 1993. Puts recent economic attitudes such as capitalism and Communism in a historical perspective to highlight their virtues and flaws.

Frieden, Jeffry A. *Global Capitalism: Its Fall and Rise in the Twentieth Century*. New York: W.W. Norton, 2006. A thorough account of the economic challenges facing global markets in the last century, with an emphasis on how proponents of capitalism managed to oust other ways of life, focusing on globalization at the beginning and end of the twentieth century.

Interlude 2: Capitalism and humans

In the early twenty-first century, most workers worldwide enjoyed a higher standard of living than in all of history. In rich and poor nations, everyday people enjoyed material comforts and food unimaginable in 1900. Hunger—once an ordinary occurrence—was less a problem than overeating and the side-effects of processed food. Poverty has been reduced more in recent decades than in all human history. Given the abject horrors of anticapitalist regimes in the past century, whether Communist or Fascist, capitalism today is often accepted unquestioned as normative.

Since there is now no organized system to replace capitalist life in the modern world, capitalism seems normal to most people. There is little historical memory of how capitalism as a system became "normal." Young people are taught of capitalism's obvious victory, its spread around the world, and the failure of its chief alternative, Communism. Yet only in recent decades has economic life become premised on the notion that people live in order to gain comforts like clothes, homes, cars, vacations, and other spoils of modern life. The capitalist model dug up the earth's resources and pushed human labor to produce countless forms of goods, bereft of appreciation for the environmental or social consequences of living life for "things."

An undisputable facet of twentieth- and twenty-first-century capitalism is that it created more material wealth in recent decades than humans enjoyed in the whole human past. Increasing returns from investment, trade, and financial markets made billions of people, in every region on earth, affluent. Most citizens in developed nations are rich in material terms by any standard compared to 1900. Nearly all technological, scientific, and economic innovation for product development and consumer goods stems from wealthy states, often employing venture capitalism or investment from the rich. Though many worldwide still struggle in poverty, wealth seeps from rich nations to provide comforts, services and jobs.

Is inequality unjust?

Though Communism failed, the "success" of capitalism is nonetheless open for debate. Neither system displayed sympathy for the casualties of economic growth. Money, as it always has in capitalist societies, creeps upward: the rich get richer, as the cliché goes, inheriting past advantages and exploiting new ones first. Technological gains, better wealth, health, education, and other benefits unmistakably go to fortunate members of society, offering their families and children further opportunities for future success. This component of Western capitalism has prompted a century-long debate over wealth distribution and the role of government intervention to counter disparities.

Those who believe in state intervention in the economy—usually progressives, Liberals or Social Democrats—argue that people born to historically less successful families, less accomplished parents, or those with historical disadvantages, contribute more to an economy when offered the opportunity. Conservative economists and most Western elites continue to claim that all people have an equal opportunity in democracies, regardless of history, ethnicity or class. Hence the government should let people compete to thrive.

> In 2015, the progressive presidential contender Bernie Sanders noted:
>
> *The United States is No. 1 in billionaires, No. 1 in corporate profits, No. 1 in CEO salaries, No. 1 in childhood poverty and No. 1 in income and wealth inequality in the industrialized world. From a moral perspective, from an economic perspective, and from a political perspective, we have got to do better than that.[21]*

Poorer people have always had limited chances to flourish in life. But today, those without means are more aware of how much others have. Workers in wealthier states are dissatisfied because of relative comparisons to the global rich. Many have lost hard-won worker protections and must endure job market instability as an accepted element of a globalized economy. Corporations weakened unions globally, so longer hours are expected to keep a job and help companies compete.

Inequality levels are high in all LDC nations, but they are also similar across South America, Russia, China, and the United States. Only European states show a propensity to equalize wealth: Scandinavian nations have been repeatedly found to be the most equal, prosperous, and safe places on earth to live.

The fact remains that the past century produced more economic activity than all previous eras. Statistics show that GDP worldwide in all industrialized nations has boomed since the 1950s. This success story stems from capital-intensive productive technologies, increased literacy and more efficient labor regimes. Capitalism clearly

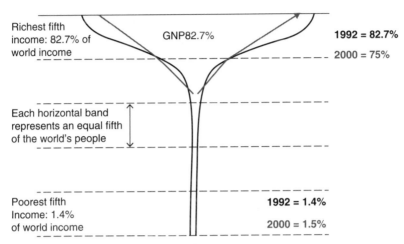

"World Income Distributed by Percentiles of Population" 1992 and 2000   1/10

Richest fifth income: 82.7% of world income

GNP82.7%

1992 = 82.7%
2000 = 75%

Each horizontal band represents an equal fifth of the world's people

Poorest fifth Income: 1.4% of world income

1992 = 1.4%
2000 = 1.5%

Figure 2.14 Increasing wealth accumulation.

Source: http://hdr.undp.org/sites/default/files/reports/221/hdr_1992_en_complete_nostats.pdf

creates comforts; it also leaves less and less time to stop and pause for reflection. Business today is not only a highly sought-after college degree, it is the source of everybody's busy-ness, a mental question.

Busy-ness: Time is money

Cultural critics, intellectuals, low-paid employees, and overworked executives often ask the same question, "Why do we live this way," or as one recent article in the *New Yorker* put it, "How did we get so busy?"[22] The wealthiest country in the world, the nation that has reaped the most economically from capitalism, with by far the most resources, is also the nation that works the most and enjoys leisure time the least. American life is ostensibly run by a small number of corporations with great political influence. Long work weeks are expected to keep the economy going and shareholder profits high. The consequences of overwork, stress, and busyness are little studied or understood.

Even among Western capitalist nations, variations exist in attitudes to economic life. Prosperous industrial nations such as France, Germany, and Britain and all of Scandinavia offer workers at least a month's paid vacation to rest and recuperate from the work year. In the United States, none is guaranteed, and at best a week's vacation is common for new employees in the private sector economy. The US model is spreading however, not Europe's. As the global economy integrates more, most nations are bent on imitating the American model. Everybody in the world wants high-energy goods such as fridges, cars, electricity, and air conditioning. As a result, the BRIC nations rush headlong into the same economic behaviors the United States has propagated in the last century. China's economy booms, with vast inequality and environmental damage -millions work maniacally in a mad rush to modernize. As Brazil and India move forward at the same pace, Russia uses oil exports to become a great power and, in the supposed workers' paradise, ignores workers rights.

While everybody looks to America's high standard of living, few consider quality of living. Americans panic daily about economic life, even though the economy is vast as compared to others. Perpetual crisis seems to be the modus operandi of a capitalist economy; capitalist media report daily of serious financial crises.

The poorest of the poor

Clearly, the nations and regions that dominated the world in 1900 are still the wealthiest and safest places to live. Most regions that were dominated remain poor or unstable, and a gap in relative inequality grows between poorer societies and rich states. Every poor nation on earth today was hampered by colonization or Cold War geopolitical interference. Most endure tyrannical despots with little interest in their people's welfare. Pervasive economic questions persist: How much is global poverty due to powerful capitalist states? How can human society distribute its wealth to the fairness of all? How can smaller, poorer nations with historical disadvantages compete in this system?

Life for many worldwide means poverty and social injustice far beyond that imaginable in the West. With greater connectivity, the poor of the world are no longer blind to the comforts of developed nations, and with increased literacy, they become more aware of the entangled pasts of rich and poor states. Dissent toward American style capitalism is pervasive in the United States, across Europe, and in Latin America. China and Russia remain convinced that American capitalism is corrupt, the root of their historical problems. Radical terrorists dissatisfied with American capitalism kill innocents to express themselves, even while Arab elites gain greatly from the system and elites in the Muslim world, as in China or Russia, do very well from ties to global finance. Violent opposition comes pointedly from terrorist groups such as ISIS across the capitalist world. The historical consequences of European colonialism and the Cold War clearly still linger for billions.

Nonetheless, most African, Latin American, and Arab economies remain archaic, with limited infrastructure, cultures of inequality and authoritarian elitism. In Africa, China, and the Muslim world, a stark income gap is so firmly established that it is barely an issue. Today as in 1900, the global South still depends on the North economically. As in 1900, constant civil wars in poor nations suggest that leaders are unwilling or unable to find a path to peace and democracy.

Change or continuity?

In many ways, little has changed over the century. Many of the world's largest companies today existed in the First World War: Exxon Mobil was a hugely influential corporation by 1900, as was its parent company, Standard Oil. Two of the largest companies on earth, Royal Dutch Shell and British Petroleum, were scouring the earth for oil in 1906. The major US auto companies all produced cars by 1914. One of the largest companies on earth, General Electric (GE), originated in 1878. Heinz, Kodak and many others were prosperous monopolies a century ago. More than twenty-five of today's top Western corporations are, unsurprisingly, larger than almost all nations economically.

Money and migration

While insecure job markets and lost worker protections increase in developed nations, a major consequence of Third World poverty is that individuals and whole families are forced to move to wealthy states as documented or undocumented migrants or refugees. One of the most far-reaching contradictions of neoliberal economics is that, though monies, ideas or goods *must* move freely worldwide, people are prevented from doing so, due to Conservative, anti-migrant ideologies. Since the 1980s, desperate economic insecurity forced people to move to Western societies. Impoverished humans accept low-paid but steady work in wealthier nations, even when unwelcome. Even with xenophobic prejudice, movement of peoples around the globe has proven unstoppable, characterizing a major feature of the last 50 years.

Some critics note that increased wealth and trade has brought neither fair distribution nor easier work anywhere. One writer notes:

> It is, to say the least, disappointing that things haven't turned out (this) way—that inequality has grown, that leisure is scarce, that even the rich complain of being overwhelmed. And yet so much of what we do, collectively and individually, suggests that we still believe more wealth is the answer. Re-examining this belief would probably be a good idea—that is, if anyone had the time for it.[23]

In recent decades, hundreds of millions of migrants moved for work and millions more move as refugees, always contributing greatly to economies through cheap labor. Such insecurity affects women worse than men. Inequality in poorer nations always hurts women the most. When men leave to find work, vulnerable women remain at home with families and no income other than remittance of currency.

Uneducated migrants do jobs that native workers refuse to do in all developed countries. And even though educated migrants played a major part in shaping Silicon Valley in California, migrants are mistakenly labeled a drag on rich nation's economies. Part of the reason for antagonism to migrants in wealthy countries is that work became increasingly contingent or part-time in developed nations as we have seen. As semi-free workers made more goods in China by the 1970s, jobs were lost in rich nations. The West lost manufacturing jobs to cheaper labor in India or China due to the Wal-Mart phenomenon—cheap goods produced globally for and by lower paid non-unionized workers.

Inequality persists even though economic life changed incalculably since 1900. Indeed, new metrics appear to better evaluate economies. Century-old economic methods become increasingly dubious in appraising "the economy," the worth of a company or the value of human labor. Human Development Indices (HDI) now attempt to grasp how humans *truly* live economically, incorporating social and environmental costs into dry numerical spreadsheets. One nation, Bhutan, evaluates its society's worth by GNH (Gross National Happiness), measuring spiritual and psychological health rather than material worth or employment levels. Economic measurement is ultimately a gauge of relative well-being, and how much the past century's economic growth and rising inequity impacted human well-being is an open question. It is to a century of intellectual history we now turn in Chapter 3.

3

Twentieth-Century Thought: Philosophical Uncertainty

Situating the chapter

This chapter explores the major streams of thought, value systems, and metaphysical approaches that governed twentieth-century history. Dramatically new intellectual movements aimed to explain being and existence, directing how humans should conduct their affairs worldwide. Unsurprisingly, most new worldviews were extensions or alterations of long-standing systems of thought, serving to both complement and challenge centuries-old religious and philosophical traditions.

Figure 3.1 "Blackville," 1878. A post-emancipation debate on Darwinism. African Americans are here caricatured in a racist fashion as illiterate and ape-like. (Print Collector/Getty Images.)

This was a century however, when new ideas confronted entrenched mind-sets more than ever, aspiring to diagnose social ills and solve human problems. Even as centralized governments obliged citizens to consent to established nationalist or religious outlooks, for the first time in history, masses of people attained literacy, critical thinking, and the ability to question ruler's opinions. This persistent tension between conformity and confrontation was a central component of twentieth-century intellectual life.

By the end of this chapter, readers should be able to:

- Explain the major intellectual trends of the century.
- Consider the role of religion in contributing to both peace and conflict.
- Grasp the role of the state in propagating new ideas about the world.
- Describe the major figures whose ideas disseminated widely.
- Discuss the gendered role of thought and the emergence of female leaders.

The story

Traditional certainties and new worlds

In 1900, most people on earth viewed the world through narrow windows. They accepted the cultural traditions in which they had been raised, typically framed in religious or ethnic terms, and nearly all believed firmly in the shared wisdom of their local worlds. This had been the case for centuries, even millennia. Questioning existence, the universe's origins, the existence of the God or gods people were raised to worship, or indeed the intellectual elites who swayed their thoughts, was rare. Pervasive religious and ethnic beliefs found in 1900 remain influential worldwide today; a majority of humans claim they are religious to some degree and believe what people did in 1900. In this regard, little has changed.

Yet ideas have to originate somewhere, and since then, billions worldwide abandoned traditional, regional, religiosity in favor of a more earth-based humanity. New, universal, values such as equality, environmentalism and human rights emerged to supplement past traditions. Such views transcended established sectional or regional identities based upon birthplace, nationality, or religious faction. This has been the central intellectual transformation of the past century, as a willingness to contemplate alternative viewpoints developed, slowly, to supplement longstanding belief systems.

Although most humans continued to identify with traditional perspectives, by end of the century the earth was increasingly *secular* and materialistic. This aligns with patterns in the other strands we explore: *political* representation and modern statecraft were premised more often upon the separation of church and state; *economic* life, particularly capitalism, proceeded free of concern for injustice, actively disinterested in morality; *technology* intrinsically developed through an evidence-based, forward thinking research basis; and while twenty-first-century *environmental* attitudes drew on traditional themes of coexistence and respect for nature, they were grounded in a new, global, non-spiritual mindfulness of earth and its occupants.

Though centuries-old worldviews continued to guide people, most cultures confronted a barrage of new views, challenging the accrued ideas of ancient belief systems. Along with the encroachment of modern industrial technology, for the first time ever, vast masses of humans became educated or literate. Particularly in developed states, individuals from the lower ranks of society partook in governance, influencing and contributing to national culture, and shaping beliefs. More interactions among societies and cultures took place than ever before in history. In such circumstances, new political rights, new technologies, and new attitudes to the environment conjoined to undercut the perpetuation of ancient religions and philosophies, shaping new cultural attitudes, often threatening established cliques.

What then is culture? In this chapter, we consider how various societies and philosophies altered their culture to explain the world. E. B. Tylor, an influential nineteenth-century anthropologist, considered culture "that complex whole which includes knowledge, belief, art, morals, law, custom and any other capabilities and habits acquired by man as a member of society."[1]

By 1900, nineteenth-century certainties, both religious and secular, had to contend with new streams of doubt, new attitudes of relativism and pragmatism that pierced ideological absolutes. Intellectual open-mindedness and flexibility permeated the century, disputing certainties and totalizing systems of thought. Novel, often confrontational ideas offered new guiding principles toward society, life, existence, and other humans, unsettling many and creating considerable conflict, while at the same time improving countless lives.

1. A century of fear and loathing?

As the twentieth century loomed, perhaps the most significant intellectual legacy of the nineteenth century was the firm belief that some societies and people were genetically, racially superior to others. Such views justified horrific acts of violence and intensified hostilities worldwide, setting humans on a course toward the immense miseries of the twentieth century, where hundreds of millions of human beings would be killed because of prejudiced ideologies.

People with differing religious beliefs had long considered others infidels, barbarians, or at best misguided. The successes of nineteenth-century Western imperialism convinced many Westerners however that they were both racially and religiously superior to all others worldwide. Westerners' readily apparent control of most regions on earth served to sustain the notion. The Victorian era thus amplified discriminatory ideas found worldwide, in which nations, tribes, empires, or religions professed superiority over others. By 1900, Westerners (and soon Japanese nationalists) formed long-standing animosities through a hateful, colorized prejudice. Skin color or race indicated lowliness; white people were supreme and the darker peoples of the world were inferior. Japanese regarded the Japanese "race" superior to other Asians. Intellectual trends, religious or secular, found no room to question this worldview in 1900. It supported those in power, so masses of people were acculturated to such thinking through education, sermons, or a burgeoning mass media.

Racism and social Darwinism

Given European worldwide domination in 1900, it is partially understandable why racism became so entrenched in Western identities. Chinese imperial identity had long been premised on arrogance toward barbarian "others." Mongols never doubted who was supreme during the time of Genghis Khan. Hindus and Muslims in India had long considered their group superior to each other, as had Christians and Muslims for a thousand years. As soon as Japan became militarily powerful, its population fell foul to deep-seated prejudice toward others. Indeed, even in colonized societies, hierarchies of superiority and inferiority based on attributes other than skin color were ubiquitous. Westerners might conceitedly invente a philosophy of superiority, but they certainly weren't the first to do so.

Even as xenophobic racism became entrenched in the West, criticism arose. Before 1900, the author Joseph Conrad criticized Western imperialism, exploring the destructive domination of colonized people in the famous novel, *Heart of Darkness*. Sigmund Freud too doubted European civilization had so much to be proud of, predicting that its dark side would prove its undoing. Freud postulated that a thin veneer of civilization overlay the barbarity of human potential, and would be proven correct.

> Gandhi famously pointed to Western arrogance. When asked what he thought of Western civilization, his reply was, "I think it would be a good idea."[2]

Though critics of racism and imperialism existed, their voices were usually ignored until the postwar era. Through the twentieth century, ancient animosities worldwide would accelerate, as well-oiled political propaganda systems used deadly weapons and new technologies of statecraft to add fuel to the fires of difference, inciting more murder and misery than in previous centuries.

The late nineteenth-century European *Civilizing Mission* claimed to bestow good governance, economic growth, and spiritual advice on inferior peoples unfit for self-rule. Christianity and capitalism would civilize the barbaric races of the world through colonization and guided cultivation. In 1900, the ideal man, the ideal human, was Christian, capitalist, and scientific; he brought progress through industrialization and urbanization. This modern, masculine ideology would prevail over people in all corners of the earth, whether they liked it or not. French colonists would edify backwards Algerian peasants, British governors would civilize Indians, and American businessmen would save Filipinos from barbarism.

Supposedly superior Westerners were also the chief proponents of two ideological systems that prompted so much enmity and death in the century, capitalism and Communism. Though the pursuit of profit may not seem particularly philosophical, both ideologies and their associated intentions overruled other worldviews in practice. In 1900, Western capitalism was ascendant, and the most powerful economies and militaries on earth were all Western European and Christian. Communism spread from Russia worldwide, to bring great misery. Communism rejected traditional worldviews in favor of a supposed workers' paradise. Most of the world was damned whichever system they were snarled in: "superior" democracies brought industrial capitalism, exploitation, and conflict; "divine" authoritarian rulers brought Fascism or Communism.

The 1900's—Metaphysical uncertainty

In the early 1900s, philosophers religious and secular grappled ancient questions. Ethical concerns remained central even while international violence beckoned. Masculine views dominated, with very limited female input or concern for environmental or social justice. Important men did not purposely neglect the importance of women or the life-giving nature of the earth; they simply had limited viewpoints and could not conceive of such notions.

In the nineteenth century, most thinkers fit into two broad camps—those with a *realist* attitude, where actual matter is all that matters, and those with an *idealist* view, where the mind or thought more deeply explained human existence. Idealists had long depicted the whole universe as no more than thoughts, constituted by the mind and ideas. Realists saw reality only in physical matter and visible objects. Western thought in 1900 derived from a combination of British utilitarian (or practical) realism and German idealism. Both these outlooks would be rejected in the twentieth century.

Akin to the certainties of traditional religions, an overconfident *positivist* mind-set emerged after 1900, disparaging idealism, in particular, as speculative nonsense lacking relevance to reality. This scientific view presumed that much is black and white, true or false. Simplistic explanations based on supposedly objective "experience" could universally explain nature or other societies. Scientific reasoning could offer a guide to truth it was supposed; the world could be understood in absolute terms. Many European thinkers committed to this worldview fled to the United States in the 1930s and 1940s, fleeing authoritarian states and influencing American political philosophy.

Yet, following the horrors of the First World War, some began to recognize the relative nature of complex questions and the overconfidence of positivism, noting how cultural values influenced observations, of society or of "facts." Scholars and scientists whose emphasis lay outside of the religious or political realm—in physics, biology, or chemistry—found life was not quite so simple to explain. Their experiments and conclusions would alter frameworks for understanding the self, society, and the universe. Such ideas spread through communication technologies and colonization to most parts of the world, affecting understandings of traditional worldviews everywhere.

Seeds of relativism

Even as some societies were deemed inferior, they became a subject of study for Western anthropologists. Explorers of Africa's interior in the nineteenth century couldn't help but notice how incredibly diverse human cultures were on that one continent. Curiosity and condescension thus instigated the intense study of colonial societies. In the first decade of the century, the influential anthropologist Franz Boaz criticized overconfident Western arrogance, emphasizing that all cultures were accomplished, but in different ways, relatively speaking. He argued that humans in all societies were talented and adapted; none were superior to others in some fictional racial hierarchy. He also argued that though long-established religious views or cultural norms perhaps seemed "natural" to their inhabitants, they were a mere veneer on a common universal humanity and intellectual capability. The influential Claude Levi-Strauss later reinforced this view, proclaiming that all cultures operated upon similar societal norms and systems.

Though familiar today, this was a shocking approach to understanding the world at the time, suggesting that the ideology of racial hierarchies was a shallow philosophy based on imperial oppression. Only after the Second World War would Boaz and others' ideas develop into a new mind-set, of cultural *relativism*. In this view, all societies and people could, with the right circumstances, achieve similar levels of development on their own terms. Racial hierarchies were nonsense in this view, as was the certitude of Western imperialism.

As new ways of understanding human language developed, the Sapir-Whorf thesis posited that language shaped available thoughts and ideas, limiting some cultures while offering others an advantage, and indeed affecting social behavior. This insight presumed that certain cultures possessed limited options for understanding questions such as time and space. This view would prevail until the 1960s when Noam Chomsky countered that no rigid linguistic structure constrained any one culture as compared to another. Nonetheless, a belief in concrete differences among races and cultures prevailed until recently, and many in power dismissed the idealism in Boaz's view as a naive wish for equality.

Though some questioned the view of absolute differences between men and women, sexual inequality remained customary—men were simply assumed to be relatively superior to women. However, seeds of opposition to chauvinism were planted, as women's rights groups challenged misogyny after 1900. Celebrated authors like Virginia Woolf protested women's conditions through her pointed narrative form. Why were all the great thinkers male, she asked? What held women back? Powerful scenes and beautiful prose from playwrights and novelists opened minds, identifying women's unquestioned oppression, in the West and elsewhere.

Forward thinking turn-ot-the-century male writers like Henrik Ibsen concurred, scandalously questioning women's marital subjugation in *A Doll's House*. Ibsen also questioned the role of women in the home and in public, criticizing the general absurdity of gendered social norms. Such ideas seeped from cultural and political elites into the wider culture over time, first in industrial nations. Ibsen's use of stagecraft to shape worldviews established the seedlings of a permissive culture, where young people were committed to enjoying the freedom to think for themselves.

The ideas of scientists were abstruse, but they too changed attitudes. In 1905, Albert Einstein's theory of relativity (among other theorems) depicted a complex universe that though measurable, had no simple, rational logic to it. No creator stood behind its origin, the earth was inconsequential in the grand universal scheme of things; the sun a mere dot in one of many universes! Once understood, Einstein's physics were plainly relativistic, lacking absolute certainty. Just like cultures and social relations, space and time were relative, in an infinitely more complex world than had been previously understood.

Scientific discoveries rattled established certainties about the world. In 1911, Ernest Rutherford discovered tiny, heavy nuclei in atoms. His work suggested, abstractly, that the whole universe—from the minute to the unimaginably massive— was quantifiable, but mysteries abounded. In 1919, Edwin Hubble's telescope revealed images of a deep universe that shook existing verities about nature. Humans could now view deep into the unknown in ways that the naked eye never could. Baffling and beautiful images spread around the world in ensuing decades, offering mystical images of the universe. When in 1931, Godel's theorem proved that uncertainty was indeed fundamental to all mathematics and science— numbers morphed, providing alternate answers depending on the context—it appeared the world was fundamentally uncertain and unknowable. This tension between intellectual certitude and humility would become a central divider in worldviews as the century passed as well as the basis of the computer science revolution.

Such complex views, based on evidence and calculation, inadvertently undermined certainties passed on through the ages, and provided little comfort for those wishing to find simple meaning and purpose. The century though would be one of statistics and mathematics, and discoveries in physics would undermine the notion that history, or life, had inherent direction. Humans simply wandered through existence, then disappeared into the soil. No objective reality in fact existed.

Innovative philosophical systems derived from mathematics did though bring meaning for some. Great thinkers such as A. N. Whitehead and his celebrated student Bertrand Russell offered a new view of the universe in 1910's *Principia Mathematica*. Though not antireligious, this treatise explored reality in a world where religion had scant relevance. Russell wrote and influenced public discourse for over 60 years, until his death in 1970. A. J. Ayers' work on language, truth, and logic would later build on this, asserting that only verified concepts could be meaningful. Without evidence, meaning was lost. Both thinkers grappled with the enduring question of whether humans were born with innate ideas or were blank slates on which to inscribe beliefs. Meaning and purpose now streamed from science and mathematics, not just inherited traditions.

The developing philosophy of science took a resolutely logical approach toward the exploration of numbers. For Russell, the logic of mathematics helped explain metaphysics and knowledge itself, and mathematical theory would in time influence crucial twentieth-century fields such as philosophy, logic, economics, the social sciences, and indeed computer science, shaping prevailing views in almost all walks of professional life. The pursuit of mathematical meaning enabled technologists to develop machine technology in the service of the state, freeing innovators from limitations based on convention or traditional authority.

Long before TV series about aliens or science fiction comics, the explorations of numbers and knowledge posed the possibility that many worlds existed. Eastern philosophies had long posited multiple perspectives and interpretations of reality, and key thinkers since Voltaire in the eighteenth century to Schopenhauer and Nietzsche in the nineteenth were exposed to India's ancient Upanishads. Thus, the practice of incorporating multiple perspectives became slowly integrated into Western approaches to science and society. Isaac Newton's pre-Einsteinian view of the universe, like Western racism in general, was exposed as too simplistic, too tidy, and too omniscient. A new messy, hard-to-fathom uncertainty, less comforting than inherited creeds, nonetheless opened pragmatic possibilities for contemplation on life's meaning and the universe and application to everyday life.

1910s—Pragmatism and pluralism

Influential American thinkers proposed a middle ground between extreme certitude and relativism, when a particularly American philosophy (*Pragmatism*) emerged in the 1900s. Its founding father, Charles Peirce, grounded mathematics in a philosophy of pragmatism. He concurred with physicists that spontaneity explains the universe, not rigid, absolute laws. Ironclad rules based on broad assumptions about societies or human nature were also abandoned in this view. Straddling the excesses of sweeping positivism and the simplicity of relativism would be an endeavor for many through the century.

Pragmatism emerged in the United States while the country developed into both an economic and intellectual powerhouse. William James, a leading proponent of Pragmatism, offered a truly modern worldview that acknowledged truths could work differently for different societies—there was no one truth based on one god, nor even one sole form of knowledge. James experimented with hallucinogens, as healers had in indigenous societies for millennia, to form a deeper understanding of nature. Instead of leaning toward one absolute certainty, or one truth, Pragmatists intimated

Figure 3.2 John Dewey (d.1952), American philosopher, physicist, and educator. (Bettmann/Contributor.)

life should be measured by the consequences and results of ideas, not vague, hard-to-prove notions.

Pragmatists argued that the self, an individual's identity, developed from behavior and experience, not from any preset personality or set of traits. Importantly, this meant people (and societies) could change, that people were not damned, fixed in character or forever flawed. Both people and cultures could develop, after 1900 through state-led policies such as education, cultural refinement, or social edification. The American educator John Dewey applied this optimist view to schooling, arguing for a *pluralistic* worldview, premised upon an acceptance of diverging, opposed ideas and ultimately of human diversity in world societies.

For the first time, it was recognized that most people tended to believe anything they were taught, including proscriptions on how to behave, cults of monarchy or autocracy, the superiority of nation or deities. For Dewey, philosophy, knowledge, belief, allegiance, thought—all were subservient to education. Such ideas were planted in the 1910s, paving the way for more sophisticated approaches to the mind that would eventually emerge after the Second World War. This laid the foundation of new approaches toward tolerance and diversity in the 1960s that questioned suppositions about class, race, gender, and about progress, power, and prejudice.

1920s—Experimentation meets tradition

The First World War brought intellectual as well as physical consequences. The horrors of warfare exposed the magnitude of nineteenth-century prejudices, belying ancient assumptions that obedience to authority was positives. Young men were slaughtered by the millions in the name of imperial and nationalist values like faith, patriotism, and heroism, yoked to the orders of supposed superiors. Destruction stemming from wartime aggression impoverished colonial populations, increasing disillusionment about indigenous viewpoints. Leaders in Turkey, India, China, and elsewhere realized that modernization was the only option available to undo the burden of foreign domination.

Turkey's new leader Kemal Ataturk was scathing toward traditionalists, as he modernized the remains of the collapsed Ottoman Empire. After he secured total power in 1924, he declared contempt for sheikhs, imams, and other religious leaders:

> In an age when inventions and the wonders of science are bringing change after change in the conditions of life, nations cannot maintain their existence by age-old rotten mentalities and by tradition-worshipping . . . Superstitions and nonsense have to be thrown out of our heads.[3]

In Europe, the psychological impact of slaughter in the trenches had a deep impact on survivors, heralding new attitudes and behaviors. Following incalculable suffering and harrowing effects of war, Westerners demanded greater rights, education, and justice from ruling cliques. Women pushed for relative equality, though most men resisted the idea. Workers contended for higher pay and better conditions, though this would meet the wrath of business owners and state militias. Both aspirations—women's and worker's rights—demanded freedoms of a new kind, the liberty to enjoy material comfort, to avoid hunger, and to assert personal opinions. The new principle of equality slowly became enshrined in Western minds. Particularly in cities, people expected basic necessities, as well as a more materialistic, pleasing way of life. Men and women experimented with new attitudes to sexuality in the 1920s, including partial acceptance of same-sex relationships and more tolerant attitudes to homosexuality.

More provincial village outlooks and long-standing belief systems prevailed for most people outside of cities and across the developed and colonial world, though they were slowly challenged. New radio and TV technology, and the disruptions of warfare troop movements, meant that people from colonies and the countryside were exposed to ways of life far beyond those previously known. Colonized people were slowly exposed to new forms of identity, associated not with local cultures, but with a desire for greater material comfort, self-determination, and rights.

Though most worldwide remained provincial in worldview, unconventional thinking spread, and American artists led the way in the 1920s. Postwar modernist artists and writers in the United States and Europe rejected all conventions and norms, questioning consciousness and reality through surrealist art and stream of consciousness literature. Visual artists pushed radically unconventional ideas into the consciousness of the masses, though the upper realms of society absorbed them first. Picasso presented a new visual world of fragmented reality and absurdity, with no obvious meaning or straightforward explanation. Abstract artists, like physicists, entertained the notion that reality did not in fact exist, that reason was impossible, and hence no absolute standard existed with which to judge taste, or for that matter morality and ethics.

New music styles appeared. Jazz music brought an inventive and original approach to sound, horrifying traditionalists. Composers proposed new tones or tempos to affect emotions in original ways. Similarly, blues music drew on specifically African rhythmic styles, stirring movement, ecstasy and emotion—no longer did staid nineteenth-century mores suffice. Both forms of expression would shape the path of music forms worldwide into the present.

Jazz and Blues also challenged the received notion that people of color were inferior. Meanwhile, black leaders in the United States such as W. E. B. Du Bois formed the Pan-African Congress in 1919 to denounce racism, beginning a grueling struggle to alter nineteenth-century views. Such intellectual and artistic movements

spread worldwide, beginning in the cities. Indian, Chinese, and Af
exposed to new sounds, and mixed modern ideas with local cultur
found huge audiences in 1920s Japan and the Philippines.

People were receptive to the irrational and novelty after th
of war. New styles of art and music pushed frontiers of thought, deci...
neither rationality nor tradition offered an all-encompassing explanation for being.
Philosophers and scientists, conceded the complexity of existence. Henri Bergson
critiqued excessive trust in evidence and factuality, elevating intuition. He posited
a universal human understanding of what he called "*duration*" with many forms of
time and experience, a multiplicity of realities, underlaying the physical universe.
In line with Darwin's view of the disordered chaos of evolution, Bergson rejected
customary, all-explaining dogmas, offering a kind of world spirit he called "elan vital."
In his view, nature predisposed humans to creativity—intuition explained actions,
not intellect or reason, and humans must unleash creativity to reach a universal
consciousness.

Persistence of convention

Such new worldviews of course had to contend with tradition and custom. Traditional
thought systems persisted all over the world amid this flurry of inventiveness. Most
people in Asia remained committed to Buddhism, Confucianism, or Daoism; most
Indians accepted Hinduism; Middle Easterners followed Islam; the majority of
Westerners remained Christian; and most Africans practiced local beliefs infused
with either Islamic or Christian tenets. Modern ideas did not replace worship, and
most people worldwide, in small towns, villages or rural areas, were not exposed
to such concepts. Most people remained uneducated, illiterate and were content
to believe in superstitions or demons, and received wisdoms passed down from
authorities.

Indeed, modernist ideas often produced a backlash. In the 1920s, Christian beliefs
revived in places like the United States, employing scientific modes of communication
such as radio, introduced in the United States in 1924. A revival of *fundamentalism*
was partially a reaction to the new attitudes of the 1920s, where sexually charged
music, designed to entertain, transported millions away from the mundane but also
the sacred. The rise of Christian *Evangelism* was central in American politics and
culture in the 1920s, promoting a traditional view of life that prevails. In 1925, the
state of Tennessee banned the teaching of evolutionary theory, prompting a dispute
that persists in the United States—the only developed nation where powerful people
consider biblical notions of time and space equivalent to scientific explanations.

Paradox best explains this decade. International Christian organizations such
as the Fellowship of Reconciliation generated support for pacifism across Western
Christian denominations, in line with the peace-seeking exhortations of many

religious leaders worldwide. Meanwhile Social Darwinism justified white domination over "inferior" peoples. The influence of the distinctly Christian Ku Klux Klan reverberated in 1920s America, as over 4 million official members held sway, shaping attitudes throughout the halls of power and in rural areas, even as urbanites turned to black music, tolerance, and diversity.

Japanese modernizers imbibed Western fashions and musical styles in the 1920s while conservatives and militarists suppressed counterculture voices with force, repressing freedom and movement. For millennia, much Asian philosophy had been premised on the conviction that contrary forces complemented each other to explain the natural world. Instead of the Western tendency to think in terms of black and white dualities such as good/evil or right/wrong, most non-Western outlooks accepted contradiction and inherent ambiguities as part and parcel of the human state. Arthur Schopenhauer had introduced Asian philosophies to the West in the nineteenth century, and by the 1920s, they were diffused through influential scholars such as Friedrich Nietzsche, Carl Jung, and the extraordinarily influential Sigmund Freud.

As societies in the 1920s wavered between convention and innovation, autocracy and democracy, hatred and tolerance, dark currents approached, to demonstrate the lights could go out on civilization very easily. Diverse schools of thought that emerged in the 1920s established it was both logical and rational to believe that existence was illogical or irrational. The global economic depression of 1929 helped nobody, and the 1930s would bear out the irrationality of humanity.

1930s—Militarism and the mind's inside

The 1920s brought forth a new, experimental intellectual outlook in the West—which both explored the interior of the human mind and exploded into hateful ideologies. Sigmund Freud changed introduced the idea of the psyche, unlocking a new world of thought, analyzing the mind in novel ways and shifting understandings of humanity's moral essence. Freud opened the mind to examination, while forwarding the notion that civilization had a dark, dangerous component. Freud's method of *psychoanalysis* moved the study of ethics away from priests and prayer to the psyche and to patient treatment. His daughter Anna later reshaped attitudes to child psychology in fundamental ways.

Freud's idea of the subconscious changed attitudes to issues as varied as childhood, reproduction, and personality. Humans, he claimed, succumbed to inner drives that required release, stemming from experiences of sexual repression, dreams, or childhood experiences. Freud's repertoire of concepts—including regression, repression, sublimation, and transference—became common tools to describe the human condition. Freudian concepts such as the libido, id, ego, and superego were embedded in everyday language. He introduced the modern study of the brain and mind, though he had many detractors. Freud had cynical attitudes to women and like most males, regarded women as inferior. Like many thinkers, his approach was Positivist, overconfident in aspiring to understand the mind wholly.

Freud's student Carl Jung broadened his concepts to posit the existence of a universal human mind, a *collective unconscious* that connected all humans through all of history. The originality of Freud and the optimism of Jung permanently changed views of human nature, impacting global consciousness. Unlike Jung, Freud, did not envision a collective humanity; he feared that civilization's thin veneer could split asunder at the slightest tug. Like Nietzsche and Schopenhauer before him, Freud thought humans were driven by violent, irrational desires, by an uncontrollable blind will that neither reason nor conscience could counter. Events soon proved him right.

Mindless violence

By 1930, the world was in global economic depression. Soon some of the most powerful, sophisticated states on earth entered a realm of madness, led by men Freud might have considered abused children. Societies from Russia to Japan, Germany to Italy, seemed to support Freud's fears, as violent governments ran amok, killing those they considered inferior. In Asia, Chinese and Japanese thinkers incorporated Western ideologies such as Communism, nationalism, or imperialism, reconciling them with local traditions - violence was the outcome everywhere.

In 1930s Europe, deep-rooted nineteenth-century racism coalesced with patriotic, nationalist doctrines, shaping aggressive ideologies that brushed away the liberal, broad-minded imagination of the 1920s. *Totalitarian authoritarianism*, in both its right-wing Nazi and left-wing Communist guises, were the dominant ideas of the decade. Proponents of both systems aimed to eliminate those who questioned authority or differed, whether artists, intellectuals, liberals, Jews, gypsies, or homosexuals. Fascism spread in Japan, Italy, and Germany, across Europe from Spain to Romania, into Latin America. It tolerated no difference: conformity was king, as cultures succumbed to conformist obedience.

Such militant mentalities soon sanctioned the mass rape of Chinese and Korean women by Japanese soldiers, followed by the murder up to 7 million Jews in the Nazi Holocaust, 50 million dead from Stalinist terrors, and innumerable other offenses to humanity in regimes that abandoned liberal democracy. In Communist China, malice toward intellectuals, entrepreneurs, or anybody who questioned state slogans and central office banalities, killed up to 30 million more by the 1970s. In its postwar Southeast Asian forms, Cambodian Communism slaughtered millions of innocents in a frenzy of hatred, as a Buddhist state converted to authoritarianism. Though imperialism certainly exposed the duplicity of democratic states such as France, Britain, and the United States, this was different.

Ideas of racial superiority and national hatred did not arrive out of thin air. Nations and empires had long believed in their superiority: in times of power Greeks, Romans, Arabs, Mongols, and Chinese all sat secure in the assumption that they were superior. Japanese Fascists were assured that they were superior toward other Asians. Ottoman Turks routinely slaughtered Druze or Christian minorities. Barbaric Japanese acts toward the Chinese in 1930s and Koreans through the 1950s suggested that racist supremacy was deeply engrained in Asia too. Cultural superiority had validated Chinese attitudes toward other Asians for centuries. Russian hatred toward minorities from Uighurs to Chechnyans existed long before Communism. Cambodian and North Korean rulers after 1945 imprisoned and murdered countless people considered unfit to live, with no immediate connection to nineteenth-century racism.

Nevertheless, ideologies of hate reached new levels of fanaticism, employing greater technology and power in this era. Friedrich Nietzsche's disdain toward conventional thought found a welcome audience in Germany by the 1930s. Nietzsche had dared proclaim, "God is dead," openly arguing that Christianity was a religion of the feeble, and democracy for the weak. Society he claimed needed an Ubermensch, a man of power and action. His provocative opinions unsettled many, though they provided a blunt, honest assessment of the world as he saw it. The idea that humans should apply will to overcome obstacles and to attain glory was not necessarily a call for Nazism. But his ideas inspired some Germans to aspire to world power through aggression, and Nazis found justification for their actions in his ideas. Just as Darwin's neutral statements about the fitness and adaptability of species were used to vindicate Western superiority in the Victorian era, so too were Nietzsche's witticisms and provocations misused to support the bizarre claims of totalitarian regimes.

In the 1930s and into the 1940s, the irrationality of "civilization" and human beings demonstrated a truly dark side to humanity. The Second World War was even worse than the Great War. It seemed that great minds had indeed offered a static, overly confident categorization of human nature from the nineteenth century. In the 1940s, over 50 million people would die from war and disease, and usually over ideas. Neither traditional nor modern ideas seemed to explain human existence.

1940s—Despair and doubt—power over thought

Freud investigation into the intricacy of the mind seemed to suggest that primitive violence was a driving motivation for the species. The period between the late 1930s and the 1950s was one when authoritarian ideas took hold, in industrial powers and weaker states. Power mattered, not thought. Nazism in particular, in its mercifully brief period of infamy, posited an absurdly malicious anti-Semitic ideology, premised upon a rejection of diversity or difference. Much of the planet suffered through autocratic rule in the 1940s, through military regimes in Europe and Latin America, colonized rule or local despots in Africa and Asia. Democracy was rare in the 1940s—there was no reason it would survive the decade.

This descent into dictatorial madness brought a prohibition on dissent or critical thought. The difference between two historically similar cultures such as Britain and Germany is significant. In the grim 1930s, literacy increased in Britain. Ideas and discussion proliferated, as the democratic British state encouraged the publication of cheap books. From 1935, Penguin Books brought the classics of literature into the consciousness of people at all levels of society, not just the highbrow elite. In a decade when Britain's National Archives built up a mammoth repository of the past, to reflect on the world's societies and question the nature of civilization, Germans both religious and secular fell foul to ignorance and hatred. Nazi Germany burnt tens of thousands of books considered subversive to the regime, at once polluting Germany's remarkable literary past, closing minds and silencing criticism.

Yet, even in this darkest decade, great minds persisted in proposing the possibility of human cooperation. H. G. Wells anticipated a "global unity of the mind" in his celebrated 1930s radio series. Wells was famous for his 1897 *War of the Worlds*, in which alien forces invade planet earth, forcing humanity to think as a unified body. He died in 1946, in the worst decade of war in human history, as national, ethnic, or religious differences exploded into carnage, the very calamity Wells wished to transcend. His idea of a World Brain that might connect people of all nations and religions to bring peace spread. Knowledge and ideas, Wells believed, could spread through a "World Encyclopedia," a concept uncannily comparable to the Internet.

The 1940s brought grave concern for civilization's survival, and disappointment at traditional ethical systems. In none of the autocratic states did champions of tradition or faith thwart the rise to power of malevolent regimes. The Catholic Church usually supported despots, while the organized Protestant churches in Germany feebly resisted Nazism. Austria's head of government Engelbert Dollfuss was a fanatical Catholic, as were many Nazis. Hitler referenced Christianity frequently, replacing the orthodoxy of traditional faith with authoritarian devotion to him as supreme leader. Hitler relied upon Christian symbolism and the acquiescence of religious elites to legitimize the Nazi Party from its outset. Mussolini in Italy enjoyed the unopposed and tacit support of the Catholic Church hierarchy. German Nazis, like Italian Fascists, made agreements with the church through a Concordat in 1933, promising that Catholics would be safe if Nazis could control society. From Romania to Poland, Hungary, and Spain, religious authorities bowed to autocratic power, often sustaining it.

The 1930s and 1940s exposed the weakness of existing moral and ethical systems. German and Russian perpetrators of violence were brought up in cultures suffused with Christianity. Hitler was brought up Christian, and though he apparently abandoned organized faith, he considered his actions as just and ethical nonetheless, writing in 1923:

> *Hence today I believe that I am acting in accordance with the will of the Almighty Creator: by defending myself against the Jew, I am fighting for the work of the Lord.*[4]

Joseph Goebbels, a key Nazi leader, was explicit on the religiosity of Nazism:

> *What does Christianity mean today? National Socialism is a religion. All we lack is a religious genius capable of uprooting outmoded religious practices and putting new ones in their place. We lack traditions and ritual. One day soon National Socialism will be the religion of all Germans. My Party is my church, and I believe I serve the Lord best if I do his will, and liberate my oppressed people from the fetters of slavery. That is my gospel.*[5]

Organized religious institutions were unwilling or unable to stand up just when humanity needed them most. Of course, many brave believers offered principled opposition, and already in 1937, the apparent cruelty of Fascism prompted the pope to speak out against Nazism. The distinguished Protestant leader Martin Niemoller remonstrated with Catholic bishops regarding the widespread murder of handicapped people in Germany, and many priests, pastors, and nuns protested vainly, enduring abuses and humiliation. Many Christians were sent to concentration camps for dissent against the annihilation of Jewish people.

Still, the churches' propensity to remain "apolitical," to stand by as murder spread far and wide, left many people embittered toward organized religion. After war ended, new philosophies developed that were founded on a certain skepticism regarding human nature and old traditions. The failure of nerve on the part of religious elites aligned with an increase in suspicion toward all received authorities. This opened a path to new worldviews such as *nihilism*, where nothing really mattered. Modernity—or at least the modern world—seemed soulless, lacking goodness or purpose. A meaningless world of banal drudgery and absurd chaos appeared to exist. Nothing in modern life seemed to satisfy humans sufficiently.

A less severe, but equally skeptical view of life, emerged through *existentialism*. Key thinkers like Jean Paul Sartre aimed to raise consciousness through a practical pessimism, using all available means to awaken the masses, through fiction, film, drama, or lectures. Existentialism was a response to both the horrors of war and existing authorities and institutions, with a focus on the self, on blunt honest communication as a retort to the veiled hypocrisies of political, economic, or religious

Figure 3.3 A group of child survivors behind a barbed wire fence at the Nazi concentration camp at Auschwitz-Birkenau in southern Poland, on the day of the camp's liberation by the Red Army, January 27, 1945. (Alexander Vorontsov/Keystone/Hulton Archive/Getty Images.)

elites. It made sense in the context of a Cold War that threatened to destroy humanity at the foolish push of a button, and it offered an activist impulse amid the bedlam of everyday existence. Postwar Westerners (and later young people worldwide) were greatly affected by Sartre's existentialism. For Sartre, all were free to choose the right path, and must do so themselves, as individuals. Humans, he argued, were not controlled by environment or irrational drives. The individual had to create meaning, since all else had failed.

rtre was nonetheless uncertain about the possibility of positive change, at least ...e short term. Others, notably Albert Camus, argued that human thought must be used to affect transformation for the good, for a better existence. Most of these postwar thinkers had little to say about religion or gods, dismissing or ignoring faith altogether. Sartre believed neither gods nor a supposed rational human nature had proven itself worthy of any ethical standard. The Catholic Church prohibited Sartre's books, putting his ideas on the same list of forbidden books that Galileo and Darwin occupied, remaining in effect until 1966. Few thinkers however influenced as many young minds as Sartre did in the postwar years.

Organized religion persevered along with new strands of thought. Christians, Muslims, Jews, Hindus, and many others adapted to social and cultural change, confronting modernity out of necessity. Vast numbers of people still found solace not in new ideas, but rather, in reinterpreting ancient ones. The Dead Sea Scrolls, discovered in the Judean desert in 1947, revitalized the mystery of ancient Judeo-Christian faith for millions. Likewise, when modernity filtered into African societies, India, and the Middle East, it was met by long-standing traditional views that remained central to the majority of minds.

The postwar decades were, however, to become increasingly secular, particularly in the developed world, but also worldwide once literacy spread. Postwar ideas encouraged humans to freely choose appropriate values, rather than to inherit fixed sets of ideas. Existentialism and skepticism opened a door to actively deliberate, to take the position as outsider or iconoclast. In the postwar era, a new search for truth turned into a comprehensive philosophy of life via popular culture. Questioning tradition was one thing; living a life of criticism was another. True freedom was the goal now, not subscribing to decrees passed down from elders.

The postwar era brought a new intellectual age, where a life of action, of talking and doing, changed people and the world through art, music, and literature. Morality, it had been shown, was independent of religious faith; it had to be fashioned continuously. While relativists proclaimed that there were no absolute true values or ethical choices, existentialists argued that humans *could* at least choose, based on phenomenon and experiences that made sense individually. Either way, something had to give following the Holocaust, the war, and over 50 million dead. Absolute worldviews and absolutist thought had brought nothing but torment.

1950s—Consumerism and conformity

Ideas such as existentialism would not spread wide until the 1960s, and most people wanted a return to normalcy after the scars of war—tradition provided a place for many after widespread war. The United States, the most powerful and influential postwar culture, represents well the paradox of these interacting and contradictory strands of thought in the 1950s, in which conventional thought wrestled with modernity.

Growing American faith was grounded in anticommunism. The US produced a culture of conformity and stultifying deference toward authority, exported abroad by a American propensity to topple or intimidate regimes that differed with American values, or indeed capitalism. The McCarthy era required ideological compliance and quietude. Traditional American racism endorsed an aversion toward difference, providing pride in a self-conceived blessed nation, whose power could and should reach worldwide. This meant that any group in the United States or overseas that countered American values, even as subtle as through the promotion of workers' rights, was wicked. While US military and business elites supported authoritarian regimes overseas through the CIA, the FBI enforced compliance domestically. The FBI threatened artists, progressives, and "alternative thinkers" with the power of the state, keeping vast numbers of files on those considered subversive. The "Red Scare" was also a "Lavender Scare," in which gay people were exposed or humiliated as supposed Communists. Democratic states could threaten freedoms too.

Though overtly Christian in culture, a pro-business materialism was the true dogma of 1950s America. *Consumerism*, the notion that people should acquire material goods to live happily, submerged religiosity or philosophy. Thinkers such as Oral Roberts and Kenneth Copeland shaped a new "Prosperity Theology," convincing millions of Americans that the road to heaven was through affluence. Jesus's social gospel, that pitied the poor and unworthy, was replaced with the prosperity gospel— to be rich was good. The environmental or social costs of consumerist capitalism would not enter the conversation until the late 1970s.

With a revived Christian presence in the halls of power, consumerism nonetheless became the central goal for Americans in the 1950s. The expectation of material comfort and the pursuit of products through shopping was normalized in the United States, then other Western states, and thereafter almost worldwide. Even those who professed a respect for austere religiosity lived lives revolving around obtaining comforts. Hope for material progress became a new creed. Like Sikhs and Hindus in India, many American Christians were converted to the gospel of wealth—self-help and the pursuit of prosperity paved the path to heaven, particularly for those with power.

With ongoing US and European interventions in the Muslim world, Middle Eastern thinkers detected an existential threat to Islamic identity in the 1950s. Muslim thinkers adopted Western ideas to unshackle their societies, trying Arab Nationalism or Socialism to unite Muslims, though both failed to unify diverse Muslim populations. Others argued fundamentalist Islam ought to guide Muslim life. Iran's Ayatollah Khomeini and Egypt's Sayyid Qutb cited Muslim traditions as a guide to morality. Formed in embryo in the 1950s, premised on unguarded abhorrence for Western imperialism, consumerism, and *secularism*, these purist philosophies would

Figure 3.4 Iranian Revolution citizens hold a portrait of Ruhollah Khomeini during a pro-Khomeini demonstration in Tehran. (Christine Spengler/Sygma/Sygma via Getty Images.)

later develop into anti-Western, jihadism. Osama Bin Laden would reshape Qutb's ideas to inspire Al-Qaeda in the 1980s.

In the 1950s, conformity was required worldwide, particularly in Communist nations where counterculture ideas were impossible to express. In 1957, China's Communist elites persecuted intellectuals mercilessly in the Hundred Flowers Campaign, condemning half a million people who would not conform to Maoist ideology to a life of hell in labor camps. Soviet critics dared offer timid opposition only after Stalin's death in 1953. The proudly anti-intellectual Nikita Khrushchev allowed thinkers, artists, and writers such as the long-suffering Alexander Solzhenitsyn the freedom to question power, though only moderate dissent transpired. A stifling compliance pervaded all Communist societies, but also many Western cultures like Ireland, Poland, and much of Latin America. There, ancient ways of thinking persisted through conservative, patriarchal rule and the inflexibility of the Catholic Church. The 1950s "return to normalcy" demanded passivity, not questioning authority, in Western and Communist nations.

Of course, some questioned conformism and consumerism in the 1950s, often reshaping ancient denunciations of greed into secular ideologies. The Frankfurt School, led by Theodore Adorno, reworked Marxist critiques of capitalist consumerism. Adorno pointed out that US culture was in fact an industry that kept people satiated with products to deflect minds from complex thought, numbing the human intellect to focus on gratuitous acquisition instead.

The ideas of the Italian Antonio Gramsci surfaced in the 1950s to promote cultural dissent. Gramsci died fighting the injustice of imprisonment by Fascists in the 1930s, and his philosophy, like Sartre's, was one of practice rather than mere contemplation, inspiring young people to question materialism and power. His influence became more apparent in the 1960s, amid a wider recognition that subordinates in all societies accepted their lowly position as if it were natural. The masses, it was argued, blindly offered their consent to ruling elites in the West such that force was rarely required. Capitalist, Communist, religious elites—all hoodwinked the masses into complicit conformity. In line with these new approaches to understanding power in the 1950s, the Anglo-Russian thinker Isaiah Berlin reclaimed the notion of liberty, expanding it to mean freedom not just from overt oppression, but also the freedom to direct one's life path through personal choice.

Such thinkers countered the *dominant paradigm*, the common sense, everyday worldview that seemed natural, sensible and obvious to most people. This skeptical worldview would become common currency by the end of the century. Similarly, subversive thought emerged in the guise of influential rebels in colonized nations, whose central existential predicament was a lack of power—the struggle to gain sovereign independence from Western intrusion. Colonized peoples from India to Africa to Southeast Asia dissented against the status quo in an all-encompassing ideology of post-colonialist upheaval in the 1960s.

As the 1950s ended, a revolution in thought brewed that would disperse worldwide. American universities and popular culture provided the wellspring for new attitudes toward others that would flower in the 1960s. Whereas prewar, most Noble Prizewinners in physics, chemistry, or medicine were European, postwar American researchers dominated research and ensuing acclamation. College-educated people, particularly in the United States, were slowly inclined toward a healthy distrust of any type of certitude.

Given that important scholars like Martin Heidegger supported Nazism and its all-encompassing ideas about existence, postwar uncertainty seemed preferable to any grand, sweeping theory of life. The psychologist Steven Pinker sums up the dangers of affirming totalizing worldviews over pluralistic approaches:

When it comes to the history of violence, the significant distinction is not one between theistic and atheistic regimes. It's the one between regimes that were based on demonizing, utopian ideologies (including Marxism, Nazism, and militant religions) and secular liberal democracies that are based on the ideal of human rights.[6]

1960s—Counterculture and criticism

In a century where absolutist views predominated, sparks of light emerged in the 1960s. Even while American, Muslim, Soviet, and Chinese elites propagated conformity and conservatism, Western culture brought alternatives to tradition. American films and music, long censored by traditionalists to maintain middle-of-the-road tastes, promoted new ideas and new forms of behavior, premised on a trenchant criticism of convention. Rock 'n' roll music and film conveyed an emotional yearning for a new type of freedom, forming a counterculture identity that proclaimed difference as a norm, and which would convert millions after the 1960s.

Critical thinkers, adolescents, and mischief-makers all over the world would emulate Hollywood genres, obsessively caricaturing characters invented in the minds of US playwrights and writers. American music would transform world music. American culture would become so universal it could be only labeled Coca-Colonization. The notion of an "American century" was palpable by the 1960s, even if much of the art was from Europe and the music of African origin.

The United States had of course been racist from its inception and remained so, its prosperity partly premised upon indigenous annihilation and lucrative slave labor. American authors like James Fennimore Cooper had influenced the young Adolf Hitler, advocating murderous ways to eradicate inferior native peoples in the 1880s. American culture did though respond to the questions raised by Nazi Germany's genocide. It had to. African American soldiers returned from fighting against Nazi prejudice to life in a segregated, violently intolerant nation—a paradox they pointed out to white people in power. President Harry Truman desegregated the US military in disgust at Nazi doctrine, but the international community mocked postwar American racism. The Soviet Union, in particular, reproached American bigotry toward those of color (overlooking Communist intolerance of course).

Nevertheless, a new worldview took shape in 1960s America, with African American civil rights activists leading the way. 1954's *Brown v Board of Education* legal ruling prompted colossal cultural conflict, with progressives working to challenge institutional racism in defense of human rights and respect for difference. Civil rights leaders like Martin Luther King influenced millions, changing worldviews through peaceful means, influenced by Mahatma Gandhi, whose nonviolence had ejected the British from South Asia.

Intolerance came under the spotlight in the 1960s unlike never before. In 1964 the Democrat president, Lyndon Johnson, passed the Civil Rights Act, as the previously racist Democrat Party subsequently supported minority rights. Black activists and other counterculture groups inspired a reevaluation of US military policy, which at the time was crushing Vietnamese peasants in the name of anticommunism. As US foreign policy created enemies all over the world, accusations of hypocrisy beset US culture both within and outside the nation.

American culture was split down the middle thereafter. The white South left the Democrats in droves for the sin of supporting civil rights, and many in the South committed intensely to revivalist conservative Protestant thinking. Between the 1930s and 1980s, explicitly antiscience, antievolution preachers such as Billy Sunday and Billy Graham shaped the views of tens of millions of Americans, frustrating the spread of evidence-based ideas on the human species, human history, and attitudes toward others.

The civil rights movement of the 1960s, with its radical new conception of human rights and equality, invited great violence and a bitter backlash from conservative whites. While American cities and universities became bastions of new ideas and ethical schools, mainstream culture did not. Protestant movements had long imposed racist Jim Crow laws and harsh anti-immigrant views, preserving a racist culture in much of the nation. The determined organization of the Ku Klux Klan revived in the 1960s, dismissing ideas of racial equality, swaying millions of white people, even when they had no official connection to the organization.

Also, in the 1960s, arguably the most influential religious institution on earth, the Vatican in Rome, began to acknowledge change and respond to secular, counterculture critiques. Surprising millions, Vatican II in 1959 accepted the virtue of other faiths, encouraged dialogue and recognized that the modern world necessitated change for humanity. The pope declared that the church must focus on freedom, human rights, and social justice, not just mere faith. The papacy's new *Liberation Theology* finally aimed to help the poor and to advocate for global human rights, in line with secular programs. Though the conservative Pope John Paul II reversed course in the 1970s, Vatican II espoused perhaps the first liberal doctrines in Catholic Church history.

Some religious leaders such as Gandhi criticized extremism and intolerance. Gandhi believed in a universal truth force, *Satyagraha*, greater than all people and religions:

> *What Is Hinduism? If I were asked to define the Hindu creed, I should simply say: Search after Truth through non-violent means. A man may not believe even in God and still call himself a Hindu . . . Hinduism is the most tolerant of all religions. Its creed is all embracing . . . Hinduism can and must coexist with all other worldviews.*[7]

Traditional religions maintained traditional views on the roles of men and women however. Gandhi's Hindu culture, like Christianity and Islam, remained orthodox toward the question of women's rights. But in the 1960s *feminism* emerged as a central cultural force in the West, targeting the eradication of long-standing customs that perpetuated inequality and injustice toward women. The movement infiltrated every aspect of life after Simone de Beauvoir published *The Second Sex* in 1949. The revolutionary claim that "the personal is political" derived from the feminist movement; pointing out not only to women but to all subjugated people that political engagement was necessary to alter personal status. The effects of this transformative approach to society, family, and the nation have since forced a reexamination of gender norms worldwide. It is possibly the greatest intellectual transformation of the past 50 years.

New technologies such as print literature, television, and radio circulated new principles like feminism or human rights globally. Artists, activists, musicians, and reformers questioned simplistic claims that freedom had been achieved in the capitalist West, let alone elsewhere, pointing out how few enjoyed autonomy. Even with the inevitable backlash to such positions, they spread irresistibly in ensuing decades.

In the 1960s, deference toward traditional thought diminished like never before. Millions of young people, many derisively labeled hippies, focused on attaining new forms of freedom, aspiring to a life of joy, of hedonism, love, and understanding. Ideas from Indian traditions and Eastern philosophy, that long preceded Christianity and Islam, augmented Western worldviews for the first time. Some, including elites like Timothy Leary at Harvard, instilled veneration for drug

Figure 3.5 Members of the National Women's Liberation Movement, on an equal rights march from Speaker's Corner to No.10 Downing Street, to mark International Women's Day, London, March 6, 1971. (Daily Express/Hulton Archive/Getty Images.)

culture, taking mind-altering chemicals to release the stress of everyday life, to access deeper levels of consciousness, and heighten awareness. Though all cultures had long found ways to alter the mind, drugs were no longer the realm of shamans but were now readily available in cities. Though the health effects were largely negative, drug usage opened minds to new possibilities, new potentials and new levels of understanding.

The 1960s brought a vast generational shift, creating more open attitudes to sexuality, experimentation, and the enjoyment of pleasure in general. Guilty feelings passed down from 1950s conservative culture were resisted, as higher expectations and self-gratification become a motivating force in ensuing decades. Rejecting inherited wisdoms, many people found a break with the past ordinary rather than alarming. But the abrupt 1960s critique of received wisdom predictably provoked a backlash from those concerned about excessively free attitudes and unrestrained opinions. Traditional understanding did not vanish, and major religions continued to shape the world in the ensuing decades. Indeed, the largest religions responded vigorously in the 1970s, adapting to social change, bringing revival among Christians in the United States and Muslims worldwide.

1970s—Revival of established ideas

Though the most fervent adherents of Christianity and Islam continued to depict followers of other faiths as infidels, there were deep similarities in the two major world religion's approaches. Spiritual leaders in both the Muslim and the Christian worlds feared experimentation and modern ideas immensely. American Conservatives reshaped the world's most powerful country into a highly religious culture, where a non-Christian president remains unimaginable. Fundamentalist Muslim leaders meanwhile planted the seeds of a global jihadi movement that would bear fruit after the 1980s (largely in response to US overseas interventions).

Adherents to both faiths grew in the 1970s. Much of the north and east of the African continent was already Muslim, having been converted in recent centuries. In the century before 1970, more than half of the African continent had been converted to Christianity by Western colonizers or African evangelists. Following the First World War millions of Africans were raised Christian, as the continent shifted from local customs to Christianity. The African continent remains a central site of conflict for ethno-religious and tribal conflict, with political divisions exacerbated by Christian–Muslim hostility. While religious elites are often Christian or Muslim, tribal animism still infuses life for most people, with scarce attention paid to issues such as civil rights or equality.

Protestant Christianity surged in the 1970s, as US based Protestant sects found converts in Africa and in Latin America, and pastors deliberately challenged the Catholic Church's centuries of intellectual influence in that continent. Nevertheless, most people in Latin America remained Catholic, while most in India were still raised Hindu, and those in Southeast Asia as Buddhist.

> In response to the 1960s, Protestantism revived under newly energized and increasingly politicized American Christians, firmly convinced of the conviction that Jesus's return beckoned. Jerry Falwell, the extremely influential leader of millions of evangelical Americans, wrote in 1984:
>
> > *If we are going to save America and evangelize the world, we cannot accommodate secular philosophies that are diametrically opposed to Christian truth . . . We need to pull out all the stops to recruit and train 25 million Americans to become informed pro-moral activists whose voices can be heard in the halls of Congress . . . I am convinced that America can be turned around if we will all get serious about the Master's business . . . We need an old-fashioned, God-honoring, Christ-exalting revival to turn American back to God. America can be saved!*[8]

Officially atheist Communist states coincidentally faltered by the 1970s. Though religion was officially banned in the USSR, Orthodox Christianity persisted in providing meaning for people in Eastern Europe. Catholics in Poland worked successfully to oust Communists after the late 1970s. Though Communist antipathy to religion lessened Christianity's official influence until the 1980s in the USSR, the church remained a powerful presence. Orthodoxy immediately rebounded when Communism fell in 1991, reemerging as a conservative force for antidemocracy in support of authoritarian leadership. Orthodox churchmen had always countered freethinking and independent thought, and the establishment continues in this vein into the present, often in suspiciously similar ways to their Communist predecessors—countering heterodox ideas, civil rights, and human rights.

Religious extremists generally spread intolerance worldwide after the 1970s. Muslims working toward peace with Israel met with hostility from Islamic jihadists, one of whom murdered Egypt's president, Anwar Sadat, in 1981 for aspiring to peace with Israel. Middle Eastern militants inspired millions of people to focus their minds on an anti-Western ideology, culminating in the September 2001 attacks in New York. Millions of disenchanted Muslims found purpose in fighting to undo historical injustices, threatening civil society worldwide through ISIS and Al Qaeda.

The Muslim world suffered most from political and religious extremism. Though instability in the region was impacted by Western intervention, long-standing divisions within Islam intensified the violence. Conflict exists in every place where Muslim societies intersect with Christians, Hindus, Jews, or secular cultures. And majority Sunni Muslims fought with Shiite Muslims for over a millennia prior to Western involvement; Sunni Turkey and Saudi Arabia both exist in opposition to

Shiite Iran. For centuries, Sunni Ottomans dominated much of the Middle East. Turkey's "modern founder" Kemal Ataturk had pushed Islam out of politics and society and secularized the state in 1923. Turkey thereafter became the most powerful, literate, and wealthiest Muslim nation. Turkish women gained voting rights, the veil was no longer required, polygamy was banned, and civil rights were expanded.

This was the exception, however. Vast areas of the Muslim world have not modernized, suffering from economic and intellectual poverty as well as the interventions of more powerful states. Though there have always been forward thinking scholars, they rarely hold power. Enlightened Islamic thinkers had long tried to advocate tolerance and modernism. In 1900, the Iranian philosopher Al-Afghani blamed Muslim religious leaders (the Ulema) for resisting modernity, arguing that those who pretended gas, modern medicine, and physical science were of no use failed to understand the principles behind the modern world. He, like many moderate Islamic thinkers since, railed against *fundamentalist* attitudes espoused by many religious leaders.

Fundamentalism—political, economic, secular, or religious—is perhaps the greatest challenge to peace in the modern world, and little-known thinkers often shape the minds of millions. The thoughts of one Muslim scholar, Sayyid Qutb, have convinced groups such as Al Qaeda and ISIS that the only way to live life is through the conversion of infidels and violent resistance. Qutb wrote:

> *When Islam makes it declaration for the liberation of mankind on earth, so that they may only serve God alone, those who usurp God's authority try to silence it. They will never tolerate it or leave it in peace. Islam will not sit idle either. It will move to deprive them of their power so that people can be freed of their shackles. This is the permanent state of affairs which necessitates the continuity of jihad until all submission is made to God alone.[9]*

The outcome of such thought was the attack in September 2001 that killed 3,000 American citizens, which has in turn beckoned the US military into Afghanistan and Iraq since. Al Qaeda was rooted in decades of Muslim humiliation in the face of twentieth-century Western power. Islamic terrorists, like many Americans, saw 9/11 as a religious matter, intertwined even as it was with long-standing geostrategic, political, and economic tensions. The attacks prompted a colossal and immediate response from the US military, encouraged by a Congress where over 90 percent profess to be practicing Christians, ordered by a president, George Bush, who was openly evangelical and who used the term "crusades," harkening back to a thousand years of Christian–Muslim enmity.

As monotheistic fundamentalists fought to maintain traditional beliefs, other ancient traditions such as Daoism and Buddhism spread their influence, altering lifestyles and spiritual attitudes in industrial nations. Physical pastimes such as yoga and meditation spread from East to West, replacing prayer or churchgoing to attain mindfulness. A new appreciation of Eastern wisdom seeped into minds worldwide, as greater cultural interaction came from cheap air travel, communication technologies, and intensified interest in other societies. TV documentaries were produced and aired with the express purpose of inciting curiosity toward other people, other worlds, and other mind-sets. By the 1990s, the Internet opened up the possibility of learning about any culture in seconds.

The Cold War disrupted traditional belief systems considerably. Western capitalism undermined global traditions through both resource extraction and intellectual innovation, while Communism brought non-religious Marxist ideology. In the face of this juggernaut of modernity, indigenous leaders worldwide fought to maintain long-standing cultural traditions. But in societies from Africa to the Middle East and Asia, trust in the social guidance and wisdom of elders diminished when modernity arrived. For indigenous people forced to move to cities for work, trust in the visions of ancestral leaders did not always hold up in the face of scientific modernity. Faced however with the disruption and intellectual trauma of modernity, literacy levels remained low in most traditional societies.

In Communist states, a callous disregard for life stained the century. A certain irony exists here, as Russian authors had long asked some of the deepest questions about existence. Writers such as Leo Tolstoy and Fyodor Dostoevsky led the twentieth-century inquiry into truth, consciousness, and the unpredictable nature of being through powerful works of literature read worldwide. Soviet postwar culture however, hindered individual freedom of thought, even though it provided education and appreciation for (Soviet) theatre, art, and film.

Communist rulers firmly closed avenues for critical thought and dissent. Though Hitler normally leaps to mind, Stalin and Mao were numerically far worse murderers. Both brought physical sufferings on more people, quieted thought for longer, and killed in far greater numbers than even the Nazis. In the USSR, even though scientific thought thrived due to Cold War competition, Stalinist orthodoxy murdered over 20 million people who dared to defy authority. Russians and minorities throughout the USSR endured decades of paranoia, where state spies inhibited creative thought. Writers and artists were sent to prison gulags through the 1970s and human rights abuses were ubiquitous. In China, even more were killed than in the Soviet Union. Maoist ideology wiped out the intelligentsia, as thinking people had to worship Mao or remain silent. In Mao's 1960s Cultural Revolution, teachers, scholars, engineers, and other contemplative people were executed en masse. The sound of party platitudes silenced thought, while the modern world left China behind.

While new intellectual approaches swept the postwar world, intemp/ worldviews also grew, driving people to commit deadly acts with no regard for life. There was however a growing proportion of religiously unaffiliated people worldwide, reflecting disenchantment with all kinds of ideologies, religious or secular. Cultural changes seeded in the 1960s instilled a new appreciation for a pluralism of worldviews, and universal principles such as equality and environmental justice spread slowly. By the late 1970s, openness and dissent in democratic nations reached new levels, pushing forward possibilities for human creativity and countering elite ideas worldwide. Since the 1980s, respect for environmental conservation, women's rights, minorities, gay rights and difference in general spread worldwide.

2. Since the 1980s: Critical Thinking and its consequences

This tense dance—between customary certainties and intellectual possibilities— continued after 1980, bringing immense and predictable disagreement. The central innovation in postwar cultural criticism coalesced under the umbrella term Critical Thinking, which seeped into minds of millions though education, communication, and media technologies. Critical Thinking shaped new attitudes to evaluating truth or falsity, and it foregrounded new principles of human rights and equality.

Critical Thinking

Probing received wisdom

Between 1900 and the 1970s, time-honored understandings of the human experience were routinely questioned. Everything formerly held dear was considered anew, and both religious and secular leaders were obliged to speak to more literate, curious populations. Both rational science and blind faith had led humanity down the path of war, gulags, and genocide. By the 1980s, all overarching theories succumbed to criticism, and all intellectual systems rooted in one specific region seemed unconvincing to thinkers with a more global approach.

Recognizing the regional biases motivating ancient worldviews, a new approach to learning and understanding developed after the 1960s, broader in scope, multiethnic, gender neutral, and universal. *Critical Theory* emerged as an expression of various new ways of critical thinking, emanating from universities and thought leaders around the world. Building on ideas of earlier decades, it conceded that no single, coherent explanation for life's complexity could be attained. The contradictory nature of the human mind could not be explained by simple traditions or age-old conventions. Acceptance of ambiguity seemed more appropriate.

Language and knowledge

In the 1980s, a new, profoundly relativistic school of thought emerged, labeled *postmodernism*. Thinkers in this vein underscored the fact that all existence was subjective, everything was relative—there was in fact no "real," no "truth." Intellectuals attempted to grasp the connection between logic, language, and thought as it pertains to meaning in life; most leaned toward an acceptance of incoherence and fragmentation. Postmodernists argued that language may not necessarily offer meaning or even refer to the actual world. Language, signs, values, and symbols shifted according to this view. Science, religion, life itself—all were mere abstractions, without inherent meaning.

Ludwig Wittgenstein inspired this outlook, highlighting the extreme difficulty of expressing and explaining private thoughts, let alone whole thought systems. In his view, each culture played a game that worked for them; Western societies had their version, as did others. "What does meaning mean anyway?" was a central question for Wittgenstein. Jacques Lacan, who lectured for decades in Western universities, emphasized the importance of psychoanalysis, of exploring the psyche to understand human actions, questioning the very notion of the "self." Jacques Derrida claimed that all humans were trapped within the constraints of language, unable to clearly perceive others or meanings. Such philosophies revived claims made earlier in the century that language is arbitrary, with no firm relationship to reality. Derrida's *deconstruction* became an important method to comprehend texts or writings passed down through history. Time, space, place, or order were not part of the human condition here, but were instead part of a stuttering and unfathomable general complexity.

A mixture of pessimism and humility undergirded such theories, derived from the ideas of Einstein, who had shown that the physical world was far more complex than had been previously imagined. By mid-century, concerns about humanity motivated new study into the knowledge of knowledge - via the field of epistemology. Scholars like Edmund Gettier presented a reluctant acceptance that humans can perhaps know little with certainty, refuting the optimistic, empirical basis of much earlier thought.

By the 1960s, Karl Popper's concept of *falsification* showed that theories behind science, or anything else for that matter, could only be sustained if they could not be contradicted. Along with Thomas Kuhn, Popper noticed that systems, or paradigms, of thought were created in human minds, in societies. This included scientific knowledge as well as ancient traditions. Scientists, like religious leaders or philosophers, he noted, were fearful of overhauling established systems of thought into which they had been socialized and educated, taking for granted much that they assumed to be true.

One philosopher, Michel Foucault, influenced countless teachers w.. interpretation premised on this unpredictability. Foucault criticized prevalent assumptions in areas such as sanity, conformity, and discipline, questioning traditional morals and exposing flaws in long-accepted norms in state-enforced societies. Foucault claimed that freedom had been gained nowhere on earth, in the West or otherwise—those who dissent are always insane or dangerous to ruling elites, who propagate ideology to promote conformity. His notion of *governmentality* stimulated new questions about the capacity of states and those in power to shape the minds of those they lead. With Derrida, he popularized the notion that most modern ideas stemmed from "dead white males," though both preferred not to critique oppressive ideas outside of the Western tradition.

Postmodernists were skeptical about rationality and true knowledge. Highly influential thinkers like Jurgen Habermas criticized the postmodern intellectual turn, remaining optimistic that Enlightenment notions of rational thought still provided a path to understanding and truth. Habermas pointed out that only the democratic public sphere provided opportunity for free thought. Even if Western institutions' supposed freedoms deceived many into apathy or were at times hypocritical, they allowed for such concepts as postmodernism to flourish.

Postmodernists were also criticized for a detachment from everyday political life, and such ideas took decades to move from the ivory tower to teachers, parents, and politicians, or into mainstream thinking. All these theorists though, however abstruse their writings, believed it essential to question orthodox thought. Such thinkers therefore represented the cutting edge of a new discourse of criticism and open inquiry.

Education

Simultaneously, the half-century after the 1960s brought more state-provided general education than ever in human history, offering a heady mixture of modern ideas and faith-based tutoring in the West and industrializing countries. In poorer nations, influential thinkers such as Paolo Freire explicitly connected liberty and rights with literacy after the 1960s. Freire criticized current learning styles, where educators "poured ideas into student's heads" from a position of power to support elite control. Instead he contended, an interactive, reciprocal learning environment should take place in what he coined *critical pedagogy*. This notion of "student-centered education" derived from Freire's experiences with colonized peasants in South America, who seemingly accepted domination and the ideas of the powerful. Freire claimed that both colonized people and students in general must avoid submission and engage in active engagement with ideas. Education should activate the mind rather than fill it with information developed by those in power, whether they be rulers, colonists, or teachers. This was yet another blow to received ideas and ways of learning, and Freire's ideas soon spread to the West.

In parallel, Frantz Fanon's *Wretched of the earth* espoused a new viewpoint to energize the oppressed masses. Speaking for vast global populations who lacked a political voice, Fanon aimed to represent the world's underrepresented people. The ongoing effects of imperialism and colonialism, he claimed, kept colonized people in poverty materially but also intellectually. Fanon advocated violence to counter foreign and state oppression and supported Algerian efforts to oust ruthless French rule. He convinced many that colonized people were entrapped in a psychological colonization that persisted well after independence, though he was widely criticized for calling for violence to effect change.

Civil Rights—speaking truth to power

While Fanon's aggressive activism provided weapons for the weak, others preferred peaceful means. For decades Mahatma Gandhi advocated a higher path toward peace and truth for both the colonized and the beleaguered. He proclaimed enlightened learning came from taking the moral high road, exposing the injustice and hypocrisy of rulers such as the British in India, always speaking truth to power. Education for Gandhi was a form of moral development, not simple knowledge acquisition. Following in Gandhi's footsteps, Martin Luther King's movement to counter white supremacism in 1950s America brought peaceful resistance and a call for education with civil rights. King and other activists transformed US culture immensely, also inspiring millions of people of color worldwide.

Such ideals had to face entrenched opposition: Gandhi died at the hands of a fanatical Hindu in 1948; a white racist assassinated King in 1968. Both though, had attuned millions to a life of peaceful protest, even while suffering violent deaths. While King fought for justice, Nelson Mandela endured 24 years of unjust imprisonment in proudly racist South Africa. Mandela would be freed in 1994, becoming an international icon for peace, equality, and racial tolerance. Though two of the most principled, peace-loving people of the century died at the hands of extremists, and another endured unmerited imprisonment their ideas nonetheless resonated worldwide.

Gendered worldviews

Great men surely shaped history, but in the 1970s some noted the stark fact that men had constructed all existing belief systems. Feminist thinkers revealed that masculine worldviews had been passed down from generation to generation with little scrutiny. Female scholars pointed out that the very origin of historically literate societies had seen power wrenched away from a female-friendly, pre-state world. Even the notion

Figure 3.6 London, England, 1951. Italian educational reformer Maria Montessori, who evolved the Montessori method of teaching children. (Popperfoto/Getty Images.)

of the written word and its indelible connection to the patriarchal state had generated a male-centered view of the world, expressed over the last 4,000 years in almost all societies. In the decades following the Second World War, perspectives from the minds of influential women challenged the restricted views offered by men over the centuries. Almost all philosophers who attempted to explain existence prior to 1945 were men after all—most of whom as it happened had not married, raised children, or met people of different walks of life.

From the 1960s, a widespread worldwide assault on masculinized, sexist thought developed. Following the two world wars, men in power struggled to explain away women's contribution in industrial nations. And by the 1960s, a new generation appeared more willing to acknowledge the capabilities of women. By the 1970s, women the first time in history attained widespread education, and as education became a system of thinking into itself, women reshaped the field enormously. The nineteenth-century Swedish writer Ellen Keys had proposed that humanity had positive potential beyond warmongering and violence, and her ideas regarding attitudes to child rearing and schooling reformed centuries of masculine "punishment and discipline" approaches. Sociologists and psychologists expanded her ideas to ask how much the manner of raising shaped the nature of an adult. Theorizing childhood as a realm of potential and creativity—opposing Sigmund Freud's traumatic interpretation and welcoming Anna Freud's sympathetic approach—Keys advocated for treating all children as unique individuals. She promoted the development of *actualized* beings, through a culture of affection and education, nurturing the young to foster a better world, replacing traditional rote learning and punishment with creative learning and reflection. These were heady ideas at the time. Most men doubted their efficacy.

The enormously influential Maria Montessori also promulgated a child-centered education, promoting individual initiative, and recognition of varied style of capabilities. Most Western democracies passed social legislation to promote positive childrearing and education based on the philosophies of Keys and Montessori by the 1970s. Margaret Mead's approach to learning also bore fruit in this decade, based upon the claim that children must be taught *how* to think, instead of being told *what* to think. The UN Declaration of Human Rights provided widespread legitimacy for such ideas under the auspices of global democratic education.

Few could conceive that gender shaped outlooks before the 1960s, even though systematic ideas passed down from Confucius and Aristotle to Mohammed and Einstein were always male. Secular political and economic systems were also run by men, based on male theorists, and men dominated military and technological programs. Though faith provided succor for women, religious traditions had never focused on the condition of women materially or ethically. East and South Asian traditions, like the monotheistic religions of Christianity, Islam, and Judaism, were mostly male-dominated. This injection of female perspectives into male intellectual systems was a revolutionary transformation.

Human rights and poverty

In the last decades of the century, *feminism* affected people worldwide, be they advocates or opponents. It impacted all other fields of thought, bringing changes in sexual attitudes, power relations, work conditions, and family life. After the 1980s, feminist interpretations of society, of history and of existence began to offer wider perceptions for the first time. By the 1990s, female US writers like bell hooks popularized notions of education as resistance, criticizing male norms inherent to capitalism, gender, and racism as obstacles to true knowledge or ethics. And as female thinkers generated a new gender-neutral worldview, women's rights and educat became increasingly entwined with human rights.

Human rights activism increased enormously after the 1970s, as the global demands of liberation movements increased. The Helsinki Final Act of 1975, ostensibly a superpower agreement about Cold War issues, helped establish the idea of human rights across Europe and later the world. It provided a crucial voice for oppressed Communist peoples, then moved globally to become a transnational human rights movement emerged. The novel idea that *all* humans, men and women, possessed certain rights under international law extended globally, with advocacy from civil rights groups. New aspirational ethical norms and standards transcended past practices. International groups such as Amnesty International exposed state brutality, pressured rogue governments, and altered expectations about power and society.

As more women worldwide gain education and claim positions of power, change seems inevitable. Africa's first female head of state, Ellen Johnson Sirleaf, provocatively argued that "Women work harder. And women are more honest; they have less reasons to be corrupt."[10]

Soon, human rights were connected with the social environment. The United Nations HDI—Human Development Index—developed in Pakistan in 1990, providing new metrics to evaluate "success" such as education and life expectancy, using universal measures readily comparable across societies that transcended economic calculations such as GDP or National Income.[11]

As with past power imbalances, certain parts of the world enjoyed more human rights than others. Inequality, poverty, and gender divisions remained far greater in non-Western and nondemocratic states, with a tiny elite possessing dominion over the majority in most states. Non-Western societies remain highly unequal; presently the only Muslim countries that rank in the top forty in terms of overall population health are the UAE, Brunei, and Qatar—all small nations that reaped vast windfalls from oil sales. Education and literacy show similar indices of low development across the Muslim world; many Asian, Latin American, and African societies are similarly low in ranking. The top fifteen societies are all Western, European, or industrial nations, located in Northwestern Europe or Scandinavia.

History has shaped present circumstances. Positive scores for human rights and overall well-being are manifest in developed, industrial nations. Those parts of the world that were colonized in the nineteenth century generally embrace low commitment to human rights, and nations with a Communist history show little inclination toward extending rights. Notably, the most traditional, religious nations on earth are consistently the least committed to human rights or women's issues. Slavery still exists worldwide, though it is usually a furtive enterprise. And though serfdom is now inconceivable in industrialized countries it still pervades in poorer nations. Workers' rights drive political conversations in developed nations, though not in LDCs. The extent to which these ongoing disparities stem from the legacy of foreign domination or from local cultural tendencies is unclear. Centuries of foreign rule certainly hindered poorer nations in many ways, but vast differences exist between industrial and developing societal attitudes toward human rights and poverty, even as the decades pass.

A literate worldview

A defining distinction between developed and undeveloped nations over the century is found in literacy levels. Twentieth-century minds could cultivate new worldviews only because the ability to read rose drastically. Through education and literacy, individuals were socialized into receiving new ideas along with old ones. World literacy has almost doubled recently, from roughly 40 percent of world population in 1960 to over 80 percent by 2010. Education—higher education, particularly—became the central means of accessing new knowledge, providing more people with the means to question power. Literacy and freedom of thought became a key aspiration for modernizing societies in the past 50 years. The UN envoy, Gordon Brown, declared education as *the* global civil rights movement for the new century.

Emulating a long-standing tradition in places like Scotland and Germany, Western states required compulsory education after the 1870s, with the United States passing laws to enforce state education in 1918. Levels of education increased sharply by the 1960s, first in Western and industrial nations, thereafter globally. Consequently, musicians, poets, painters, authors, and artists of all types could scrutinize the suppositions of time-honored worldviews, daring to propose, as the poet Shelley had, that poetry, or the arts, explained the world more comprehensively than politics. The history and structure of religious texts, the use of language, turns of phrases, the purported meanings of the canons of history—all were now open for criticism, reinterpretation, and if necessary, dismissal after the 1960s.

Imagined worlds

Reading was crucial. Reading demanded thought about the human condition, opening doors of empathy toward those in unfamiliar societies or those in other social classes. Intellectuals noted that the ability to read novels altered worldviews imperceptibly, developing new ways of seeing the world. This important idea first surfaced in England at a particularly dark moment in history, when, in the 1940s, the

Figure 3.7 Colombian writer and Nobel Prize in literature winner Gabriel Garcia Marquez. (Ulf Andersen/Getty Images.)

cultural critic F. R. Leavis posited that reading literature spread universal ethics and values. In the 1960s Jean-Francois Lyotard developed the theory that the diffusion of knowledge to laypeople splintered overarching narratives, calling it a form of mass emancipation.

By the 1970s, innumerable authors invented new types of imaginary, but nonetheless forceful, worlds in affordable paperback publications. Stories now shaped the average person's mind in the manner in which traditional narratives always had, except that now readers could explore distant peoples, characters, and ideas. Where previously people only understood local cultures, they could now access far away, unfamiliar worlds.

Non-Western authors influenced a worldwide audience through acclaimed works after the 1970s. Chinua Achebe's work uncovered the impossibility of transitioning into Western modernity for tribal Africans, exploring the lived experience of colonized people on their own terms, not those of the West. Achebe too noted the power of language to exert control, particularly the language of a foreign ruler. Luminaries such as V. S. Naipaul and Jamaica Kincaid showed how Caribbean society still wrestled with the colonial experience, exhibiting how history had hindered colonized societies under foreign influence. Gabriel Garcia Marquez's mixture of reality and mysticism projected a dissatisfaction with Western impositions, proclaiming the indigenous literature of Latin America peoples, selling in huge numbers worldwide.

ghly literate cultures continued to produce great works. US literature rose to a new level of influence after the 1960s, as giants like William Faulkner and Tennessee Williams demonstrated a critical new consciousness of race, gender, and class. Williams's works were turned into Hollywood classics, exposing a wide global population to questions of sexuality, sanity, and social hypocrisy. Ralph Ellison brought new awareness of the contribution of African Americans to US culture, and James Baldwin brought activism and a commitment to social justice to the minds of millions through his writing. As a gay black man, Baldwin's work symbolized ongoing tensions between a new culture of self-indulgence and acceptance, and the persistence of restrained behavior, intolerance, and a fear of difference. More prosaic writers like Barbara Cartland and Danielle Steel sold hundreds of millions of romance novels worldwide, increasing literacy while entertaining mostly female readers.

English writers such as J. R. R. Tolkien and C. S. Lewis were also read by hundreds of millions of people, their fantasy worlds releasing minds from the drudgery of everyday life. These authors and many others pointed readers toward a humanistic, literary universalism that transcended any one state or culture. Imagination was central: repetition of past truisms was subtly rebuked. Agatha Christie introduced crime novels to worldwide audiences through the century, and as the new century turned in 2000, J. K. Rowling, a working-class woman, produced the Harry Potter series, selling more books than any other author on earth.

Of course, traditional oral histories and national folk epics were still passed down orally worldwide. Religious stories continued to explain the world to billions, whether they could read or not. Indians are still raised on a steady diet of Hindu nationalist epics that promote cultural pride. Chinese people read billions of copies of Chairman Mao's aphorisms into the 1980s, although the most popular Chinese book of the century was an eighteenth-century family epic *Dream of the Red Chamber*. Muslims, Jews, and Christians worldwide continued to learn stories from ancient scriptures at home and in school. Series such as the Left Behind books reoriented millions of Christian Americans toward a nineteenth-century biblical worldview, a probable reaction to permissive modern literature and 1960s culture.

However, the hugely popular Berenstain Bears series were read by millions of American children. These books, and TV shows such as *Sesame Street*, did not talk of faith, focusing on contemporary issues such as bullying, decision making and self-image instead, actively encouraging literacy. For adults, popular mass literature such as Readers' Digest offered new worlds of learning to those who did not attend college. Secular topics such as nutrition, stress management and healthier lifestyles filled the pages of popular journals, contributing to a general increase in health alongside literacy. Indeed, low literacy has been shown repeatedly to align with lower income, less security, precarious life chances and worse health.

The poorest nations in the world today remain those with the least educa as undeveloped nations censor new or threatening ideas to control literacy, great costs to humanity. Since the early twentieth century, wealthy industrial nations inculcated a modern worldview through mass education, patriotism, and mandatory school attendance. As the twenty-first century arrived, reading became a central characteristic of a modern human identity. Regardless of the type or quality of education, basic literacy changed conceptions of past and present, fostering transformation intrinsic to modernity.

Mind and body

Coincident with rising literacy, science and technology changed all aspects of modern life after the 1960s. Radar and basic computers helped Western democracies defeat totalitarianism, and thereafter, Western governments and universities funded research into both the inner mind and outer space, that would spread worldwide. Jurgen Habermas proposed that science and technology formed a new, systemic worldview, a form of mental organization that overrode all previous systems of thought. New research brought new perspectives. In 1953, work on the sequence of the human gene lead to the discovery of the very structure of life, DNA, meaning that both the origins of the human species and the makeup of the human body were better understood. Scientific learning unleashed new understandings of human brains, organisms and genes, providing new insights into human behaviors, derived not from regional cultures, but from the far prehistorical, evolutionary past.

New realms of knowledge—from atoms to genes, new planets to plate tectonics—determined that deeper mysteries could be found in human nature than earlier thought. In the 1980s, researchers visually mapped the structures of the brain, using computer processing power. By 2000, the Human Genome Project aimed to map all human genes, the grandest biological study in human history. Some humility reemerged regarding the extent of human knowledge. Much clearly lay unexplained in the human body and mind.

Human health

Science thus altered attitudes to well-being and improved health. In 1900, as for millennia, most people lived a day-by-day existence lacking information about health or their body and mind. They pondered questions of family, weather, food, and perhaps life's mysteries, but only a few read anything. Life was slower, and likely more violent, both publicly and privately. When illness came, even the death of a child, it was accepted with resignation. Many natural remedies worked and were used, but life was fatalistic by modern standards. Until medical technology began to counter illness in the mid-twentieth century, there was no expectation that humanity could fight sickness and disease, or find happiness.

After the 1970s, scientific research not only kept billions alive in rich and poor nations, it prompted new attitudes toward health, body, and mind. Personal fulfillment became a central concern for millions worldwide, as state policy and public programs contributed to anticipations of better health and comforts, a new and overwhelmingly positive aspiration for humanity. New research-based medicines developed to cure bodies worldwide. They built on earlier programs. In the first half of the twentieth century, Albert Schweitzer spread Western science to hundreds of millions in Africa. Along with his paternalistic Christian evangelism, he provided medical advice to those he considered backward peoples, nonetheless saving millions of lives with scientific medicine practices.

The contradictions of Schweitzer's outlook symbolize well Western influence in the past century. The discovery of insulin to treat diabetes, the emergence of antibiotics after the 1930s, and the development of new vaccines helped prevent illness or death globally. The development of penicillin in Britain and the United States has saved billions of lives since the 1940s, and by the 1960s, immunization was widely accepted as a global remedy, contributing to population growth, healthier lives and longer life spans. Institutions such as the World Health Organization educate the globe about health, as medical knowledge moved from advanced nations to poorer ones using evidence-based studies. For most of history, witch doctors, elders, healers, or priests attempted to restore sick bodies and such practices persist worldwide in LDCs. In the new century, more people turned to trained doctors, as educated professionals replaced faith healers, ritual or prayer to curing body or mind.

Given the violence of Western colonialism and ensuing Cold War dominion, it is somewhat incongruous that medicine and healthcare from those same aggressor nations supported the birth of up to a billion people in less-developed nations after 1945. Likewise, systematic scientific production of foodstuffs has both nourished and sickened people. Western eating habits, the consumption of cheap, fast-food required vast swathes of land, greatly harming the planet and the bodies of billions. Industrial workers worldwide are now addicted to sugar and red meat. Close to 40 percent of Kuwaitis are obese today due to the introduction of American fast-food since the 1991 war. Such Western eating habits spread globally toward the end of the century, both feeding stomachs and sickening populations. They also impacted the global environment detrimentally.

Environmentalism

Rising literacy and technology clearly improved understanding of the human body. It also brought greater comprehension of human impact on the land that sustains our species. In 1900 as in 1960, few considered the environment worthy of intellectual concern, just as few thought women's conditions or bodily health a pressing issue. By the 1970s, again incongruously, the most robust environmental movements developed in the same industrial nations that abused the land the most, Europe and North America.

Though many people inspired the environmental movement in the 1960s, no single person is responsible for increasing ecological awareness more in the last 50 years than Rachel Carson, who wrote *Silent Spring* in 1961. Her work changed attitudes toward the relationship between industry, wealth, and the ecosystem. Though business and government leaders heavily contested her ideas, openly insulting her assumed female frailty, her work eventually inspired movements such as Greenpeace, organizations like the Sierra Club, and the establishment in the 1970s of the Environmental Protection Agency in the United States. Carson's groundbreaking view that earth was a connected, sensitive ecosystem was buttressed by the apparent fragility of the planet revealed in the globally famous *Blue Marble* picture. Taken in 1972 from space, the image provided a new scale of reflection upon the relatively small planet humans occupied.

In concert with feminism and human rights, *environmentalism* emerged as a prevailing worldview in the final decades of the century, overlapping with traditional views, while standing above various cultural perspectives. The need to react to potential species termination required a new approach. The recognition that the human species could wipe itself out derived partly from new scientific understandings of the role of other species in the environment. Human similarity to animals, demonstrated by genetic studies, signified a new understanding of the wider environment and humans' tenuous position in ecosystems. Although animal rights activism appeared mostly in Western societies, it too represented a striking expression of the extension of environmental awareness and growing rights movements. This new environmental approach somewhat ironically recalled ancient, indigenous practices in preindustrial societies, where animals and plants were central to understandings of life, rituals and practices, not separate from humans.

Knowledge and truth?

The quantity of information flowing into human minds increased so greatly since 1900 that is it almost impossible to measure the shift. The United Nations estimates that in the next few decades more humans will receive formal education than in all of human history! The role of high school and higher education in altering perspectives is easily overlooked, and spending on social infrastructure (such as schools, parks, or housing) is now taken for granted as a function of a modern state.

In the past century, those parts of the world with a culture of education and technical research developed technologies that fed more people and provided a higher quality of living. Those lacking the infrastructure for schooling and university remain mired in poverty for the most part. Since the Second World War, the United States, Western Europe, Japan, Canada, New Zealand, and Australia, and more recently East Asian nations, surged far ahead of the rest of the world in levels of education and living standards, usually with a concurrent commitment to toleration and pluralism, and far greater levels of stability.

Throughout the century, far more information was transmitted into the minds of citizens in modern nation-states than in traditional societies. Informed citizens in turn changed industrial societies. Compulsory education purposely shaped popular views and norms, but ironically could not contain the ensuing criticism of prevailing views that emerged. State education has been criticized for impinging upon individual creativity, for shaping passive consumers and citizens, but the alternative, having no education at all, seems far more dangerous.

National wealth clearly correlates with literacy; nations with low literacy are almost universally impoverished. Poverty and illiteracy are so closely intertwined that 98 percent of the worlds illiterate live in LDCs, and women represent two-thirds of this number, suffering the subsequent pain of poverty and oppression. Calls for literacy as a human right expressly aim to improve life, particularly for women and families, in nations mostly in the Middle East and Africa.

Outside of industrialized nations however, literacy is a relatively new way of shaping opinion. Many LDCs around the world began expanding the spread of literacy only in recent decades. East Asian states such as Japan, Singapore, and Korea supported education and implemented high-tech social and economic systems, rapidly enriching their populations. Japan, in particular, welcomed modernity after 1900 without hesitation, after centuries of isolation. China's population remained low in literacy until the 1970s. Only since 2000 have large numbers of Chinese had access to online information, and many sites remain restricted. Access to education remains low in Eastern Europe after decades of mandatory ideological Communist instruction. Post-Soviet Russia opened the path toward democracy in the 1990s, but since 2000 Russia, while a literate society, has reverted to its traditional control of information, with a surge in orthodox thinking, homophobia, and sexism supported by official church-business-state collusion.

India instituted mass education after independence in 1947, while Pakistan and Central Asia still suffer a general dearth of higher education. Through the end of the century, outside of elite universities, most of Latin America maintained a conservative worldview influenced heavily by the Catholic Church, trusting information from populist and demagogic elites. As in the Muslim world, Central Asia and much of Africa, poorer Latin American nations lack broad higher education, suffering the attendant negative consequences of increased violence and poverty. Just like political power and economic wealth, intellectual mindfulness and information flow were very unevenly distributed on planet earth, in 2017 as in 1900.

The most pervasive means through which vast streams of information flooded human minds since the Second World War was through science-based electronics. Basic expectations for learning changed after 1945, shepherded by revolutionary new forms of information diffusion such as print media, radio, and TV. Since the 1980s, the Internet developed into the most pervasive conveyor of free information in history. Early prototypes had developed in Europe; Britain had free information through Teletext by 1973, and France's renowned Minitel was widespread by 1978. In the 1990s, most Western people spent vast amounts of time on the Internet accessing information at will, a practice almost considered a human right by the twenty-first century.

3. Conclusion: Transformation or permanence?

Undeniably, the past century produced a profusion of hateful and fearful thought systems, both old and new. Minds filled with the deeply held beliefs of many traditions, customs, religions and ideologies, and minds polluted with newly invented ones, conspired to kill an estimated 170 million people since 1900, ruining the lives of countless more. This was a dark century for humanity, and mere ideas motivated much conflict.

Yet in a world historical context, these numbers pale in comparison to the sheer number of people born, as the human population grew from roughly 1 to almost 8 billion in a century. By 2018, everyday people worldwide gained from the spread of information, literacy, awareness and international laws. Ideas of justice spread to shape new norms like antiracism, antidiscrimination, gender equality, environmental sustainability, human rights and animal rights. Freedom of thought became a central expectation for many, even if it remained a dream in some societies.

The violent competition of the twentieth century caused untold miseries, the scale of which was previously unimaginable. Yet life after 2000 for most people was far superior to their ancestor's in 1900. Even in wealthier nations in 1900, most lived in cold, uncomfortable circumstances, deprived of electricity, heating, gas or security, lacking the comforts taken for granted today. Today's developing nations were all poorer in 1900, threatened by disease and famine without hope or solutions. Most of the world's population was illiterate in 1900, and few were accustomed to the notion of using critical faculties to question their position in the world. Few could understand the earth's origins or patterns of development, and most could not envision democracy, civil and human rights, or anticipate economic improvement.

The proportion of people living in poverty continues to decline worldwide, and literacy keeps rising. Even with the horrors of violent conflict, this has been a century of improved conditions for billions.

In both industrial and less-developed nations, a culture of individualism has spread globally. This has conceivably fostered greater selfishness, but a world of selfies and a complicated sense of self also bring more awareness of personal flaws, more selflessness, as well as more self-concern. Although it is an ancient question, we are only beginning to illuminate the inner self, the mind, and our humanity. Many of the ideas explored this century, though innovative, were reworked from earlier antecedents—Plato's insistence on the importance of the inner life, and the difficulty of accessing our own thoughts, still resonates; ancient Indian and Chinese notions of self-worth and a meaningful life never vanished; Buddhists, along with all the Abrahamic traditions, spoke to sympathy, ethics and understanding—such ideas are now repackaged as social or environmental justice.

Indeed, since the 1960s truly global ideas and values merged for the first time. Eastern philosophy and Western began to assimilate, forging new possibilities and asking new questions. Supplementing Western cultural values, Eastern influences such as meditation, yoga, herbal medicines, and natural remedies spread along with more ancient philosophical systems. A new universal consciousness seemed to emerge expressed in the environmental movement.

By the twentieth-first century, a cross fusion of ideas never before seen permeated worldwide, spread quickly and easily by communication technologies. Postures employed by African women to maintain healthy backs informed injured Western workers; the inclination of Asians to squat rather than sit on chairs highlighted the ills of the modern workplace; a slower pace of life in undeveloped nations underscored the frenzied nature of modernity; natural and homeopathic remedies from indigenous societies were found equal or superior to industrial-pharmaceutical drugs: all these notions questioned Western arrogance and assumptions, and complemented the search for satisfaction and meaning in life.

All was not tranquil, of course. Cultures of openness are challenged by those committed to conformity, censorship, and closed rigidity. Cognizant of massacres wrought by Western states in past decades, Al Qaeda and ISIS represent a dissonance with modernity, refusing to accept changing global culture, willing to kill to make the point, to return to some imagined pure Islamic past.

The philosopher Umberto Eco noted in 1980, just as the new fundamentalism was emerging: "People are never so completely and enthusiastically evil as when they act out of religious conviction."[12]

Yet some spiritual leaders recognized human diversity and the need for inclusion and justice. Pope Francis noted in 2013:

> *Men and women are sacrificed to the idols of profit and consumption ....if a computer breaks it is a tragedy, but poverty, the needs and dramas of so many people end up being considered normal. . . . When the stock market drops 10 points in some cities, it constitutes a tragedy. Someone who dies is not news, but lowering income by 10 points is a tragedy! In this way people are thrown aside as if they were trash.*[13]

Through the twentieth century, religious, secular, and philosophical worldviews merged to form new combinations. Pragmatism, relativism, modernism, and nationalism burned new thoughts into millions of minds in the first few decades. Ideologies of homicidal, nationalist militarism terrified humanity in the interwar decades. The post-Second World War era brought a period of rebuilding and conformity, and in the 1960s, a monumental decade of change questioned assumptions anew, overhauling all previous norms. Since the 1970s, cultures of critical thinking have opened possibilities for new beliefs—in human rights, equality, literacy, and education. The idea of terminating poverty and finding peace both within the body and among societies is no longer inconceivable. As such, the philosopher John Rawls recently posited a new ethics of social justice, applicable to all humankind, where consuming, believing and competing must be seconded to consideration and toleration.

In the twenty-first century, much was very wrong with the world, as it was in 1900. As in the political and economic spheres, so much changed, but much endured. Yet a palpable commitment to the global environment, both ecological and social, overrode particularistic views founded on specific religions, nations or ideologies. Both consumerism and environmentalism were the consummation of a century of violence and absolutist thought, yet Critical Thinking, premised on the idea of free thought in an open society, offered hope for pragmatic progress for all humans. Ideas clearly matter. Yet, it seems technology will likely underscore whichever path humanity takes, and to this we turn in Chapter 4.

Key terms

Social Darwinism [160]
Utilitarian [152]
Positivist [152]
Relativism [153]
Pragmatism [156]
Pluralism [157]
Evangelism [159]

Further readings

Barry, Peter, *Beginning Theory: An Introduction to Literary and Cultural Theory*. Manchester University Press, 2009. A short introduction to a complex field of the theories behind modern philosophy that students can grapple with and understand.

Solomon, Robert C., and Kathleen Marie Higgins. *A Short History of Philosophy*. New York: Oxford University Press, 1996. Accessible and detailed analysis of the major philosophical fields, incorporating the importance of non-Western worldviews.

Hedstrom, Matthew S. *The Rise of Liberal Religion: Book Culture and American Spirituality in the Twentieth Century*. Oxford: Oxford University Press, 2012. Intriguing study of religion in the United States and its intersection with popular culture, reading and media. Follows the course of American Protestantism and its interactions with the modern world.

Interlude 3: Certainty

Ideological certainty, fanaticism, and the quest for pluralism

The past century brought relentless efforts to grasp an understanding of existence on earth. Since 1900, such endeavors have restructured human thought in myriad ways, changing humanity and notions of life's purpose. A century ago, the vast majority of humans were acculturated into a restricted regional outlook, based upon homegrown metaphysical certainties. Geographically localized worldviews, informed by place of birth and parental influence, were reinforced by political or religious elites, usually to shape loyalty to tribe, culture, religion, or nation. It is safe to say that most humans' internalized social norms and beliefs about existence unquestioningly, with little new information ruffling their feathers. Today similarly provincial mind-sets endure worldwide, but they are increasingly exposed to a more fragmented, ambiguous understanding of the human environment, incorporating broader perspectives.

Philosophical and intellectual worldviews have changed more since 1900 than in all previous centuries. Traditional views vied with an onslaught of new viewpoints, in particular nationalist ideologies. Technologies such as radio and TV empowered leaders to spread crude, stirring messages to "the people," as centuries-old faiths were submerged by new beliefs in the national superiority or inferiority of different peoples. Philosophical distinctions over issues such as the nature of governance, economy, or society inspired the slaughter of hundreds of millions of humans. Ideas mattered more in the past century.

Twentieth-century totalitarian regimes conveniently substituted conventional religious belief systems with new political ones, namely, Fascism or Communism. Dictator-led regimes outwardly disparaged traditional religions, then replaced them with fanatical new belief systems, essentially imitation religions. Authoritarianism flourished particularly in the Catholic world. Nazism developed in a mixed Protestant-Catholic Germany. Worldwide, Communists were as devoutly fanatical to their thought systems as the most zealous preacher or believer. Rulers in totalitarian states became replacement gods, and knew it all too well: Stalin had studied in a

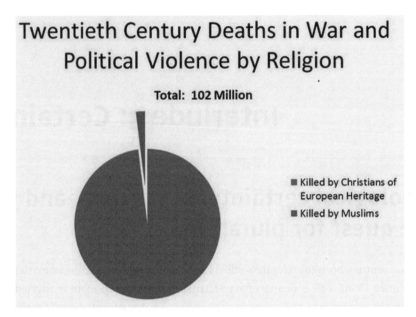

Figure 3.8 Juan Cole's argument about the propensity of Christian states toward violence.

Source: http://www.juancole.com/2013/04/terrorism-other-religions.html

religious seminary, growing up in a fervent Russian Orthodox state; Hitler grew up Catholic in a devoutly Christian nation; and the murderous Communist Pol Pot was a practicing Buddhist, who also studied in a monastery and Catholic School. The scholar Juan Cole points out how much violence stemmed from western, Christian nations in the past century (Figure. 3.8).

Indeed, once the glue of Communist rule fragmented in places like Yugoslavia, religious differences immediately resurfaced. Catholic Croats and Slovenes, Orthodox Serbs, Muslim Albanians, and Bosnians set upon each other, prompting societal collapse and ethnic cleansing. This is perhaps not surprising, given the historical record of religious warfare. Germany's slaughter of 7 million Jews was the result of long-standing religious hatred of Jews for Christians. In 1947, the Indian partition triggered over a million deaths over religious difference; Muslims and Hindus were simply not willing to live together in peace. In places like Afghanistan and Iraq, tribal conflict between Sunni and Shiite Muslims, or even sects within the Sunni tradition are ancient and persist.

Of course, human tribes of diverse sizes had always fought over ideas and resources. The scale of violence increased in the twentieth century, as ideological disputes and nationalist competition aggravated existing religious differences to induce unseen levels of slaughter. Religious, political, military, and intellectual elites through the century promoted the tendency to hate, essentially training ordinary people to kill.

Ironically, Western nations, responsible for most conflict in the first half of the century and many of the most lethal ideologies, have enjoyed 70 years of stability

Regional Distribution of the Unaffiliated
Population by region as of 2010

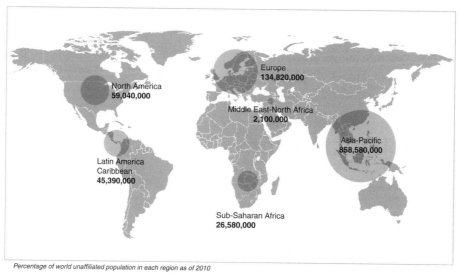

Percentage of world unaffiliated population in each region as of 2010

5.2	4.0	12.0			76.2%
		Europe	0.2 Middle East-North Africa		Asia-Pacific
Latin America					
Caribbean		2.4			
North America		Sub-Saharan Africa			

Population estimates are rounded to the ten thousands. Percentages are calculated from unrounded numbers. Percentages may not add to 100 due to rounding.
Few Research Center's Forum on religion & Public Life • Global Religious Landscape, December 2012

Figure 3.9 One billion people unaffiliated worldwide. (Pew Research Centre's Forum on Religion & Public Life.)

Source: http://assets.pewresearch.org/wp-content/uploads/sites/11/2012/12/08_un-map.png

and tolerance since 1945. Since then Western, secular, and industrial states, far more accepting of cultural difference and dissent than most, have profited from democratic rule and tolerant cultures. The most unstable, violent societies are all exceptionally religious or authoritarian, and are accordingly impoverished, lacking education, diversity or literacy. Though serious ideological and religious conflict is rare today in the First World, it persists worldwide, where opposing views of one sole "truth" shape identities and foster animosity.

Much of the Middle East, North Africa, central Asia, Southeast Asia, and Russia remain centers of religious or ideological violence. Parts of Africa suffer from ongoing animosities based on tribal differences exacerbated by faith. In the Sudan, Christian and Muslim militias habitually slaughter populations. In 2013, two Islamic militants of African descent butchered British soldiers in the name of anti-Christian radicalism, shocking a peaceful democracy.

Christians and Muslims of course persecuted Jews for millennia. Now, with Israel the most powerful nation in the Middle East, punitive attitudes toward Palestinian Muslims sustain hardline Israeli policy, justified by Arab terrorism. Russian oppression of Muslim minorities in the former Soviet Union persists, with murderous attacks on Chechnyan rebels conceived as terrorists. Hindu nationalists regularly persecute minority Muslims in India, and in Southeast Asia Burmese Buddhists commit continuing brutal violence against Rohingya Muslims, detaining religious opponents in concentration camps. A half-century of Chinese domination of Tibet is strategic in nature but enflamed by Communist disdain for Tibetan Buddhism. ISIS is today without doubt the worst example of religious fanaticism; horrific attacks on innocent people persist in the streets of Europe at the time of writing.

Metaphysical self-assuredness

Though nearly all such conflicts have a religious or ideological element, economic or political factors also intrude. The vast majority of religious people today, presumably as always, do not hate others for their beliefs. Notably, most conflict occurs in impoverished societies with low literacy. Belief in one local, national, or supposedly universal thought system has for millennia provided a comfortable certainty for most humans, serving to vindicate resentment and violence in otherwise ordinary people. Religious and nationalist certainty continued this tradition through the past century, enabling humans to kill over different ideas. We still deal with the consequences.

In the longer historical view genes, people, and societies have in fact always mixed. Ideas and beliefs merged as cultures formed and were named. Humans have nonetheless always accepted negative stereotypes toward those who differ. Education more than anything softens such views—the more information available, the less likely people act dogmatically. But education is a luxury, and global inequality continues to contribute to philosophical fanaticism.

Already in the century before 1900, Western imperialism forced people worldwide to confront wholly different thought systems from those that they were raised with. Though there was much syncretism and cross-pollination of beliefs and ideas, Western imperialists were ideologically assured their worldview was "right," and twentieth-century nationalist competition undid any hope for peace and prosperity. By 1900, many, weary of religious conflict, openly stated that religious worldviews were no longer pertinent, and the philosophical systems of influential thinkers such as Friedrich Nietzsche and Karl Marx undermined arguments for religion altogether. This prompted many of faith to dig in their heels and stand by traditional worldviews; it also, however, prompted those with totalitarian tendencies to give up on morality altogether, bringing great harm to humankind through authoritarian ideologies.

The American psychologist John Dewey noted that for millennia, most philosophers came from the leisured class and failed to explain the world accurately, more often playing baffling thought games bereft of meaning for most people. Perhaps this is why received wisdom passed down from elders from century to century has failed to bring peace. Maybe we are still grappling in search of a system of thought that makes sense for all of humanity.

Once again, perhaps little has changed since 1900. Few can manage to grasp a universal human worldview. Local mentalities struggle to comprehend variations in cultures and diverse norms worldwide, holding on firmly to regional beliefs. Pragmatism—a particularly American philosophical system in a particularly American century—posited that philosophy and religion needed to catch up with science, through evidentiary and practical demonstrations of reality. To some extent this has occurred, but humanity still struggles with the whirlwind of ideas derived from tradition and innovation. Arguably, the only unifying element all humankind now commits to is technology, to which we now turn.

4

Twentieth-Century Technology: Fear and Euphoria

Situating the chapter

Around 1900, many important thinkers considered technology as a purely positive source of progress, unquestionably improving life on earth for humanity. A century later, things are not so clear: the use of technology to detonate nuclear weapons; to murder millions in concentration camps; or to spread misinformation has been far from benevolent. Even less malevolent matters such as screen addiction demonstrate technology is not a simple good for humanity, and information warfare now concerns all who cherish democracy.

Technology's impact on human life is plainly ambiguous. Technical innovations boosted postwar economic productivity far more than planned or free-market

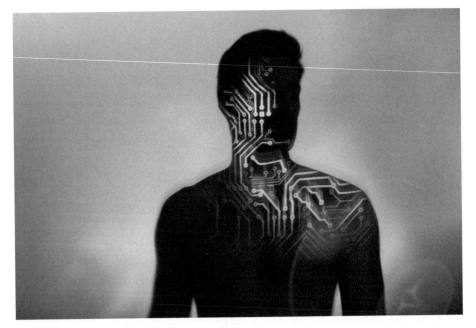

Figure 4.1 Cyborg. (Credit: Liam Norris.)

government policies, creating astonishing levels of wealth and comfort. Technology also helped industrial nations impoverish traditional societies. It enabled governments to educate millions of people, while providing easy means to spread lies. Technology fed billions of humans, ruining vast swathes of lands.

In the past century, a waltz transpired between technological positives and negatives: technologies polluted the environment, worked humans harder, and murdered millions; technological solutions saved lives, created inexpensive creature comforts, and fed billions. This chapter will explore how this occurred.

By the end of this chapter, readers should aim to:

- Understand how humans transformed the world through technology in the twentieth century.
- Offer ways in which different populations benefitted from technology.
- Explain the consequences of the global dispersal of technology.
- Evaluate whether technology was positive or negative for humanity.
- Consider how future uses of technology might impact life on earth.

The story

Technology is not an isolated area of human endeavor or accomplishment. Technological innovation is intertwined with and reliant upon certain political and economic circumstances. It necessitates a social and working environment where individuals can tinker, test and think freely, where he or she must be able to function free from the constraints of convention. One important example of this, from countless possible examples, is the life of the Croatian inventor Nikola Tesla (1856–1943), after whom today's dream machine for millions, the Tesla, is named. Without Tesla's exertions, we would have a very different world today – possibly bereft of miracles such as wireless, robotics, motors, radio, X-rays, alternating current in electrical grids, even remote controls!

Notably, Tesla was encouraged by his scientifically minded mother as a child, at a time when most women worldwide were forbidden to think freely, let alone encourage innovation. He had to ignore his conservative father's command to join the Orthodox priesthood as a young man, at a time when deference to males, particularly those with religious authority, was obligatory. Tesla hence represents well the changed circumstances humans have managed to create since the 19th century with regard to modern technological innovation and freedom of thought.

Understanding technology

Nonetheless, most humans don't understand technology. How do computers work? What is wireless, and how does it send data? Yet, technology now influences humanity more than the other four realms we explore here: politics, economics, ideas, or nature. Indeed, in the 1950s, the British novelist C. P. Snow had warned that industrial nations were cleaving into two separate cultures. In one sphere, engineers and scientists pursued practical and material interests. In the other, teachers and thinkers focused on the humanities, and life's meaning beyond immediate gains. Snow and other writers, teachers, and artists sought to comprehend life's purpose, to foster the use of technology, science, and engineering for humankind, for humans. It remains unclear how successful they were.

The application of human intellect to develop scientific theories since 1900 has brought about a pace of historical change so remarkable that it is difficult to measure its impact. The speed of technological progress and the worldwide spread of technology is incomparable to any previous era. It is near impossible to determine which innovations are most important: the organization of information and data for managing society; the development of vast transportation systems that move and feed millions; the synthesis of ammonia to produce abundant food through cheap fertilizers; the application of penicillin to combat sickness; the electrification of homes and cheap transmission of energy or heat? The list of modern marvels is too long to pinpoint one dominant technological application.

Since 1900, technology improved the quality of life for billions of humans, in a manner unknown in all of history. While hundreds of millions died in dreadful technology-induced conflicts, billions more were born and thrived due to medical technologies. Twentieth-century innovations built on centuries of accrued knowledge. Most complex societies today, whether in Asia, Europe, or North America, had already forged ahead technologically by 1900. They hence enjoyed a huge head start in competitive advantage over LDCs. Though East Asian states innovated in the 1980s, most of the century's technology originated in Western societies. Nations in Eastern Europe, China, the Middle East, Africa, and the rest of the world have thus had to respond to or emulate Western technologies. From the 1960s, Third World elites sought legitimacy by adopting Western know-how to build dams, reroute rivers, distribute food, and engineer large-scale governmental projects. Few spread the benefits of technology to those below.

1. Industrial states and the technology gap

As we saw in Chapter 3, the foremost change in philosophical approach since 1900 was the ardent adoption of a scientific worldview to shape civilization. In 1900, most societies functioned as they had for centuries or millennia. Application of the *scientific method* since then has effectively provided solutions to human problems more than any previous, even as it created new problems. Observation and measurement dictated understanding more in the past century than belief and guesswork.

This shaped new attitudes in all aspects of everyday life. For most of history, people accepted that death could come any day—from other humans, animals, or sickness. Bad weather might bring famine; a group of men on the horizon could bring death; or a simple fever could end a healthy person's life. People functioned, if not in constant fear, nonetheless in a state of awareness that life might end any time. Today, except in war zones or failed states, this is not the case. Many in the developed world expect to live close to a hundred years; people in LDCs live decades longer than most did in 1900. The primary reason for this development is use of the scientific method to preserve health and life through the use of technology.

Since the ancient world, almost all previous uses of technology were based on experimentation or observation, lacking theoretical underpinning. Through the 1800s, though energy was produced by manipulating chemicals, metals, or machines, industrialists had little understanding of the processes actually occurring; chemistry, metallurgy, or the laws of thermodynamics were not clearly understood. After 1900, more developed scientific theory began to improve results. Government-supported laboratory research in wealthy nations, chasing both profits and practicality, soon created a huge technology gap between a few Western nations and the rest of the world. Europeans and North Americans surged ahead, followed by Japan in the 1920s. German and American technologists in particular, successfully developed chemical and electrical power generation, to be put to use for industrial, military, and economic gain.

Since innovation is self-reinforcing, building upon itself, those states already prone to technological innovation in the nineteenth century excelled. Western technologies were far ahead in 1900. Western tinkerers and engineers accrued more than a century of practice in applying the lessons of the Scientific Revolution and the Enlightenment to understand and exploit nature's properties. Organized mass production and assembly-line technologies provided industrial nations with enormous levels of efficiency as compared to mostly rural LDCs, where products were still created through arts and crafts rather than the industrial application of knowledge. Technological advances came almost exclusively from urban environments in nations with vast capital investment capabilities and stable government. Innovations stemmed from university or government-sponsored research in circumstances rarely found outside industrial nations.

Twentieth-century technologies rapidly increased global disparities in power. By 1900, railroads connected people across continents worldwide, laid by and for the commercial benefit of industrial powers. The Suez Canal linked the Red Seat to the Mediterranean after 1869 to enhance British rule. In 1914, the Panama Canal mixed the waters of the Pacific and Atlantic to increase American influence. These earth-shaping technologies did not bode well for traditional societies. Both canals were built by colonial labor in colonized locations (North Africa and Central America). Locals did most of the physical work, while profits went to Western investors. In industrial nations too, the subsequent increase in trade and competition required factory workers to spend longer days in appalling conditions, to maintain profits or a nation's competitive edge. Twentieth-century technology quickly showed its downside.

Technology and war

By 1920, industrial technology had sent tens of millions to their graves in the First World War, prompted by economic and military competition. Already in 1900, the world's most powerful nation had made extraordinarily efficient use of the first machine gun, the Maxim Gun. The 1898 Battle of Omdurman in Sudan saw forty-seven British soldiers die: 12,000 African warriors were slaughtered with supreme ease at the pull of the trigger. The more mystically inclined indigenous fighters, encouraged by tribal shamans, believed that they were immune to bullets, ending up dead or writhing on the ground.

Whereas wars had long been fought between armies of relative parity, the difference between two factions by 1900 was often vast due to industrial technologies. No longer did strategic decisions on the battlefield, soldiers' morale, valor, or luck determine the victor. Instead, a preposterous disparity between those with or without industrial-scale metal machine power determined success. In such circumstances, Latin American, African, Asian, and Arab societies could not compete, and suffered humiliation upon humiliation through the century.

Writing about the Maxim Gun in 1902, Hillaire Beloc famously, and mockingly, wrote:

> In dealing wid de Native Scum, Yo' cannot pick an' choose;
>   Yo' hab to promise um a sum, Ob wages, paid in Cloth and Rum.
>   But, Lordy! that's a ruse! Yo' get yo' well on de Adventure,
>   And change de wages to Indenture.
>   We did the thing that he projected, The Caravan grew disaffected,
>   And Sin and I consulted; Blood understood the Native mind. He said: "We must be firm but kind."
>   A Mutiny resulted. I never shall forget the way, That Blood upon this awful day, Preserved us all from death.

He stood upon a little mound, Cast his lethargic eyes around, And said beneath his breath:

> Whatever happens we have got
>   The Maxim Gun, and they have not.[1]

By 1910, Western nations slid into the savagery of war and the gap between modern nations and the world at large was tremendous. Huge metal ships, impervious to most artillery, built in the first decade of the century, carried guns that could intimidate coastline ports. Heavy metal "dreadnoughts," developed in Britain, made all other navies obsolete and were immediately imitated by Germany, the United States, France, Russia, and Japan. Like nuclear bombs later, dreadnoughts and Maxim Guns forced those without them to concede military disadvantage, with all the negative consequences therein. By 1913, Britain's navy possessed twenty-seven of these huge ships and could confidently sail where it pleased, except for waters near Germany or the United States.

Once invented, technologies will be used. Britain engaged in at least one military campaign for every year of Victoria's reign (1837–1901). Revealingly, the United States would be at war somewhere on earth for the whole of the twentieth century once ascendancy moved across the Atlantic. Neither states were the peace-loving liberal democracies as proposed in nationalist rhetoric.

Levels of militarization differed among industrial powers, and Germany mobilized far more, with more destructive intent. Already ahead in the development of chemicals, medical technology, and electronics by 1900, German scientists applied research to industrial and military aims. By 1916, they developed huge Howitzer guns, weapons that could fire shells over great distances to kill enemies or break up defenses. In the First World War, powerful tanks—new technology incomprehensible

Figure 4.2 Replica of First World War battle tank in London. (Amer Ghazzal/ Barcroft Images/Barcroft Media via Getty Images.)

in undeveloped nations—provided capabilities for swift attacks, overcoming open trenches, barbed wire fences, and opponent machine guns. Though tanks were used to limited effect in this war, they presaged decades of tank warfare to come.

The First World War was at root a technological contest between a small number of Western states, that dragged the world into the quagmire. Soldiers from colonized regions, in the Arab world, India, Asia, and Africa were pressured or forced to enlist, as the fighting impinged upon colonial lands and economies. An overwhelming 10 million people were slaughtered, as new technology provided the means to murder more efficiently. A worldwide influenza epidemic followed, that killed 20 million more, since researchers had not yet figured out how to fight viruses.

Between the wars, technology strengthened authoritarian rule. Spanish, Italian, German, and Japanese right-wing governments mastered methods of control through propaganda and science. Production of tanks, trains, and planes in preparation for total war became the sole intent of dictatorial governments. By the 1930s, an authoritarian arms race developed in Europe, with German industrial might leading the pack, followed by Italy and the slow-moving USSR.

This was not just a European compulsion. Industrial technology motivated Japanese workers to produce artillery, guns, shells, tanks, planes, and railroads for military expansion. Limited by its island resources, Japan pursued total control of China in the 1930s, and Southeast Asia by 1940. Japanese aerial technology developed at a fast pace, enabling its air force to send high-speed planes into the heart of the US Navy in Hawaii in 1941. Pearl Harbor brought US involvement in the war. It also demonstrated incredible innovation in aerial expertise.

Conversely, none of the democracies had planned for large-scale war in the 1930s. Western rulers focused more on social issues such as poverty, so they were ill prepared when war came in 1939. Sensing threat in the 1930s, the French devoted huge technical energies to build the defensive Maginot Line, a vast wall of concrete along France's eastern border intended to keep Germans out, which ultimately failed. French policies, like that of other democracies, were inward looking, attending to domestic conflict instead of international warfare.

Britain devoted intellectual resources to develop new scientific computation techniques. Its ability to stand alone against German expansion and then defeat Axis powers in the second war owed a considerable debt to sophisticated research and development in the 1930s. The brutal war machines of 1914–1918 were transformed into a war of radio wireless and code-breaking in the 1930s, personified by the gifted minds of *Bletchley Park* in England, where radar technology was developed. The development of radar and computation technology would decide the war in favor of the Allies, as much as armies or even US support. Radar helped the British reverse early German victories, as electronic information informed operators where enemy planes were located at any given moment.

In the 1940s, technical knowledge destroyed physical German targets, and early computers plugged into electrical circuits shaped the outcome of the Second World War. Enemy flights could be tracked to provide security for Allied combat pilots and help wear down Germany. Historians estimate that the war was shortened by up to 4 years, saving unknown numbers of lives, as a result of new computer technologies developed mostly in Britain. Information technology would soon contribute to postwar American technical supremacy, as universities and research labs in Allied states shared information openly. In the decades after 1945, military technology moved from earthly competition to rivalry in outer space.

Technology and physics

From the ashes of the Second World War came astonishing new technologies, as applied engineering and scientific principles used to bomb people also showed the way to depart the earth's atmosphere. By the 1950s, rocket technology and nuclear bombs were science fiction become real. Cold War competition built on German rocket designs initially intended to destroy Europe. The Nazis excelled in the physics of guided missiles, dropping thousands of V1 flying bombs on Britain in 1944. German engineers were building more lethal V2 rockets even as they lost the war.

However, the first use of atomic power came from the United States, whose leaders in 1945 decided to drop two bombs on Japan. With Britain's agreement, the bombings killed up to 150,000 Japanese civilians in Hiroshima, followed by 80,000 more in Nagasaki three days later. Deemed necessary to end the war, these bombs served as the first shots in the Cold War. Whether justified or not, Hiroshima and Nagasaki shocked the world - to the extent that technology came under scrutiny from international organizations such as the United Nations, as well as pacifists and environmentalists. The strikes also made clear to Stalin that the United States meant business, provoking his paranoia and ensuing mutual Soviet buildup of long-range bombers and missiles through the 1950s.

The Cold War was in essence a race for technological supremacy. Compared to all other nations, the superpowers occupied a separate realm scientifically and militarily. Already by the time of the Yalta Conference in February 1945, US nuclear warhead research had advanced ahead of all rivals. The first tests came later that year in the Pacific Islands, without due concern for native populations. Britain detonated its first nuclear bomb in 1952; France followed in 1960. Each bomb generated radioactive fallout in the testing and manufacture process, spreading pollutants into the atmosphere for thousands of miles. China would detonate its first nuclear weapon in 1964, though its space program lagged behind.

Industrial nations also used nuclear power plants to provide peacetime energy, starting with Russia in 1954, followed by Britain, France, the United States and then India. All these countries, at one time or another, succumbed to unintended radioactive leaks and forced people to flee homes. All tested bombs in areas populated by indigenous people without their consultation. All ignored protests from environmentalists and created envy among rivals lacking the same power.

Military and intergalactic competition proceeded together between 1945 and 1989, when the USSR collapsed. In these decades, the USSR committed its greatest minds to science, shocking the United States by putting its Sputnik satellite in space in 1957. Applied understanding of battery power, light metals, and radio transmission empowered the Soviets, demonstrating the power of dictatorial rule to focus industrially and militarily. The USSR added further humiliation by orbiting the first human, a Russian astronaut, around the earth in 1961. This propelled US scientists to aim reach the moon first, which they achieved in 1969 when three men landed safely. In recent decades, even with massive budget cuts, the United States has remained far ahead of all rivals in its ability to explore space, sending satellites to Mars. By the twenty-first century, the United States possessed a colossal military budget and continued to spend far more than other nations technologically.

The furious arms race in the decades between the 1950s and the 1980s produced massive numbers of nuclear arms. The military doctrine of MAD—Mutually Assured Destruction—instigated the production of at least 40,000 nuclear warheads for both superpowers, all capable of wiping out a city in one attack. By the 1980s, Ronald Reagan and Conservatives in the US military industry had assembled a vast supply of arms to deter their Communist counterparts. Reagan even aspired to place nuclear weapons in space in the far-fetched Star Wars program. Fortunately, by 1985 and 1986, meetings in Iceland between Reagan and Mikhail Gorbachev showed leaders responded to peace protestors, environmental and nuclear critics. Both powers agreed to limit the production and shipping of ballistic missiles, with the goal of eventually eliminating them. After 2000, US administrations reduced weapons and arms, focusing instead on new drone technologies. By then, the USSR had collapsed, leaving a massive stockpile of rusty weapons in unstable ex-Communist republics.

Industrial states also applied technical knowledge to propel chemical and biological missiles at enemy populations. Chemical weapons were employed by both sides in the First World War, and British soldiers used chemicals to fight Malayan independence fighters in the 1950s. During the Vietnam War in the 1960s the United States demonstrated an enthusiastic use of chemical firepower to kill Vietnamese combatants and civilians. Chemical technology produced *Agent Orange*, burning the skins of thousands of innocent children and families, eradicating food crops as an act of war. By the 1960s, military technology had facilitated biological murder without even the risk of proximity. Middle Eastern regimes have not hesitated to use biological and chemical weapons on enemy populations in recent decades.

While the West and the USSR modernized, leaders in China spent the postwar decades coercing laborers to work as substitutes for machinery, forcing millions of peasants to employ ancient food production practices in place of technology. Through the postwar decades, Chinese Communist Party elites focused on agricultural and ideological efficiency; Mao's fictional utopian ideals replaced scientific knowledge to produce food or industrial growth. Only in the late 1970s did China turn to the West for technological help, borrowing monies from the IMF and ideas for rationalizing industry, science, and technology. Prior to this, Soviet advice had been sought on and off in a tense relationship. Moscow advised China when it suited the Soviets or wanted to antagonize the West.

Technology and the Third World

From the perspective of the West or the USSR, the Cold War was a technological contest for survival against ideological adversaries. Seen from a world perspective however, client states of both nations were manipulated and harassed, to the detriment of the world's poorest people. Soviet technological goals were to maintain the power of Stalin, the Kremlin, and later leaders. US actions were always in the interests of Washington, US influence and affluence more than global democracy or fair trade.

During the Cold War, Soviet power and prosperity increased, Europe enjoyed 50 peaceful years and the United States became the wealthiest society in history. However, in Central and Latin America, Africa, Asia, and the Middle East, wars continued. While populations in developed states saw the material benefit of industrial and technological competition, the fight for global domination after 1945 spread, as the Cold War powers sent military technology to those who collaborated with them.

Cold War history beyond the usual story of two vying superpowers shows immensely negative effects worldwide. Developing nations, often struggling to break colonial shackles, were subject to decades of Cold War interventionism abetted by superior technical prowess. US and Soviet intrusions into already impoverished states destabilized all continents. The Vietnam War was the most obvious case: proxy wars fought in Cuba, Afghanistan, Angola, and Ethiopia, to name only a few, wreaked havoc on the lives of millions of colonized people. Routine regime toppling in Latin America wrought Cold War violence. By the 1980s, when the great powers turned toward relative amicability, the damage had been done worldwide.

In 1979, Iran and Afghanistan collapsed due to internal conflicts aggravated by Cold War meddling. Iranian religious fundamentalists thrust off US influence, overthrowing Iran's pro-West dynasty and reverting to pure Islamic practices. Regaining control of essential economic assets, the new theocracy swore to wage war against the American "Great Satan" thereafter. That same year, Afghani Marxist rebels killed and overthrew Afghanistan's president, prompting a murderous civil war between Soviet backed rebels and Islamic mujahedeen. As in Iran, an Islamic state repelled what it perceived as Western (including Russian) subjugation. The present threat of radical jihadist extremism stems directly from seeds planted in the Cold War.

Figure 4.3 A 11-year old Vietnamese boy badly burned in an accident sent to the United States for treatment by the COR (Committee of Responsibility). (Larry Burrows/The LIFE Picture Collection/Getty Images.)

Indeed, radicals everywhere—Far Leftists in Europe and Latin America, Marxists in Africa or Islamists in the Middle East—shared a common grievance toward the superpowers. Both powers spoke of peace but sent military technology worldwide to ensure their client states remained docile or compliant. From the perspective of radicals in the Middle East, these decades vindicated the most striking and shocking use of technology in recent years. The horrific events of September 2001 in New York were the desperate actions of deranged, dispirited, fundamentalist Muslims—using Western airplane technology to fight Western domination. Technology did not bring security to the undeveloped world.

Technology and health

The effects of technology reached both positive and negative extremes of course. While the lives of millions of Vietnamese were ruined, and while chemical warfare spread cancerous toxins onto lands worldwide, technological advances from the developed world also brought the miracles of science worldwide. In the postwar era, research into vaccines and antibiotics countered the common flu that had killed millions in 1920. In the 1950s, chemical industries in rich nations produced synthetic fertilizers to feed billions worldwide (albeit using DDT which, while killing insects, polluted the food chain.)

As powerful Western states extracted resources and selected favorite rulers across Asia and Africa, they also healed communities with medicines far superior to folk remedies. Scientists had found ways to preserve food or provide supplementary nutrition for populations worldwide, so millions could now survive childhood and live longer in poorer countries. Since 1945, the much-criticized United Nations has worked as a global force for good, preventing war and monitoring rogue states, saving countless lives in poor nations and delivering necessities through technology.

By the postwar era, technological "progress" provided both the means of murder on a mass scale and the ability for doctors to save lives inexpensively through the miracle of antibiotics. Around 109.7 million people died in the twentieth century from military conflict, compared to estimates of only 19.4 million deaths in the nineteenth, and 7 million in the eighteenth centuries.[2] While guns, tanks, planes, and shells killed, billions more were born to live longer, healthier lives thanks to medical technology. Indeed, the impact of technology on public health has mostly been a public, or global, good. Death rates plummeted worldwide due to developments in

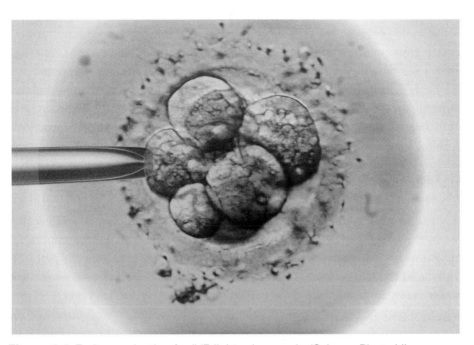

Figure 4.4 Embryo selection for IVF, light micrograph. (Science Photo Library, ZEPHYR.)

health care. Synthetic aspirin, produced by 1900, became the most used drug in world history. Even simple, low-cost Band-Aids, developed in the United States in 1920, prevented widespread infections. Pharmaceutical research produced cheap and safe antiseptics and anesthesia to deaden the unimaginable pain of past infections. Since the 1980s open-heart surgery has become ordinary; surgery saves lives routinely. Along with antibiotics, penicillin saved millions of lives, becoming affordable in most nations.

Refrigeration and transportation technologies kept food fresher, shipping produce worldwide to offer diverse diets, while the mechanization of food production produced bounties of nourishment unimaginable prior to 1900. Particularly after 1960, scientific crop production offered immense gains in yields. Since the 1980s genetically modified crops have grown in use and sale, prompting concern but feeding many. Clean water supplies through technological storage and distribution systems kept disease at bay to end the daily disease regime of the past.

Though travel to the skies in the 1950s astonished humanity, equally exotic worlds were shown to exist inside bodies, cells, and organs. Much of our knowledge of the human body derives from Anglo-American scientific work, which in 1953 revealed the existence of DNA and genes in the human body. By the 1980s the technology of genetic engineering emerged along with the manufacture of precision instrumentation. Nanotechnology developed in the 1990s to the point doctors can now explore sick bodies, monitor how they function, how they feel, and how they interact with other humans. Minute instruments inside the body provide data about well-being, lifestyle, and social interactions.

Technology shaped human demographics. Uncontrolled population growth caused great suffering in societies that always struggled to feed mouths, and high birth rates have thwarted prosperity in LDCs. The revolutionary invention of the birth control pill in the 1960s prevented unwanted children and attendant suffering for those without secure homes or opportunities. By the 1980s, in vitro fertilization brought laboratory-made babies, for couples unable to procreate. Technological innovation now enables doctors to monitor embryos and ensure safe passage into life, something unknown in the past when women so often died in childbirth.

Scientists even began manipulating human embryos by the end of the century, entering uncertain moral territory. The discovery of chromosomes and genetics meant that along with new understanding of the human body came aspirations for replicating or "improving" humans. The famous cloning of the sheep *Dolly* in 1997 introduced the idea of human cloning. The aim to create perfect people went too far for many. Some questioned the perils of intervening in nature's process, even if it were to prevent sick babies or children born with diseases; others considered the magic of technology a worthy replacement for the mysteries of the past, finding no reason for concern.

2. Manipulating matter

The cloning of another species of mammals represents an extreme exan technology manipulating matter. This was the culmination of a centur engineering of various sorts of matter—first metals, woods, and fossil fuels, then later bits of information that would create digital films, songs, and online content. The sophisticated engineering feats of the postwar era made past achievements seem rudimentary. Atoms and molecules were restructured for use as solids, liquids, and gases, to be manipulated into practical products and materials. A century of technological breakthroughs enabled 8 billion people to survive on earth, as nutrition, water purification systems, and medical technology diffused worldwide from research laboratories.

Good or bad chemistry?

German researchers were first to master chemical technology and produce *synthetic materials* before 1900. Centuries of efforts to extract natural sources (usually from colonized societies) ended when Fritz Haber synthesized ammonia in 1909. Chemical industries could now use *synthetics* instead of natural resources to produce clothes, paints, plastics, and rubber, and later to feed billions of humans. After the 1950s, the use of fertilizers produced huge food surpluses in the West. Engine-driven tractors yielded vast levels of food production in wealthier nations, and high yielding crops produced growing populations worldwide.

Better-fed people worked more productively in a positive feedback cycle. As chemical technology fed billions and prevented disease, early twentieth-century work on the use of chemical microbes and filtration to treat sewage in Britain became the global standard for preventing urban disease outbreaks. Greater food supplies harnessed more human brainpower, molding more literate societies: ideas spread quicker in better-fed societies. American domination after the Second World War, like Britain's before that, came from a well-fed, highly literate and numerate society, trained to think in terms of words and numbers to work for national advantage.

Technology brought new problems, however. When proteins were extracted from crops through the use of fertilizers, they absorbed increased amounts of nitrogen from soils, damaging them. Besides increasing food supplies, chemicals such as ammonia produced gunpowder and explosives, the perfect symbol of technology's paradox. When the Haber-Bosch plant succeeded in producing large volumes of cheap synthetic fertilizer after 1912, it meant that Germany could fight longer during the war, prolonging violence through 1918. Chemicals were also part of the reason a young Adolf Hitler, traumatized after suffering temporary blindness from Allied armies' use of mustard gas in 1918, swore revenge on liberal democracies. His loathing for free nations was only surpassed by his hatred for Jews, and of course chemical technology was the horrific means by which 7 million Jewish people were gassed in the Third Reich.

By the end of the century, chemical warfare was a genuine global threat, realizing the fears of 1950s sci-fi films like *Godzilla*. The USSR and United States produced enough chemical stockpiles in the Cold War to destroy much of the earth, and as we have seen, the United States used Napalm to bomb Vietnam for years. More recently, Saddam Hussein gassed minority Kurds in his Sunni Arab realm in the 1990s and Syria has used chemical weapons on rebel factions.

Metals and machines

Industrial states manipulated matter exponentially after 1900. Engineers converted raw ores from the earth's innards into metal ships, bridges, railroads, and large buildings. Mass production during the First World War prompted a huge increase in shipping trade, which increased through the century. Each achievement prompted further innovation, improving upon earlier engineering techniques. The connection between technical innovation and profit increased investment and jobs in industrial nations, but also required overseas influence in undeveloped regions. The key motivation for control and extraction of foreign resources was to profit from cheap supplies. Increased transportation and shipping of products created pollutants, as the effluents of fossil fuels contaminated waterways and poisoned the air.

Yet, by the Second World War, revolutionary new organizational technologies such as containerization facilitated simpler logistical movement of global goods. In the 1950s, this American innovation moved materials more quickly and easily to more people. Metal container cubes made of thin steel and aluminum were placed on ships, trains, trucks, and ports like Lego pieces, for intermodal movement from origin to destination. The technology of storage and distribution changed the lives of billions, lowering the average costs of goods by over 90 percent between 1950 and 2000. Made of cheap metals, being both reusable and practical, this simple, little recognized, technical solution fed and clothed billions, increasing global trade while lowering costs.

Steel and aluminum

Without cheap steel and aluminum, most modern home and office products could not exist. Stainless steel was developed in England and Germany around 1913. Comparable to electricity in impact, the mass production of steel reshaped the world. Advanced metal technology spread to all industrial states after 1945, becoming a source of national prestige, visualized in skyscrapers, bridges, or other monuments of modernity.

Steel symbolically represented the power of Communist and autocratic nations in their challenge to capitalism. Stalin ("man of steel") changed his birth name for a good reason. While capitalist nations produced greater quantities of cheap steel for construction, infrastructure, and transportation, despotic states abused laborers to keep up. Steel became ubiquitous, transformed from earth's ores to reinforce concrete in foundations, build freeways and dams and lay city streets. Steel suspension bridges crossed rivers to connect people and markets, and steel made landing gears and essential parts for all machines.

Like steel, aluminum products like canned goods, toasters, fridges, and water heaters became abundant. Earth's most abundant element and metal, aluminum, was processed on industrial scale after development by French and American metallurgists around 1900. Made from the ore bauxite, aluminum became cheap worldwide after 1945, providing material for packaging in food preservation or the bodies of cars and planes. Building materials for construction and homes became affordable due to this proliferation of metals, whether shaping impressive steel structures in state capitals or holding up aluminum roofing in ghettoes worldwide.

Metal changed the heart of city life and increased national ambitions. After Chicago's Home Insurance Building was erected in 1885 high-rise buildings constructed of steel soon rose above cities like urban temples. For centuries, cities were centered around the tallest edifice, typically a church or other sacred space, but after 1900 civic buildings such as city halls and skyscrapers represented the center of city life. Developing and developed nations today compete for the tallest possible building for prestige.

Metal permeated the twentieth-century world. Iron internal combustion engines were secured onto the steel chassis of buses, tanks, airplanes, and trains. After producing bicycles of simple metal frames at the turn of the century, the Wright Brothers turned their interest to flight. By placing engines in front of rudimentary airplanes they put humans into air for the first time in history in North Carolina in 1903. Until the 1920s, planes were made of light woods, fabric, and thin steel, but were soon transformed into machines of heavy steel wrapped in aluminum, capable of flying passengers around the earth or to bomb societies into submission. Airplane technology used for bombing civilians provided the means of global travel for millions by the 1960s. By the 1980s, international passenger air-travel descended from first being a privilege for the wealthy, then becoming affordable for ordinary people.

The magical manipulation of metals represented the surest symbol of progress by the 1950s. Engine-driven tractors could produce more food than ever before, to be shipped to poor nations. Improved mass production techniques offered more possessions to the masses, as scientifically scrutinized, repeatable processes lowered prices and spread commodities worldwide. Machines automated manufacturing, offsetting human error.

Though steel productivity was measured in terms of positive industrial growth, its manufacture did not always represent progress. Metal technologies were used to kill people in wartime, and for laborers in factories and foundries even in rich nations, industries grew and declined, meaning that jobs were lost and livelihoods were threatened. Workers in autocratic nations were labored to death's door to produce metal, and the manufacture of repeating rifles, trains, cannons, and steamships empowered industrial states to overcome weaker societies.

The earth's ores and minerals were reshaped into vehicles for public transportation, products for farming and machines for warfare in the twentieth century. But as steel built railroads, it conquered space and people. When Western engineers laid tracks in colonized regions to export raw materials, indigenous and local populations lost control of their own space and resources. The only non-Western nation whose natural reserves were not extracted by foreigners was Japan. Lacking abundant natural resources, Japanese engineers made use of hydroelectric plants while importing necessary ores and materials. Its scant natural ores also prompted imperial aggression, for which China and Korea suffered terribly.

Oil and gas

Overseas ventures for resource extraction were one of the hallmarks of the century. All the machines mentioned above needed oil to run, and many essential twentieth-century products would be made from oil-based materials. Oil as it happened was most abundantly found in the Middle East, and once discovered in 1908 in Persia, its extraction became a fundamental component of international relations between Western superpowers and Arab states.

Perhaps no starker example exists of the costs of manipulating molecules than in the production of crude oil—or petroleum—in the past century, as ancient fossils lain dormant for hundreds of millions of years were reshaped from petroleum byproducts into household products, heat, gasoline or Vaseline! In both world wars control of oil impacted military calculations, and Cold War competition for supplies only increased the strategic necessity of fossil fuels. Oil derricks epitomize humanity's technical skills, as metal straws struck deep into rocks and oceans to extract oil and gasoline for modern life.

Momentously, in 1912 the world's superpower Britain switched its navy from coal to oil to for military advantage. In July 1914, just prior to the war, the British government acquired a majority stake in the Anglo-Persian Oil Company, and British agents secured concessions in Iran and Iraq. The British admiralty thus ensured access to cheap Middle Eastern oil, fighting Turks and Germans during the First World War to maintain supplies. Most Arabs had no say, or knew this had occurred.

The rest of the century would follow this pattern, as drilling and extraction technologies developed by Anglo-American companies brought production and

Figure 4.5 Soil pollution in Egypt. (DeAgostini/Getty Images.)

subsequent conflict. Particularly after American oilmen found vast supplies in Saudi Arabia in 1943, access to cheap oil became essential to US postwar geopolitics. This new chapter in technological history would not serve the Middle East well, as conflict in the region heightened from its possession of fossil fuels. It is important to note that Arab and Persian elites made great fortunes from new Western connections, and Western industrial innovation permitted production in the first place. By 1913, Western petrochemical industries had effected the means of eliminating almost all waste from the extraction of crude oil (ignoring the environmental side-effects until the 1970s).

Derivatives of crude oil refining included gas for heat and power, but also plastic, a revolutionary, world-changing product. In 1907, Leo Baekeland altered the molecular structure of plastic polymers to create the modern plastics industry. From Tupperware containers to binkies or toys, life on earth as it is would be unimaginable without the flexibility of plastics. Nail polish, fertilizers, soap, umbrellas, trash bags, and duct tape are all plastic based. After the 1950s, mass production of plastics brought unrivaled convenience. Only in the 1990s did environmental critics reveal that plastic trash took centuries to break down, activists exposed the mountains of garbage created and massive gyres of debris appeared in the world's oceans.

Oil production increased through the century, providing the means for industrialization, prompting ceaseless conflict, contributing to massive pollution and climate change. Today, almost half of the world's crude oil is transformed into millions of everyday industrial products, as homes and businesses worldwide are filled with the byproducts of oil extraction. But perhaps the ultimate symbol of twentieth-century oil extraction is the gas-motored automobile, the ultimate consumer item, impossible to imagine without the bounty of oil that flowed after the 1900s.

Automobiles

The definitive mass-produced product, automobiles propelled humans forward, using metal engines and the byproduct of oil refining to ignite engines. Like the plane, cars were modeled after the bicycle, when the pioneering German automakers Benz and Daimler developed simple two-stroke engines in the 1870s. A three-wheeled version emerged in 1886, as French engineers improved the design to move people minus a horse-drawn carriage. Automobile sales in the West took off after the German-Jewish businessman Emil Jellinek opened a dealership in 1902, securing the rights to sell the car in Europe and North America, and naming the first automobile trademark after his daughter Mercedes.

Though the automobile is the ultimate symbol of modernity, few anticipated its global impact. The engineer Rudolph Diesel died in 1913, convinced that his high-efficiency diesel engine would fail commercially. Engine technology nevertheless developed to move people at unheard of speeds. In a few short years, humans, after millennia moving at foot speed, took to slow-moving bikes, then to unimaginable rates of propulsion in automobiles and airplanes. This was a dizzying change.

W. E. Henley expressed the common impression that technology brought near religious experiences, in his *Song of Speed*, from 1903:

A SONG OF SPEED

In the Eye of the Lord
By the Will of the Lord,
Out of the infinite
Bounty dissembled.
Since Time began.
In the Hand of the Lord,
Speed! . . .

. . . Speed, and the range of God's skies.
Distances, changes, surprises;
Speed, and the hug of God's winds
And the play of God's airs.
Beautiful, whimsical, wonderful;
Clean, fierce and clean.
With a thrust in the throat
And a rush at the nostrils;
Keen, with a far-away.[3]

Since so many raw materials for automobiles were sourced from non-Western regions, colonized or nonindustrial areas were increasingly pressured to export commodities to the developed world. Like oil and gas, the rubber required for motor vehicles came from colonized regions, in Southeast Asia, Africa, or South America. When the French Michelin brothers famously mapped the roads of France to provide infrastructure for cars, they also engineered remarkable new soft tires of rubber, providing comfort and moving heavier loads. Booming tire production brought more global intervention. Faster trucks, tanks, and planes increased the murderous mechanized efficiency of world wars.

Cars were mass-produced in huge numbers after the war, and the automobile became a huge success when Henry Ford revolutionized its production. Setting up the Ford Motor Company in 1903, he employed the remarkable new mechanized technology of assembly-line production, pre-shaping interior parts such as chairs and windscreens. New industrial processes replaced the endless and inefficient tedium where one worker performed the same motion repeatedly. This allowed vast increases in production levels, as thousands of parts were made more quickly on assembly lines, speeding up manufacture and making the car cheaper to sell. Ford paid his workers well, so they could buy their own products. His famous Model T appeared in 1908, offering a reliable, affordable car that changed the United States and the world.

Figure 4.6 1894 Paris to Rouen race. (Peugeot National Motor Museum/Heritage Images/Getty Images.)

Ford's production line also spurred new innovations in sales and marketing to stoke desire for cars in the minds of men and women. American advertisers manipulated people psychologically, using Freud's insights to increase sales through targeted marketing. By the 1940s, working men could proudly offer their families a car. Americans covered more geographical space, took more vacations far from home, and produced everything more rapidly in a modern lifestyle contingent upon the supply of cheap oil and mined metals that brought geopolitical and environmental consequences few comprehended.

The magic of electricity

Cars also required battery power, and the scientific principles of electricity provided this mystery force. Some innovations underwrite almost all others, and electricity, which in 1900 seemed as bewitching as any cleric, imam, or shaman's rituals, impacted almost all subsequent inventions. The flow of electrons that characterize electricity seemed both baffling and beautiful in 1900, as invisible forces seemed to pervade the world as much as solid matter.

Scientists had been working to understand electricity since the seventeenth century. Michael Faraday's work on induction in the nineteenth century made it possible to apply electromagnetic force for use in modern life. His work on generating AC (alternating current) is the basis of almost all modern appliances. James Maxwell's translation of Faraday's theories into workable mathematical equations enabled twentieth-century technologists to push science forward in practical terms. Maxwell's equations clarified the nature of magnetism, showing how force fields acted upon solid masses.

After 1900, innovators surged forward with frenzied energy to understand these new forces, with vast practical consequences for humanity. By 1910, Max Planck developed instrumentation to observe atoms invisible to the naked eye, aiding application of electrical energy. Using magnetic rays, he demonstrated that atoms were not like solid billiard balls as had been previously thought. Instead, they interacted in an immeasurable and unexplainable fashion. Long believed to be the smallest physical unit of material in the universe, atomic study was further revolutionized when the physicist J. J. Thomson discovered the electron, to explain electrical conduction. Theodore Hertz had showed in 1886 that electromagnetic waves were longer than light waves but shorter than sound, knowledge which enabled ships to use Morse signals to communicate across oceans. Radio and television stations could not transmit sound or light across distances without this insight. And though Einstein's equations or his theory of relativity might not mean much to the non-mathematical masses, the physical and electrical application of his calculations were real, obliterating two Japanese cities in 1945 through the use of atomic energy.

The production of cheap electricity through commercial power generation also presented a boon to humanity. Humans had always used natural resources to shape their lives, and sources of natural energy usually dictated how a society functioned. Energy had always come from human and animal muscle or the manipulation of water and wind. Prior to 1900, faint light emitted from wax candles or stinking oil lamps, requiring the slaughter of huge numbers of whales for whale oil. Electrical light changed this, empowering workers and factories to continue production into the night. Light bulb design has barely changed since 1900 in fact.

Electricity is the only source of energy easily converted to motion, heat, light, and chemical potential. It was exceptional in its simplicity and ease of distribution over wide areas. By the early twentieth century, electrical batteries could store energy, using voltaic piles of two metals to power machines, cars, and planes beyond human capabilities. This was a new world of power production. It literally lit the world, as brightened nights meant that humans could work longer, could read more, think and produce more—in industrial states.

Electricity boosted industrial efficiency incalculably, particularly after the inventions of Thomas Edison sent electrical power to most corners on earth. By 1902, Edison's station in New York used steam engines, boilers, steel stacks, employing industrial armies of thinkers and tinkerers. Edison devised the concept of central stations to transmit power near Wall Street as it happens, a street fast becoming the center of world finance and power. Indeed, the connection between power generation and wealth was snug; the first light was turned on in 1882 in the financier J. P. Morgan's New York office. Captains of industry enjoyed access to the benefits of technology first, using existing capital to exploit revolutionary new technologies. Powerful states made use of the magic to maintain position worldwide.

The power of power

By the 1930s the United States was the most electrified nation on earth, with all the attendant benefits in quality of life and productivity. The process of patenting was essential to motivating theorists and generating new research in a mostly open society. The United States had granted its millionth patent in 1911, fittingly, for a car tire. By the end of the century, the transmission of low-cost electricity to the vast majority of humans on earth was considered humdrum, its magic faded, the technology behind it somewhat prosaic. Yet, this technology enabled easier and better living for billions, providing light, safety and warmth for a low sum per person through the century.

By the twenty-first century, technical instrumentation could measure light on an electromagnetic spectrum to indicate how far away or how old a star, or even galaxy, might be. As researchers sensed information far beyond ordinary human sight—in the skies, under the seas, and inside of the earth—scientists seemed able to grasp the mechanics of the universe.

Yet scientists also acknowledged the existence of complexity beyond human understanding. The universe seemed composed as much by random chaos as by measurable order. Einstein and others had showed in quantum theory that nature was unpredictable, and modern scientists calculate that subatomic particles can be in more than one place at a time! Hence, rational understanding and quantifiable solutions were not always apparent. The universe remained as mysterious as the mind itself, even after a century of technological manipulation and practical application. Nevertheless, the electrification of technology fundamentally altered the basic principles of human experience—in sound, vision, and sensory reception of information. Technology now brought the miracle of the galaxies to the human eye. By manipulating electromagnetic radiation through curved glass, placed inside a metal frame, the astronomer Edwin Hubble in 1929 showed the human eye stars and galaxies beyond imagination. The universe was now in plain sight, shattering human perception of time and space, and indeed of life on earth. New images, premised upon scientific understanding of an expanding and dynamic universe, inspired alternative cosmologies. Hubble showed that galaxies were born and died—with perhaps our own proceeding along a similar process. Perhaps earth's history was a very ephemeral process?

3. Sound and Vision: Computing, communicating, conquering space

Human sensory perception entered a new realm after the 1920s. Film theaters revealed new worlds of inspiration to those who read little or never, visual stimulation altered perceptions and stoked imaginations. In the same decade, broadcast radio brought voices from across the planet affordably into the home. In developed nations, inexpensive magazines like *National Geographic* transported the wider world into the living rooms of millions. This was a brave new world. After the Second World War, magical exploration of the skies was complemented by mind-blowing entertainment for hundreds of millions of humans. In the postwar era, mass communication through different mediums would change how people learned, listened, and connected.

Mass media

In the 1920s, new forms of entertainment emerged in France, Britain, and the United States to change the visual and auditory perspectives of humans permanently. Electronics exploited the relationship between electromagnetic and light waves to produce signals for the radio. Known as wireless, radio sent signals anywhere worldwide where a transmitter could receive them. Wireless developed from the work

1920's -1930's
Europe

of technologists in various European nations: the Serbian émigré to America, Nikola Tesla, created the AC system for electrical current that made radio possible; the Italian G. G. Marconi developed electrical transmission technologies to send sound securely and clearly. In 1900, the Canadian Reginald Fessenden sent the first radio message to a friend a mile away in Maryland, asking, "1,2,3,4, is it snowing where you are?"

New concepts appeared such as *broadcasting* (derivative of broad seed spreading in eighteenth-century agriculture). In the 1920s, broadcast radio dispersed information widely at unfathomable speeds, scattering new ideas at the speed of sound. Electrified radio wavelengths conveyed sound and information through speakers for the pleasure of crowds or homemakers. Britain's BBC began transmitting in FM by 1933, to transmit more clearly nationwide, as voice and music was broadcast to millions at once, replacing small gatherings in village squares.

People were easily led by new information. The famous 1938 radio show *War of the Worlds* caused widespread panic in the United States, with its storyline of alien invasion so convincing that thousands believed it was real. Misinformation could clearly be manipulated intentionally or accidentally. A year later, when Germany invaded Poland to start the Second World War, radio transmission was central to political and military control. Many Germans had been indoctrinated into Nazism through broadcasts by 1939.

While men in power broadcast a hyper-masculine message of war, women played important roles in developing technology, though few received recognition. During the Second World War, remarkable women such as the actress Hedy Lamarr helped challenge gender norms in the science community (tellingly her fame was for her beauty, not her intellect, even though she had worked on code-breaking devices to defeat the Germans). Male and female technologists in Britain and America gathered information on Nazi and Japanese movements at the extraordinary top-secret Bletchley Park complex near London. They would break German cipher codes, ultimately facilitating victory. The requirements of war provided new opportunity for women to show that they were scientists too. Bletchley Park harnessed the outstanding efforts of a mostly female workforce, who preserved liberties for millions through their intellectual endeavors.

Telegraph, telephone, and television

By the 1950s radio was commonplace, and technologies based on similar principles such as film and television enthralled people more, supplying wondrous storylines at the theater or in homes. Television transmitted images to any home on earth with electricity. Like radio and film, it molded ideas about how to live, sending information across nations and continents, and shaping consciousness.

Communication technologies developed first in the West because for decades before 1900, industrial powers had moved information over vast distances. By 1866,

Britain and the United States had laid copper cable across the Atlantic Ocean, wrapped in colonial rubber. Cables, utilizing the electrical theories of Faraday, connected great powers across oceans, offering advantage to those states who controlled information. In peacetime and in war, those with the best information outmaneuvered opponents. Through the First World War, Britain controlled most of the world's cables and could easily cut German communications; Britain's use of radar provided crucial advantage in the Second World War.

More impressive even than the telegraph in its ease of use and clarity, telephone communication, invented by 1904, crossed the Atlantic in 1915. Westerners could now connect to discuss politics and business without cumbersome Morse code required for cables, through regular human voice. They could also quickly communicate to colonial officers to control subjugated peoples.

But television had the greatest impact. Scientists across the industrial world worked in tandem to develop the TV. The Russian Boris Rosing first transmitted murky images through tubes before the First World War, and the Scottish inventor John Logie Baird pioneered working televisions, building on earlier efforts. By 1929, crude images of actual were sent from Britain to the United States. TV signals could soon be extended over great distances thanks to the invention of the outdoor antenna in Japan in 1926, when the inventor Yagi Uda sold his invention in Britain and America. Until the 1950s, only the wealthiest homes in the United States had televisions, while middling families aspired to own one. Thereafter, most Americans had access to TV.

The TV and film industries were controlled exclusively by men, ensuring that women were objectified and demeaned through sexist visual representations on screen. People of color would be consistently caricatured, as white males dominating the industry shaped the roles available for women and ethnic minorities, and also influenced their expected roles in society. In 1928, the TV station CBS (Columbia Broadcasting System) broadcast dramas to middle-class housewives, usually selling housekeeping products such as soap in the breaks (hence the term Soap Opera). By the 1950s six major TV stations reproduced life as US executives conceived it should be. The introduction of color TV in 1954 was revolutionary, and sound was improved through the introduction of Dolby stereo technology in 1956. By 1967, Satellite TV could transmit the most famous band on earth, The Beatles, live worldwide—the first event transmitted globally.

Television transformed the world and the way that people imagined and thought, it as it spread globally in the 1960s. This small box of electronic gadgets changed perceptions of others and of reality, creating a new transnational worldview and laying the foundations for globalization thereafter. TV, like film, transmitted the images, music, norms, and emotions of Western cultures worldwide. Western TV truly went global in 1980 when Cable News Network (CNN) offered news worldwide all day long, providing a constant stream of visual data to shape views, distract or influence voters.

Film and Camera

This visual means of communicating was both new and not so new. Most societies had communicated traditionally through visual symbols and images as much as words. Established worldviews had been disseminated through images of gods, heroes or saints; stories were supplemented by visual characterizations of significant figures. Though this was a century of literacy, words clearly did not eliminate visual means of communication.

Film and pleasure

Edward Muybridge's famous film of a trotting horse in California marked the beginning of film in 1887, and new modes of graphic communication built on earlier innovations. *Motion pictures*, as they became known, developed the nineteenth-century technology of photography into a dynamic world of moving images to entertain, inform and persuade. 1927's *The Jazz Singer* was the first movie with dialogue and sound. It proved a massive success, introducing mass audiences to the magical pleasures of visual storytelling.

Finance and profit motivated the spread of film. Economic position correlated with high levels of literacy, meaning that richer nations more easily sent great volumes of

Figure 4.7 High-speed sequence of galloping horse and rider. (Eadweard Muybridge Collection/Kingston Museum/Science Photo Library.)

information, print and visual, to citizens and workers. Information literacy spread through schools and churches, but also through mass-produced comics, which fused humor with storytelling. Wealthier nations saturated consumers with low-cost graphic illustrations, spreading knowledge and shaping minds.

The economic prospect of film was thus capitalized upon most in wealthy America. Film studios like Paramount were profitable by 1912. Using newspapers to generate interest, producers rehashed older theatre plays or novels to create new shows in the Hollywood suburbs of Los Angeles, still the center of the film industry today. Films made enriched many people and delighted many more in ways never before seen.

Developed nations meticulously documented the past and present of both Western and non-Western societies. In the 1910s, the billionaire Alfred Kahn travelled and filmed the world, preserving for the first time what he feared were dying traditional societies.[4] Portable and usable cameras were available only for the rich in 1900, but after 1945 the middle classes could own one. In 1975, Kodak produced the first affordable digital camera, and of course since then, digital technology replaced traditional photography, spreading images worldwide in seconds.

Film entertained and provided escape, but it criticized authority and technology too. 1927's German classic *Metropolis* revolutionized both visual effects and plotline development, confronting real issues of class differences, inequality, and attacking the immorality of greed in a futuristic state of worker bondage. Charlie Chaplin's *Modern Times* in 1936 similarly critiqued industrial work life while providing mass entertainment.

Film and opinion

Soon after it emerged in France in 1898, commercial film would shape and reshape perceptions of life for billions of humans. Though a medium for pleasure, its propaganda potential easily conscripted people to murder or hate. Racists in democracies were quick to use film media to shape views. The very first movie screened in the White House celebrated racial chauvinism. The white supremacist silent movie *Birth of a Nation* did not need dialogue to make its point. Shown in 1915, it depicted black Americans as inferior and violent, idealizing and perpetuating a bigoted white version of American history. A great commercial success, it demonstrated the monetary as well as ideological value of the new medium.

Authoritarian states made even greater use of film, to convince gullible masses of national greatness, relying upon doctored images to create fake stories. Nazis used film to sway Germans to the horrors of German nationalism, demonizing Jews, leftists, and foreigners. Communist states used film to control the minds of millions into the 1980s. Indeed, revelations of the horrors of the Nazi Holocaust were brought to the world via film images that could not be doctored. Allied and Russian cameramen thankfully found it crucial to film the death camps - to convince an unbelieving world that the Holocaust had occurred. The Second World War was partly a cinematic competition, as Allied powers and authoritarian states used movies to convince people what to believe. Film told stories people immediately believed, influencing everyday actions, capturing their conscience and cementing preconceptions.

After the 1950s, film (and filmed news media) replaced passed down, oral information to represent experience and form beliefs. The subject of technology itself is central to movies today; innumerable films and documentaries confront the pained question of whether or not humans will shape a dystopian or utopian future. A spectrum exists between end-of-the-world dystopias depicting the end of humanity and imagined utopian worlds that may provide a life of leisure and pleasure. Subjects such as inequality and injustice have long been explored in film, raising the consciousness of millions, and documentaries now alter political or religious beliefs by demonstrating complex arguments visually.

 Since film derives from the West, it has transmitted Western norms and values to colonized nations, checking the opposite flow of cultural norms. Only in recent decades Westerners have begun to learn of faraway places though film and documentary, as others have learned of the West. Films can also provide a pollutant effect: Al Qaeda and ISIS now use technologies such as film or Internet video to recruit in their violent quest to fight what they see as corrupt Western morals.

For better or worse, film has presented crucial questions about the human condition. Worldwide film industries now exist, though Western films are still craved globally, demonstrating a global urge for cultural products emanating from more literate societies. Few can escape the power of imagery and storytelling. Hitler apparently adored the Disney classic *Snow White*. Dictators collected Western films obsessively, from Saddam Hussein to Idi Amin in Uganda and North Korea's dictator today. ISIS recruits live on a diet of YouTube clips, as much as the rest of the world.

Sound and freedom

Technologies derived from the telegraph and telephone also produced the phonograph, or record player. By placing tinfoil on a waxed cylinder, Thomas Edison found that he could record and reproduce sounds, and by 1902 two-sided disks played up to ten minutes of music. Prior to the twentieth century, most people could live their whole lives only hearing local live music, even in the developed world. Better-off patrons might hear Beethoven or Haydn's symphonies a handful of times in their life. Now music was reproducible, pervasive, and affordable.

In the interwar years, music became a means of relaxation at home, providing immense personal pleasure and melodious entertainment. After 1924, audio recording using hi-fidelity sound enchanted the ears of listeners, and when magnetic tape was found capable of storing data in 1927, tape cassettes appeared. The LP (or Long Player) appeared in 1948. Musical artists could now produce a full hour of musical concepts for eager audiences. By the 1980s, when the Compact Disc, or CD, appeared in the United States, music became ubiquitous in almost all societies, as the digitization of sound made it cheaper and easier to distribute.

Like radio and film, music shaped identity, particularly in the 1950s. Already in the 1920s, novel styles of music—that is, not classical or spiritual—shocked conventional society, but radio also broadcast spiritual messages to religious populations, forming opinions about others. Particularly in the United States (but eventually everywhere) enthusiastic preachers utilized radio to deliver fire-and-brimstone messages, to convert or keep the faithful devout. By the early 1950s, African American musical styles such as the blues and jazz were appropriated then transformed into the mostly white cultural movement of rock and roll. Scandalous, energetic compositions offered new freedoms— to change one's character, to express individualistic, often brash forms of language, to sing loudly and dress, dance, and behave unconventionally. Though hard to fathom now, The Rolling Stones' "long" hair horrified establishment figures in the 1960s.

Emerging first in the United States, rock and roll proved a cultural juggernaut across the West, even prompting violence in opposition and in favor of its expression. By the 1960s, British music pushed boundaries further: men grew hair as long as women, who now dressed in very short skirts, expressing sexuality and originality in the new faith of popular music. New attitudes derived from musical technologies signaled the decline of deference to authority at all levels. Such new attitudes to life spread throughout the Americas and West, spreading then globally in the 1980s.

A new culture emerged in which the masses enjoyed considerable freedom of expression, reshaping everyday language, bringing horrified responses from upholders of convention. Predictably, dictatorial and traditional societies restricted access to radio and music. In authoritarian states, radio shows repeated the droning diktats of those in power; listeners received only officially sanctioned music, with no room for creativity or taste preference. Long wave radio enthusiasts even risked imprisonment across the Communist world to hear Western music.

In the 1960's Herbert Marcuse argued that like authoritarian states, liberal societies used technology to coerce, in what he depicted as the "dictatorship of freedom":

By virtue of the way it has organized its technological base, contemporary industrial society tends to be totalitarian. For "totalitarian" is not only a terroristic political coordination of society, but also a non-terroristic economic-technical coordination which operates through the manipulation of needs by vested interests , , ,. Not only a specific form of government or party rule makes for totalitarianism, but also a specific system of production and distribution which may well be compatible with a "pluralism" of parties, newspapers, "countervailing powers," etc.[5]

Marcuse referred principally to the distraction of consumerism ar
media, which he argued prevented true political mass opposition
Popular music certainly brought distraction from serious issues, but
world nonetheless brought also freedom from conformity. Technology in the po
democratic world provided the means for self-expression to millions, including
women and other long-oppressed populations, who gained new freedoms in the
decades to follow.

As far as is known, all societies have sung and produced music. But after the 1950s,
technology transformed natural acoustic human and wood/metal instrumentation
sounds, broadcast through radio and television. By the end of the century, it would
retransform, into digital, computerized media. Though respectable society frowned,
and repressive states censored, music was an unstoppable cultural force. Freedom
of expression abounded, channeled through accessible communication technology,
particularly in democracies.

At root, music is a form of information, and information technologies create
opportunity for thought and expression to the detriment of those in power.
This explains frequent attempts to prohibit or control it. Though classical and
Communist music appreciation certainly grew in the USSR, creativity and
originality did not. Non-Western, autocratic societies still use radio and television
to constrain opinion and thought. Fundamentalist societies prohibit unrestricted
musical expression; the Taliban in Afghanistan famously banned music, and will
kill to enforce the law. Al Qaeda similarly banned music, though they used tape
cassettes in the 2000s to spread jihadi commitment to murder for faith. ISIS today
behead for the offense of listening to music, while using social media and Twitter
to recruit malcontents.

These inventions and attendant joys, now taken for granted, sprang from the
workings of free-flowing minds in open societies. Whether understanding the atom
or charting the cosmos, improving the camera or the car, manufacturing televisions
or CD's, technical improvements derived from human thought experiments.
Twentieth-century technologists benefitted immensely from and helped create a
culture of free exploration, where new avenues of opportunity and possibility were
explored without constraints.

A musical globe of haves and have-nots thus emerged by the 1970s. As technological
progress developed computing power, it widened power disparities worldwide. By
1947, American physicists learned to exploit the conducting properties of natural
elements such as silicon., and through this accomplishment, the transistor would
change the world via improved radio, telephone, television, and eventually computers.
The little transistor, the basic device through which all electronics functioned
thereafter by switching current or amplifying signals, enabled modern technology to
take the course it has.

Computer technology and free-flowing information

After Western countries defeated authoritarianism in the 1940s, a new form of information technology developed, stemming directly from wartime circumstances. Huge, bulky machines of metal and glass were built to compute and manipulate data, to transmit numbers and letters electronically. Democratic technologists first processed information to defeat Fascism, then to improve government and business administration.

By 1958, integrated circuits (small wafers that amplified and conducted electronic information) were used in America. Chips composed of silicon—one of the most abundant elements in the universe—evolved into the microchips that power modern computers. By the 1970s, offices and some homes used smaller computers with chips functioning as tiny engines. In the 1990s, faster processors sent music, film, bills, files and words over networks at low cost. The internet, a near imitation of the brain's neural network, soon connected computers worldwide to shape a new global society seeped in social media.

The cheap transmission of digitized data on affordable computers reshaped life worldwide. Once electromechanical technologies such as television, telephone or radio were converted into electronics, a revolution ensued, and all components of modern life were computerized the new century. Personal and professional life required computer literacy, and people or societies without it were generally condemned to poverty.

How this new style of computerized existence became so common and widespread stems largely from technological advances in the same industrial nations with global power in 1900. The origins of the computer revolution began early in the century in the United States and Western Europe. Punched cards used in the nineteenth-century textile industry to feed threads were substituted into holes in cardboard which signaled yes or no, in effect the first binary computers. By 1889, machines could compile data using paper strips on a plate, with wires embedded onto a switchboard, and by 1918, the Flip-flop circuit introduced vacuum tubes, which could store information in Random Access Memory (RAM). This was extremely costly, and only after transistors were invented in 1948 could technologists develop electronic circuits to make cheaper devices.

New computing technologies derived from human conflict as much as clever minds. In 1915 two naval officers in Holland invented the *Enigma Machine*, which provided the wherewithal to cipher and decode information on enemy German movements. The Allies could now communicate messages without detection. The first usable machines, essentially large typewriters, were available commercially by 1923, and in the 1940s German operatives used advanced versions of the machine to predict the movement of the Allies. Constructed with lights, wheels, keys, and plugs, the machine was a prototype electronic calculator that foreshadowed personal computers by transmitting current through keys to wheels. Messages could be sent in many billions of combinations for analysts to decode, making it near impossible for enemies to understand it. After the war, such machines were used by commercial enterprises to gain advantage over competitors who might wish to discover how a product was made or why it was priced at a certain level.

American and English technologists in particular won the war by computing more effectively. The hugely important Englishman Alan Turing designed the famous Turing Machine in 1936. Created as war approached, it was a clear forerunner to modern personal computers (PCs), making near infinite calculations based upon simple on and off switches, moving from 1 to 0 and back. By printing data on a spool, information could be sent to faraway military and official decision makers.

Turing's ideas were developed at Bletchley Park, where mostly female computer scientists decoded the German Enigma Machine to detect Nazi movements and plans. Information was shared with US military leaders working on parallel technologies. Indeed, American women like Grace Hopper were deeply involved in the computer revolution. Hopper famously coined the term "bug" to describe computer problems in 1945 (when an actual bug, a moth, impeded the function of a large machine!). Women worked through the war and postwar decades both as scientists, and even as human calculators in offices run by men. Katherine Johnson was only one of many women of color whose mathematical genius computerized and developed the US space program, culminating in the US moon landing in 1969.

> Many unsung women were part of the computer revolution, and the lives of women worldwide were in turn changed immensely by new technologies. One scholar argues that, "Women's liberation could have not succeeded if science had not provided them with contraception and household technology."[6]

Scientists and scholars from the highly interchangeable academic worlds of Britain and the United States cultivated and habituated Western politicians to the possibilities of "computing" for strategic and economic gain. Businessmen were of course quick to notice the opportunity for profits. IBM had incorporated in 1924, evolving into the first large profit-seeking technology business. Initially named Computing-Tabulating-Recording Company, IBM eventually employed millions of men and women, becoming a vast enterprise using dials, tapes, keys, and other simple mechanical moving parts to transmit and manage data for those in power. IBM was so central to US national development that it managed data on American social security records during the 1930s New Deal. The company also contributed to the war effort,

ng a core partner in US military efforts to counter totalitarianism in Europe
)an. In addition, it managed essential military information on armaments and
)duction in the Arab World.

American creativity

In democracies, business and government had long worked together both to control and advance technology. Small-scale tinkerers had driven science and technology since the seventeenth century in Britain. Bell Labs was incorporated in the US in 1925, after decades of experimentation in the family home of company founder Alexander Graham Bell, who had won $50,000 from the French government to invent a workable phone. But in the twentieth century, well-funded state research in the name of national competition and prestige pushed developments.

After 1945, the US military successfully harnessed the expertise of the best engineers, mathematicians, and scientists from Britain and the United States, but also Germany, to improve processing power and crunch data. By 1947 *ENIAC*, the first usable computer, was funded and researched by the US government (using so much energy when first turned on, that it dimmed the lights of Philadelphia). By 1950, the first personal computer, *Simon* was marketed for everyday home use, costing $600 (roughly $6000 today). Through the Cold War, Western states used computers to compete with the USSR. A major conference was held in 1957 in Rome to maximize the possibility of mainframe power. Soon, the first commercial computers emerged, filling large rooms they were so bulky. German engineers at vast enterprises like Siemens developed ideas from British engineers, using financial and intellectual support from the US military, to develop new products such as calculators and typing machines.

Western universities were also essential in developing computing technology. In 1957, forty slow, cumbersome PCs were hooked up across several university campuses in the United States—American engineers had linked the first network. By1964, the program BASIC was designed at Dartmouth College: now computer programmers could customize software and develop practical computer programs (beyond mere math or data collection). This provided the impetus in the 1970s for companies such as Microsoft, who would develop graphic programs such as MS Word or PowerPoint.

The British inventor Tim Berners-Lee transformed how we live by designing what would become the Internet. He wrote:

The web is more a social creation than a technical one. I designed it for a social effect—to help people work together—and not as a technical toy. The ultimate goal of the Web is to support and improve our weblike existence in the world. We clump into families, associations, and companies. We develop trust across the miles and distrust around the corner.[7]

Though Soviet leaders proudly displayed successes in space travel, the United States enjoyed huge advantage over the USSR (and the rest of world) by the 1960s, both in computer processing and innovation. Unlike in the United States, the purpose of Communist technological growth was to bolster state pride rather than to aim for commercial application. In the USSR, state decrees stimulated attempts to improve technology militarily rather than for consumers or profits. Engineers and scientists focused energies on space travel and medical advances, but frequent purges and oppression shackled the brightest minds.

Research was funded by the military in the United States too, but with unconstrained university engineers doing the actual science. By the 1970s, the USSR had no equivalent of *Arpanet*, which crisscrossed US universities to create computer networks. The Arpanet architecture was the forerunner of TCP/IP, which would connect devices globally by 2000. The word Internet was first used in 1973, and communication via electronic mail slowly emerged; the first email messages were sent in 1965 but were used only on campuses or for government use. Decades passed before mainstream use emerged in the 1990s.

By the 1990s, PC's were pervasive in developed nations. The first Word Processor, Word 1.0 released in 1989, facilitating textual writing on a screen. This changed the way that most people spent their days at work; authors no longer used typewriters but instead wrote lengthy tracts on white screens; office workers now sat in front of screens to perform job tasks; those in warehouses or in sales teams used computers and Microsoft Office to track their work or maintain information. The Internet and PCs became ubiquitous after 1994, using essential components such as microchips and semiconductors invented after the war. By 1980, no nation on earth could match the infrastructure of university research, government support, and private sector innovation of the United States. Most of the groundwork for the information revolution was thus laid there, with essential inputs from Western Allies.

Late twentieth-century microchip technology opened new vistas for understanding human existence. The transmission of electricity and computerization slowly enveloped the planet, bringing power and potential to populations worldwide. Urban, modern life is justly critiqued for its pace and for forcing billions to sit at desks all day, as humans with bad posture process tedious computer information for hours on end. But few would prefer to be illiterate, impoverished, or live without connectivity. Computer technology shaped a new kind of personal and professional existence, delivering economic growth, new avenues for social criticism, and immense access to information. In the 2000's, enterprises such as Facebook and YouTube became principal mediums for humanity's social and business affairs. Billions of people worldwide now go to the same sites and communicate directly, sharing pictures, offering opinions, and revealing attitudes to the world.

Join or die

During the American Revolution, Benjamin Franklin famously galvanized Americans to fight perceived British tyranny, leaving no choice but to "Join, or die." Though death has not always been the consequence, since 1900 nonindustrial and non-Western societies worldwide have been left with similarly limited options, forced to join the race for technological advancement. Those that did, such as Japan and most of East Asia, prospered; those that didn't suffered mightily. LDCs had no chance and have been second- and third-class global states for a century now.

Clear advantage fell to societies that first developed and utilized modern technology, with dire consequences for the majority of people worldwide. Trains exported ores from poor societies to rich ones for manufacturing purposes through the century. Planes provided military advantage to demolish fighters on foot. States that colonized developing societies continue to extract raw materials or exploit cheap labor today. Even when colonization declined after the 1960s, Soviets and Americans fought a technological war in the 40-year-long Space Race, imposing their will on the Third World. LDCs heavily influenced by Washington and Moscow suffered political and economic disruption, receiving little if any of the technological gains and all of the pressures.

Western inventions have been thrust upon the developing world. A Malaysian writer spoke of the introduction of television into a small village in the 1970s, highlighting the magic of the screen:

When Pak Ali bought the TV set, he knew he was buying it for the whole village . . . the villages 300 families are all Indian film fans. The elders talk of religion and rubber, of politics and the new village chief. Though their eyes are fixed on the TV set, they keep up a dignified discussion, for they do not quite approve of the love scenes in the film. The women with babies are frankly enthralled. Standing far back in the shadows are the villages young men and girls. There are very few, for most have gone off to town to chase the dream of a better life.[8]

Whether this reads as a lamentation or a celebration is for the reader to decide.

Many therefore question whether technology promotes or constrains freedom or democracy. George Orwell's widely read novel *1984*, published in 1948, depicted a terrible world where technology enabled government officials to control populations more easily. Orwell presciently argued that technology could shape political views, philosophical outlooks, even beliefs about correct actions. He observed that technological inventions changed not only the pace of life, but also the very nature of humanity's outlook toward everything. Twentieth-century technology clearly provided modern governments with the means to control populations at home and societies abroad. It also permitted the exploitation of nature's resources in ways that had never been seen before.

Orwell also asserted that historically and geographically, diverse cultures enjoyed different means of existence, but now technological advance moved culture only in one direction, from traditional to industrial societies. If nineteenth-century imperialism afforded powerful modern states economic and political advantage, twentieth-century technological innovations only widened that gap.

Technologies developed in industrial nations reinforced economic, military, and political domination, emerging with few exceptions from laboratories in the United States, Britain, France, Germany, or Russia. Western states formed organized societies committed to technological utility, enabling them to apply power with ease. If in 1900 societies worldwide were forced to join a capitalist, industrial Western-dominated world at a disadvantage, by 2000, most of those same societies were bit players in a Western-shaped world of Facebook posts, Google searches and Microsoft programs. When after 1945 the Allied powers forbade Japan from remilitarizing, Japanese leaders dedicated massive national and intellectual capital into modernization and computer electronics. By 1980, it was the wealthiest society on earth. Engineers in Korea, Taiwan, and Singapore soon emulated the Japanese, producing world-class products that filled homes with electronic gadgets. Such nations enjoyed affluence and security by copying the Western capitalist model of production through technology. By the 1970s, electronics industries sprouted across East Asia, and created reciprocity in goods and ideas between North America, Europe, and Asia, putting these regions in positions of wealth and power incomparably higher than the rest of the planet, a condition that persists today. This shows that high national funding and research for technological innovation correlates almost perfectly with higher wealth and stability. Perhaps the only option is to join or die.

4. The Information Age

The influential Austrian economist Fritz Machlup, working in the United States after fleeing Nazi Germany, predicted that after the war information would become a key financial resource. A century-long transition from an industrial to an information economy indeed transpired thereafter. Wealth, for centuries based upon the control of land, labor, and capital, was now built on information and knowledge. Facebook, Amazon, and Google—companies that functioned in physical offices but nonetheless profited by transmitting information globally in milliseconds—replaced metal machines in enormous factories.

Communication of information over distance became a central component of twenty-first-century life. Since information produced wealth, nations with higher levels of technological literacy dominated those without. Once again, the West was far ahead: nonindustrial, ex-colonized regions had to respond rather than lead in the computer revolution. Ex-Communist states played catch-up too, as habits of dogma held back the minds of millions unaccustomed to critical thought.

The proliferation of computer technology required highly literate and numerate populations. The basic ability to read and compute were essential skills for industrial urban life even before the Second World War. Owning a bank account, the ability to manage money and credit, and the ability to understand words, were expected in the developed world. The consequences were severe for those who could not. The inability to read contracts meant that citizens could be duped into bad loans or indebted for life, in developed or traditional societies. The inability to read meant that people were more easily led, more prone to follow the diktats and decrees of others. In the new century, a global digital divide demonstrated starkly the vast disparity between industrialized, literate nations and developing nations with low literacy.

Computer literacy

Literacy of any type is at root the ability to communicate and comprehend. It is therefore central to human history, especially since 1900. Reading literacy rates increased vastly over the century, a necessary component of industrial development. While 80 percent of the world was illiterate in 1900, less than 20 percent were by 2000, living almost entirely in LDCs. The poorest nations on earth today neatly correlate with low levels of literacy. Wealthy nations have long enjoyed high literacy; Western states were already close to universal literacy in 1900. Well before the Second World War, a huge paper industry existed in Britain, feeding a literate culture of book and magazine reading. In Europe and the United States, widely read, affordable magazines such as Readers' Digest spread ideas nationwide, creating information dispersal mechanisms to those without formal education, increasing literacy while entertaining. In 1900, post offices distributed letters across developed nations, promoting reading and writing, increasing communication by using the written rather than the spoken word.

By 1933, simple machines such as the typewriter aided the spread of ideas (good or bad) over great distances, in turn increasing the need for high literacy in developed societies. Countries with standardized methods of communication shared more information more efficiently. Barely noticed inventions such as standardized fonts conveyed information clearly and globally. The font used here, Times New Roman, was created in 1932, and became a potent symbol for communication and standardization. The Xerox machine, invented in 1959, enabled firms to copy and share vast amounts of information among their ranks and with partners around the world. Businesses thus performed tasks more cost-effectively, increasing profits and production.

In the last few decades of the century, built-up industrialized wealth funded new research, which in turn fostered greater literacy. Higher education levels and administrative efficiency enabled developed states to produce more, to gain further advantage over traditional, less precision driven societies. Third World nations that endured colonization, or authoritarian states focused on militarism, did not exploit their intellectual resources or innovate. Cheap or free education in wealthy nations enabled citizens to count and calculate faster. The accurate measurement of production and of productivity provided information to hire more people or boost output. Industries such as banking fashioned a new world, where ordinary people used checks and credit cards, or invested through computers.

Computer technology changed life, work, purchasing, even eating and drinking. It shaped leisure time, enabled people to find partners, socialize with family, and debate politics, history or religion. By 2000, information flow represented a prime source of leisure and entertainment. By processing and transmitting data Netflix conveyed thousands of movies to homes at low cost; Xbox, Amazon, and many others provided people with the means to play games with people worldwide.

Greater literacy brought the freedom to interpret information autonomously, and new technologies provoked recipients of information to question authority. Documentaries became relatively cheap to make, enjoying wide viewership and reshaping attitudes toward life, economy, politics, or beliefs. Information literacy increased human curiosity, initiated an insatiable desire to study nature, to question truths, and to find new ways of thinking and doing. The power of information management reached to the skies, as satellites provided data to developed states to predict weather, prepare for disasters, understand climate change, and help to avoid the consequences of drought or flood. Humans had for millennia merely responded to nature; they had controlled and exploited it through industrial methods for two centuries; by 2000, they manipulated it through information technology.

Too much information?

None of the "progress" outlined above came without costs. Only recently has the field of Information Technology embraced the study of ethics to attempt to humanize the apparent benefits of technology. An array of technological negatives, from psychological, personal, or physical ailments to economic, military, and environmental abuse, persist in troubling much of humanity, adding to the horrors wrought since 1900.

Psychological impact

Technologists have long feared their own creations. *Frankenstein* turning on his inventor has been a central trope in modern literature, and Alfred Nobel's guilt over inventing dynamite prompted him to create the Nobel Peace Prize. Einstein feared that his work had served the rise of Nazi power, and Robert Oppenheimer famously doubted his exertions after seeing its fruits in the first atomic bomb test. Appalled at the destructive power his research unleashed, he cited ancient Hindu scripture, "I am become Death, the destroyer of worlds." Arthur C. Clarke, who first devised satellites circling the earth in 1960, also feared of the consequences of his idea.

As long ago as 1921 the Czech author Karel Capek expressed similar concerns. Capek invented the term *robot*, suggesting (at least in fiction) that artificial people might one day perform menial labor. The word "robot" in Czech stems from "drudgery or menial labor" and of course now robots clean homes and much more. They have produced automobiles since the 1970s, they stock warehouses, fight in wars, and dispense cash. The theme of machines taking over became prominent in twentieth-century sci-fi novels in Capek's wake.

The concept of AI—artificial intelligence—was coined in 1955 when computer scientists intentionally aspired to improve machines to make human-like decisions. Computer technology has not only created incredible wealth for modern, technical societies, it appears to be imitating the human brain. By the new century, PCs could process information so quickly that they beat world champions at chess, and have now beaten champions in the East Asian *Go,* which requires adaptive thinking far more than chess! It has been suggested that AI might be the last invention humans ever make.

More fundamentally, some worry about technology's impact on the human mind. Alvin Toffler's 1970 bestseller *Future Shock* warned millions of readers that too much change too quickly could have detrimental effects on humanity. Few, he opined, grasped the psychological effects of—at that time—rather limited data flow. Even the world-famous singer Sting bemoaned the pervasiveness of information technology, singing in the 1980s, "Too much information, running through my brain. Too much information, driving me insane."

Privacy

Computers now make decisions regarding human tastes, interests, and wishes, using math-based Internet algorithms to predict social desires more accurately than governments, militaries, or businesses ever could. This has major implications for privacy, since citizens cannot prevent their personal information being used for commercial, legal, or pernicious purposes. Intrusions into privacy, whether online, through telephones or televisual habits, provide massive amounts of data to authorities, sharing personal actions, location, and opinions. Privacy scanning technology in the hands of officials working for the state or the private sector can impinge upon the rights of law-abiding citizens. Edward Snowden demonstrated that

Figure 4.8 Attendees wear Oculus Rift virtual reality (VR) headsets during the Intel Corp. press event at the 2017 Consumer Electronics Show. (Patrick T. Fallon/ Bloomberg via Getty Images.)

the US security apparatus was willing to spy on foreign leaders and its own citizens under the guise of "security." Crime prevention technology such as CCTV is also used for the greater good. In London, England, cameras are placed on almost every corner—the average person is filmed thousands of times a day in public.

Government might reasonably be expected to control some degree of information, yet businesses also gain access to it now. There has long been a dubious relationship between scientific technology and profit seeking. Whereas during the Scientific Revolution and Industrial Revolution tinkerers and home-based innovators worked alone for the sake of experimentation, most scientific research is today performed in large expensive laboratories, chasing profits. Billions of dollars flow into government-supported labs or universities, who enjoy grants and close relationships with officialdom. Profit seeking or grant chasing scholars often work not for the common good but for the bottom line, or for their own ideological or geopolitical goals, financially influenced by large pharmaceutical or engineering corporations. The stakes are higher than just privacy rights though. Vested economic interests explain the willingness of a tiny minority of scientists to doubt climate change data and global warming, even though overwhelming consensus exists.

nmental collapse

h-century paradox - of technology's immense benefits, and its negative ...pact on the human and natural environment - is palpable. Thrilling automobile technology by 1900 quickly transformed into lethal tanks and bombers by 1918. Fast-moving tractors that produced so much food in the 1920s despoiled lands to cause the Dust Bowl in the 1930s. Technology produced vast quantities of food in the postwar Green Revolution; now over 8 billion people populate the planet, pressuring resources. The chemicals that provide nourishment for billions are used in biological weaponry. Computers and printers require billions of pages of paper via industrial forestry; pollutant chemicals bleach pages white. Satellites provide entertainment for billions, and useful information to those in power. Millions of broken satellites clutter the skies, dropping debris that hopefully burns in the atmosphere before landing. Digital addiction is now a major concern for parents raising children, and society in general.

Environment devastation is a major consequence of technology, whether through water-guzzling, air-conditioned server farms for Silicon Valley companies, or the extraction of rare minerals in Africa or Central Asia for smartphones and tablets. The United States is a representative example of the problem: at just over 4 percent of the global population, Americans use up to 25 percent of the world's key resources such as coal, aluminum, oil, and copper to enjoy its ultra-technological lifestyle.

The ultimate symbol of American, Western and now global success, the automobile, is also the definitive contradiction environmentally. Life without cars may seem unimaginable, but they are mechanically inefficient machines that waste huge amounts of energy. Cars are built with vast quantities of natural resources such as water, metal, glass, rubber, and plastic. They endanger humans, ecosystems, and have killed 1.3 million worldwide people in 2015, more than any other cause aside from disease, far more than in war!

Energy is still produced inefficiently; scientists do not know how to apply fertilizers to wheat or rice without impacting soil quality; and technologists struggle to find efficient battery power for hybrids or mass electric vehicles without scouring mines from mountains. Resource extraction, like climate change, impacts poorer societies more than rich ones, working many to the bone, creating millions of climate refugees.

There is hope of course. In the United States and Western countries, environmental regulations and official restrictions on the use of coal or wood helped clear the air in many cities as long ago as the 1950s. Environmentalism after all began in the United States, but the US Environmental Protection Agency (EPA) has an awkward relationship with business, offending financial elites by constraining polluters. It is currently threatened with extinction. Its report back in 1973 expressed pressing concerns:

> Our contemporary culture, primed by population growth and driven by technology, has created problems of environmental degradation that directly affect all of our senses: noise, odors and toxins which bring physical pain and suffering, and ugliness, barrenness, and homogeneity of experience which bring emotional and psychological suffering and emptiness. In short, we are jeopardizing our human qualities by pursuing technology as an end rather than a means. Too often we have failed to ask two necessary questions: First, what human purpose will a given technology or development serve? Second, what human and environmental effects will it have?[9]

5. Conclusion

Since 1900, a vast concatenation of innovations, creations, and inventions increased the impact of humans on earth exponentially compared to all earlier history. This continues apace. Technology improved the quality of life for billions in ways inconceivable 100 years ago. Billions more people now live and alter nature as a result of improved medical technology, ravenously demanding access to material wealth derived from nature. Information is readily available as never before; the world's knowledge is searchable on a smartphone. The application of "Big Data" in fields such as genome research modifies how humans conceive of themselves.

On the surface, this seems to be for the general good. Through information technology, more people know more about what is happening in society and can find information to solve problems. Though many still lack Internet access, most people in 1900, as for most of history, had no access to information about other people, other histories, or other ways of seeing the world. Most people simply heard the voices of their families and neighbors, or those in power. The Internet demonstrates how the whole world lives—it may introduce new attitudes, new awareness, and more acceptance of difference. A key issue remains regarding access to information; will less literate poor people enjoy the gains of information as much as the educated and wealthy? Will those in power abuse information to control as they did in the past?

Regardless, most people cannot get through their day now without technology, and few wish to. Technology is the means through which we understand the very problems that beset us: we would be blithely unaware of climate change without technology; the nutritional qualities of foods would be immeasurable without technology; gathering troops on a border could take us by surprise, as they did for millennia, without technology to monitor aggressors. This is the archetypal paradox; modern technology is both liberator and oppressor.

Indeed, modern technology originated in military research and wartime anxieties. On a global level, nations now engage in cyber wars, competing for industrial or political knowledge. Evident distrust between the United States and Iran, China, or Russia is undergirded by covert practices of information warfare. Governments now spy on each other for competitive advantage. US elections succumb to influence from foreign agents, making Cold War spy games seem quaint in retrospect. As usual, history provides context. From the time when Britain shot ahead in industrial power, Western nations engaged in espionage and technological competition; this underwrote the German and British race to militarize that prompted the First World War. Envy of American or any other nation's technological prowess has motivated most non-Western societies for much of the past century.

However, we often overlook the fact that all technologies, however advantageous, derive from raw materials, consume energy and impact the natural environment. While great material wealth and comfort comes from the technology-driven production and transportation of clothes, foods and countless household products, most of it ends up in landfills or oceans as garbage or is shipped to poor nations for disposal. Since modern societies are built on fossil fuels, subsequent climate change may be the major global consequence of all this progress. As in the past, LDCs pay the price of industrial nation's development.

Fear of the apocalypse is of course as old as humanity. Now as in 1900, humanity seems addicted to technology. Only the scale has changed. It is obvious that the Internet and information technology have changed world history however. As every student knows, the Internet offers an exciting new world of opportunity—to learn, to collaborate globally, to communicate with distant family, to enjoy entertainment, to start businesses, to distribute food and water to conflict-ridden regions. Like roads connecting cities in the ancient world, ships sailing oceans in the early modern era, canals and railroads in the nineteenth century, like electricity, and the telegraph and the telephone after 1900, the Internet represents a new iteration of cultural connectivity for humanity. Its components however all come from nature, and so it is to the environment and its recent history that we will turn to, after the Interlude, to conclude, in Chapter 5.

Key terms

Scientific Method [204]
Bletchley Park [208]
Agent Orange [210]
Synthetics [215]
Broadcasting [225]
Motion Pictures [227]

Enigma machine [232]
ENIAC [234]
Arpanet [235]
Robot [240]

Further readings

Smil, Vaclav. *Creating the Twentieth Century: Technical Innovations of 1867–1914 and Their Lasting Impact*. New York: Oxford University Press, 2005. A fascinating explanation of the major innovations and inventions in the late nineteenth century, addressing ongoing effects on modern life.

Buchanan, R. A. *The Power of the Machine: The Impact of Technology from 1700 to the Present*. London: Viking, 1992. Excellent long-term historical perspective on how humanity arrived at twentieth-century engineering advances.

http://www.unep.org/ For an international perspective on issues facing humanity today, this is an excellent resource, with data on climate change, conflict, governance and resource use.

Interlude 4: Freedom

Technology and power

In one of the defining moments of the century, on December 25, 1991, Moscow abandoned Soviet Communism. The economic and political underpinnings of Communism had been discredited globally. In a meeting with fellow world leaders televised worldwide that day, Mikhail Gorbachev attempted to sign the document to abdicate and concede the demise of Communism. In front of the world and the cameras of America's burgeoning televisual giant, CNN, Gorbachev's pen didn't work! Though those present reacted with humor, few could help but notice how the moment symbolized the disparity between the efficiency of Western technology and the corrupt, fictitious production figures and technological limitations of Soviet— indeed all Communist—societies.

Soviets and Americans had spent decades insulting each other, proclaiming the exclusive virtues of their own system. In a struggle more technological than military, both claimed that their people enjoyed more freedom and a better way of life. Both sides produced massive firepower; both sides abused the powerless militarily. Though the war was fought mostly in the rhetorical battlefields of space research and nuclear power, the Cold War was won and lost in shopping malls. The desire for material comforts and consumer joys converted people away from Communism, showing Western democracies produced far superior technologies.

Power and control

Between 1945 and 1991, sophisticated technological prowess enabled the United States and the USSR to control, or at least influence, almost all regions on earth. Soviet elites controlled all aspects of society in a modernizing techno-state, constantly telling people they were free, even as they lived lives ranging from the dreary to the nightmarish. Orwell's *1984* had forewarned of such a society, where humans lose all meaning in life through conformity, obedience and trained hate - trusting the propaganda those in power spread so adeptly via the state apparatus.

Figure 4.9 Poster from a BBC TV production of George Orwell's classic novel *1984*. (Larry Ellis/Express/Getty Images.)

Though the Second World War was a victory for democracy, critics worried that elites in open societies also numbed the minds of the masses through propaganda, inducing an addiction to consumption as a substitute for real thought. Business advertising and state propaganda socialized Westerners into consumption, using "soft power," arguably even more effective than more transparent totalitarian propaganda. In 1931, Aldous Huxley had forewarned of this in his renowned *Brave New World*. Huxley proposed that a mixture of pleasure and indolence, doled out like a drug with official approval from a state-sanctioned entertainment complex, could subdue critical thought through affordable pharmaceuticals, purposely numbing societies into unquestioning obedience. Postwar sociologists such as Theodore Adorno suggested a society of advertising and acquisition was not better than an authoritarian society.

These were serious warnings. Orwell cautioned readers of the abusive manipulation of history and memory that pervaded modern statehood, famously writing, "Who controls the past controls the future. Who controls the present, controls the past."[10] Huxley foresaw a world where technology and entertainment rather than political violence would undermine democratic life, writing, "Democracy can hardly be expected to flourish in societies where political and economic power is being progressively concentrated and centralized. But the progress of technology has led and is still leading to just such a concentration and centralization of power."[11]

Technology and its uses

yes – 30 sec
prof. commercials

We undoubtedly grapple with such issues in our newly globalized techno-world. Technology certainly created haves and have-nots in the past century, provided the means for officialdom to pull the wool over people's eyes—in autocratic and "free" nations—and it empowered vast state machines to use firepower to kill millions. Authoritarian regimes deployed files and data to efficiently plan the eradication of millions of people.

A central question in the new century then is how states should use technology. The prevalence of technology and its ability to obliterate humankind makes it a subject of interest and concern to all. Governments in the past century used technologies to bolster national prestige or maintain power. But information technology has now become a way of waging war, between states and inside them. Hackers working for states use data to undermine structures of governance, including military, security, or bureaucratic computer systems. Hackers working alone aim to disrupt society for the sake of it; some gleefully disrupt democratic elections. 3-D printers now manufacture houses and bicycles using carbon printing filaments—they also make guns. Bionic bodies are now commonplace, though biomedical advances raise new questions of ethics. The manipulation of genes alters people now as humans altered corns and grains in the past.

Technology and freedom

Technologies also help resist power. The literary technique of reading—only for the rich and powerful a century ago—rises globally. In the twenty-first century, blogs enable millions to write for wide audiences, online publishing provides nonacademic and professional writers the ability to share their thoughts. Rising literacy spreads more critical viewpoints; questioning authority becomes customary instead of terrifying. Internet technologies enable those who suspect politicians intentions to connect over great distances.

Critical Thinking

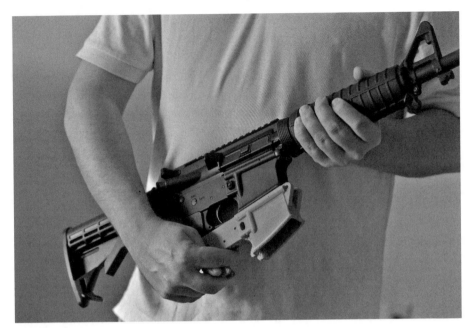

Figure 4.10 Assault rifle parts made with a 3-D printer. (Jahi Chikwendiu/ *Washington Post* via Getty Images.)

Other benefits are obvious too. Families separated by the demands of work or those split by voluntary or forced migration can inexpensively see each other and talk on video. Travel around the globe is cheap enough for millions to fly daily. Few live without the Internet, instant international communication spreads daily. 4D TV promises to make home entertainment akin to live experience, and films and series galore are available to homes in the developed world. Regardless of its virtues or hazards, we may be unable to stop technology. The concept of technological determinism—that there is no stopping the advance of technology and science—might well be our destiny.

Visualizing new worlds

At root, human ingenuity was the source and inspiration behind modern governance and technological innovation. Technology has done great harm, but it has provided the opportunity for humans to express themselves more in the last century than ever before in history. Indeed, the most popular blockbuster movies and TV series continue to question technology and human future, altering the mental worldviews of billions of people. In 1999, the famous *Matrix* series emerged, suggesting how humans might blend with computers. Recent blockbusters continue such themes. *The*

Hunger Games in 2012 cautioned that trust in authority is a slippery slope, exposing the short path between necessary state security and autocratic overreach. This dystopian story was especially important for female audiences weary of male authors, male protagonists, and male heroes. Its central star was a teenage girl, not wearing pink or acting as the princess, but fighting for freedom. The film's interpretation was purposely broad, ranging from liberal and secular ideas, contending that societies need agitation and diversity, all the way to conservative traditionalism, proclaiming the need for more faith.

Technology also exacerbated national, class and racial divisions from 1900. There is some concern those who control technology could become a master race, enslaving those without access. 2009's *Avatar* addressed crucial issues of how humans relate to each other and to nature in this technological world. It futuristically adapted themes of historical imperialism and racism to foresee future forms of domination on different planets among different species. The writers questioned the mass tendency to passively accept huge armies and technological militarism—notions long sold by those in power.

Elysium, made in 2013 but set in 2154, approached the environmental question of overpopulation, ever worsening due to recent technological advances in health care, nutrition and prolonged lifespans. In *Elysium*, citizens download data to control minds or access personal and financial information. Seemingly affable, apparently caring leaders manipulate the masses, deflecting them from questions of material inequality in a supposedly moral, materially abundant world.

These futuristic scenarios are hardly far-fetched. For the past century, control of technology has permitted rulers worldwide to block disadvantaged populations from agitating. Technology now allows democratic or autocratic nations to fire missiles worldwide without going near enemies, using computer-controlled drones, combat is increasingly automated. What does it mean when soldiers raised on video games can obey their leaders and kill for country, from a computer, without leaving home?

Technology, pleasure, and peace

Yet, for all the fears surrounding evolving intelligence, screen addiction, instant consumerism or potential authoritarianism, humans worldwide increasingly idolize our gadgets. Technology now encroaches into every aspect of life, from apps that monitor newborns to means of keeping people alive longer than nature perhaps intended. Through Internet technology, global spectators explore films and documentaries bringing new meaning in life, addressing all manners of topics.

Upon reading the daily news (online) it might seem like the world is about to end, but plenty of people find solace in modern life. Though the media display the horrors of global humanity each day through technology, most people live more peaceably than ever before. Though some claim video games increase violence, there

Figure 4.11 Mushroom cloud from the first test of a hydrogen bomb, 1952. (Photo by SSPL/Getty Images.)

is evidence violence is on a steep decline worldwide. Stephen Pinker claims these are the safest times in human history. Jared Diamond and others note that in places where technology has NOT spread, life is as dangerous as it was 3,000 years ago, conspicuously more than in advanced states. Indeed, states with the most advanced technology not only have the longest life spans and highest standards of living, but also the safest everyday existence, even accounting for class and racial biases. Those that don't, usually in the undeveloped world, live with similar levels of fear as in the past.

Technology and living things

Since 1900, human minds have reshaped atoms, altered genes, changed the chemical and physical nature of life on earth, and can now perform precise biochemical analyses of all living cells on earth! They have prolonged life, countered famine and disease and turned the homes of billions into pleasure domes. The very genes that constitute our bodies are now under scientific scrutiny. When Watson and Crick described the structure of DNA and its functions in the 1950s, most people then, as today, could not comprehend its meaning or impact. DNA, a substance found in all cells in living organisms, contains the genetic code of human beings. What does it mean to observe the well-known double-helix image of our DNA? What does it suggest that we have the ability to alter it? It's hard to tell.

From the stick to the plough, the water mill to the nuclear bomb and the Internet, technology has shaped us more than we presently understand. Since the Industrial Revolution in England in the late eighteenth century, almost every advance in technology has harnessed the power of nature, propelling certain societies into positions of power, prominence and influence. It provided some with vastly more comfort and wealth than others, easily maintained through greater information access. Technological advance also ruined millions of lives, murdered millions, injured those doing most of the work, impoverished non-industrial nations, and desecrated the global environment.

Perhaps the most frightening symbol of the immense human proficiency for technological advance is that we can turn the basic knowledge of atoms and molecules into nuclear bombs. We can manipulate natural resources and processes to destroy whole cities, or in sufficient scale, life on earth. Technology has changed politics, economics, beliefs, opinions and life itself in ways unimaginable a century ago. Its greatest impact however may ultimately be in the way it has affected the environment, the source of all human life. We now turn, in our final chapter, to explore the environmental history of the world since 1900.

5

Twentieth-Century Environment: Ecologically Unequal

Situating the chapter

Our final chapter covers the most important issue humankind can conceivably face, the potential for ecological catastrophe and major climate change, arising from historically shaped *political* opinions, *economic* desires, *technological* innovations, and the deep-seated *beliefs* underlying them. Since 1900, immense quantities of pollution wafted into and around the planet due to political ambitions, material aspirations, and resource extraction. Technology brought immense environmental contamination and destruction. Religious and philosophical sensibilities failed to counter these everyday aspirations, as a focus on the afterlife or ideology seemed to precede concerns over the present.

By 2017, scientists, experts, and informed citizens feared that the environment was on the verge of disaster if human behavior did not change. Massive opposition to environmental conservation from businesses, lobbyists, and Conservatives, particularly in the United States and Russia, obstructed efforts to repair ecosystems and control pollution. At the same time, important dialogue took place globally about the state of the planet and how to counter climate change. The G20 group of nations, who produce 80 percent of world trade, have committed to fighting climate

Figure 5.1 Beijing pollution. (Credit: DuKai photographer.)

change, (with the exception of the United States). This chapter explores how attitudes toward and exploitation of the natural world has changed since 1900.

By the end of this chapter, readers should be able to:

- Explain how states and societies have exploited the environment since 1900.
- Distinguish between industrial and less-developed societies' impacts on the earth.
- Compare the different effects of environmental exploitation on poor and rich people or countries.
- Evaluate how and if human attitudes to nature have changed in the past century.
- Summarize the impact on the earth from industrial growth in the last century.

The story

"The health of nations is more important than the wealth of nations." Will Durant.

The technological, economic and political history of the past century depended entirely on converting natural materials into products or energy. Nevertheless, the importance of the earth, its soils or inhabitants went unaccounted for in the race for national wealth, as the scholar Will Durant implied just after the Second World War with his famous quotation. Durant, one of the most read historians of the century, hoped to unite people worldwide through world history and philosophy, and at the heart of this aphorism was a belief that nations' focus on accruing economic power brought serious hidden costs.

Perhaps the clearest expression of humanity's focus on politics or economics instead of the environment is the fact that the widely known and well-studied First World War slaughtered around 20 million people, while the Spanish flu epidemic that followed killed (it is now estimated) up to 100 million humans! Which, one wonders, is in fact the greater story?

1. Belief in the future

Much of what humans make of the world is, and has been, based on some mixture of *belief* and *knowledge*. Politically, as Chapter 1 showed, nations fought each other due to differing beliefs over political organization, whether imperial, tribal, democratic, autocratic, or dynastic. Chapter 2 explored how humans willingly killed over economic beliefs concerning free-market capitalism, Socialism, or resource extraction. Chapter 3 demonstrated enduring differences in belief systems, both profane and sacred, bringing consternation, hostility, even genocide. Chapter 4 explored the deep-seated belief that technological proficiency was positive, even when so often used for negative purposes. Different sets of beliefs, dependent on relative location in time, space, or background, clearly benefitted some and hurt others.

Epistemologists fall into two broad camps: a knowledge-first group and a belief-first one. The first side claims that factual knowledge is all humans have to go on, based on empirical data—that beliefs are of little use in studying the physical world. The other claims that beliefs are as justifiable as knowledge, and question established facts or consensuses. Both groups, however, agree that once internal beliefs move from the individual and are externalized to others in the world, we can practically determine whether those beliefs are precise, correct, useful, or applicable as knowledge. Here for instance, climate change deniers have only their beliefs to go on, all the evidence supports the argument climate change is occurring.

Hence, differences in belief concerning the environment, formed historically and passed on, are potentially catastrophic for all humans. If diversity in beliefs regarding politics, economics, ideas, or technology may harvest great violence, this could be negligible when compared to the prospective environmental devastation humans face. Many believe that the environment is already ruined, while others believe that it mends itself, arguing it is presumptuous to attempt to even measure the human impact on earth. Either way, the vast majority of environmental scientists, NASA, scholars, and the most educated members of all societies concur that human actions are changing the planet's temperature—quickly. Experts rely on observable data regarding sea levels, temperatures, the size of ice sheets, glacial disappearance, and other objective factors to form this knowledge; beliefs do not interfere in their conclusions.

From bad to better?

One central claim of climate change deniers however is accurate—the environment *has* always changed. Through all of history, societies have used and abused their surroundings. Use of resources is after all how states, societies, and empires formed in the first place. But as we have seen recurrently, the twentieth century was different, in population numbers, resource use, violence, and in the scale of technological and economic rivalry. The planet is now warming faster than ever: environmental change is not the same as the minor modifications humans made to their environs prior to industrialization and globalization.

Already in the nineteenth century, humans had transformed the physical environment more than ever before in history. But other than Romantic writers or naturalists, few questioned the destruction. By the 1950s, states polluted the earth at unprecedented rates: many endured unbreathable air in cities; rivers worldwide were poisoned with chemical runoff; urbanization encroached upon wildlife; and governments laid cement and tarmac over green lands. The scale of air pollution or water contamination only became apparent in the 1960s and was not addressed through broad policies until the 1970s. Since then, though conservationists point out the despoliation of nature worldwide, more and more societies have consumed goods, and businesses compete to produce and pollute, neglectful of the consequences of industrial practices.

Tragedy of the commons

Hence, only as the twentieth century waned did those in power become cognizant of the hazards of climate change. Slow progress was made with international agreements to address melting icebergs and rising rivers in the 2000s. Success had been achieved in the 1990s to close the hole in the atmosphere known as the ozone layer. But the aspiration for individual nations to prosper prevented unity or progress, particularly the opposition of special interests in the US Congress, the world's most powerful state, and greatest per capita polluter. A combination of powerful lobbying in the oil, energy, and automobile industries, and remarkable contempt for the scientific consensus on climate change, remain the chief obstacles to US cooperation.

Certainly, the aspiration for material progress is in keeping with the past century, where business and government leaders in industrial societies, and then LDCs, targeted a better standard of living for their people. Though few in 1900 could have imagined the harm that societies could do to the planet, few could have imagined the world of abundance, comfort, and longer life spans that so many would attain. Everyday life today would have seemed utopian a century ago. In the First World at least, a life of travel, technology, and entertainment is taken for granted by billions, who rarely worry about hunger or disease. Humans are taller and healthier than they have ever been. Even though billions of people remain poor, they too live longer than their ancestors and are often relatively better off.

Evidently, industrial societies have harmed the environment most while gaining the most. The vast majority of societies historically, and many since 1900, touched the environment only lightly. For millennia before the eighteenth-century Industrial Revolution, humans used nature and learned from it, only dimly aware of ecological changes such as deforestation, drying riverbeds, or climate changes. In the nineteenth century, the scale of human manipulation of nature surged, producing a focused craving to make products, commodities, and goods, generally understand as *Industrial Capitalism*. By 2000, nearly all societies aspired to emulate the high energy, high polluting standard of living of industrial nations.

For most of the century then, environmentalism played little to no part in policy making, until concerned citizens recently raised awareness. A male-dominated world of industrial and military exploitation that persisted into the 1970s transformed into one where female voices were heard, incorporating more diverse analyses of ecosystems, profound questions about consumerism, and a greater awareness of mother earth and her fragility. The two approaches now sit uneasily at a historical juncture.

2. Belief in power—politics and nature

Through the century, vast swaths of nature were despoiled due to the political belief that nations must compete for resources, either at home or (preferably) on foreign soils. Well-organized industrialized nation-states brought large-scale ecological destruction, in war, through building infrastructure projects, or in goods production. After the 1960s, LDCs and colonized societies repeated the pattern in their attempt to industrialize or modernize, and continue to do so.

The power to pollute

By 1900, Western democracies extracted oil, rubber, and other essential raw materials from overseas regions to maintain domestic stability and prosperity. Soviet Russia followed after 1921, dominating adjoining regions, exploiting tens of millions of subjugated workers through forced labor for Communist gain. Japan industrialized at breakneck speed, rapidly exploiting other nations' resources, particularly China's. And, after 1949, China prolonged a century of environmental disaster through economic incompetence, enormous projects, and the exploitation of cheap labor. From the 1970s, colonized regions of the world from Latin America to Africa modernized, exporting raw materials to industrial states with great environmental damages. Like rulers in industrial nations, elites in ex-colonized states displayed very limited aptitude to address the despoliation of nature.

For over a century, in democratic, autocratic or ex-colonized societies, the earth has been scraped, polluted, and reshaped more than ever before, leaving enduring environmental problems. Centralized states fundamentally wrought environmental devastation to achieve economic growth or political stability. Leaders needed legitimization to maintain position or compete with rivals, and huge state-led infrastructure projects brought prestige, wealth, and power, free of concern for long-term effects on the lands or populations directly impacted. Even when critics expressed opposition, the instant gains from energy supplies or economic growth overrode ecological concerns or calls for social justice until recently.

Democracies utilized environmental resources most efficiently. Ironically, the nation that uses the most resources globally today was also the first to venerate the natural environment. In 1901, Teddy Roosevelt was the first world leader to implement policies to protect nature, through the US National Park system. He of course also chased cheap labor and natural resources in South and Central America, famously "wielding his stick" in the 1904 Roosevelt Corollary to gain access to the resources of weaker states. His cousin, Franklin Delano Roosevelt, later steered the United States through the Depression by harnessing the resources of a booming industrial American state—circumstances in which dirty rivers, dead soils, or polluted air were hardly of concern. Similarly, the first superpower Britain conserved nature domestically while abusing it overseas. Winston Churchill famously switched the British Navy from coal to oil in 1910, preserving British dominance while incorporating the Middle East into Western conflicts.

Like democratic leaders, authoritarian elites built dams, mines, and vast irrigation projects to create energy and improve living standards. Critics though could not oversee or limit such infrastructure projects, lacking the voice that opponents have in democratic states. Second and Third World leaders sustained their position or exploited public support by using natural resources. Grandiose schemes to harness nature for national pride harmed both local and foreign environs. Stalin, Hitler, Mussolini, Nasser in Egypt, Deng Xiaoping in China and many other autocrats in smaller nations earned legitimacy by extracting resources through control of the environment. Autocratic rulers today still reshape the environment at will.

Figure 5.2 The Palm Jumeirah in Dubai, Dubai, United Arab Emirates. (Credit: Nikada.)

Sources of energy sustained Fascist power, since authoritarian states that harnessed nature's power best could more easily dominate others. Italy became an industrial power when Mussolini made use of technology to harness river valleys. Massive hydroelectric plants in northern Italy exploited the power of the River Po for the whole nation, employing millions, developing the economy while legitimizing Fascist policies. Germany made use of its natural resources in the 1930s, though it also exploited the labor of millions of Jews, working them to death in the 1940s, as well as enslaving 4 million Russian laborers.

Twentieth century independence struggles were fought over national resources as much as political sovereignty. The Mexican Revolution in 1911 was largely a fight over oil resources. The oil boom in the 1910s provided income for the new state, empowering leaders to push US interests out of the market and legitimize the new government. The story of the state of Israel, though steeped in religious and political discord, is also one of effective exploitation of lands inhabited by Palestinian Arabs prior to 1948. By 1947, Indians wanted control of a vast continent's resources, following centuries of British management. As in established states, industrial exploitation and widespread pollution prevailed after independence. Wars fought for national independence were violent for large swaths of society, but the cost to wildlife, rivers, and soils were seldom considered worth quantifying.

Since they could not repel imperial powers, weaker nations, in essence, fe
ones. Japan's elite controlled Korean and Chinese resources through dec
expansionism. Focused on bolstering Japan's limited island reserves, authoriti
rarely concerned with human or environmental health. After Japan industrialized
in the late 1800s, lands were polluted, heavy metal waste from mining and metal
production pouring into rivers and rice paddies. When farmers protested, the state
usually ignored them. As elsewhere, the peasant population suffered horribly.
Both world wars and the Cold War saw huge militaries executing strategies in
an unregulated and unquestioned environment, plundering lands in the name of
combat. Following vast quantities of artillery dropped in the world wars, the Cold
War brought even more despoliation. Though the Vietnam War was a nightmare for
both the US military and the Vietnamese people, its negative impact on farmland
and paddies was immeasurable. Some critics have labeled it an ecocide. Huge
nuclear stockpiles built by the United States and the USSR in the Cold War remain
underground, at risk to surrounding environs in US deserts and ex-Soviet republics.

Nature also shaped political history. Weather intervened in world wars, as in all
past wars. Weather patterns could easily determine the victors and vanquished: the
escape of British and French armies in 1940 from Nazi aggression at Dunkirk was in
part due to calm seas; Germany's invasion of Moscow in 1941 met a terrible winter
and subsequent failure.

The environment, and its persistent destruction, has been a central story of the past
century, as pollution intensified, from regional disasters at first to cross-continental
catastrophes. Tens of thousands of oil spills from ships and rigs worldwide have killed
inestimable numbers of animals and sea life. Explosions from chemical plants have
continued through the century, from England to India to the USSR. The *Chernobyl*
disaster in the Soviet Union in 1986 sent contamination and radiation across all of
Europe, and Japan's nuclear reactor meltdown in 2011 sent tainted chemicals as far
as America's West Coast. In comparison to the political and economic stories of the
century, a barely noticed litany of environmental calamities warranted only limited
attention in the minds of most people or politicians.

Political energy

Of course, many would contend that such damage was necessary for national
security or prosperity. But humans used more energy in the last century than in all of
previous human history, as cheap energy became the foundation upon which modern
states were built. The most powerful states indeed used the environment the most.
Colossal quantities of oil, gas, and coal powered life in wealthy nations. Without
such extraction of natural and often overseas bounties, Westerners could not have
traveled in automobiles or airplanes or lived in heated, cooled or well-lit homes. Nor
could they have fought two world wars with each other. Just as Europeans accessed

more energy than other cultures in the nineteenth century, the United States did so after 1900.

The most powerful and energy rich society since 1945, the United States, harnessed natural and human resources efficiently by using domestic and foreign resources. From its origins, the United States had exploited free slave labor and enjoyed easy access to native lands. In the twentieth century, the nation grew rich by employing cheap immigrant labor and accessing a continent of nature's bounty. Extraction of domestic ores and minerals combined with assertive extraction of overseas fossil fuels, to maintain prime position.

The United States thus secured global domination through effectual energy extraction. Oil production was crucial, and the precious liquid increasingly shaped policy making after 1918. Already by 1900, cars, trucks, and planes needed oil for internal combustion engines (ICE), thus beginning a century-long essential role in moving military machines, private and public transportation. Developed first in Germany, the ICE was most fully developed in the United States through Ford's automobile production revolution.

By the Cold War era, the United States, Western Europe and their allies needed to import oil to maintain their lifestyles. Since geological forces had placed most of the earth's oil in the region around the Suez Canal and Middle East, those areas became supplier nations, exporting oil for their economic existence. Aside from political instability, the Persian Gulf and Mediterranean region suffered massive pollution from continuous oil leaks. Beyond that region, oil producers worldwide simply spilled waste into riverine water systems. Only in the 1980s did legislation begin to halt polluting practices, first in the West, contested vigorously by business interests.

As oil became the world's fuel of choice, electrification in developing nations required hydroelectric and coal power, usually by damming rivers to harness stored power for electricity. Coal production worldwide went from 762 million metric tons in 1900 to well over 5 billion tons by 2000.[1] This relatively sudden shift from steam to fossil fuel energies sent particulate matter into the air in unprecedented quantities in order to electrify nations.

Dammed if you do, damned if you don't

Dams for electrification altered nature's rhythms enormously, as river systems and habitats that took millennia to form were suddenly transformed by the insertion of enormous man-made concrete walls. State planners built over 30,000 dams worldwide in the century, to exploit river power, remaking huge tracts of land for industrial energy in the process. Particularly between the 1930s and the 1980s, massive swaths of land were inundated with water for power. The exploitation of water from dams reached its maximum in the 1970s, when one was being built every day somewhere on earth. Those nations that dammed the most —China, the United States, and the USSR—accordingly harnessed the most power for their populations.

Though democracies despoiled lands, authoritarian rulers did so without pressure from critics, worsening the effects. Terrible costs for humans and ecosystems followed, as populations suffered impoverishment or sickness for the sake of national goals. Though power fueled industrial growth and homes, dams and reservoirs have displaced over 50 million people since 1945. From Brazil to India to China, villages and cities were inundated for national dams; just in the 1990s, China's Three Gorges River Dam forcibly displaced over a million people.

Dams became targets in water wars. Chinese military leaders flooded millions of hectares of lands in 1938, opening the dikes on the Yellow River in an attempt to repel Japanese invasion. Thousands drowned in the process, sacrificed for country. India and Pakistan fought for water rights over Indus Valley irrigation immediately after independence in 1947. In the Korean War, the United States attacked North Korean dams to cut off supplies. The Middle East conflict between Israel and Arab lands has been as much about water as principles, and conflicts on the African continent persist over attempts to control water.

By developing such immense energy, elites increased food supplies and modernized societies, and d a huge increase in food supplies occurred worldwide for people at all levels. In the developed world, obesity replaced hunger as a major health issue. Even in undeveloped societies, starvation was eradicated for the first time, except in regions where political and religious conflict provokes food insecurity.

This paradox—improved food supplies and worsened environmental damage— symbolizes the past century in world history. Ransacking the environment became a national pastime, often unplanned or in obliviousness. By the 1950s, in the West and then worldwide, electricity provided prodigious levels of comfort, generating warmth in homes, piping clean water, and offering modern conveniences such as fridges and washing machines. Machinery run with electrical power made goods quickly and cheaply with less labor. Inexpensive items were now available for the masses instead of royals or the rich. This was a world of wonders.

Going nuclear

Perhaps the most potent symbol of humanity's transformation of nature is the capacity to harness nuclear energy. Building on the intellectual efforts of scientists, atomic bombs were devised during the Second World War, with grave consequences for the environment. After the 1950s, humanity could breathe its last if too much nuclear power was released mistakenly or in anger. The United States exploded the first hydrogen bomb in 1952; Soviet Russia followed in 1953; Britain tested a bomb in 1957; and by 1970, France and India were nuclear powers. All tested bombs in isolated locations, sacrificing local populations for the furtherance of geopolitics.

Only after 1963 were limitations enforced on such practices. France still refuses to compensate Algerians for bombing in the Sahara, and Britain has tested bombs freely in the Pacific Ocean. Russia and China refuse to compensate test victims in Central Asia. Only the United States has compensated Pacific islanders, as well as Native Americans in Nevada for testing bombs in the desert region.

Political and economic competition, expressed through nationalism and national development, formed the chief threat to humanity in the past century. After the unprecedented depredations of the Second World War some wished to transcend this model, to aim for global equity and a broader system of international relations that might not condemn billions to poverty. Transnational institutions thus emerged in the postwar era to fight for the rights of weaker peoples through the United Nations and regional organizations. In the 1950s, procedures were introduced to hold world leaders responsible for human rights abuses, both within nations and internationally.

In that decade, United Nations specialists introduced a new legal concept, "War crimes against humanity," aiming to reach a higher level of global jurisprudence. The context in which the United Nations became acceptable and respected was thus the end of the worst war in history. Soon, burgeoning independence movements fought through the United Nations to win sovereignty for the vast majority of humanity for the first time. This new international perspective transcended the petty disputes of separate nations and even extended into the world's oceans. The UN-inspired Law of the Sea Convention of 1982 was a first endeavor to pressure nations to share the spoils of the seas without plunder. Pushback predictably ensued, but the ideas were now public, to broaden narrow attitudes about the national power and supremacy that had brought such awful environmental damage in the first place.

Air, water, and soil

The air we breathe

Increasingly after 1900, Europeans produced vast amounts of coal, steel, and iron, all of which sent particles into the airborne environment. Air pollution did not originate in the twentieth century however. Port cities for centuries produced bad air if winds did not send pollution out to sea. Indeed, large industrial urban areas like London and the Midlands in England, Pittsburgh and Chicago in the United States, and the Yangtze Valley in China, suffered filthier air in 1900 than they do today. But the sheer scale of output would grow exponentially after 1900.

It is impossible to measure the overall harm done to individual lungs or to green belts of land in the past century. Some events though stand out in severity. Britain was the site of the filthiest air pollution event ever, when the *London Smog* disaster of 1952 brought four days of stagnant polluted air. Killing over 10,000 people, this was the worst environmental disaster of the century in sheer number of deaths. The

Figure 5.3 London Smog in 1950s. (Credit: Don Price.)

1980s epitomize the low point regarding environmental abuse. The 1980 Love Canal disaster in New York sent chemical waste into water supplies, prompting a surge in cancer rates and birth defects. The 1984 Bhopal industrial disaster in India killed over 2,000 people, and the USSR's 1986 Chernobyl nuclear catastrophe threatened the health of everyone in the northern hemisphere, all of whom received doses of radiation from it.

Since then, criticism from environmental activists slowly stirred national leaders to action, and cries for change surged in the 1980s. Thanks to both lone voices and group efforts, air quality slowly improved after the 1960s across the West. Legislation passed in England in 1956 was a harbinger of regulation to curb smoke emissions from home chimneys and factories. Los Angeles, a region designed for cars, was until the 1970s infamous for its automobile exhaust and stagnant air, though it has improved since.

Developed nations slowly improved overall air quality by the end of the century, as forward-thinking leaders succumbed to a gradual realization that the destruction of nature may be irreversible. For a century before the 1980s, company's dumped toxic wastes straight into ponds and rivers without considering the environmental or social consequences. As one indicator, lead levels in children's blood peaked in the United States in 1977, declining by almost 95 percent in the ensuing 20 years, as health advocates uncovered the bodily effects of environmental abuse. In less developed and autocratic states, action was less feasible due to an absence of activists or media pressure.

> Very small numbers of people have changed attitudes toward the environment. The anthropologist Margaret Mead famously argued that the ideas of small numbers of people could overcome huge challenges in the wider world:
>
> *Never doubt that a small group of thoughtful, committed citizens can change the world; indeed, it's the only thing that ever has.*[2]

Communities realized in the 1980s that environmental problems transcend recently formed political entities such as nations. Environmentalists showed that air pollution was oblivious of borders or economic goals, and cannot be contained within one state or region. By 2007 more people on earth lived in cities than in the countryside, meaning that more people were exposed to bad air. By the twenty-first century poorer nations suffered the worst air. The center of ancient Western civilization, Athens, remains famous for its dirty air, its ancient statues crumbling from toxic erosion. Many Chinese cities emit filthy smog most days of the year, and the poor in cities like Mexico City and Sao Paolo suffer most from respiratory problems due to polluted air.

Technology both caused and facilitated understanding of industrial waste. Through television, worldwide audiences learned of sizable environmental disasters and negative health effects, exposing the outcomes of unregulated industry. A gradual shift from leaded gas to unleaded in the 1980s showed Western legislators responding to environmentalists, as business and political elites realized they could no longer hide the effects of profit-seeking enterprises or prestige projects.

Drinking water

Though the quality of air has generally improved, water pollution persists. Dense populations have always settled near coasts or rivers, and most ancient societies originated around flowing rivers with fresh water. Though few were aware of it in 1900, the human body is 80 percent water. Since humans require water to survive, societies made use of rivers or oceans throughout history, but complex states exploited water resources on a far greater scale since 1900. A century ago, water was mostly used for irrigation. Twentieth-century industrialization, including today's computer server farms, use colossal amounts of water. The most powerful states use far more water than the rest of the world. Rich nations use ten times more water per person than in 1900.

Water management has been a central measure of success for modern states. Through the century, national policies depended on water supplies; water management became central to leaders strategies. Today nations vie for fresh, consistent water supplies to support increasingly complex water delivery systems. Water is needed for irrigation to grow food, to keep industry running, and to clean cities. Its finite nature makes it a source of conflict.

Nor is water equally distributed, either to different nations or to populations within them. The rich have access to water while the poor do not. Water is dotted unevenly round the earth, most of it settled in deep aquifers or in difficult-to-access glaciers. Less than 1 percent of the fresh water on earth resides in lakes and rivers (a quarter of that in one place, in Lake Baikal in Siberia!). The reality of disparate amounts of fresh water is a problem that affects developing nations most. People in much of Africa and the Middle East have less access to fresh water. South America has ample water but remains mostly impoverished and unequal, so millions suffer hardship from dearth . Asia sits in between: Northern China has always been dry, as are large parts of South Asia, while South China gets ample moisture and Bangladesh gets too much water from monsoon systems. Notably, most of Europe and North America are blessed with ample rainfall and enjoy great volumes of rainwater annually.

This was also a century of substantial mishandling of water supplies. After 1970, the USSR destroyed the vast Aral Sea region, hindering thousands of years of mountain drainage in order to produce cotton export goods. Today, it has all but vanished due to over-production, shrinking to 10 percent of its size in the 1970s. Soviet scientists were oblivious to the fact that evaporation induced less snowpack in the mountains, and thus even less water. Zealous planners with shortsighted national goals undid millennia of natural processes in Communist and autocratic states, often for personal gain.

Democratic states brought water disasters too. The whole Western region of the United States, including Silicon Valley and Hollywood, was settled by reshaping water flows in California valleys since the 1920s. The huge population growth in that state occurred after the Dust Bowl disaster of the 1930s. Environmental disaster thus populated California, where growth has now pushed numbers upwards, and drought is always on the horizon. The Colorado River has been sucked dry for creature comforts in Western states for decades. Colorado has twenty dams controlling its rivers, flowing into cities for crops, air conditioning and suburban life. The Snake and Columbia rivers in the American west have been heavily dammed, and in the Midwest, the Ogallala reservoir has been drying for decades due to overuse, with no replenishment in sight. The Mississippi has long been controlled and channeled by levees, and the tragic 2004 New Orleans' flood, long predicted by geographers, demonstrated how unstable water patterns are in the richest nation on earth.

Access to water prompted frequent conflict through the century. Since water, like oil, is an essential gauge of modern life, religious and economic clashes mix with water conflicts in newly formed states. The ongoing Israeli–Palestinian conflict is centered on control of already inadequate water supplies. The Jordan River basin is the main source of water for various countries in the Middle East, leading to water deprivation for the neediest populations. Water scarcity is prevalent in the poorest regions of the world, from Africa across the Middle East to India, all societies that suffer from low rainfall or fresh water supplies. Conflict beckons as Egypt's military avidly defends access to the River Nile. Much of the Ganges is so polluted that Indians have limited access to fresh water. India and Pakistan continue to fight over waters around the Indus River.

Growing populations in poor regions also abuse the environment. Poorer regions with rising populations put great stress on water supplies, and bad governance usually ignores the problem. Poverty induces fishermen in undeveloped states to overexploit waterways to make a living, while market demand from wealthy societies encourages them to deplete seas by overfishing. Fishermen worldwide recall far more fish in the seas when they were young. Waste is sent from rich to poor countries to such an extent that products made cheap in Asia are now sent back to send to Third World landfills or seaways.

Figure 5.4 Scavengers collecting recyclable materials from a mountain of garbage, Manila, Philippines. (Credit: Stuart Dee.)

Industrial capitalism put pressure on international waters through the century. Already by the 1940s the International Whaling Commission was forced to pressure nations such as Japan and Norway to preserve dying whale populations, traditionally used as a source for heat and food. Particularly after 1945, huge quantities of ocean life were poisoned by industry freely washing metals, oils, chemicals, and other pollutants into seas. Environmentalists have slowly forced industrialists and politicians to monitor waste output, and the greatest per capita abuser, the United States, has cut back on water usage since the 1980s. Only in recent decades has awareness grown that the oceans produce weather patterns and rain cycles.

The oceans are in fact so vast that they could feasibly absorb human misuse. However, wetlands are more fragile, and throughout over the century worldwide, wetlands were converted to cropland to feed hungry mouths. Overused wetlands

Figure 5.5 The Blue Marble—Earth as seen by Apollo 17 in 1972. (https://en.wikipedia.org/wiki/The_Blue_Marble, accessed August 19, 2017).

ow faster water flows through deltas, removing nutrients from soil and drying ut regions. Particularly in Southeast Asia, the Philippines, and India, huge tracts of wetlands were lost. When logging is added to the mix, wildlife vanishes, and whole regions are deforested. Diversity has been lost and water supplies constrained enormously since the 1950s. Ocean acidification is a genuine threat due to pollution.

Humans worldwide use about twice as much water per person now when compared to 1900, and growing global populations need even more water. Only since the 1980s has some awareness of this potential catastrophe seeped into the minds of leaders and laypeople. The famous *Blue Marble* image, taken in 1972 by the US space program, demonstrated to humanity for the first time both the planet's fragility and its watery blue appearance. Thus space technology, combined with the growing environmental movement, recently introduced an appreciation that water is the source of life, in a century of unprecedented plundering.

Soil of the nation

Air and water in fact combined to constitute the main components of the thin layer of dirt that sustains all life by covering bedrock to make soil around the world. US President Franklin Roosevelt, in the wake of the terrible 1930s Dust Bowl, famously said, "The nation that destroys its soil destroys itself." Coincidentally, at this time, blood and soil became the common motto of Fascist parties worldwide, fostering the belief that pureblooded nationals possessed the ground under their feet. These two approaches to soil—one to preserve it and share its bounty, the other to own and exploit it—worked in stark tension through the century in both democracies and autocracies.

Military struggles assaulted soils in ways unimaginable before 1900. Belgium's Flanders region, like many in Europe, was turned into a muddy, poisoned metallic conflagration after 1914. From Gallipoli in Turkey in 1915 to Tobruk in Libya in 1941, battles in the world wars devastated colonized lands as well. Leaders worldwide believed that the exploitation of lands was necessary to make nations great. Hence influential officials ruined rivers, air quality, and soils in the search for national wealth in war and peacetime. Soil depletion occurred worldwide as policy makers seized resources in an international race to the bottom.

Forests were cleared to build homes or create space for food production. The broad redwoods that covered the San Francisco Bay Area were depleted through the 1990s, with only a few stands remaining. Boreal forests from the United States to Russia continue to be exploited and Japan has deforested lightly wooded lands for industry and fuels. Tropical forests shrunk in size through the century, as LDCs exploited resources to become affluent or to export to international markets. Rulers in ex-colonized regions worsened earlier damage committed by colonial powers. Indonesian forests depleted for centuries by the Dutch were exploited for international profits after independence, with rewards going to local elites. African dictators and Islamic leaders despoiled lands won back from colonial powers in an effort to gain legitimacy, increasing desertification in already arid regions.

By 1980, grasslands, forests, and soils worldwide were laced with industrial metals and toxins. Only since then have environmentalists managed to focus the minds of elites on the true cost of depleting the thin layer of soil covering the earth's mantle. Less developed nations leaders argue today though that they cannot afford environmentally friendly policies, pointing to the damages already committed by industrial nations. Many people expect the same standard of living regardless of the cost to the earth. In an effort to eradicate the material inequalities of the recent past, LDCs and nations such as China despoil land recklessly, free of regulations often found in the West.

More food

But there is light in this dark century-long story of environmental misuse. After the 1970s, better land management methods emerged from scientific and academic research. Forests returned in many places, especially wealthy northern nations, and Japan, North America, and Western Europe began reforesting. Indeed, temperate forests have expanded since 1945, rebounding in places like the American eastern woodlands after centuries of chopping. Policies improved through grassroots efforts more than officialdom or corporate culture. Businesses turned "green" only when customer growth or profits depended on it. Today in some states, a new generation of politicians with greener credentials seems to realize the necessity of green policies.

State leaders responded to growing populations by expanding cropland for greater food supplies. Tractor technology and food production fed and bred taller, broader humans, who in turn demanded more food. Inventiveness and better technologies have doubled the amount of cropland on earth compared to a century ago. In the past three decades, food has become cheap for most people, reversing the trend in all of history, where food was expensive and famine frequent.

Food prices went down, but social or environmental costs were only occasionally measured. Western fast-food companies leased or bought huge tracts of land in South and Central America to produce cheap burgers after the 1960s. An enormous increase in heart disease, obesity, and nutritional disorders partnered this dietary change. Vast increases in livestock worldwide mean that people globally not only expect, but now consume, more meat every day. Far more meat has been eaten over recent decades when compared to traditional grain diets of wheat, rice, or barley. The ecological cost is great, and it is unclear if the earth can sustain billions of burger eaters.

30, US President Jimmy Carter was voted out of office in a humiliating
lide, ridiculed for his broad sympathy for poorer societies and environmental
rstanding. Carter believed that humans must use their brains to harness
the sun's power, doing no harm to nature or the people in it. He wrote in 1979:

> If we do not learn to eliminate waste and to be more productive and more
> efficient in the ways we use energy, then we will fall short . . . but if we use
> our technological imagination, if we can work together to harness the light
> of the Sun, the power of the wind, and the strength of rushing streams,
> then we will succeed.[13]

In 1981, Ronald Reagan removed the solar panels that Carter had installed on the
White House roof. He supported automobile companies and their allies in the oil
industry, who enjoyed a business-friendly 1980s, which purposely dismantled the
emerging electric car revolution—stalling progress for 30 years. A generation of
environmentally friendly automobile production just beginning in the 1980s was
thus set aside for decades in the world's most influential and prosperous economy.

All societies have damaged the air, waters, and soils of the earth since 1900.
But more powerful states damaged the earth far more, both at home and abroad.
Environmental sustainability today is still challenged by an incessant desire for
material well-being, founded on a century-long belief that economic growth is
infinite, the sole measure of happiness. When Jimmy Carter tried to point to a
higher cause for humankind—its shared environment—he paid a political price.
Short-term political, and economic, aspirations may prove to be the story of the
century.

3. Belief in profit—economics and nature

The primary reason humans ruined nature so much was at root the desire for national
economic development. This became an unquestioned truism, cemented in belief over
the century. Traditional patterns such as maintaining a light footprint, reverence for
nature, or simpler lifestyles, were all pushed aside after 1900, as industrial capitalism
and state development became the new mantra.

Certainly, many were dubious of endless extraction of wealth from earth's
environment. *Mahatma Gandhi's* call for ecological sustenance was essential to the
core of his spiritual worldview, derived from Hinduism and Buddhism. Prominent
Indians like Rabindranath Tagore criticized British capitalism, proposing alternative
economic and political paths as early as 1910. Tagore derided Western "progress,"
recommending that individuals adopt conserve and respect nature in their mad rush

Figure 5.6 Biologist and author Rachel Carson. (Alfred Eisenstaedt/The LIFE Picture Collection/Getty Images.)

for wealth. Generally oblivious to such traditional views, Westerners were slow to heed the real cost of industrial progress, though critical voices in the nineteenth century West disdained materialism too. Henrik Ibsen condemned the repressive nature of industrial life in 1900, and Fyodor Dostoevsky in Russia bemoaned a lack of spirituality toward mother earth.

Developed states only recognized the cost of economic avarice in the 1960s. Authors like *Rachel Carson*, who overcame serious illness and chauvinistic attacks from powerful businessmen, comprehensively exposed the cancerous agents entering American waters, air, and soils. Showing that capitalism was killing nature—and people—in the name of industrial progress, Carson transformed beliefs about food, nature, and humans' relationship to the environment. She highlighted clearly, along with powerless nations, the spillover effects—or negative externalities—of global capitalism.

In *Silent Spring*, Carson popularized the idea that industrial life was polluting not just air and water, but also human bodies. She wrote in 1961:

A Who's Who of pesticides is therefore of concern to us all. If we are going to live so intimately with these chemicals eating and drinking them, taking them into the very marrow of our bones—we had better know something about their nature and their power.[4]

By the 1960s, industrial life had exposed billions to lead in paints, asbestos in buildings, and toxic industrial waste. Cancer rates increased, as did miscarriages and birth defects from chemicals. Until Carson published her critique, few considered the issue worth worrying about in developed nations, let alone LDCs.

Belief in excess

One reason why Carson's views were so roundly ridiculed was that industrial elites were then incapable of understanding ideas such as growth without destruction. For almost a century, economic progress had been the stated goal of almost all state leaders. In the modern era, leadership depended on improving lifestyles, which meant competition with others, to the death if necessary.

Though all societies have extracted nature's fruits, Westerners, in particular, controlled nature in recent centuries, in Europe, the Americas, and in colonies around the world. Driven by a Judeo-Christian cosmology that promoted the use of "God's green earth," Western elites developed industrial capitalism as an all-encompassing ideology, rationalizing imperial expansion as a "civilizing mission" for the good of humanity. A linear, historical view of the world derived from Christian beliefs impressed upon Westerners that they must go forth and multiply, - to convert the inferior non-Christian peoples of the world, with no thought of consequences or alternative perspectives. The main critique of Western religiosity, the Enlightenment rational tradition, also motivated industrial exploitation of nature - brushing aside the Romanticist critique to idealize nature.

Both world wars and the Cold War were extreme environmental disasters, premised upon excessive commitment to economic beliefs. 1914 brought colossal pillage of nature: soldiers rotted in muddy holes infested by rats, while vast fields were shelled, destroying their fertility. The Second World War was worse. Though Westerners thought that they had mastered nature, they were wrecking it. The United States and the USSR pursued the same path in the Cold War, sacrificing ecosystems for ideological economic opposition until 1991.

The century brought relentless munitions production. Along with oil, metal ores for steel or iron were essential for armaments. Chemicals, minerals, and ores culled from mines were transformed into bombs, propelled from planes and ships onto military and civilian targets. The effects on humans and soils were appalling, In the First World War, civilian noncombatants were only 5 percent of deaths; in the second it was close to 50 percent. As millions of bombs hammered humanity, surrounding environs became uncultivable. Every explosion left contaminated soil and water. Millions of animals died in the process. Hence, the main conflicts of the century saw powerful, sophisticated societies fighting, while making use of the lands of powerless peoples, despoiling natural resources, ending lives and killing crops.

A philosophy of abuse

By 1917, the Western worldview of Industrial Capitalism met its first stiff opponent, in anticapitalist, workers' organizations and mostly, in Communist Russia. Inspired by Karl Marx, worker's groups contended that the foundational premise of capitalism was exploitation of human labor and the abuse of power for the good of the few. True or not, Communist states then committed as much if not greater harm to human and natural resources over the century.

Capitalism required the exploitation of people worldwide, and of the lands of the colonized principally. This was Vladimir Lenin's point when he argued in 1917 that capitalism inevitably led to imperialism. But Communism, though fundamentally opposed to the abuses of capitalist excess, proved even worse for the environment. The USSR's incompetent abuse of nature and brutal neglect of human rights ruined lands and lives from the 1920s to the 1980s, lacking even the corresponding gains in material wealth. When Soviet Communism collapsed in 1991, a ruined and crumbling landscape throughout Soviet satellites and republics remained. China's growth in recent decades has been similarly devoid of environmental regulation. Since the 1950s, shortsighted development brought the large-scale poisoning of people and plants in all Communist nations. Both ideologies purported to offer better lives to their citizens. When capitalists proclaimed the virtues of material prosperity, Communists pointed to its obvious exploitation. Both systems required large-scale transformation of nature through the manipulation of atoms, elements and molecules.

"Better living through chemistry"

The famous Du Pont Company slogan above (used until 1982) expresses well the role chemical industries played in producing modern life. The first nation to adopt an industrial lifestyle, Britain, had been extracting ores worldwide since the eighteenth century Industrial Revolution, and British development was soon emulated by the United States, the USSR, and Germany.

The *Second Industrial Revolution* emerged in Germany and the United States, introducing new chemicals, synthetics, and plastics into human life around 1900. Celebrated chemists like Haber Bosch shaped German industrial chemistry, putting chemical industries at the service of growing German power. Massive volumes of chemical nitrates derived from Chilean guano deposits increased Western food production before 1900, but once German chemists such as Bosch created synthetic nitrates for food fertilizer, Europeans no longer needed Chilean exports. Nitrates were also a basic ingredient of the explosives that killed or maimed so many in war. Synthetic textiles and fabrics were not magically made from thin air: they derived from the byproducts of coal, gas, and oil. Chemical fertilizers depleted soils worldwide for decades. Since the 1970s a huge increase in fertilizer use has impacted land negatively in poorer countries, often forcing the migration of peasants.

More than any other society, the United States created great wealth by advancing chemical industries. American businessmen discovered oil in Pennsylvania in 1859. American reserves were supplemented by Iranian sources after 1906, and for the rest of the century, relations with the Arab world were premised on attaining oil. The British Royal Navy, the most powerful on earth, switched from coal to oil in 1910, initiating Western intervention in Middle Eastern lands. By 1914, American, British, and French entrepreneurs controlled oil extraction in the Middle East.

Oil ran the machines of modernity in war and peacetime. The need for oil drove the decisions of national leaders and economic advisors, necessitating regime overthrow if powerful nations did not get their way. Already by 1919, wealthy states could not produce food for their growing populations without oil. By 1945, oil provided the raw materials for synthetics and plastics, for chemicals required in fertilizers to boost food supplies, and almost every other product in supermarkets. Petroleum jelly from oil healed cuts on children's hands, as oil fueled cars, planes, and tanks.

Chemical innovation had political consequences, but it also produced vast amounts of food. The development of artificial fertilizers in Germany helped hundreds of millions worldwide access reliable sources of food to live longer. And everyday products derived from chemicals, such as stockings, socks, or rayon (artificial silk), were as exciting 80 years ago as the Internet or HDTV today. An understandable desire for material comfort underwrote humanity's newfound addiction to affordable goods, filling homes and providing gratification for consumers through the century. Plastics, furniture, crockery, carpets, and soaps, and much more found in the home and office, all contained chemicals. Almost all went unregulated until the 1970s in the search of better living standards.

American dream

The two chief sources of chemical pollution since 1900 were also two features of modern life that most people cannot imagine living without: the automobile and industrial manufacture. Both were pioneered in the wealthiest nation in world history, the United States, improving on German and British production techniques. American businessmen pioneered a new ideology of industrial efficiency after 1910: the notion that production should and could keep rising was supported by *Taylorism* (where the scientific analysis of business tasks produces more and more), and *Fordism* (speedy assembly-line production to make product faster). Both systems improved production levels, neither considered human or environmental costs.

America matters so much because the main goal of societies worldwide after 1945 was to attain US-style consumerism. In the United States, more than anywhere, ores turned into cheap steel, aluminum and iron provided sturdy housing, impressive buildings, and bridges—the necessary infrastructure of a modern state. Ores built chassis for oil-driven trains and cars, easing life for all. The systematic logging and transportation of forest products built homes, laid floors, and made furniture. Redwoods and oaks chopped down by the million made homes, - areas like Oakland in California that were once oak forests were transformed into urban concrete jungles.

Gains derived from mass production made goods affordable but also polluted lives in rich and poor nations. Fossil fuel combustion, required to generate the energy for modern life, produced vast air pollution. Fossil fuels emitted enormous amounts of carbon and other gases into the atmosphere, changing weather patterns, contaminating the air that humans, animals, and plants breathed. Industrial products came packed with metals, chemicals, and plastics, and the manufacturing process left debris in rivers and soils, as well as in the bodies of those consuming items. Fridges, a dream product for most people in the 1970s, emitted CFCs that poked a hole in the ozone layer that sustains human life.

Much of the materiel for industrial products derived from lands in LDCs and would be exported back as waste. Rubber from colonial estates offered magical new goods such as tires for trucks or bikes, waterproof clothing and boots, requiring plantations in tropical realms. After 1915, arable land worldwide was paved over with cement and tarmac for cars and other forms of transportation. This created easily traversable city streets capable of transporting workers and citizens at high speed, a basic necessity of modern life, modeled on the US system.

Speeding up

Belief in the virtue of consuming nature's fruits was one thing, but doing it as fast as possible was another. By increasing the speed of manufacture, humans became both more productive and more destructive over the century, bringing insatiable aspirations to access earth's energy and resources. Farmers have long known that depletion of soil nutrients lowers plant development and agricultural yields—the foundation of all food supplies. By using tractors, machines, and gleaning more from land, the earth's soils were damaged for crop production, vast mines scarred lands, and erosion of soil layers ruined whole regions.

Global droughts in the 1920s and 1930s demonstrated how little understanding nations possessed of the true cost of increased food production. The *Dust Bowl* in the United States shocked a country supreme in confidence of its approach. Along with massive unemployment, people went hungry, and 2.4 million migrants were forced to leave home in the 1930s, moving out West in desperation. Foolhardy profit-seeking decisions regarding crop choices, the overuse of machinery and ravenous land usage brought a high price. The same mistakes would occur in Russia and China in the 1950s, when tens of millions actually died from famine. Midwestern hunger was one thing; massive starvation was another.

Nevertheless, the overuse of land for economic gain spread worldwide by the 1970s, as developing nations emulated the American pursuit of profit without regard for nature. Booming international trade meant that everything from coffee and bananas to beef moved quickly, from undeveloped regions to distant markets, as growing demand prompted erosion of fertile tropical ex-colonized lands. Industrializing nations such as China, Brazil, Australia, and Japan produced vast quantities of ores and commodities for export to imitate American prosperity. Nations that industrialized more recently—Mexico, Indonesia, and India—are often the worst abusers of the environment. Increased urbanization—industrialization's natural partner—prompted global pollution, as almost every aspect of city life demanded products harmful to the environment.

After the Second World War, Western economists and the policymakers they convinced believed, from a narrow industrial capitalist viewpoint, that profits and supply/demand charts justified the fabrication of bounties of goods. In this calculus, nature was subtracted from economic goals and production figures, as was the cost to the regions of origin. Particularly after Margaret Thatcher and Ronald Reagan took control in 1980, the Western world ratcheted up its desire for worldly goods. Thatcherism regarded the poor as idlers, who suffered the consequences of their own laziness, with no mention of environment in her policies. Many of Reagan's American advisors and supporters believed through their particular strain of evangelicalism that the apocalypse was coming, that the rich were good in the eyes of God. Preserving the earth for future generations mattered less than prosperity today. Neither of these hugely influential leaders accepted that everyday use of CFCs impacted the atmosphere until vast damage was already done. Both regarded environmentalists as an irritant. Both Thatcher and Reagan were supported by white Conservatives in their respective nations; those who benefitted most from their policies.

The hugely popular 1957 Broadway musical *West Side Story* symbolizes the moment US music began to outshine its European cousin, and the United States began to shape the world's culture significantly. Here immigrants expose differing views of life in the thriving new world power:

ANITA / GIRLS
   Skyscrapers bloom in America.
   Cadillacs zoom in America.
   Industry boom in America.

BERNARDO / BOYS
   Twelve in a room in America . . .

> *GIRLS*
> *Life can be bright in America.*
>
> *BOYS*
> *If you can fight in America.*
>
> *GIRLS*
> *Life is all right in America.*
>
> *BOYS*
> *If you're all white in America.*

This exposes the contradiction that is modern America: for many, it is the perfect society; for many others, it is a dark place. The same could be said for Western society at large, particularly for those forced to move as migrants from countries previously colonized. The worldviews of leaders like Reagan and Thatcher, and many worldwide who imitated them, ignored global environmental or social costs. Life was a race to the top, barely different to nineteenth-century social Darwinism, where stronger states dominated powerless ones and stronger people conquered the weak.

Colonial subordination

The century-long accumulation of wealth in both democratic and autocratic nations depended heavily upon the cheap labor or cheaply extracted resources of LDCs. First and foremost, powerless peoples lost control of their environment to stronger states. Whether through colonization, Communism, or capitalist expansion, hundreds of millions lost ancestral lands, and great powers had little concern for the ecosystems of colonized locations or for previous practices or traditions.

From 1900 to the 1960s colonial powers made decisions in less developed regions regarding land use, labor conditions and investment patterns, in the name of efficient commerce or governance. Rarely were these decisions for the good of the local populations. The United States, Australia, and Canada were already established white settler states with dispossessed minorities by 1900. By then, the French, Dutch, and British had extracted as much as possible at lowest cost for decades from Africa and Asia. In the imperial era, resistance was met with cruelty. Mussolini used poison gas to attack Ethiopia in 1936, prolonging patterns of violent Western rule. French colonizers controlled Algerian lands until 1963, the British controlled India's resources until 1947, (and as we have seen, into the late 1940s Japan exploited Korea, Taiwan, and China mercilessly for economic gain). US control of the Philippines until 1947 brought economic development through forest clearance and sugar plantations. In the postwar era, timber companies explored and exploited forests globally so that cheap woods could be sent to thriving consumer markets.

Yet, after Western powers departed, environmental abuses continued, in the Phillipines and elsewhere, where dictators eager to demonstrate their power took control of new national resources. Once freedom from colonization came, the rush to develop inspired even worse despoliation, as pressure to connect to capitalist markets meant further abuses. Following independence in the 1950s and 1960s, autocrats who took control of undeveloped nations rarely considered the poor and continued similarly exploitative practices.

Since decolonization African environments have suffered enormously. "Big Men"—dictators in newly independent states continuing African tribal traditions—sought personal prestige on the international stage in vain attempts to reverse past humiliations. Rulers rarely understood the ecosystems they had inherited and displayed little interest in equality or the environment. The Niger River in Mali was rerouted for irrigation to feed and clothe populations, with terrible, if unintended, ecological consequences in the 1960s. Seven major droughts have ravaged Africa since 1970 alone. North and East Africa endured terrible drought in the 1980s, devastating millions of lives and killing close to a million. Lake Chad today is a fifth of its postwar volume, as four major countries drain it for sustenance. Ongoing civil war in central Africa for the past 30 years has ruined crops, animals, and flora, along with millions of people's lives. Pervasive air pollution across the continent is worsened by overpopulation and deforestation.

Governmental mismanagement often brought inadvertent disasters. In 1956, Egypt's ruler Colonel Nasser took the Aswan Dam from European powers, offering reliable water flow to win the hearts and votes of Egyptians. Yet Egyptian independence brought greater ruination of the Nile, prompting higher evaporation, limiting the river's flow from Ethiopia due to overuse in producing cotton. Ethiopian soils then eroded for a decade, forcing new reliance on (Western manufactured) fertilizers.

As the brutality of colonization recedes in Western minds, the great wars of the century are recalled with pride, ignoring the ecological destruction, particularly of colonized lands. After 1950, the Korean War—ostensibly between China and the United States—killed a million Koreans and ruined fields and lands. The Vietnam War was an environmental catastrophe due to the sheer numbers of bombs dropped and persistent chemical warfare. Agent Orange sprayed from US planes blinded thousands of Vietnamese, ruining plants and animals over vast tracts of land. One of the war's many negative outcomes, the murderous regime of the Khmer Rouge, left so much land live-mined that Cambodia became known as the "Killing Fields."

Since Soviet Communism fell, much of Central Asia has endured awful pollution, widespread disease, and poverty, including Afghanistan. The already dry Middle East suffers from persistent climate related conflict. The decades long war between Israel, Lebanon, and Palestine has ruined countless lands and lives, both urban and rural. The post 9/11 response of the United States, the invasion of Iraq and Afghanistan, eradicated any hope of environmental recovery in the region due to ongoing violence.

Figure 5.7 Vietnamese children flee from their homes in the South Vietnamese village of Trang Bang after South Vietnamese planes accidentally dropped a napalm bomb on the village. (Bettmann/Contributor.)

Climate change, as it is presently understood, threatens the developing world far more than the industrial, a painful historical irony.

The female environment

Industrial pollution has clearly been a male-driven process. Though environmentalism is certainly not an exclusively female concern, men in power had little time for questioning progress until recently. The environmental movement emerged only in the 1960s, as women gained a voice in economic and political life. In the 1970s the Indian environmentalist and women's rights activist, Vandana Shiva, popularized the notion that industrial agriculture impacted the world's women most. Men in power, as well as ordinary men, believed deeply through the century that women were inferior, and that this idea was fixed and natural. As inequality between nations persisted, so too did gender inequality within nations.

The condition of women is normally closely related to the state of society and its environment. The nations with the worst environmental records today disregard the issue of women's rights or equality, meaning that women suffer most, as they have for centuries, because men control income, power, or wealth. In developed and traditional societies, women remain severely impoverished when compared to men, who benefitted most from accrued wealth and environmental exploitation.

Masculinized mind-sets such as military and industrial rivalry, two facets of social behavior linked to warrior virtues such as bravery and virility, were considered ordinary and pervaded twentieth-century thought. The effects of warfare and pollution spread disease into the lives of men and women, but women's suffering was less apparent. War impacts women directly, even when they are not on the front lines. Every war comes with attendant abuses of civilian populations, particularly women. Japanese soldiers raped tens of thousands in Nanking in 1937, forcing Korean women into sexual slavery during the war decades. Russian soldiers are said to have raped up to 100,000 German women upon taking Berlin in 1945. The same occurred when the Balkans collapsed in the 1990s and African women suffer in today's conflicts.

One of the earliest critics of our rush to exhaust the earth for material gain was however a man, the American writer Henry David Thoreau, who anticipated Theodore Roosevelt's conservation movement. In 1861, Thoreau highlighted male hubris, blissfully unaware that soon after his death, men and women would be able to fly and attack each other in the process:

> Most men, it seems to me, do not care for Nature and would sell their share in all her beauty, as long as they may live, for a stated sum—many for a glass of rum. Thank God, men cannot as yet fly, and lay waste the sky as well as the earth![5]

Thoreau's calls were barely heeded however, until the 1960s, when women in industrial nations gained greater voice in affairs of state and industry. The rise of environmental awareness overlapped with second wave feminism, led by Simone de Beauvoir. Her 1947 book *The Second Sex* became the new bible of women's rights, countering centuries of beliefs in women's inferiority and subservience. Introducing bold new attitudes to improve women's rights, her ideas seeped into broader issues

such as women's living and working environment, as well as the impact of
priorities on women. By showing that gender roles and identities were co
de Beauvoir opened the door to understanding how to change harmful
not only socially and economically, but also toward the environment.

After the 1950s, movements for women's liberation sprouted in industrial nations,
linking women's rights with ecological awareness. Women led the largest organized
movement on earth in the 1960s, the Campaign for Nuclear Disarmament, placing
front and center the need to save Mother Earth from macho nuclear violence. India's
Chipko movement fought for women's rights and raised awareness of deforestation in
the 1970s, and activists like Marjory Stone Douglas spent a lifetime fighting industrial
development in the Florida Everglades, fiercely fighting a male-run sugar industry.
As we have seen, the modern environmental movement owes its origins to the
unrecognized female biologist Rachel Carson. Inspired by these prominent women,
activists like Lois Gibbs spent 40 years fighting industry and government abuse of
lands, in particular exposing the Love Canal toxic dump which lay underneath the
homes and schools in New York, her home state. While men received the accolades,
women like Marie Tharp mapped the ocean floors for the first time, enduring ridicule
and sexism even as she revolutionized our grasp of the planet's geological makeup.

The feminist movement was an essential component of the shift toward
environmentalism and human rights after the 1960s. Since then, increased funding
toward education and the empowerment of women has had a hugely positive impact.
Worldwide, women's education has lowered birthrates, preventing overpopulation
and helping attain equality in the home, the office and ultimately in the corridors of
power. Arguably, greater gender equality may be the only way to alter the masculine-
led domination of earth since 1900.

Women recognized, earlier than men, the necessity of preserving "mother earth."
In recent decades, women worldwide have been at the forefront of shifting attitudes
to political, economic, religious, and technological mind-sets with regard to nature.
Africa's foremost feminist Wangari Mathai has fought to improve women's rights
through communities and landscape improvement for decades, and continues to
alter stereotypes about land usage and women in society. China's Mei Ng and Russia's
Maria Cherkasova continue to expose the effect of industrial globalization on women
and families.

Since 1900, nationalist expansionism and political and economic competition
brought incalculable environmental disasters. But there is hope: 1997's *Kyoto
Accords* and the ensuing *Paris Climate Accords* of 2016 suggest a new awareness of
the connected nature of lands and the consequences of national goals. Women are
prominent in these international negotiations. Most powerful countries agree that it
is time for change, and industrial conglomerates such as Ford and British Petroleum
now recognize the need to reduce emissions. Women have been front and center in
this transformation.

4. Beliefs about nature

The notion of reshaping attitudes to gender, like new ideas about the environment, met with obstinate opposition through the century. Men believed that women were to raise children and listen to men. Well into the 1960s, Western women were expected to work in the home, tending to the house and children, while men worked in industry. This remains the norm in many traditional and religious societies, where production is often the realm of men and women either tend fields or reproduce.

Indeed, reproduction was one of the stories of the century. Humans procreated like weeds, growing from roughly 1.5 to 8 billion people in a century, each person requiring natural resources. While at the outset of the century, belief in high birth rates was the norm, by 2000, a new commitment to the benefits of population control had set in, as population and birth control became necessary. As a rule, where population growth is high, so too is poverty and inequality.

Rank	Country/Territory	Population c. 1900[6]
–	World	1,700,000,000
1	Qing China	415,001,488
2	Indian Empire (UK)	280,912,000
3	Russian Empire	119,546,234
4	United States (US proper only)	75,994,575
5	Germany	56,000,000
6	Austria-Hungary	51,356,465
7	Dutch East Indies (Netherlands)	45,500,000
8	Empire of Japan	42,000,000
9	United Kingdom (Including Ireland)	38,000,000
10	France	38,000,000

Population growth

Three general stages of population change were identified a century ago, known as the *demographic transition*. In the first phase, typically found in traditional societies, deaths balance births, with a low growth rate over time. In the second phase, improved medicine, nutrition, and education boost populations, leading to quick increases, as in nineteenth-century Europe and the Third World since 1945. In a third phase, usually found in developed societies, people have fewer children, women assert more control over their lives and bodies, and populations then level off, often requiring immigration to sustain an economy.

Political desire for larger national populations, constant economi[c]
improved technologies facilitated the greatest environmental change i[n]
increase in world population to 8 billion people. World population [grew]
moderately over the thousand years before 1700, doubling from aroun[d]
in 1600 to 600 million in 1700. Industrialization brought exponenti.. ....
lives: in the eighteenth and nineteenth centuries worldwide population grew to a
billion. Abundant food supplies and medical advances prompted high birthrates over
the past century. The United Nations estimates that roughly 15 billion humans will
be living on earth by 2050. Human procreation may be the greatest threat to the
environment.

The national family

A century ago, both modern and traditional societies purposely promoted high
fertility rates. Industrial nations feared that too few people would lessen their
competitive edge, while traditional societies considered unrestricted births natural.
Great states needed soldiers to fight and workers to toil in factories. After the First
World War, leaders in France, previously one of the most populated countries, were
extremely concerned about population loss from decreased fertility and wartime
deaths. German and Italian elites compelled families to produce more citizens and
soldiers through the fascist years.

White Westerners populated the world's continents in large numbers in the century
up to 1900, with over 5 million Britons alone moving to the Americas, creating large
families of European origin. Between 1900 and 1920 up to 3 million more Britons
moved to Canada, New Zealand, and Australia, Anglicizing those nations. European
migrants moved to the United States to create a mixed population of Central and
South Americans, Asians, Native Americans, and African Americans, among others.
Europeans peaked in reproduction around 1900, and have since stopped breeding
when compared to other groups. Since the Second World War, populations in Africa,
Asia, and Latin America have increased rapidly, mostly in unstable states.

Though modern urban nations exploited nature the most, they also addressed the
issue of uncontrolled reproduction and women's equality first. Population control
in wealthier nations came through social choices made possible by urban industrial
cultures. Medical advances such as industrially produced latex condoms meant that
by 1920 women could choose to avoid pregnancy. Women made their own choices
for the first time, instead of being considered breeding machines as was tradition
(and still is in much of the developing world). Women's rights thus coincided with
lower population growth. When high birthrates are not the national goal, women are
empowered and can limit childbirth to pursue personal and professional goals.

The region that has declined the most in numbers is Europe. After doubling in
the nineteenth century from 188 to over 400 million, European births decelerated

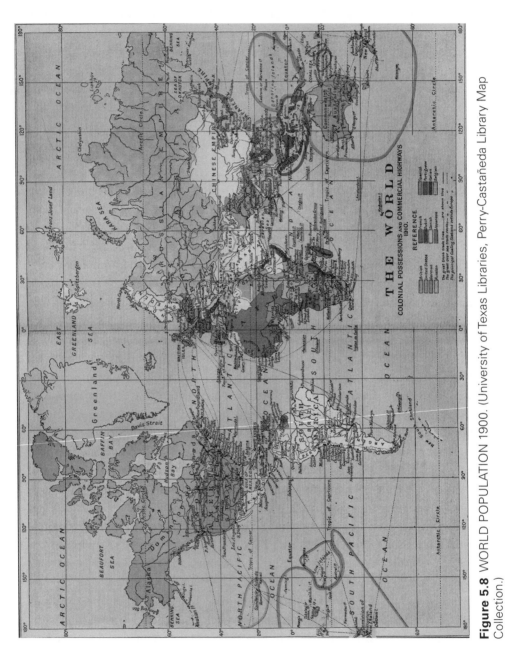

Figure 5.8 WORLD POPULATION 1900. (University of Texas Libraries, Perry-Castañeda Library Map Collection.)

since 1900, through warfare and personal choice. From roughly 25 percent of world population in 1900, Europeans now constitute less than 10 percent. While US population has been sustained through immigration, Europe's numbers declined rapidly. Without immigration, neither the United States nor European population rates can meet replacement levels.

Second World—producing comrades

Birthrates in all developed nations slowed after the 1950s, while Communist states continued to produce high numbers of children. Populations in the USSR and China grew in number over the century even as both lost millions to warfare, mismanagement, and hunger. Both eventually industrialized to create safer conditions for childbirth, in spite of the fact that men with limited education and little interest in women's rights dominated both states. Mao, like most Communists, had only a high school education; Stalin was not formally educated; and Khrushchev directed Russian policies in the 1950s with only 4 years of primary school. All dictated traditional views on women and childbirth.

At the same time, due to ideological commitments to equality derived from Marxism, Communist states made health more of a priority than Western ones. Cuba, China, and Russia provided broader health care than most capitalist states, including free basic health coverage. Women in postwar Communist nations typically enjoyed more access to outside work, education and relative cultural equality as compared to Western or traditional societies.

The USSR in fact saw a population boom in the postwar decades, similar to Third World nations. This has leveled off since the 1990s and, like other developed states, Russia now sees declining birth rates. China added over 200 million people to an impoverished population between 1961 and 1972 as a result of increased food production, mostly from nitrogen fertilizers. Indeed so many Chinese were born that in order to prevent overpopulation, the Communist government implemented a one-child policy in 1980, penalizing those with a second child, compelling abortion if a third was born. The Chinese state sterilized up to 10 million women in recent decades in an attempt to control births.

Poor Children

LDCs produced high numbers of children and large families through the century and high population growth occurred in poorer countries particularly since 1945, due to the belief in the value of large families (and lifesaving medical technologies). Large numbers of people thus reached maturity lacking education, sophisticated medical care, or government support. The poorer parts of the world have thus added the most people in recent decades, correlating with less inclination towards women's rights, widespread illiteracy, poverty, ill health, and at times radical terrorism.

Africa, the Middle East, and South Asia have soared in population since 1945, amid ongoing instability or poverty. Third World families typically generate more children to help bring in income or to work the land. Traditional gender attitudes from religious or political authorities increase births, and most cultures attached great importance to having male children. The Muslim world, most of Asia, and Latin America traditionally bestowed great pride in producing sons to continue family lines, and places like China and India are now stuck with a huge gender imbalance, meaning that men are forced to migrate to find work or partners in difficult circumstances.

Religious leaders in poorer regions also prohibited planned reproduction or sex education. By the 1960s contraception became freely available in North America, Europe, Japan, and China, but it was forbidden in much of the Third World. In Latin America, where a postwar population boom continued amid great poverty, the Catholic Church governed questions regarding sex or the family, instead of doctors. The church refused to consent to birth control, inhibiting women's rights in the process. Today, massive illiteracy and poverty persist on the continent, even in richer states like Brazil, Chile, and Argentina. Only in the past decade or so have birth control methods and sex education spread globally, to slow down birth rates in Asia, Africa, and Latin America.

Already in 1900, lower mortality rates for child and mother prevailed in Western nations, a trend that continued through the century. Unequal access to women's health persists to dispiriting levels in the Third World, where people eat far less than those in rich nations. But even with huge population growth, thanks to medical technology, life expectancy has increased in all regions, and even the poorest eat more than most did a century ago. Consequently, even with well over 100 million deaths from conflict and other causes, billions of new births constitute the main environmental story of the century, putting pressure on lands and ecosystems as never before. Only recently has spiraling population become as great a concern as warfare or disease. The very concept of the earth's *carrying capacity* was unfamiliar just decades ago.

Family values?

Population control is now perhaps the only course forward for humanity, a stark contrast to a century ago. Early in the twentieth century, family planning became a prevalent concern for the first time in history, in developed nations. In poorer countries, nature ran its course with regard to sexual activity. Women suffered the consequences of bearing large numbers of children, which prevented participation in public life and perpetuated supposed family values. The forces of industrialization and urbanization altered this dynamic, changing what the notion of family meant altogether.

Through the century women suffered far more from a patriarchal and legal value system that enshrined power and wealth in male hands. All over the world in 1900, small groups of wealthy men owned most of the land. Industrial workers in modernizing states had long lost their lands to elites. They were forced to move to cities to live and work in the eighteenth and nineteenth centuries, and rent from landlords who profited from their labor. In northwestern Europe, working families lived in cheap but shoddy state-provided housing, while in white settler societies (such as the United States, Australia, South Africa, and Canada) the working classes gradually won home and land ownership, prospering with each subsequent generation. In these states, migrants from colonized societies and indigenous people of color enjoyed no such privilege, either remaining in dire poverty or suffering outright dispossession well into the postwar era.

In Eastern Europe and Catholic nations like Spain, Italy, and Portugal, a tiny number of families owned vast tracts of land, passing on wealth and influence since 1900. Inefficient agriculture lay in the hands of wealthy potentates who hired families to labor for them. Everywhere, people lost access to land in the first half of the century, as peasants worldwide found land they had used for generations turned over to control of the state. These patterns prevailed in Latin America where very few owned land, or in Communist states where nobody (theoretically) owned it.

The Communist Revolution slogan of "Peace, land and bread" proclaimed the new Soviet utopia would share land with the families of the nation. This turned out to be false, as the state, run by a tiny elite, owned all land. Some lands seized from pre-Communist elites were certainly distributed to loyal peasants, but the vast majority remained landless. Other Communist revolutions also promised much but delivered little: China after 1949 persecuted millions of landowners of means, for "being bourgeois." Before Cuba's revolution in 1959, American capitalist interests owned 75 percent of the land, and Fidel Castro's ensuing reforms put land in the hands of the state to benefit mostly well-connected Cubans. For most worldwide, select male ownership of lands meant a life of economic insecurity, with limited control over their one's destiny.

Disease

Sickness has of course always directed human history, possibly more than politics or economics. Until the nineteenth century, few believed much could be done to prevent it. Death was just part of life. In 1900, cold, exhaustion, pain, or hunger were everyday facets of life for people all over the planet, bringing disease regularly. Yet, scientists in advanced nations in the nineteenth century posited a newfound conviction that disease could be controlled or prevented. Methods derived from medical technology, such as vaccination and research-based treatments, would save billions of lives thereafter. Millennia of fatalism, of belief in miracle cures, slowly gave way to scientific medicine, though the benefits were unequally distributed along the lines of rich and poor, male and female, within nations and among them. A key contributing factor to booming human populations since 1900 was thus better disease control.

Industrial disease

After 1900, urbanization spread around the earth. Millions of people streamed into towns in both rich and poor nations, prompting a new need to counter disease through sustained research. Fortunately, epidemiology had already emerged as a field in Western medicine before 1900. The spread of diseases was in fact declining worldwide by the 1890s, as humans controlled pathogens more than ever and research revealed the existence of viruses to be thereafter contained.

The most powerful states, in Western Europe and North America, learned first of microbes and how to control them. As Westerners expanded globally, they brought disease, but also spread awareness of disease control to the conquered. Germany in particular, so deeply entangled in the foulest portions of twentieth-century history, was also the font of better understanding of physiology and medicine. Robert Koch changed the world forever, by discovering bacteria as the cause of sickness with his *Germ Theory* in the 1880s, ending centuries of mistaken belief in "bad air" as a cause of illness.

Generally, the most important factor in positive disease control was secular, scientific, industrial government, which facilitated the sharing of empirically based medical information among doctors around the world. Modern states specifically removed faith from policy making with regard to public health and to administer disease. State intervention spread the benefits of health technology to millions of Western workers via vaccination programs, antiseptics, or advanced surgery techniques.

Efforts to counter the mass killers - cholera and typhoid - bore fruit by the 1880s. Though few die from waterborne disease in the developed world today, in 1900 people in all towns could expect sickness or death from dirty water, as those in poorer nations still do. During the First World War, Western military medics fought staunchly to contain diseases like typhoid or diphtheria: hence the paradox that war provided a vehicle for advancing medical knowledge in the fields of infection control and surgery. Typhus killed hundreds of thousands in war-torn nations during the first half of the century, until doctors generated a vaccine in the 1930s.

Still, through to the 1950s tuberculosis, dysentery, and cholera killed millions, even in developed nations. By the late 1940s medical professionals countered bacterial microorganisms that for centuries brought grave illness, incapacitated people, or led to death without recourse. One of the most extraordinarily important discoveries of the century was the emergence of *antibiotics*, after the Scotsman Alexander Fleming discovered that mold healed infections in 1928. This led to the development of penicillin, derived from fungi but ideal for treating countless bacterial diseases. Other bacterium, discovered in places as distant as Venezuela and Missouri, were turned into the first antibiotics, creating a hugely lucrative pharmaceutical industry, while improving countless lives.

Life became enormously more comfortable in wealthier nations following such medical advances. Shadowing Fleming, others worked to understand bacteria further. The US army researched antibiotics in depth in the 1940s, and today, tens of thousands of affordable antibiotics exist to alleviate illness worldwide. After the Second World War, efforts to eradicate diseases such as tetanus, yellow fever, and flu flourished. The awful disease polio was finally controlled in 1954, with measles better managed by the 1980s. Even accounting for the horrors of colonization and warfare, such miraculous innovations, shaped by research in modern states, saved more lives than were lost over the course of the century.

Urban disease

Of course, aggregate numbers provide scant comfort to those who suffered. And people everywhere suffered from a century of warfare dictated by urbanized nations. Though bombs and mortars killed millions, more often death came from exhaustion, sickness, or disease, particularly before the Second World War. More deaths stemmed from infections than from artillery in both world wars, and enormous chemical waste and polluted sediments filtered into water systems in wartime. The Rhine, Germany's largest river and source of much of its freshwater, was polluted dreadfully from Second World War bombings. Japan suffered the horrendous effects of atomic bombs dropped by American planes in Nagasaki and Hiroshima. Though many Jews died from Nazi guns, millions also suffered diseases before dying from hunger and abuse.

Industrializing nations always dispensed great suffering to populations in the haste to modernize. Industrial cities are necessarily destructive of land, covering grasses and soils with cement and tarmac for transportation or homes. Increasingly after 1900, wealthy states coerced working people into the misery of grimy cities. Workers and families were jammed into tiny rooms, worked to the bone in factories or mines, with little regulation or safety. Waste was ordinarily sent to the street or to a dump just outside of town. Only in the 1950s did developed nations begin to address the problem of urban garbage disposal, when progressive politicians pressed compliance upon all members of the community, including businesses, to prevent disease spreading in cities. Refuse management issues still plague the poor in developing nations.

Whenever municipal or national officeholders failed to legislate, people died in great numbers. The lethargic response of Japanese leaders to the chemical pollution of major conglomerates between 1932 and 1968 left innumerable people crippled. Japanese people suffered enormously, while business elites evaded prosecution for polluting rivers with mercury. The notorious *"Cat dancing disease"* in Japan in 1956 afflicted large numbers of children with brain disease. The Bhopal region of India brought horrific injury to human life in 1984 due to a large gas leak, with at least 2,000 people dying and up to 500,000 falling prey to sickness. The 1979 Three Mile Island nuclear reactor panic in New York highlighted the risks endemic to atomic energy, with ensuing growth in cancer rates in the region.

Communist states of course paid little heed to the lives of workers, with disastrous disease prevention records. About 10 million Ukrainians and other populations died from famine in 1932, and millions more were worked to death for the state. If Stalin's merciless purges did not kill people directly, Communist life subjected them to ill-health, infirmity, or chronic sickness. Decades of irresponsible and unresponsive governance in the USSR came to a climax with the Chernobyl nuclear reactor explosion in 1986, with up to 10,000 cases of thyroid cancer in the following decades from massive radiation. Much of Soviet-controlled Eastern Europe was left a scarred environmental landscape thanks to decades of heavy industry. Ex-Soviet states and Russia still have high rates of alcoholism, suicide rates, and child mortality as indicators of long-suffering populations. Millions of Chinese peasants died in the interwar years from parasitic diseases in a nation torn by conflict. In the postwar era, sickness and disease spread after Maoists eradicated "bourgeois intellectuals" - doctors, engineers, or academics. Estimates of deaths under Mao's regime range from 15 to 45 million dead, mostly from incompetence.

Third World disease

Industrial states were thus at the forefront of modern medicine even as they killed millions in warfare and spread disease. In the last century however, most disease has occurred in nonindustrial regions, in undeveloped states across Africa, the Middle East, or Asia, where people have borne disease as they have done for centuries.

Developing nations brought both domination and improved disease prevention. The construction of the Panama Canal (to advance Western trade) also facilitated understanding of local disease vectors that had long destroyed lives. While Euro-American industrial interests colonized Panama and Columbia before 1900, Cuban and American doctors determined that mosquitoes transmitted yellow fever and malaria, the first step to fighting these terrible illnesses. People worldwide who may have died before fifty from disease lived longer with Western medicine. By 1950, malaria, yellow fever, and leprosy were mostly under control due to public health programs and modern medical science. Smallpox had wiped people out for thousands of years, killing millions in the twentieth century, but by 1980 it was contained through vaccination. Malaria persists in undeveloped tropical regions, though simple mass-produced nets now prevent mosquito bites at night.

Combined population growth and urban poverty canceled out many of the benefits, however. With so many more people living longer life spans, new cities could not cope with waste or infections and urban population growth made it increasingly impossible to maintain sanitary hygiene. As had been the case in 1900 in rich nations, urban waste and stench became a daily part of life in poor states in the postwar era. Though most large cities in developed nations are cleaner today than they were in 1900, squalor and disease from human waste persist in poorer regions.

Megacities in developing parts of India, South America, and China sprawl uncontrolled today, and officials in conurbations cannot cope with waste where overpopulation and disease intersect. Some urban areas with over 10 million people lack levels of management found in Western cities in the 1950s. In poorer nations, people live and die amid chemical effluents, in corrugated iron homes covered in tarpaulin and cardboard. Millions make a living from scouring garbage dumps for food in almost all underdeveloped nations, including wealthier ones such as Brazil and India.

Unsurprisingly, poor nations and poor people continue to suffer most from disease, and when new diseases emerge, poorer people are infected more. AIDs decimated the poorest continent, Africa, in particular. Though the virus emerged in the 1980s among gay communities in the West, most of the 25 million deaths to date have been in Africa or poor nations. Over 30 million people in Africa were infected. Women suffered the most because men refused to wear condoms, thereby helping spread disease. Cholera, measles, and malaria are still endemic in poor countries, while controlled in industrial nations.

Traditional medicine

Though poverty clearly exacerbates the disease environment, death rates since 1900 declined everywhere, and life expectation grew in tandem. Thriving numbers of humans lived longer lives, absorbing more of the earth's energy, as scientific medical advances saved countless lives. Still, the effects of colonization persisted to the detriment of disadvantaged people. Westerners spread disease to poorer nations through imperialism and war. Only after the First World War were passports necessary to travel afar, but before then explorers or missionaries moved with relative ease, often spreading disease unintentionally.

Though societies in Africa had long suffered epidemics, natural remedies developed by healers protected populations to some degree. The imperial activities of Westerners weakened populations by introducing European diseases. Land that might have grown food to strengthen immune systems was claimed by white settlers or used to export crops to Western markets and mouths. As forests or fields were ploughed over to export single crops to markets, food diversity lessened and indigenous diets suffered.

Italian armies introduced rinderpest into cattle in the Somali wars of 1880s, eliminating a key source of nutrition while grabbing land. Indians endured increased disease from the movement of people under British colonialism in the century before 1947. Poverty and inequality however persist in India as in other postcolonial states. An inefficient state and the flow of biological waste pollute waterways such as the River Ganges, worsened by the religious practice of purifying dead bodies in the water. The river is dirtier today than it was under imperial rule.

Westerners were nearly always disdainful toward traditional methods of healing. Native or indigenous medicines were mocked or even outlawed until independence. Ancient Indian practices such as yoga or meditation were considered barbaric by Western modernizers, many of whose descendants now practice both fervently. Homeopathy, acupuncture, and holistic healing, which healed people in Asia for centuries, were pushed aside in favor of industrial pharmacology.

Everywhere medicine was masculinized. Women were labeled unfit, replaced by male doctors or surgeons, even in the area of childbirth. Where midwives had long delivered babies, by 1900 men took over in hospital wards. A male-dominated medical industry manufactured medicines for profit, while women's traditional role in healing the sick was pushed aside. Arguably, masculine honor codes motivated an overly activist response to sickness—bringing excessive medication or treatment—that has been as harmful as helpful. Into the twenty-first century, male dominated parliaments and governments continue to direct funding toward diseases men suffer from more than women. Only after the 1960s did Westerners realize that indigenous systems of health and female perspectives might supplement modern medical theory. The input of women thus adjusted gendered attitudes to both the social and health environment in the late twentieth century.

Political disease

Nonetheless, the primary institution for developing lifesaving disease prevention mechanisms has been the modern, scientific state. Government-administered vaccination programs to fight viruses have saved millions of lives, first in the developed world, then globally. Powerful centralized states developed innovative solutions to disease, even as war eviscerated populations and traumatized millions. When millions of combat deaths after the First World War were followed by 20 million deaths from typhus and influenza, doctors were ordered to find ways to cure sick people. Close partnerships thus formed between medical experts, political, and military elites to better understand medicine. It was just such a partnership between medics and British army doctors that helped develop the vital typhoid vaccine in 1914.

The regulation and management of disease improved astonishingly after 1900, though the battle against disease is of course continuous and ever shifting. Disease is after all part of the natural environment, so as older viruses are eradicated, new epidemics appear. Though infectious disease declined, contemporary maladies like heart disease, cancer, and stress-induced illness have risen to epidemic proportions—mainly due to industrial living and modern pressures. Lifestyle diseases such as alcoholism, drug addiction, lung cancer, and STD's torment people worldwide, even while nineteenth-century diseases are eliminated.

Disease is still the greatest cause of death in humans. Murder from warfare peaked mid-century and has thankfully declined precipitously in recent decades. Indeed, the world has now returned to historical patterns, where most people die from disease instead of violence. The institutions of the state, more than ever historically, now control or constrain human life, for better or worse. Technology is the means by which this power is expressed.

5. Belief in technology—reshaping human nature

The positive effects of twentieth-century state-sponsored science and technology on the human and natural environment are incalculable. Lifesaving immunizations and antibiotics have made billions of lives more bearable, saving countless people from lives of suffering. Applied technology built state hospitals, filled them with machines and then trained experts to save life on a daily basis. By mid-century science provided a biochemical analysis of any living cell on earth through the work of Francis Crick.

Progress?

Building on the Industrial Revolution of the nineteenth century, science and technology provided humans with the means to see inside the body and indeed all of nature. We are now at a point where as a species, human brains will determine the path forward for the planet. The past century is clearly a cautionary tale, and contradictions abound. The same industrial lifestyle that polluted human bodies facilitated survival for far more humans who then produced more pollution. The very processes improving human health, disease, and reproduction, though they increased understanding of the human body, also pushed the world's population to potentially unsustainable levels. More humans alive brought declining biodiversity and vast landscape transformations, from dams to levees to concrete jungles. Human access to nature's fruits fed families, built homes, and provided comfortable living, but until the 1970s, few could muster the intellectual will to question the downside of growth and "progress."

Food for thought

Humans can't think without food, and in the last century technological advances helped humans grow more agricultural product to feed more mouths than in all of previous history. This is surely a force for good. Political entities like nation-states can't function without feeding the masses; economies depend first and foremost upon food production; religious and philosophical thinkers go unheard in times of famine.

Scientific analysis and technology-driven practices improved land usage and food production, bringing more efficient irrigation and far greater crop productivity to feed billions of people who might have starved in earlier times. Technological enhancements like fertilizers and pesticides cultivated abundant food supplies in developed nations, and technology transfers then brought improvements to LDCs. Since 1900, large Agribusinesses have made food more efficiently than millions of small farmers could, using capital investments and technologies such as well-equipped, faster tractors to lower the price of food for all, if not to raise the quality. Bounties of staple foods were produced to the point that mountains of food sat in warehouses in Europe for much of the postwar period. State-supported, research-driven intellectual innovations increased births, lowered child mortality rates, and prolonged lives. Human populations increased from greater technical manipulation of nature: land productivity, efficient farming, irrigation, and chemical concoctions such as genetic engineering, have made food readily available.

The Austrian Gregor Mendel used applied equations to discover genetics in the late nineteenth century. The field developed, until in the 1960s, scientists could breed new strains of wheat and rice - in essence, tricking nature to feed billions of hungry mouths. Scientists now modify the genetic coding of crops. Since the 1950s the West experienced another agricultural revolution, improving the breeding of livestock, use of fertilizers, seed selection, land use and modern machinery, to bring plenty of food to growing populations. The *Green Revolution* in the decades after the Second World War replaced the tens of millions of dead through warfare with billions more alive. In these decades, the work of the humanitarian biologist Norman Borlaugh saved up to a billion humans from hunger, from India to Mexico to the Philippines, through innovative plant breeding technologies.

However, all advances brought serious side-effects. Chemical's soaked into the land by large Agribiz enterprises depleted soils. Focused on profit, businesses ignored the negative environmental and human effects, rejecting accusations that they polluted human bodies or unintentionally laced food with toxins. Worldwide, until the 1980s, the impact of dangerous chemicals was ignored, as corporations chased profits and pressured or threatened family farmers to use their products. Large business pushed out local family farmers who had tilled land naturally for decades or centuries. Caution from soil experts was habitually ignored. Since it can take decades for the effects of chemically induced toxins to permeate into populations, CEO's could pay little heed. Short-term shareholder gains and higher food production levels overrode the risk of homogenization of earth's diverse strains of flora and fauna. By centuries end, *Genetically Modified (GM) crops* provided further more food while introducing barely understood ecological mutations. Today, farms look more like business parks, as gigantic industrial sheds cover once green pastures.

Ongoing population growth and declining biodiversity are two obvious threats to the earth, but rapid climate change is surely the greatest. In her 1971 *Diet for a Small Planet*, Frances Moore Lappe warned of the risks of climate change through wasteful food production processes. It is now readily apparent that all that human sustenance, today and throughout history, comes from land and water. Most of the world remains either uninformed of this fact or committed to overlooking it for material gain. As a result, the earth's rapidly changing climate in coming decades may affect human existence far more than political or economic systems, particular beliefs about life, or even technological progress.

Climate change

As climate change skeptics correctly note, climate has changed throughout human history. There have indeed been five mass extinctions on earth without any human participation, so if a sixth came, it may be "natural" as some claim—the question is: Do we want to invite it sooner rather than later? This is ultimately a question of faith versus knowledge, belief versus science.

The historical record also demonstrates that large-scale societal collapses are frequent. Empire after empire, culture after culture, tribe after tribe, has disappeared over time. Animals and species are often wiped out. If time is measured proportionately, microbes ruled the earth for 2 of the past 13 billion years, humans only for a few millennia. Mammals are after all a recent arrival. Indeed, 245 million years ago 90 percent of marine species were wiped out, and as most schoolchildren know, dinosaurs were eliminated 65 million years ago, providing opportunity for mammals like humans to evolve in the first place.

Since 1900, the use and abuse of land and water has expedited exponentially when compared to all of history. Population's boomed, plants and animals were driven to extinction, river systems were dammed or damaged, soils dried up—now the planet gets warmer each year. Some experts predict a sixth mass extinction will come soon. The earth has no need for humans after all; it existed long before our species subject it to our power ploys, economic aspirations, belief systems and technological skills.

ǝlieving in earth

The essential question therefore for the historically informed thinker is what do we believe we have done, and what do we believe we should do? The eighteenth- and nineteenth-century Industrial Revolution induced more transformation in the earth's environment than all of history prior to that, and since 1945 we have now changed the world far more than in those two centuries. When coal was produced in 1900 it merely polluted rivers and lands in certain regions of industrial nations. When the United States, Russian, or Chinese energy companies drill deep into the core of the earth today, they can prompt earthquakes across a continent, polluting water tables that feed millions of people.

In 2014, the *Los Angeles Times* reported that Oklahoma, a region of the United States which rarely experienced earthquakes, saw a vast increase in ground movement at the same time as recent increases in gas production through fracking.[7] The revenues from this new form of cheap gasoline extraction drove an economic boom that benefitted the wider US economy. Affordable gas and oil meant cheaper driving, lower heating and food prices food for Americans across the income spectrum. But objective studies from Harvard and Cornell universities supplied evidence that fracking did more than pollute water supplies for locals, it threatened the very geological structure of the region's bedrock. These environmental risks and the anger of homeowners who protested were mocked by the energy industry. Perpetuating patterns of behavior since 1900, the pursuit of profits and cheap energy chased away social and environmental concerns.

This story symbolizes the payoff humans worldwide have grappled with since 1900: short-term economic gains always come at great environmental and social cost. Fracking and cheap gas could end the geopolitical conflict that has embroiled Americans in conflicts worldwide for decades. Ending US reliance on foreign oil— which has prompted numerous interventions in the Middle East, Asia, parts of Africa, and South America for decades, as well as the recent Iraq and Afghanistan wars—could offer incredible rewards. Fracking is cleaner than fossil fuels, and can serve as a transition source of energy while engineers work on renewable energies like solar, wind, or nuclear fusion technologies.

But if it potentially causes swarms of earthquakes, ruins the land for those in the way of development, is it just another process that offers catastrophe for nature and humanity? The desire for short-term economic gain that drives world leaders conflicts with the purview of the historian's longer perspective. At present it seems humans do not have the intellectual capacity to consider such disaster scenarios until they occur. The most environmentally destructive nations on earth today— the United States, Brazil, and China, India, Russia, and Indonesia—race to increase wealth or modernize.

As the earth warms, and it has each year for the past three decades, la[...] for growing food, while populations continue to grow. Greenland, famousl[...] in ice for millennia, is now actually becoming green, as ice melts. It is p[...] Gulf Stream, the central component of all Northern Hemisphere weather, could fail if climate keeps getting warmer. Seas are rising, and hundreds of millions of people will no longer be able to live along coasts. Wars will prospectively result over clear air and clean water.

The current international system of state politics—democracies, monarchies, traditional societies, or dictatorships—has, for a century, disregarded stewardship of the environment. Scientists know climate change is indisputable, and a massive international consensus exists among experts. Yet economic elites and fervent religious institutions obstruct efforts to limit production of goods and exploitation of lands. The 2015 Paris Accords to control environmental destruction have lost the support of the United States due to American suspicion of climate science.

The living standards enjoyed by Americans, and emulated worldwide, are today as much a threat to humanity as nuclear war or disease epidemics. Conservatives who shape the political discussion in the United States feel threatened that their belief system might be subsumed by a scientific philosophy whose purpose is to continue using the earth for all of humanity. A very American belief that material affluence is more important than nature, that short-term wealth matters more than long term planning, continues to abuse the earth's complex ecosystem.

It is surely ironic that Osama Bin Laden, the person who posed the greatest threat to freedom and prosperity of US citizens, pointed out the hypocrisy of American (and Western) exploitation of nature's bounty. Until President Obama, using US Special Forces, assassinated him in 2011, Bin Laden was an outspoken critic of the virtues of modernity. His venomous actions notwithstanding, Bin Laden questioned American values with regard to the environment. Even murderers can make sense sometimes:

> You have destroyed nature with your industrial waste and gases more than any other nation in history. Despite this, you refuse to sign the Kyoto (environmental) agreement so that you can secure the profit of your greedy companies and industries.[8]

Visions of earth

Like many fundamentalist Christians in the United States, Bin Laden and his followers embrace a wholly different conception of earth, time, space - and hence existence - than scientists or historians do. Such groups either don't concern themselves with earth's future, or they predict that science can enable us to intervene and sustain the climate. Technology created the imbalances in power distribution that drives the likes of Al Qaeda or ISIS. It also brought the fast-paced modern world that threatens traditionally minded people. Religious conservatives from West to East, from America to Islam, today challenge technological and scientific attitudes toward the environment, while enjoying its fruits.

This is partly understandable. Only since 1969 have humans been able to see an actual photograph of the planet, altering attitudes to raise consciousness regarding nature's fragility. In 1957, Russian scientists put an artificial satellite into space, starting the Space Race in earnest. This small piece of machinery named Sputnik, composed of metals, plastics, and glass, spent three months in orbit, traveling over 40 million miles from earth, a distance barely imaginable for most of history. This fascinating illustration of human control of the environment could be seen by all worldwide, merely by looking up at the sky at the correct time.

The United States response was uninhibited and explorative. The NASA program bolstered national pride and pointed toward the ultimate goal of putting a man on the moon. Launching the Apollo Program in 1961, John F. Kennedy vowed to beat the Soviets, and by 1969 American astronauts landed on the moon and safely returned to earth. These competitive efforts revealed that the United States and the USSR could harness the powers of scientists—as well as mutual antipathy—to counter earth's gravitational pull. These advanced technologies have since brought the world satellite TV, the Internet, streaming movies and much more. As the USSR and the United States developed space technologies, they pointed hundreds of thousands of nuclear warheads at each other in a program aptly labeled MAD. For most of the postwar era, humans lived for the first time with the threat of nuclear annihilation, and the end of the world seemed possible.

Such end-of-the-world predictions existed long before nuclear technology however. Technology, particularly in recent centuries, continues to provide solutions to human problems, and while climate change, overpopulation, or nuclear warfare point toward potential calamity, there is much to be excited about in recent history. Where one person sees the past century as a litany of slaughter over mere ideas, another can highlight higher standards of living for billions of humans, longer lives and immeasurably greater creature comforts.

Perhaps technologists will find new imaginative ways to resolve resource scarcity or population pressures. In the past 5,000 years, human *cultural evolution* advanced far faster than biological evolution: while the human body remains much as it has for hundreds of thousands of years, human cultural abilities progressed at great speed over five millennia, particularly in the last century. Is the human body perhaps evolving? Or are we devolving toward senseless androids and unfeeling automatons? Will technology move from servant to master? Only time will tell.

New forms of complexity arise now that we don't fully understand. Virtual Reality, Artificial Intelligence and brain-computer interfaces change the environment like never before. Ray Kurzweil's notion of the Singularity seemed futuristic when he argued humans will eventually merge with technology in the 1960s. But Kurzweil has repeatedly predicted technologies accurately. Already genetics, biological enhancement and robotics connect software and hardware with human bodies. Virtual Reality may become normal, instead of present reality. Scientists and engineers are already devising ways to live on other planets. The International Space Station hovers 240 miles above earth, now providing conditions for long-term space life for astronauts. History seems to move at a new pace.

Key terms

Industrial capitalism [260]
London Smog [266]
Chernobyl [263]
Mahatma Gandhi [274]
Rachel Carson [275]
Second Industrial Revolution [277]
Taylorism [278]
Fordism [278]
Dust Bowl [279]
Paris Climate Accords [285]
Germ Theory [292]
Antibiotics [293]
GM Crops [299]
Green Revolution [298]
Cultural evolution [302]

Further readings

Fagan, Brian M. *The Long Summer: How Climate Changed Civilization*. New York: Basic Books, 2004. A perfect introduction to the latest research on the long-term processes that shaped our planet. Fagan devotes only one chapter to the last two thousand years, highlighting the millennia and in a long perspective.

Bsumek, Erika Marie, David Kinkela, and Mark Atwood Lawrence. *Nation-States and the Global Environment: New Approaches to International Environmental History*. Oxford: Oxford University Press, 2013. An edited set of essays from the latest scholars who work to explain the disjuncture between the interests of the nation-state and the earth itself. Environmental history is the central topic of this rather than political or economic issues.

McNeill, John Robert. *Something New under the Sun: An Environmental History of the Twentieth-Century World.* New York: W.W. Norton & Company, 2000. The first major account of the century through an environmental lens, focusing on issues for all humans as opposed to the interests of certain nations or economic systems.

Epilogue: "It's the end of the world as we know it . . . "

As the song from the college rock band R. E. M. suggested, change may be on the horizon in ways we can't imagine. For the past five chapters, we have scoured a century or so of political, economic, philosophical, and technological change, to come to an understanding of our current environmental circumstances. There has been much despair, but also much hope. Climate change seems bigger than the needs of nations, the pursuit of power, inherited creeds and convictions, economic aspirations, or the joys of innovation that spurred twentieth-century history.

History seems to suggest that perhaps the human interest in power and wealth are normal. Shocking events are surely more exciting than enduring ecosystems. People often ask, "Where were you when the Berlin Wall fell," or ". . . when JFK was shot" or ". . . when 9/11 happened?" Maybe someday humans will ask, "Where were you when the seas entered Miami" or ". . . when Arizona became too hot to inhabit?"

Politics as usual

We have seen how *political* entities that govern the world are historically recent creations—constructed nation-states run by well-connected, often self-serving elites, striving to compete in a zero-sum game of international competition. Humans have lived in states of various types for only 5,000 years, relying on and settling near rivers and water sources, exploiting soil to find food and flourish. Those in power today affect nature far more than regular individuals; history is rarely part of the conversation. The political will of most notables seems to be short term, interested more in reelection than in stewarding the environment. Stable, prosperous states that plundered the environment the most seem best suited to thwart future catastrophe. Failing states, impoverished nations, or war zones without strong centralized rule are oblivious to the needs of people or their land, often imprisoned in a harsh fight for survival. The environment is not their immediate concern. However, a younger generation of political leaders, trained in environmental understanding, might offer hope, utilizing historical perspectives.

Economic exploitation

We have learned too that a deep-seated *economic* commitment to growth, mass consumption, profits, and competition are also historically recent practices, developing only since the late eighteenth century. Industrial capitalism has been the driving philosophy, the true "religion" of the century, far outweighing the desire for environmental justice, social equality, or even peace. It has spread from one industrial nation to another, covering the whole globe in recent decades as all seek the comforts, joys, and toys of consumerism. Nature has not responded well to national economies; the latter rarely embrace the former. Fortunately, such practices are increasingly questioned now, both in value and wisdom, as nature exposes the severe social and ecological costs of excessive materialism. The Natural Capitalism movement seeks to educate business leaders about opportunities to make money while protecting nature, incorporating historical assessment.

Believing in earth

We have also learned that *philosophical* and *religious* belief systems only recently began to recognize and address the biggest question of all—earth's sustainability and humanity's continued existence. Most traditions, particularly indigenous ones outside of the West, long respected the need for earth's conservation. But the Western Judeo-Christian approach believed in making use of the earth, and nations within this tradition have been the most culpable in damaging nature worldwide, until recently. In recent decades Hindu India, Confucian China, and now Muslim Indonesia, like nations of Christian heritage before them, seem willing to set aside the lessons of moderation in their traditions, to attain economic status and sit at the table of rich nations. Environmentalism itself appears to be a new philosophy, above and beyond regional traditions, again incorporating historical perspective.

Technologies for the future

After the Renaissance, the West built on and improved Asian, Muslim, and Indian technological innovations. Twentieth- and twenty-first-century technologies have swept aside centuries, even millennia, of natural environmental processes and ecosystems. Within years, dammed rivers, ruined coastlines, and spoiled soils altered landscapes that took thousands of years to form. Technological abilities and economic expectations always overrode the conservation of clean air and water. This is perhaps changing now as technology serves to help expose our global abuse of the planet, even as it proceeds at faster pace. History can serve as our clearest guide.

Alternative modernity?

So, what to believe in? We only have ourselves to blame if we choose the wrong kind of progress, and we have a century of remarkable history to use as source material. The world is slowly learning to produce food locally and organically; clean cars and busses are increasingly used to move people around; ecological engineering, green architecture, and urban planning fill the minds of college students who will shape the new world.

If humanity cannot stop itself from destroying its habitable planet, we have had a century of warnings. Early in the twentieth century, some argued that humans seemed unable to prevent themselves from abusing nature—like naughty children who know better but cannot change. In 1920, Walter Benjamin, an underappreciated commentator on modernity (citing a painting by Paul Klee, *Angelus Novus*), cautioned regarding the rush to modernity:

> *Where we perceive a chain of events, (the angel) sees one single catastrophe which keeps piling wreckage upon wreckage and hurls it in front of his feet. The angel would like to stay, awaken the dead, and make whole what has been smashed. But a storm is blowing from Paradise; it has got caught in his wings with such violence that the angel can no longer close them. This storm irresistibly propels him into the future to which his back is turned, while the pile of debris before him grows skyward. This storm is what we call progress.[1]*

Some now question the very ethics of profit seeking, as kingdoms like Bhutan measure happiness rather than wealth production. New global metrics show the superficiality of twentieth-century metrics for analyzing the quality of life or economic success. Today's successful nations measure higher on the HDI instead of gross income levels. GDP may be losing its throne in measuring national well-being, with emphasis now on gender or economic equality. Levels of stress or happiness tell us more than the net worth of nations or people, to indicate how "successful" a society is or how much "progress" is made. Health, education, environmental sustainability, inclusiveness and equity are now bywords for those who will shape the next generation of human life on earth. This is a revolutionary historical transformation, and we are all part of it.

Notes

Chapter 1 Twentieth-Century Politics: Nationalism, Imperialism, Colonization

1 The term First World usually refers to nationalist, capitalist, Western states. The term Second World was applied to the various Communist states that existed until 1991. The Third World refers to the remaining, usually weaker, states.

2 Marshall Berman, *All That Is Solid Melts into Air: The Experience of Modernity* (New York: Penguin Books, 1988).

3 Visit https://en.wikipedia.org/wiki/New_Imperialism#/media/ File:Colonisation_1914.png for a map of European empires in 1914.

4 Alistair Horne, *The Price of Glory: Verdun 1916* (Harmondsworth: Penguin Books, 1964), p. 236.

5 The last line translates to "It is sweet and proper to die for the fatherland." https:// www.poetryfoundation.org/poems/46560/dulce-et-decorum-est

6 See the Fourteen Points at http://avalon.law.yale.edu/20th_century/wilson14.asp.

7 http://avalon.law.yale.edu/20th_century/sykes.asp

8 G. M. Gilbert, *Nuremberg Diary* (New York: Farrar, Straus and Giroux, 1947), pp. 278–279.

9 http://www.winstonchurchill.org/learn/speeches/ speeches-of-winston-churchill/128-we-shall-fight-on-the-beaches

10 Joseph B. Fabry, 1980. *The Pursuit of Meaning: Viktor Frankl, Logotherapy, and Life* (San Francisco: Harper & Row), p. 154.

11 https://en.wikipedia.org/wiki/World_War_II_casualties

12 UN Conference on Trade and Development.

13 Nate Thayer, interview with Pol Pot, 1997. http://natethayer.typepad.com/ blog/2011/11/pol-pot-unrepentant-an-exclusive-interview-by-nate-thayer.html

14 Cited in Craig A. Lockard, *Southeast Asia in World History* (Oxford: Oxford University Press, 2009), p. 138.

15 https://en.wikipedia.org/wiki/John_T._Flynn

16 Kwane Nkrumah, *Neo-Colonialism. The Last State of Imperialism* (London: Nelson and Sons, June 1966]), p. 965.

17 Cited in Prevost and Vanden, *Latin America*, (Oxford: Oxford University Press, 2010), pp. 174–175.

18 http://pro-europa.eu/index.php/en/library/the-struggle-for-the-union-of- europe/156-gorbachev,-mikhail-the-common-european-home

Interlude 1: Propaganda

19 http://www.theguardian.com/world/2002/nov/24/theobserver

Chapter 2 Twentieth-Century Economics: Natural Inequality

1   The only regions trading in silver were China and Persia, both of which were also under British influence.
2   http://labourmanifesto.com/1906/1906-labour-manifesto.shtml.
3   Karl Marx, Friedrich Engels, Samuel Moore, and David McLellan. *The Communist Manifesto*. (Oxford: Oxford University Press, 1992), chapter one.
4   Bertrand Russell, *Sceptical Essays*, (Routledge Classics, Volume 101 (Routledge, 1988).
5   General Agreement on Tariffs and Trade.
6   "Written comment on a document of the National Conference on Financial and Economic Work held in the summer of 1953." (accessed, July 12, 2016). https://www.marxists.org/reference/archive/mao/selected-works/volume-5/mswv5_30.htm
7   https://winstonchurchill.hillsdale.edu/socialism-is-the-philosophy-of-failure-winston-churchill/
8   For a full timeline go to http://en.rfi.fr/africa/20100216-timeline-african-independence
9   R. K. Prabhu and U. R. Rao, *Mind of Mahatma Gandhi* (Jitendra T. Desai, 1960), p. 219.
10 Camille Paglia *Sex, Art, And American Culture: Essays* (New York : Vintage Books, 1992).
11 http://lanic.utexas.edu/project/castro/db/1991/19910604-1.html
12 Organization of Petroleum Exporting Countries.
13 http://archive.fortune.com/magazines/fortune/fortune_archive/2003/02/03/336434/index.htm
14 Association of Southeast Asian Nations.
15 Friedrich Hayek, *The Road to Serfdom*.
16 http://www.bloombergview.com/articles/2013-09-17/vladimir-putin-the-richest-man-on-earth
17 http://www.huffingtonpost.com/eduardo-paes/polisdigitocracy_b_4044222.html
18 http://www.forbes.com/sites/faraigundan/2014/01/28/top-quotes-about-africa-at-the-2014-world-economic-forum-in-davos/
19 North American Free Trade Agreement. The current Trump administration is trying to undo the agreement.
20 http://www.theguardian.com/environment/2010/apr/21/cochabamba-mining-protests-climate-summit

Interlude 2: Capitalism and humans

21 http://www.sanders.senate.gov/newsroom/recent-business/income-inequality-06-20-2014
22 http://www.newyorker.com/arts/critics/books/2014/05/26/140526crbo_books_kolbert?currentPage=2
23 http://www.newyorker.com/magazine/2014/05/26/no-time

Chapter 3 Twentieth-Century Thought: Philosophical Uncertainty

1 E. B. Tylor, *Primitive Culture: Researches into the Development of Mythology, Philosophy, Religion, Art, and Custom.* (New York: Gordon Press, [1871]1974), p. 1.
2 http://www.ccs.neu.edu/home/will/CPP/gandhi.html (accessed May 12, 2017).
3 Quoted in A. L. Macfie, *Ataturk*, (London: Pearson, 1999), p. 138.
4 A. Hitler, and J. V. Murphy, *Mein Kampf.* (London: Hurst and Blackett, 1981), p. 60.
5 *The Diaries of Joseph Goebbels, Part I: Notations, 1923–1941*, October 16, 1928. See http://blogs.bodleian.ox.ac.uk/history/2013/01/10/newgoebbelsdiaries/
6 http://stevenpinker.com/pages/frequently-asked-questions-about-better-angels-our-nature-why-violence-has-declined
7 Raj Kumar, *Essays on Ancient India* (Delhi: Discovery Publishing House, 1993), 33.
8 Jerry Falwell, *"Moral Majority Report"* September, 1984, cited in Jan G. Linn, *What's Wrong with the Christian Right* (Universal Publishers, 2004), p. 32.
9 *Princeton Readings in Islamist Thought: Texts and Contexts from Al-Banna to Bin Laden.* (Princeton: Princeton University Press, 2009), p. 152.
10 http://www.nytimes.com/2010/10/24/magazine/24sirleaf-t.html.
11 http://hdr.undp.org/en/statistics/hdi
12 Umberto Eco, *The Prague Cemetery* (Oxford: Isis, 2012), p. 3.
13 http://www.catholicnews.com/data/stories/cns/1400862.htm. (General audience, June 5, 2013)

Chapter 4 Twentieth-Century Technology: Fear and Euphoria

1 https://archive.org/stream/moderntraveller00belluoft/moderntraveller00belluoft_djvu.txt (accessed June 12, 2017).

2 David Christian *Maps of Time: An Introduction to Big History* (California: UC Press, 2011), p. 458.
3 https://archive.org/stream/asongspeed00conggoog/asongspeed00conggoog_djvu. txt (accessed June 12, 2017).
4 Available on Youtube.
5 Herbert Marcuse, *One-Dimensional Man: Studies in the Ideology of Advanced Industrial Society*. (Boston: Beacon Press, 1991), p. 3.
6 Max Perutz, "The Impact of Science on Society: The Challenge for Education," in J. L. Lewis and P. J. Kelly (eds.), Science and Technology and Future Human Needs (New York: Pergamon Press. (1987), p. 18.
7 Tim Berners-Lee, *Weaving the Web: The Original Design and Ultimate Destiny of the World Wide Web* (London: Harper, 2004), p. 123.
8 Cited in Craig A. Lockard, *Southeast Asia in World History*. (Oxford: Oxford University Press, 2009), p. 168.
9 'Environmental Quality: Summary and Discussion of Major Provisions', U.S. Environmental Protection Agency, Legal Compilation, (January 1973), Water, Vol. 3, 1365. EPA. See https://en.wikipedia.org/wiki/Clean_Air_Act_(United_States) (accessed July 5, 2017).

Interlude 4: Freedom

10 George Orwell, *Animal Farm: A Fairy Story*. (New York : Signet Classics, 1996), p. 248.
11 Aldous Huxley, and Christopher Hitchens. *Brave New World: And, Brave New World Revisited*. (London: Harpers, 2005), p. 18.

Chapter 5 Twentieth-Century Environment: Ecologically Unequal

1 John Robert McNeill, *Something New Under the Sun* (New York: Norton, 2000), 30.
2 Commonly attributed to Margaret Mead.
3 President Jimmy Carter, Speech to dedicate solar panels on the White House roof, 'Solar Energy Remarks Announcing Administration Proposals' (June, 20, 1979).
4 Rachel Carson, *Silent Spring* (Boston: Houghton Mifflin, 2002), 17.
5 https://www.walden.org/Library/Quotations/Conservation. [Journal, January 3, 1861]
6 10.10: These are rough estimates of populations in 1900. https://en.wikipedia.org/ wiki/List_of_countries_by_population_in_1900
7 http://www.latimes.com/science/sciencenow/la-sci-sn-oklahoma-earthquakes-fracking-science-20140703-story.html
8 http://www.theguardian.com/world/2002/nov/24/theobserver

Epilogue: "It's the end of the world as we know it . . . "

1 http://modernism.research.yale.edu/wiki/index.php/Theses_on_the_
   Philosophy_of_History

Glossary

actualization – when individuals fulfill their potential as humans, expressing themselves as they best can, and utilizing their particular talents.

agent orange – chemical made from herbicides used by the United States as chemical weapon in Vietnam, sickening over a million people and defoliating millions of hectares.

age of affluence – era from the 1950s to 1970s when Western societies in particular grew constantly, bringing widespread wealth mostly through new technologies and rising literacy.

apartheid – systematic political program of racial stratification purposely designed to keep black South Africans in poverty, characterized by extreme brutality and violence, enforced between 1948 and 1991.

antibiotics – drugs that kill bacteria to prevent infections and since the Second World War have prevented billions of people from death or serious sickness.

Arpanet – The basic technological foundation of networking computers that makes the Internet work, established by the US Department of Defense in 1969.

autarky – When a nation-state attempts to function alone economically, detaching itself from wider trade networks, ideally to find self-sufficiency.

authoritarian – Societies that enforce rigorous obedience to authority, usually state authority, limiting the freedoms of groups and individuals.

Bletchley Park – The secret location for British codebreakers that during the Second World War breached Germany and other enemy power's secret communications.

broadcasting – The electronic transmission of radio or television for means of mass communications.

capital – money, land, or labor available for investment in projects or products.

capitalism – the philosophy in support of an economic system in which markets of all sorts are free and largely unregulated and assets are generally in the hands of private individuals or groups of individuals.

Chernobyl – Cataclysmic nuclear disaster in 1986 in the Soviet Union that sent radioactive materials over all of Europe and indicated the failure of the Communist regime.

civilizing mission – The argument, largely held by European and Euro-American settler societies, that they had a duty and a right to "civilize" subject peoples through colonial rule and cultural transformation.

civil rights – A movement that grew in the 1960s to counter historical discrimination and fight for broader participation in American political and social life, particularly for people of color.

classical liberalism – a commitment to fundamental liberties including freedom to choose one's religion, to speak, to assemble, to a free press, and ultimately, to the right to aspire to a life of freedom with aspirations to advance in society as well as support for free trade, individual property rights, and open markets.

collectivized agriculture – Stalin's program between 1928 and 1940 which aimed to push small farmers into large state-supervised agricultural holdings, leading to millions of deaths and immense social punishment.

colonization – When imperial powers possess or control another nation's sovereignty.

Communism – an economic system in which the means of production are in the hands of the state as a representative for the workers.

consumerism – Economic and social practice that aims for increased acquisition of goods and products and which assumes that greater consumption brings greater happiness.

corporatism – ideology that assumes a national community can benefit from major interest groups working together (i.e., military, business, agricultural, and religious) for the common good.

critical theory – A philosophical approach that criticizes society and culture by analyzing historical injustice though the lens of wider populations instead of small elite groups.

cultural evolution – Theory of evolutionary change that explains how societies change over time from simple to more complex entities.

Cultural Revolution – Social movement in China between 1966 and 1976 that aimed to purge Mao's China of capitalist elements, stalling the economy, bringing great violence, and persecuting millions of individuals.

democracy – A political system which enables citizens to replace ineffective government, participate in political life, enjoy civil rights and the rule of law.

Dollar Diplomacy – US foreign policy after 1904 which stated that the United States had the right, indeed the obligation, to intervene in the affairs of any country in the Americas.

dominant paradigm – The values and attitudes accepted by most people in a given society that most consider correct, universal, and unchanging.

Dust Bowl – Man-made environmental disaster in the 1930s that ruined the prairies and grasslands of the United States and Canada, caused by overworking soils with tractor technology, pushing millions to desperation.

ENIAC – Electronic Numerical Integrator and Computer. The earliest high-speed processing computer that from 1946 could compute many numbers at once, foreshadowing faster computers

enigma machine – One of numerous electro-mechanical cipher machines that coded and protected business, diplomatic and military information transmissions after the First World War.

Environmentalism – general philosophy that aims to protect the natural environment for the good of humanity and the ecosystems that support it.

European convention on human rights – international treaty from 1950 that aimed to protect the human rights and fundamental freedoms of Europeans and which served as a model for global rights movements thereafter.

European Union – Economic and political union of twenty-eight countries in Europe which formed in 1951 to advocate for the free movement of goods, services, people and money among member states. Twenty-seven of its twenty-eight states enjoy very high scores on the UN's Human Development Index.

evangelism – Spreading of the message of the Christian gospel to people of other faiths or none.

existentialism – A philosophy that celebrates the existence of the individual as a responsible person who can determine their own development through acts of free will and rational choice.

extractive economies – Economies typically located in undeveloped countries that depend on extracting natural resources for sale or trade for export, typically without processing or finishing.

feminism – A philosophy and movement aiming to transform attitudes toward the sexes, aspiring to equal rights and respect for women.

Fordism – American mass production approach to making cars pioneered by Henry Ford that transformed production in capitalist systems worldwide.

foreign direct investment – When people or enterprises invest in another country, either through ownership or control of a foreign business.

fundamentalism – Religious movements that call for a return to basic and original ideals, exclusive of other views or faiths.

germ theory – The late nineteenth-century theory that many diseases are caused by tiny microorganisms such as bacteria entering the body.

GM crops – Genetically modified plants and crops that alter the naturally occurring DNA of existing plants.

governmentality – Foucault's theory that the state governs, or rules, not only populations but their minds and physical bodies.

great leap forward – Mao's program to modernize China after 1958, the largest mass murder in history, killing up to 50 million people.

green revolution – Modernization program that saved a billion people from starvation in the postwar era by developing higher yielding grains.

indirect rule – a strategy by which a colonial government co-opts local leaders to support them or work with the colonial state.

industrial capitalism – A phase of capitalism in which finance was closely connected to the needs of industry, which became dominant globally in the twentieth century.

interventionist state – Government intervention in the economy to correct for market inequalities and protect the welfare of all in society.

intifadas – Two large-scale rebellions of Palestinian Arabs against Israeli occupation of the Gaza Strip and West Bank in Palestine/Israel.

Islamism – A radical ideology that demands all people to adhere to Islamic law, rejecting Western interference in particular, expanding the religion of Islam into a global ideology.

Keynesianism – Keynes's theory that government must spend, borrowing if necessary, to increase demand and pull weak economies out of recession.

League of Nations – International organization founded in 1920 to resolve disputes without conflict and improve cooperation among nations.

liberation theology – Mostly Catholic movement since the 1960s that aimed to fight social and political injustice in Latin America.

London Smog – Dense blanket of smoke and fog that covered London in 1952 and killed over 10,000 people.

Mahatma Gandhi – Indian independence hero and philosopher who popularized nonviolent protest, inspiring movements worldwide for civil rights and equality.

mandate system – League of Nations agreements among Western powers to prevent conflict in the Ottoman Empire, which created protectorates in the Middle East and is the source of problems in the region today.

moral economy – historical theory that workers and peasants enjoyed a more humane economy with ethical relations prior to modern capitalism.

motion pictures – Early twentieth-century technology that transferred still images to screen to create modern film.

mujahedeen – Muslim soldiers fighting jihadi war stemming from Afghani Islamist resistance to US and Russian interventions.

nationalism – patriotic love for one's country that assumes superiority over other nations and works toward policies that support this.

neo-imperialism – Late nineteenth and twentieth-century expansion of European, American, and Japanese power to gain overseas territories and resources, including all of Africa, the Middle East, and much of Southeast Asia and the Pacific.

neoliberalism – Application of nineteenth-century free-market ideals to modern economies, including open markets, free trade, and deregulation.

newly industrialized countries (NIC's) – When developing countries transition from rural economies to goods producing manufacture, trading more with others and usually raising standards of living.

nihilism – radical worldview that maintains skepticism toward everything in existence, typically with negative outcomes.

nonaligned movement – Coordinated group of over 100 nations who resist alignment with great power blocs to maintain independence, emerging in the postwar struggle for colonial independence.

North-South report – Groundbreaking 1980 report by Willy Brandt that highlighted the disparity between the Northern and Southern hemispheres in standard of living and called for a transfer of wealth to the south.

Paris Climate Accords – 2016 agreement among 196 nations to combat the threat of climate change on a global scale. Only the United States, Syria, and Nicaragua have not signed.

positivism – A philosophy that argues any claim can be supported rationally or scientifically by logic, rejecting metaphysical and faith-based explanations.

pluralism – A principle that insists upon diverse worldviews in a society, incorporating various ethnicities, classes, faiths, and social groups.

postmodernism – A postwar intellectual movement committed to subjectivity and relativism, refuting that reason explains reality or history offers lessons.

pragmatism – A philosophy that asserts meaning can be found through the practical application of beliefs, theories or evidence.

progress – the assumption that history moves forward toward ever better standards of living or that history has a linear motion.

Rachel Carson – American biologist whose writings jumpstarted the modern environmental movement.

Red Scare – When governments promote the fear of radical or mainstream left-wing politics by associating policies with Communism, most commonly in the United States but also in twentieth-century Europe.

relativism – The principle that truth, ethics or knowledge vary from culture to culture, that no absolutes exist.

roaring twenties – Period of urbanization, new fashion and music trends, increasing consumerism, and abandoning of traditional mores in 1920s America.

robot – A programmable computerized machine that can perform tasks automatically that humans normally accomplish.

scientific method – A process of observation, measurement and experiment to form or test hypotheses in order to understand the natural world or create technologies.

Second World – term denoting states that were Communist in the past century, mostly those under the rule of the USSR.

secularism – A view that supports the separation of religion from the political and social spheres of decision making and daily life.

social democracies – Political systems that embraces the virtues of Socialism and capitalism, blending them to pass legislation protecting the welfare for all citizens while enabling enterprises and capital to thrive.

Socialism – An economic system of collective labor in which the means of production are in the hands of workers or their representatives.

social Darwinism – A racist nineteenth-century ideology that influenced many leaders in the twentieth century to justify imperialist, conservative, racist policies.

Solidarnosc – Anticommunist social trade union movement in 1980s Poland that rose to challenge Moscow's grip on Eastern Europe.

stagflation – Little understood problem in capitalist economies where high unemployment combines with high inflation, particularly bad in the 1970s.

synthetics – Chemical compounds composed of carbon that can make rubber,

plastic, medicines, and many other useful modern materials.

Taylorism – Twentieth-century theory of scientific management that studies workflows in businesses to increase efficiency, profits, and productivity.

theocracy – A system of government in which authority derives from a god, passed through priests or imams into law.

Third World – Cold War term to designate mostly undeveloped countries that had been colonized or remained dependent upon core, wealthy, industrial states.

totalitarianism – A form of government in which dictators enforce utter conformity and obedience of all aspects of the individuals life to the state, typically referring to Nazi Germany and Communist Russia.

Treaty of Versailles – A key peace treaty concluding the First World War, which though well intentioned, served to foster conditions that lead to the worse Second World War.

United Nations – An international organization formed in 1945 to prevent another conflict like the Second World War. Its goals are to maintain peace, spread human rights, develop poor economies and prevent disaster such as famine and war.

utilitarianism – A philosophy that calls for absolute rationalism in decision making regardless of consequences.

War Guilt Clause – An article in Versailles treaty forcing Germany to take sole responsibility for the First World War, creating intense bitterness and leading to the rise of extremism in the 1920s.

warfare state – A theory that the most powerful industrial states extend diplomacy into warfare by continually pursuing advantage over others, creating a vicious circle of competition and conflict.

Index